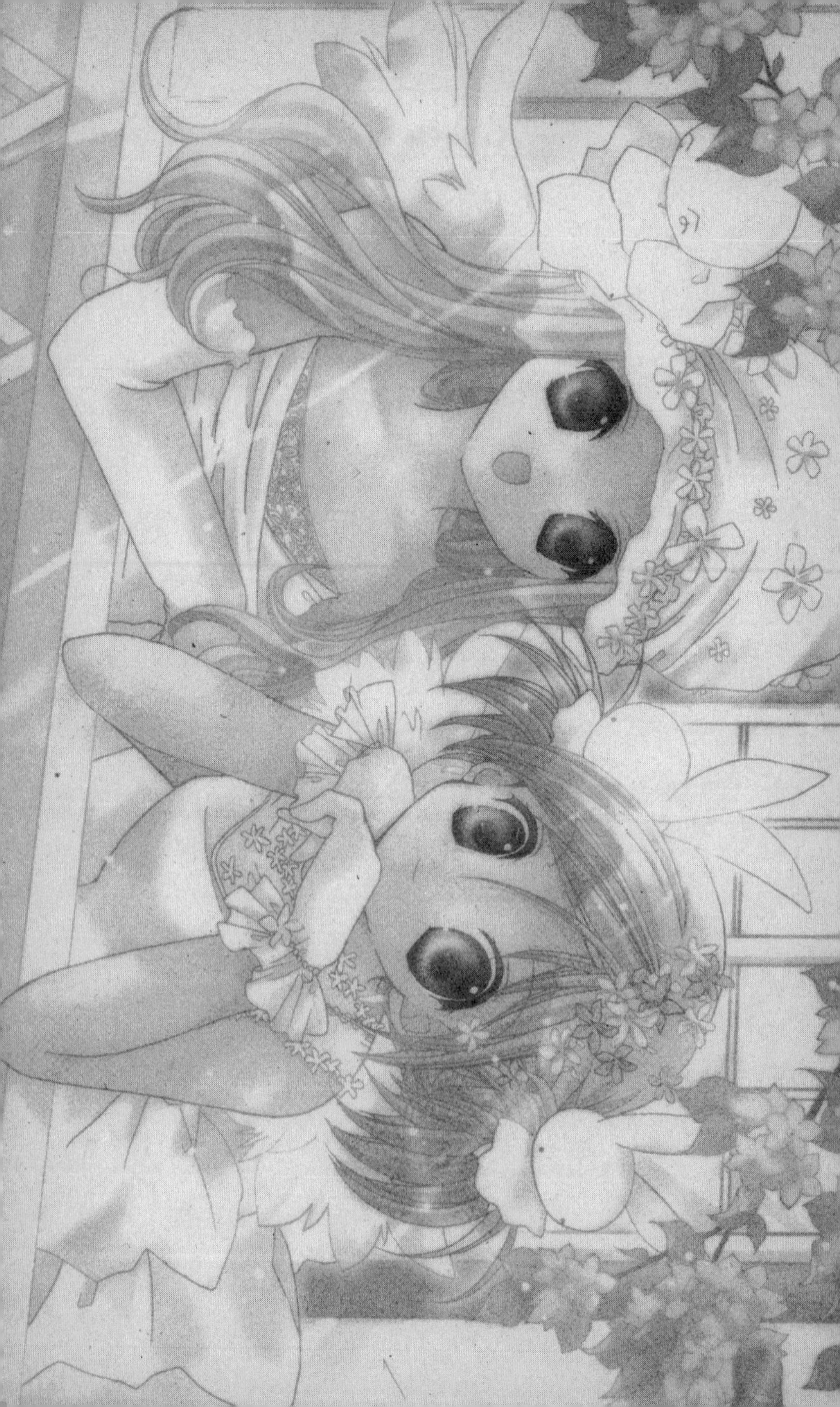

PITA-TEN

Volume 5

by
Koge-Donbo

HAMBURG // LONDON // LOS ANGELES // TOKYO

Pita-Ten Vol. 5
Created by Koge-Donbo

Translation - Nan Rymer
English Adaptation - Adam Arnold
Associate Editor - Hope Donovan
Retouch and Lettering - Abelardo Bigting
Production Artist - John Lo
Cover Design - Raymond Makowski

Editor - Paul Morrissey
Digital Imaging Manager - Chris Buford
Pre-Press Manager - Antonio DePietro
Production Managers - Jennifer Miller and Mutsumi Miyazaki
Art Director - Matt Alford
Managing Editor - Jill Freshney
VP of Production - Ron Klamert
President and C.O.O. - John Parker
Publisher and C.E.O. - Stuart Levy

A  Manga

TOKYOPOP Inc.
5900 Wilshire Blvd. Suite 2000
Los Angeles, CA 90036

E-mail: info@TOKYOPOP.com
Come visit us online at www.TOKYOPOP.com

ISBN: 1-59182-631-4

First TOKYOPOP printing: September 2004
10 9 8 7 6 5 4 3 2
Printed in the USA

Contents

Characters

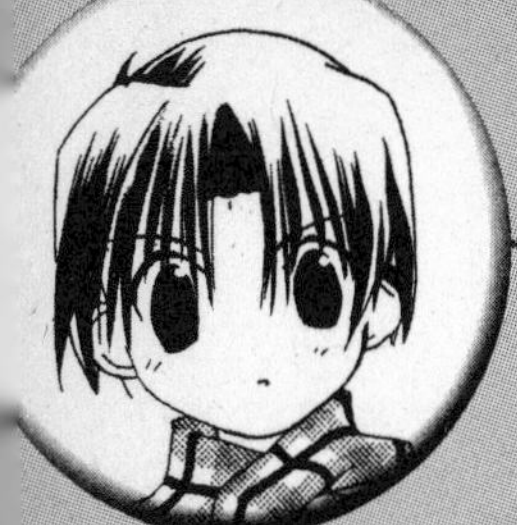

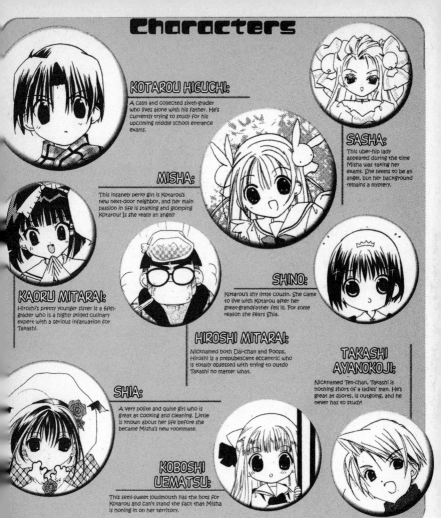

KOTAROU HIGUCHI:

A calm and collected sixth-grader who lives alone with his father. He's currently trying to study for his upcoming middle school entrance exams.

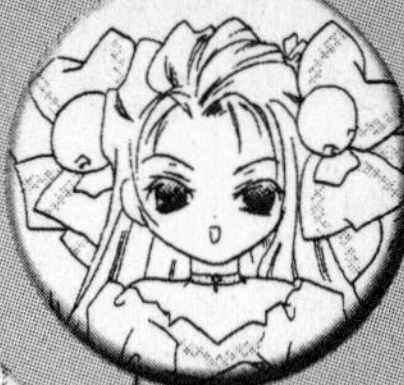

SASHA:

This uber-hip lady appeared during the time Misha was taking her exams. She seems to be an angel, but her background remains a mystery.

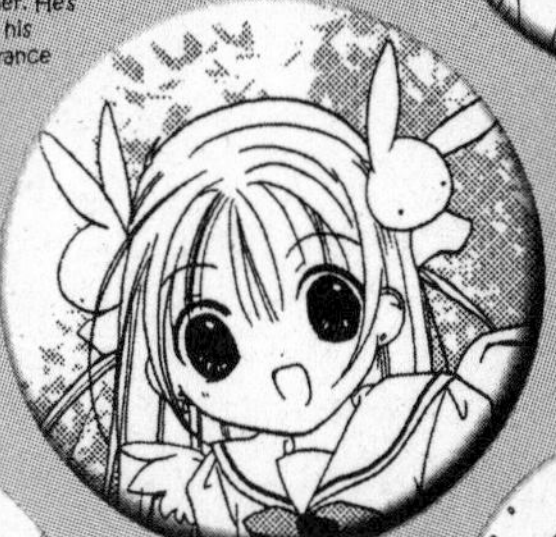

MISHA:

This insanely perky girl is Kotarou's new next-door neighbor, and her main passion in life is stalking and glomping Kotarou! Is she really an angel?

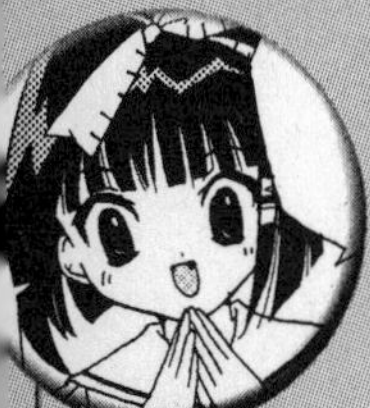

KAORU MITARAI:

Hiroshi's pretty younger sister is a fifth-grader who is a highly skilled culinary expert with a serious infatuation for Takashi.

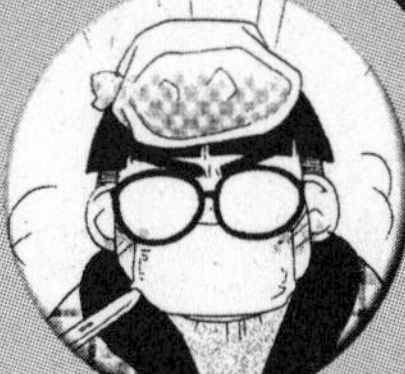

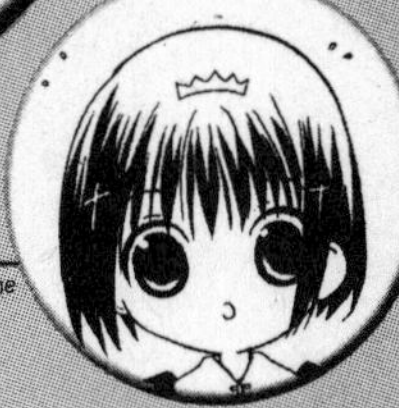

SHINO:

Kotarou's shy little cousin. She came to live with Kotarou after her great-grandfather fell ill. For some reason she fears Shia.

HIROSHI MITARAI:

Nicknamed both Dai-chan and Poops, Hiroshi is a prepubescent eccentric who is totally obsessed with trying to outdo Takashi no matter what.

TAKASHI AYANOKOJI:

Nicknamed Ten-chan, Takashi is nothing short of a ladies' man. He's great at sports, is outgoing, and he never has to study!

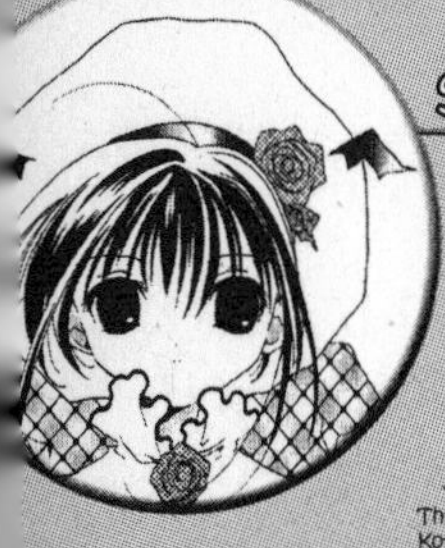

SHIA:

A very polite and quite girl who is great at cooking and cleaning. Little is known about her life before she became Misha's new roommate.

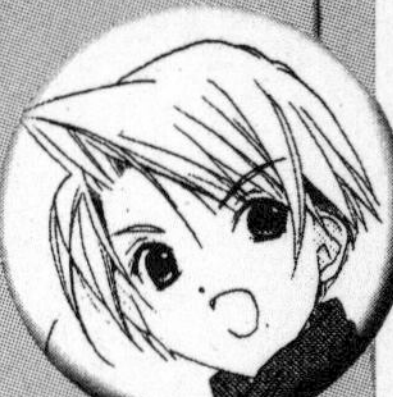

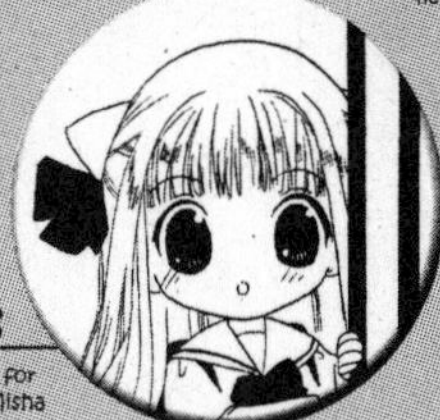

KOBOSHI UEMATSU:

This semi-sweet loudmouth has the hots for Kotarou and can't stand the fact that Misha is honing in on her territory.

'he Story Until Now:

Quiet elementary school student Kotarou Higuchi is worse off than most kids. His mother died in a traffic cident and his workaholic father is never at home. This leaves Kotarou struggling to make it to school on time, ok his own meals, go shopping and keep up with his studies.

Yet, his so-called normal life has thrown him a curve ball in the form of a mysterious girl named Misha who s not only moved in next door to him, but also started to attend the very same middle school as him! Out of eliness and desperation, Misha decides to make it her life's work to chase after, "abuse" and glomp Kotarou. t long after her appearance, another strange girl by the name of Shia appears and ends up as Misha's new mmate! Just as Kotarou manages to adjust to his topsy-turvy new life, one day Misha returns crestfallen after ring news that she failed her examinations. Kotarou tries to cheer her up, but as luck would have it, Misha s slip that she is not trying for herself, but rather for Kotarou's sake. Taken aback by her words, Kotarou grows ry and pushes Misha away.

In order to regain her self-worth, Misha seeks to make Kotarou see her finally as an angel, even showing her wings. Unfortunately, the event only serves to plummet Kotarou into further confusion. In this midst of s turmoil, Kotarou's cousin, Shino, arrives and moves in with Kotarou. Oh, and then there is the matter of an ther uninvited guest...

Lesson 26

How to Use One's Wings

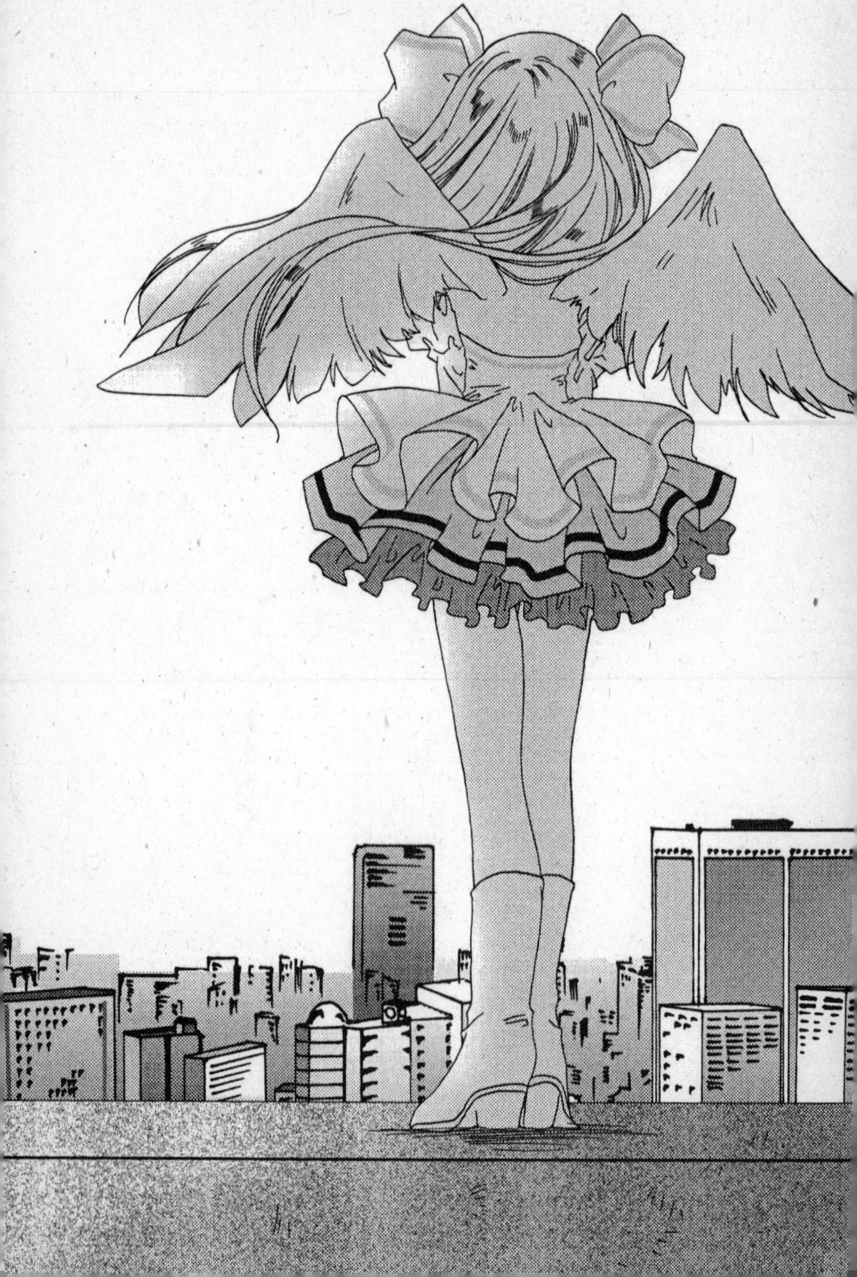

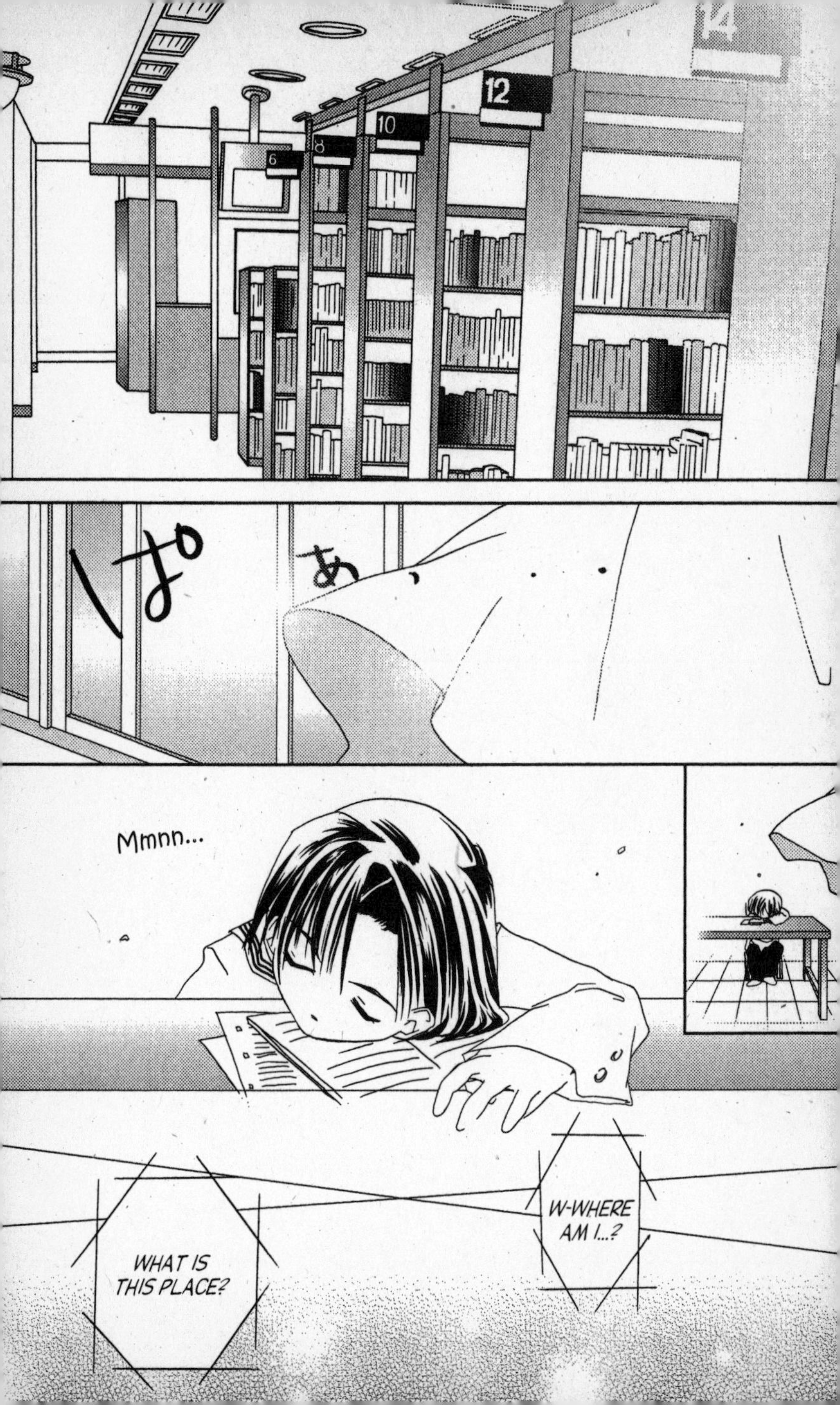
14
12
10
8
6
ぱあ…
Mmnn...
W-WHERE AM I...?
WHAT IS THIS PLACE?

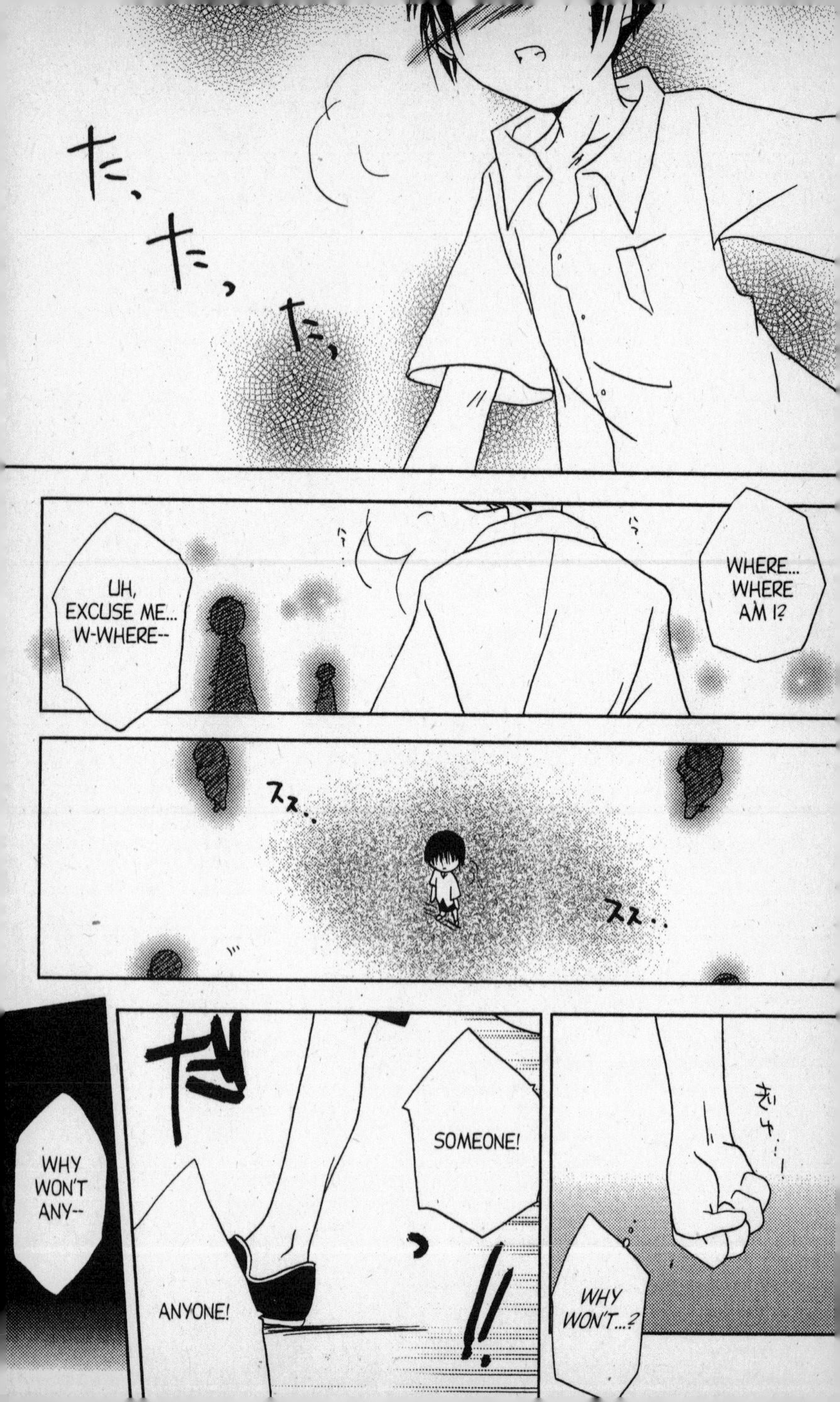

た、た、た、
WHERE... WHERE AM I!?
UH, EXCUSE ME... W-WHERE--
スス...
スス...
ぎゅ...!
WHY WON'T...?
SOMEONE!
だ
ANYONE!
っ!!
WHY WON'T ANY--

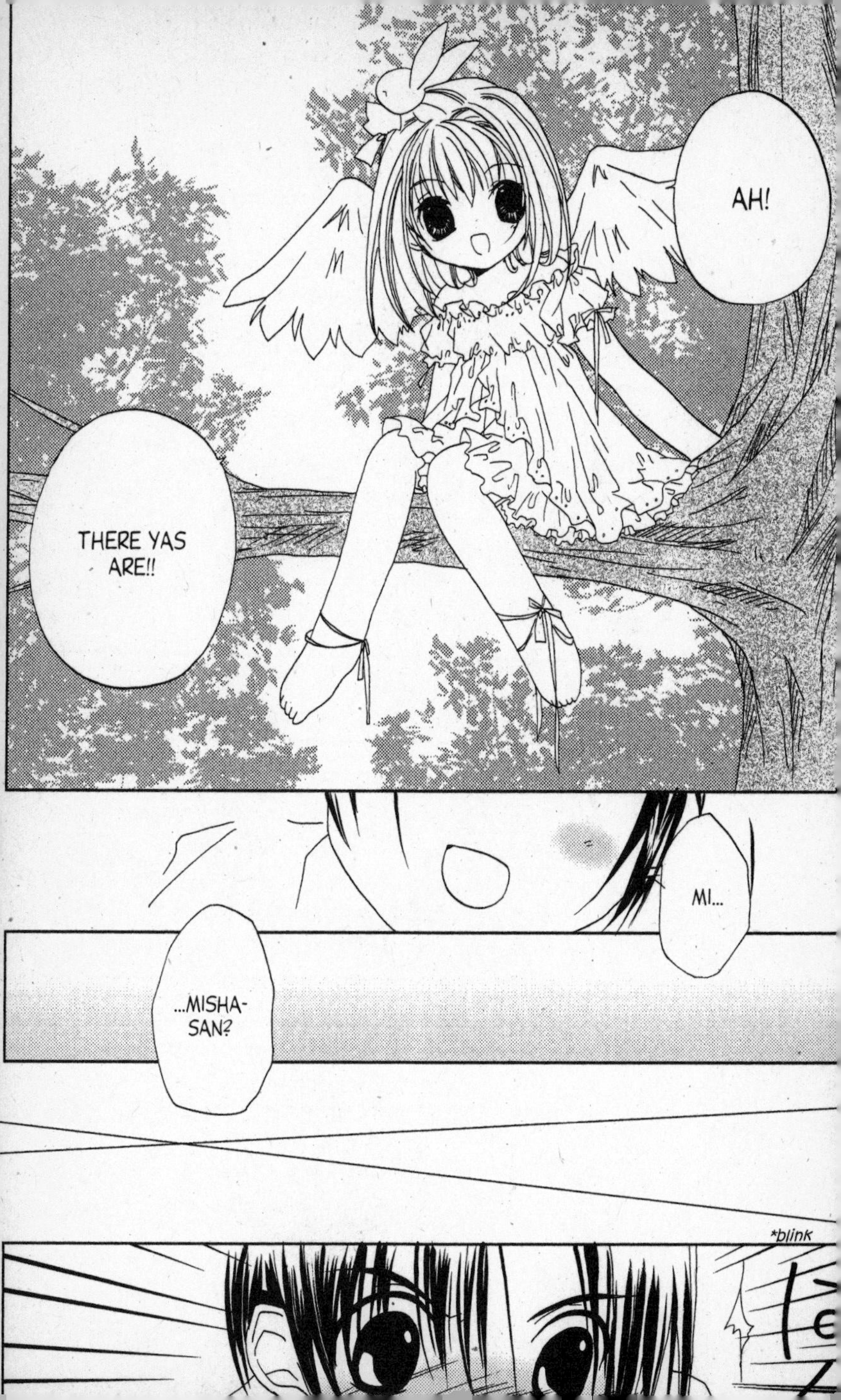
AH!
THERE YAS ARE!!
MI...
...MISHA-SAN?
*blink

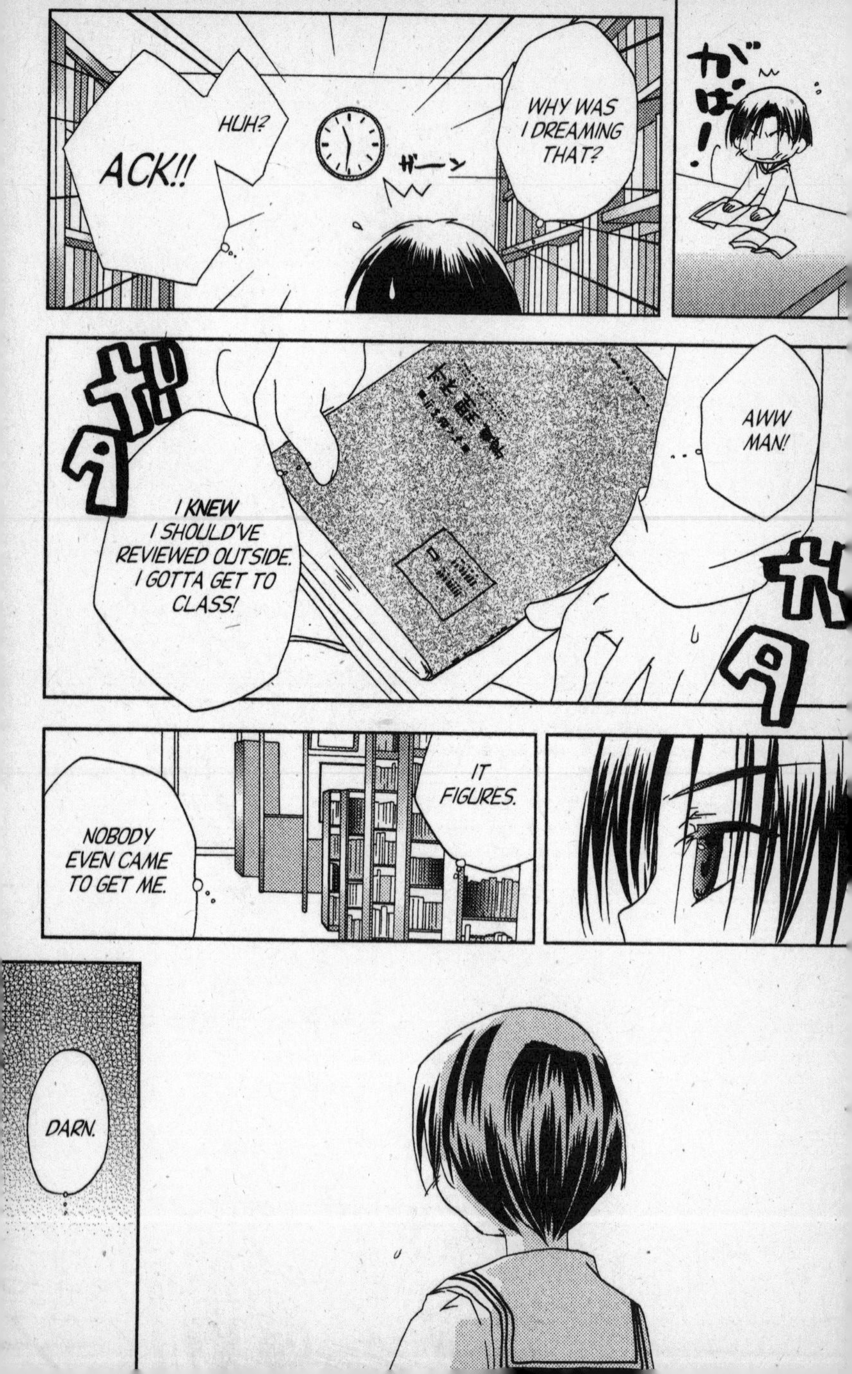
がばっ!
WHY WAS I DREAMING THAT?
HUH?
ガーン
ACK!!
AWW MAN!
I KNEW I SHOULD'VE REVIEWED OUTSIDE. I GOTTA GET TO CLASS!
ガタ
IT FIGURES.
NOBODY EVEN CAME TO GET ME.
DARN.

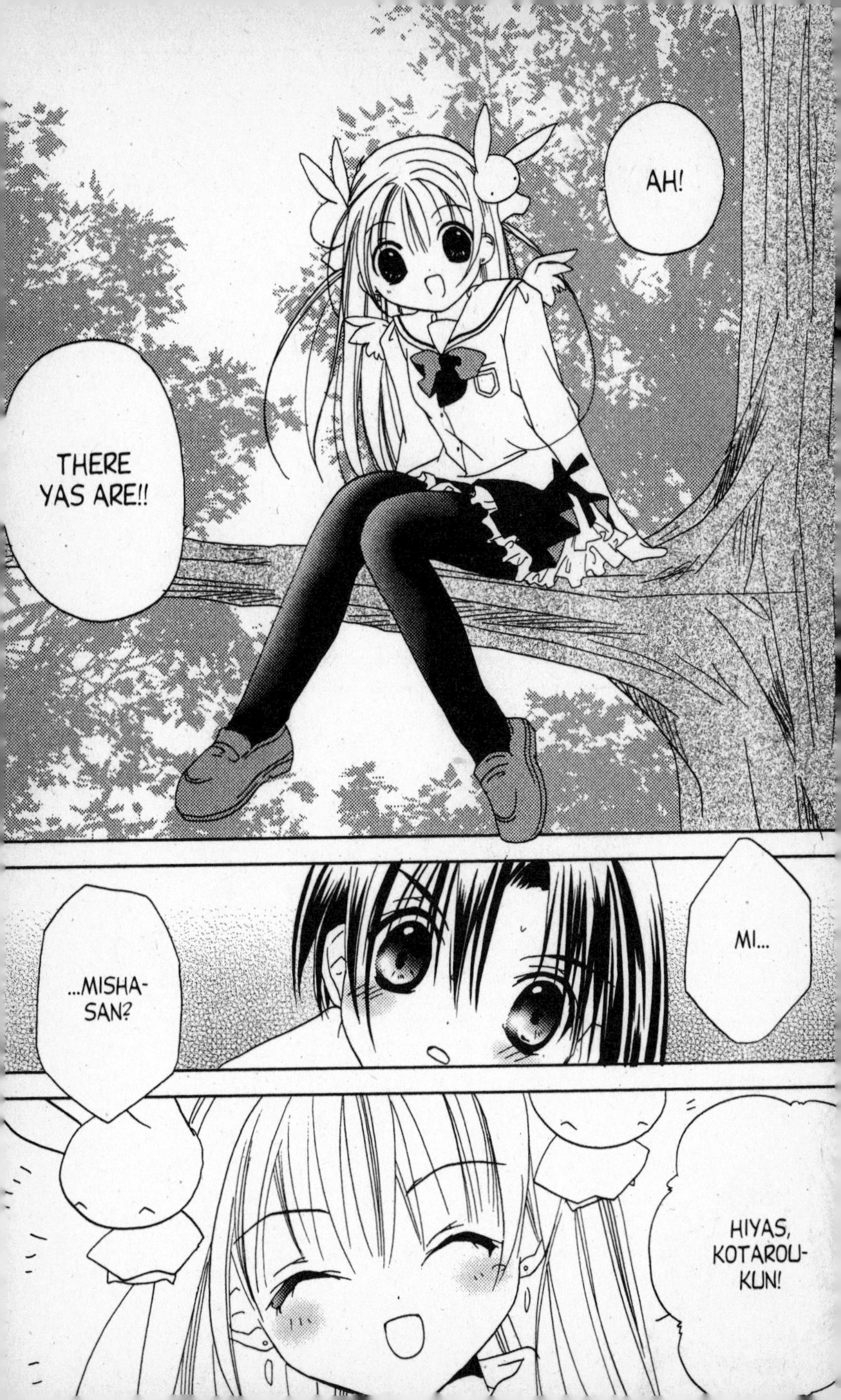
AH!
THERE YAS ARE!!
MI...
...MISHA-SAN?
HIYAS, KOTAROU-KUN!

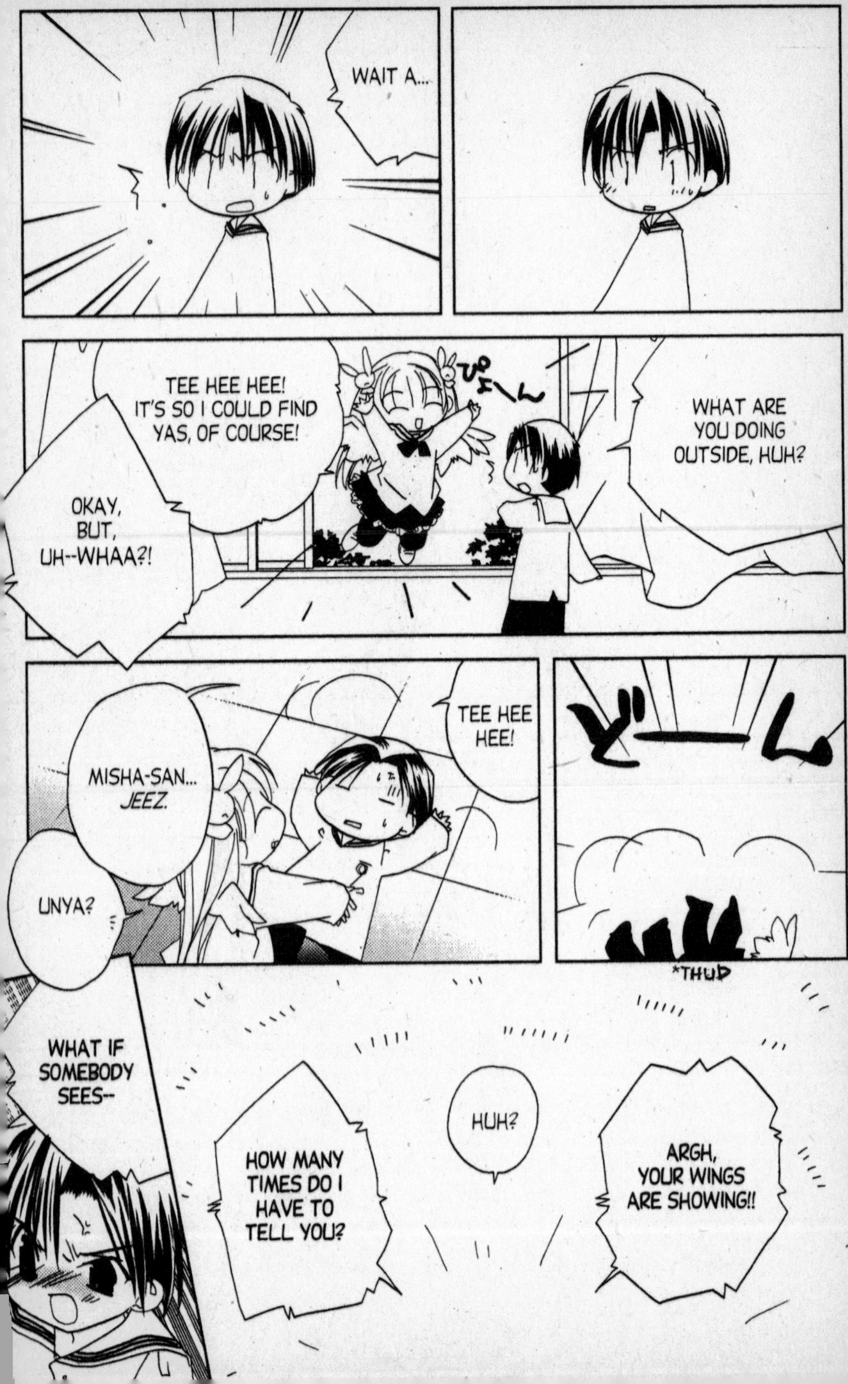
WAIT A...
WHAT ARE YOU DOING OUTSIDE, HUH?
ぴょ〜ん
TEE HEE HEE! IT'S SO I COULD FIND YAS, OF COURSE!
OKAY, BUT, UH--WHAA?!
どーーん
*THUD
TEE HEE HEE!
MISHA-SAN... *JEEZ.*
UNYA?
ARGH, YOUR WINGS ARE SHOWING!!
HUH?
HOW MANY TIMES DO I HAVE TO TELL YOU?
WHAT IF SOMEBODY SEES--

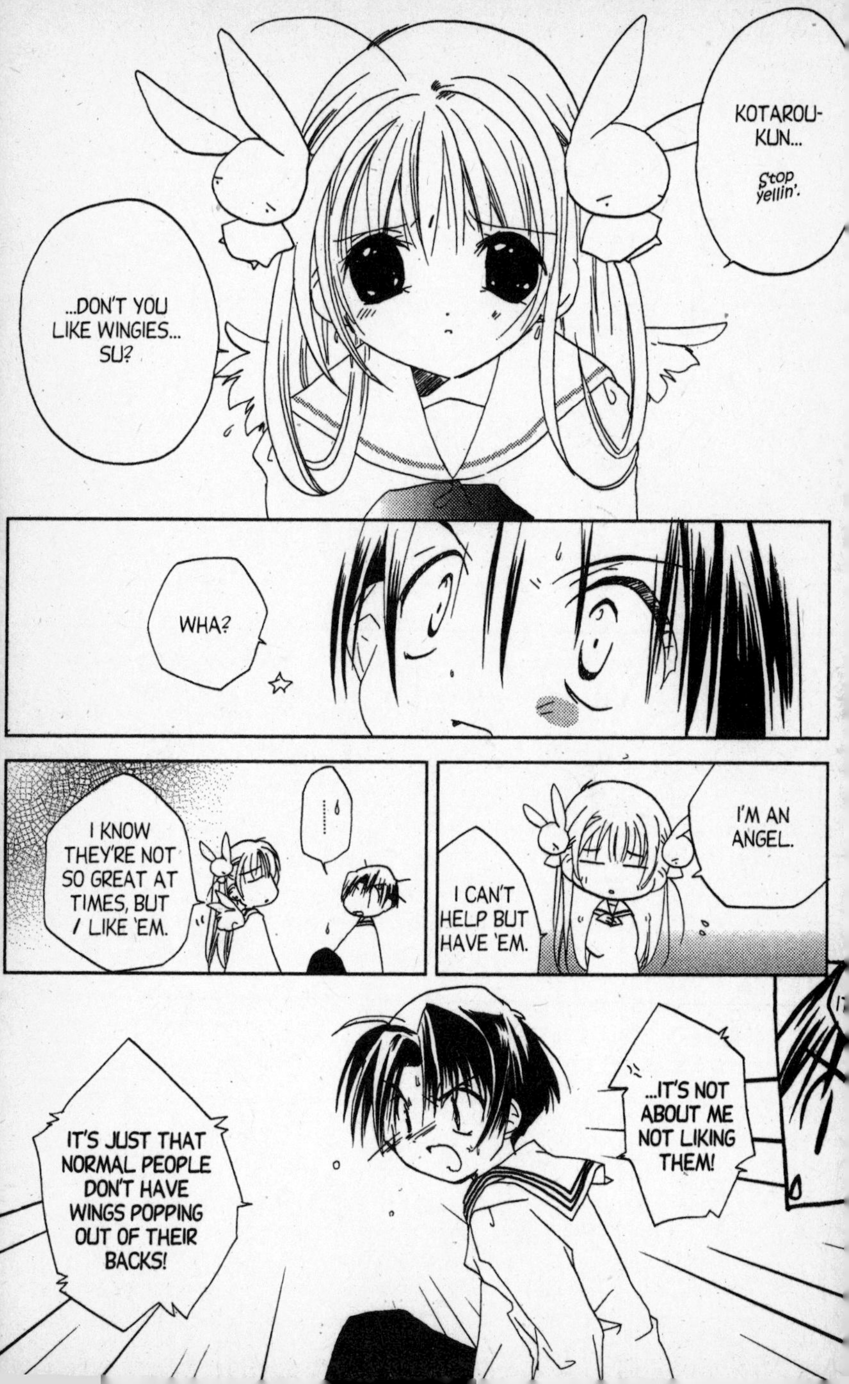
KOTAROU-KUN...
Stop yellin'.
...DON'T YOU LIKE WINGIES... SU?
WHA?
I'M AN ANGEL.
I CAN'T HELP BUT HAVE 'EM.
......
I KNOW THEY'RE NOT SO GREAT AT TIMES, BUT I LIKE 'EM.
...IT'S NOT ABOUT ME NOT LIKING THEM!
IT'S JUST THAT NORMAL PEOPLE DON'T HAVE WINGS POPPING OUT OF THEIR BACKS!

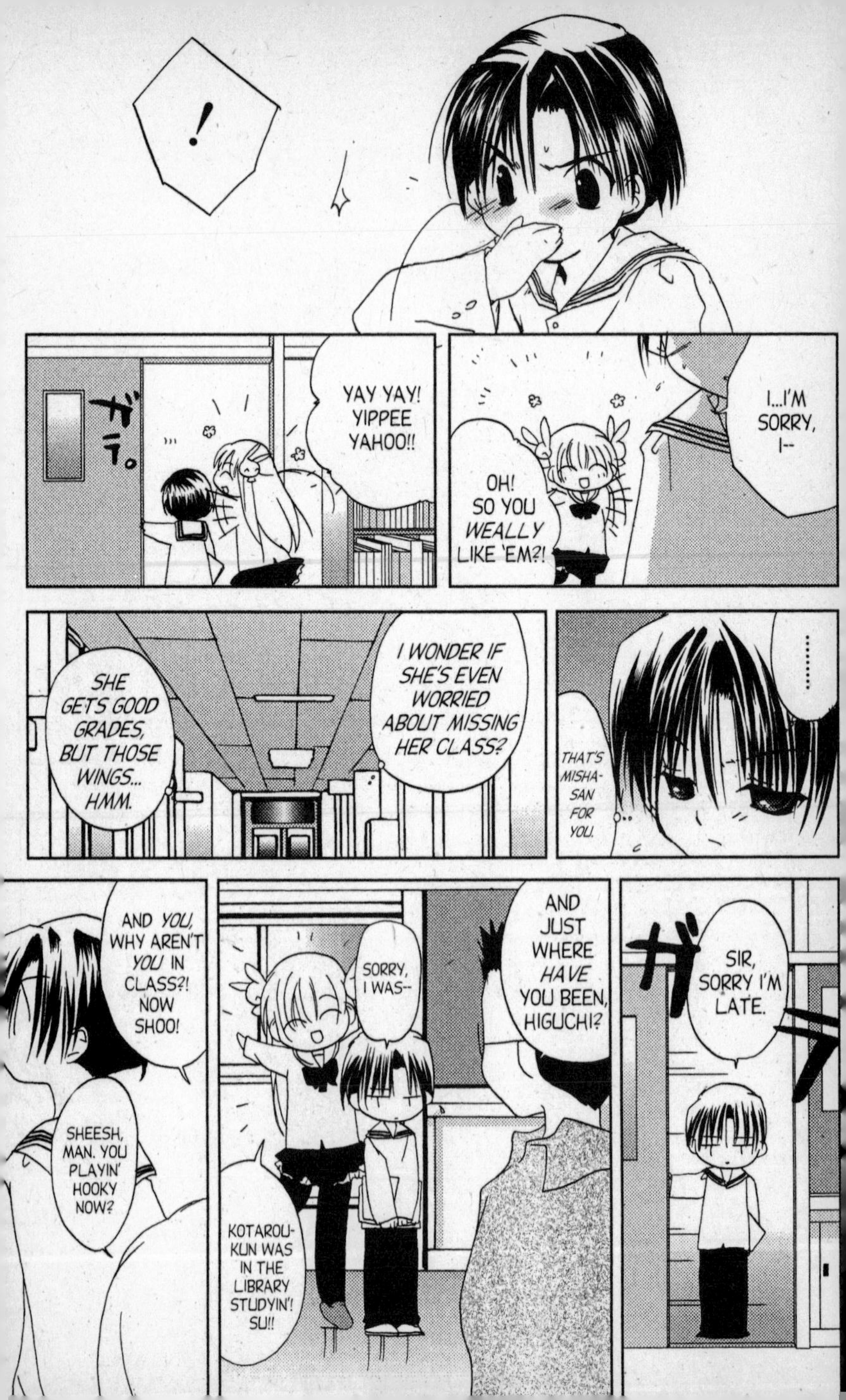
!
I...I'M SORRY, I--
OH! SO YOU *WEALLY* LIKE 'EM?!
YAY YAY! YIPPEE YAHOO!!
ガラ。
......
THAT'S MISHA-SAN FOR YOU.
I WONDER IF SHE'S EVEN WORRIED ABOUT MISSING HER CLASS?
SHE GETS GOOD GRADES, BUT THOSE WINGS... HMM.
ガラ
SIR, SORRY I'M LATE.
AND JUST WHERE *HAVE* YOU BEEN, HIGUCHI?
SORRY, I WAS--
KOTAROU-KUN WAS IN THE LIBRARY STUDYIN'! SU!!
AND *YOU*, WHY AREN'T *YOU* IN CLASS?! NOW SHOO!
SHEESH, MAN. YOU PLAYIN' HOOKY NOW?

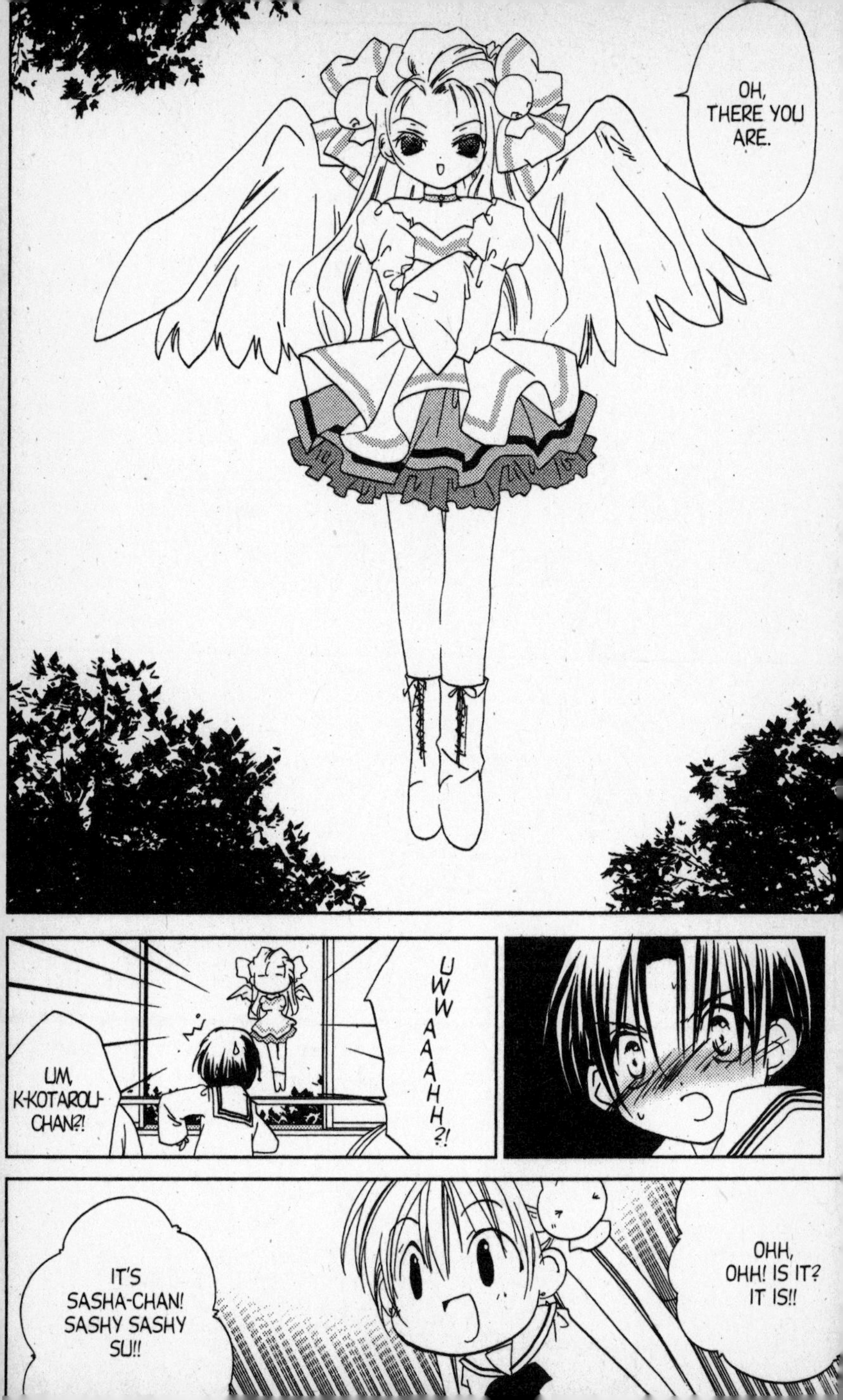
OH, THERE YOU ARE.
UWWAAAHH?!
UM, K-KOTAROU-CHAN?!
OHH, OHH! IS IT? IT IS!!
IT'S SASHA-CHAN! SASHY SASHY SU!!

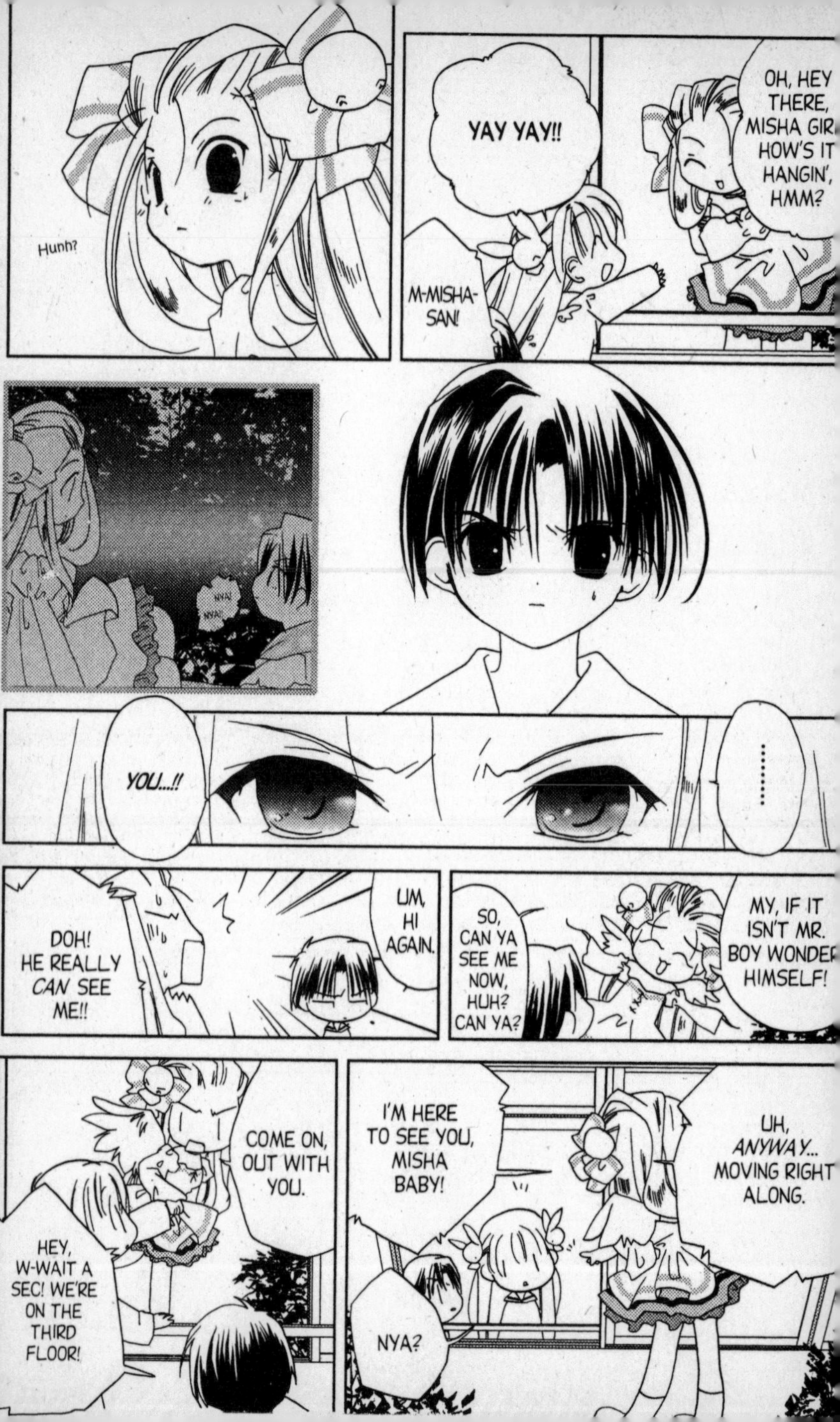
OH, HEY THERE, MISHA GIR HOW'S IT HANGIN', HMM?
YAY YAY!!
M-MISHA-SAN!
Hunh?
NYA! NYA!
......
YOU...!!
MY, IF IT ISN'T MR. BOY WONDE HIMSELF!
SO, CAN YA SEE ME NOW, HUH? CAN YA?
UM, HI AGAIN.
DOH! HE REALLY *CAN* SEE ME!!
UH, *ANYWAY*... MOVING RIGHT ALONG.
I'M HERE TO SEE YOU, MISHA BABY!
NYA?
COME ON, OUT WITH YOU.
HEY, W-WAIT A SEC! WE'RE ON THE THIRD FLOOR!

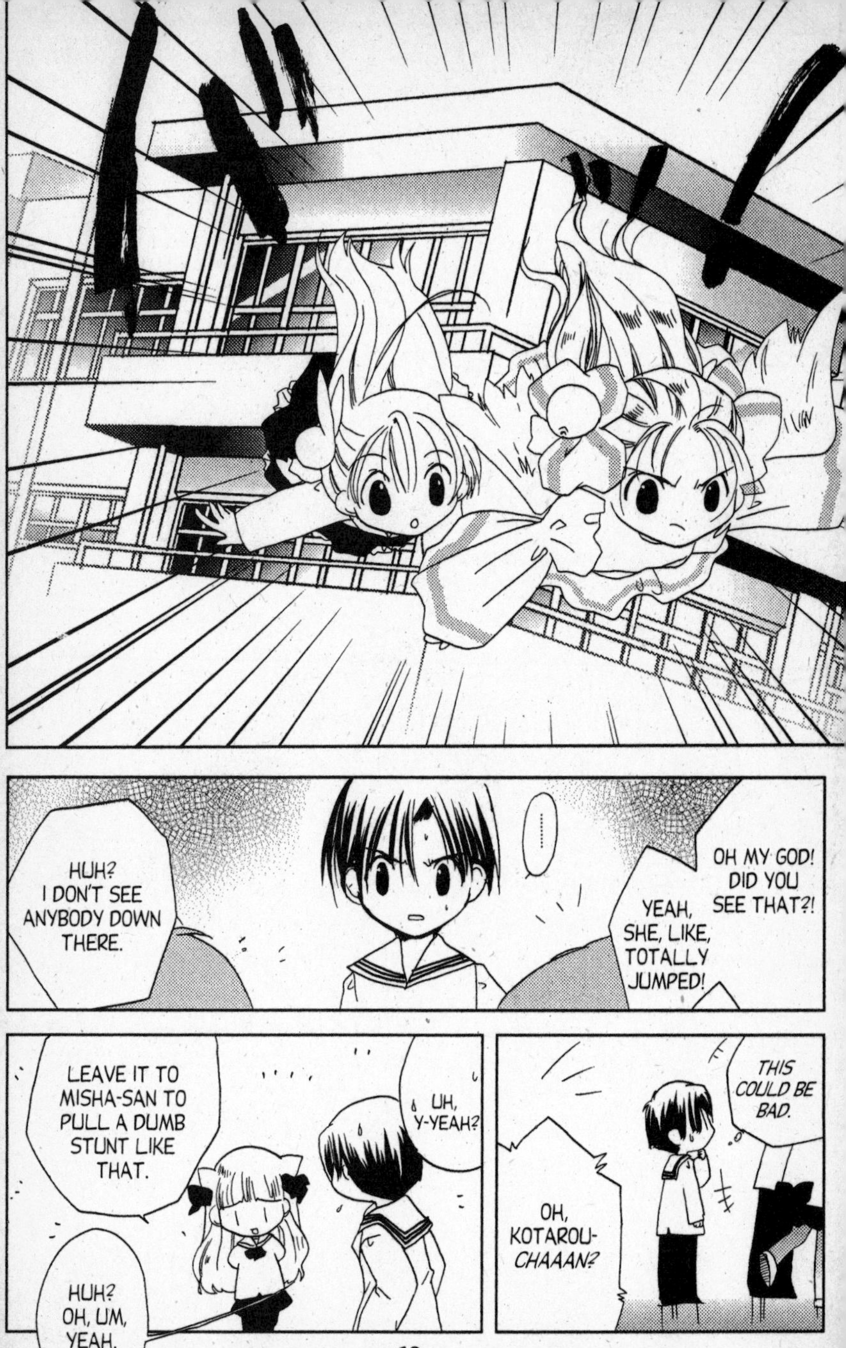
OH MY GOD! DID YOU SEE THAT?!
YEAH, SHE, LIKE, TOTALLY JUMPED!
......
HUH? I DON'T SEE ANYBODY DOWN THERE.
THIS COULD BE BAD.
OH, KOTAROU-CHAAAN?
UH, Y-YEAH?
LEAVE IT TO MISHA-SAN TO PULL A DUMB STUNT LIKE THAT.
HUH? OH, UM, YEAH.

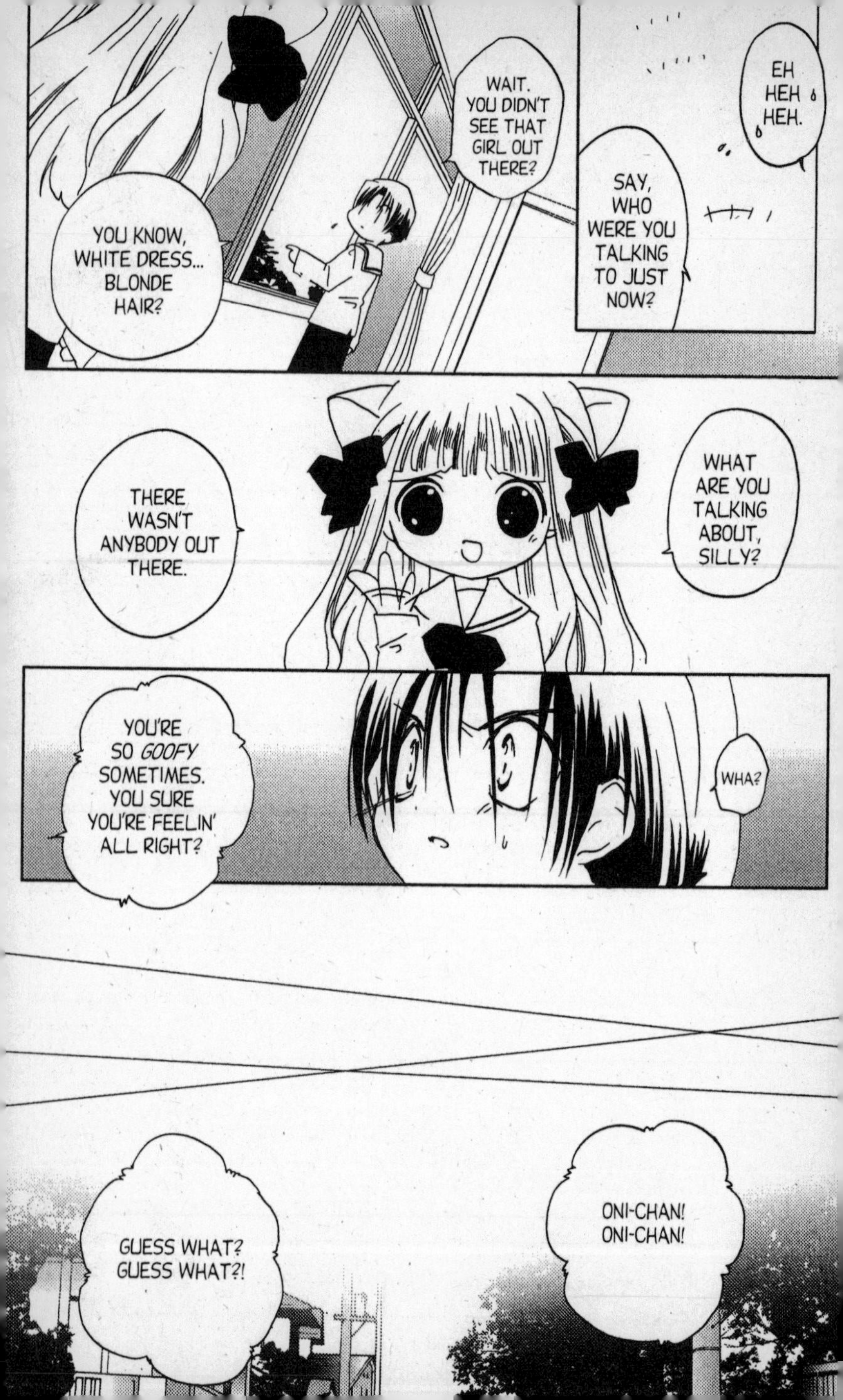
EH HEH HEH.
SAY, WHO WERE YOU TALKING TO JUST NOW?
WAIT. YOU DIDN'T SEE THAT GIRL OUT THERE?
YOU KNOW, WHITE DRESS... BLONDE HAIR?
WHAT ARE YOU TALKING ABOUT, SILLY?
THERE WASN'T ANYBODY OUT THERE.
YOU'RE SO *GOOFY* SOMETIMES. YOU SURE YOU'RE FEELIN' ALL RIGHT?
WHA?
ONI-CHAN! ONI-CHAN!
GUESS WHAT? GUESS WHAT?!

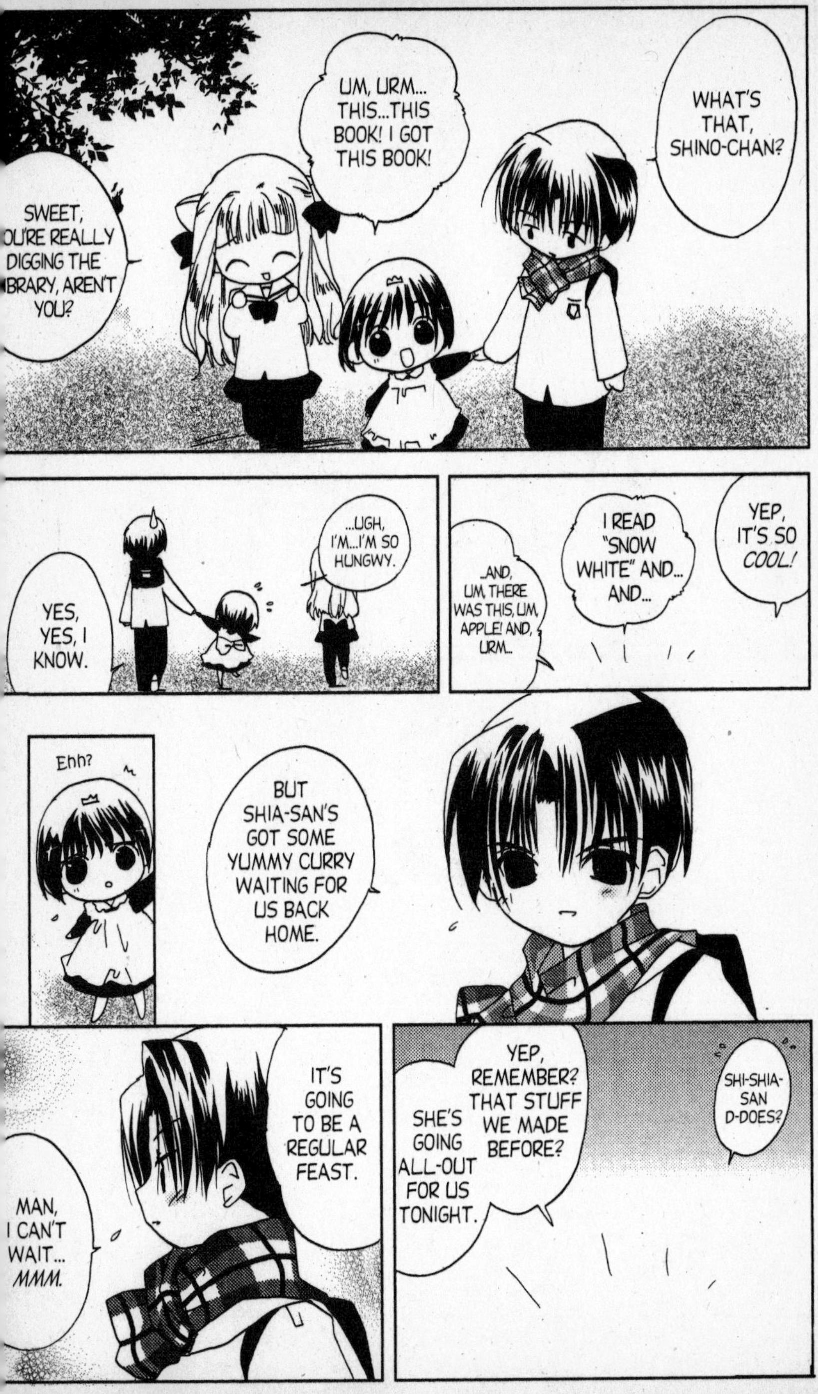
WHAT'S THAT, SHINO-CHAN?
UM, URM... THIS...THIS BOOK! I GOT THIS BOOK!
SWEET, OU'RE REALLY DIGGING THE BRARY, AREN'T YOU?
YEP, IT'S SO *COOL!*
I READ "SNOW WHITE" AND... AND...
...AND, UM, THERE WAS THIS, UM, APPLE! AND, URM...
...UGH, I'M...I'M SO HUNGWY.
YES, YES, I KNOW.
BUT SHIA-SAN'S GOT SOME YUMMY CURRY WAITING FOR US BACK HOME.
Ehh?
SHI-SHIA-SAN D-DOES?
YEP, REMEMBER? THAT STUFF WE MADE BEFORE?
SHE'S GOING ALL-OUT FOR US TONIGHT.
IT'S GOING TO BE A REGULAR FEAST.
MAN, I CAN'T WAIT... *MMM.*

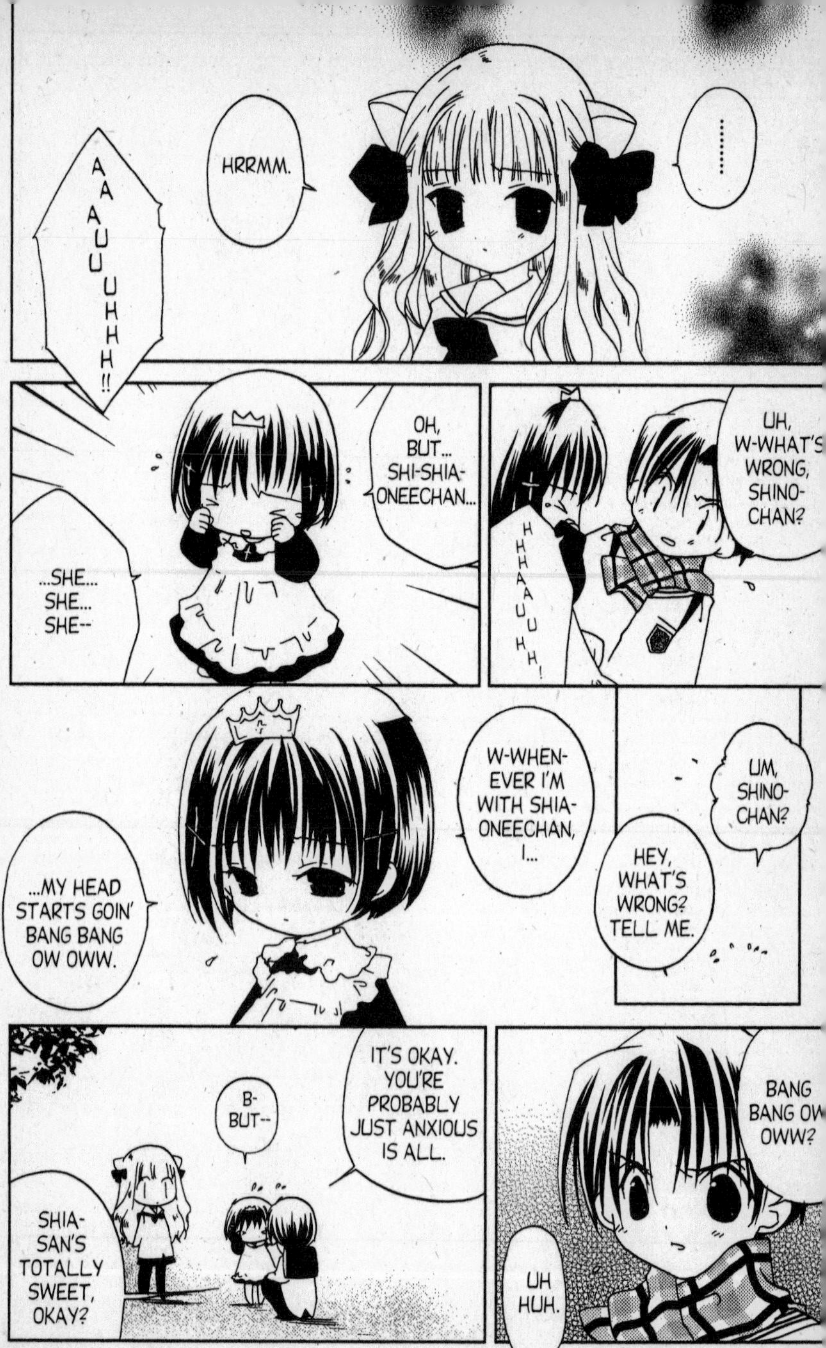
……
HRRMM.
AAAUUUHHHH!!
UH, W-WHAT'S WRONG, SHINO-CHAN?
HHHAAUUHH!
OH, BUT... SHI-SHIA-ONEECHAN...
...SHE... SHE... SHE--
UM, SHINO-CHAN?
HEY, WHAT'S WRONG? TELL ME.
W-WHEN-EVER I'M WITH SHIA-ONEECHAN, I...
...MY HEAD STARTS GOIN' BANG BANG OW OWW.
BANG BANG OW OWW?
UH HUH.
IT'S OKAY. YOU'RE PROBABLY JUST ANXIOUS IS ALL.
B-BUT--
SHIA-SAN'S TOTALLY SWEET, OKAY?

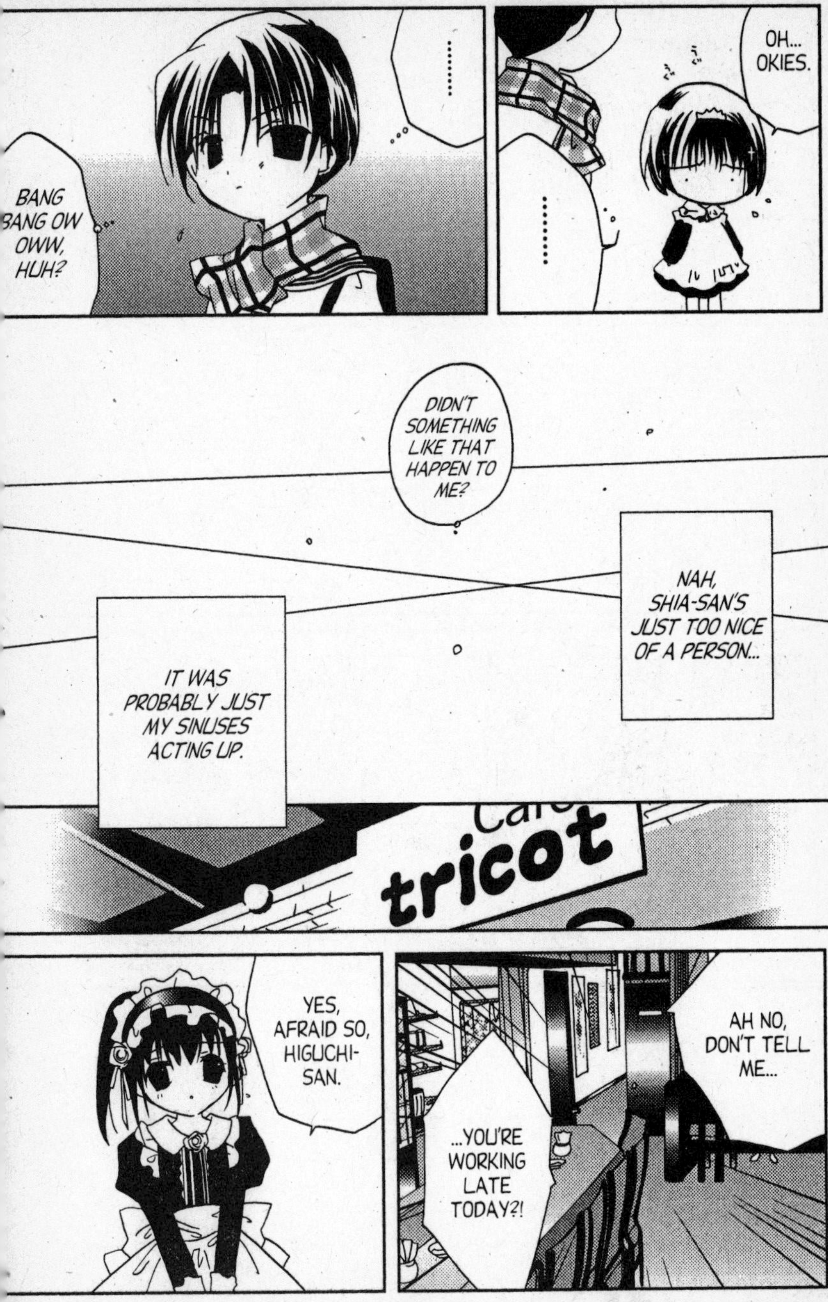
OH... OKIES.
......
......
BANG BANG OW OWW, HUH?
DIDN'T SOMETHING LIKE THAT HAPPEN TO ME?
NAH, SHIA-SAN'S JUST TOO NICE OF A PERSON...
IT WAS PROBABLY JUST MY SINUSES ACTING UP.
tricot
AH NO, DON'T TELL ME...
...YOU'RE WORKING LATE TODAY?!
YES, AFRAID SO, HIGUCHI-SAN.

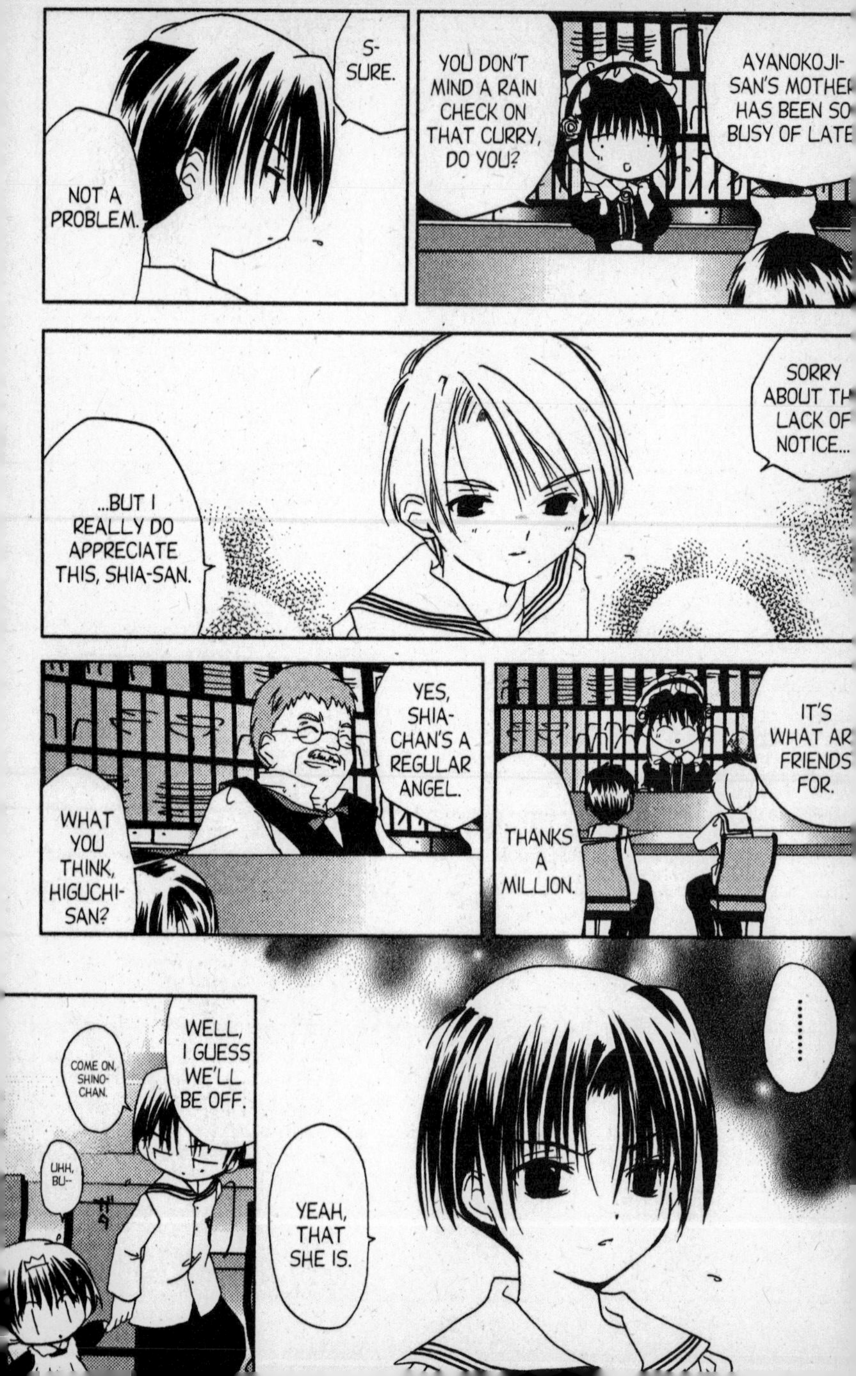
AYANOKOJI-SAN'S MOTHER HAS BEEN SO BUSY OF LATE
YOU DON'T MIND A RAIN CHECK ON THAT CURRY, DO YOU?
S-SURE.
NOT A PROBLEM.
SORRY ABOUT TH LACK OF NOTICE...
...BUT I REALLY DO APPRECIATE THIS, SHIA-SAN.
IT'S WHAT AR FRIENDS FOR.
THANKS A MILLION.
YES, SHIA-CHAN'S A REGULAR ANGEL.
WHAT YOU THINK, HIGUCHI-SAN?
....
YEAH, THAT SHE IS.
WELL, I GUESS WE'LL BE OFF.
COME ON, SHINO-CHAN.
UHH, BU--

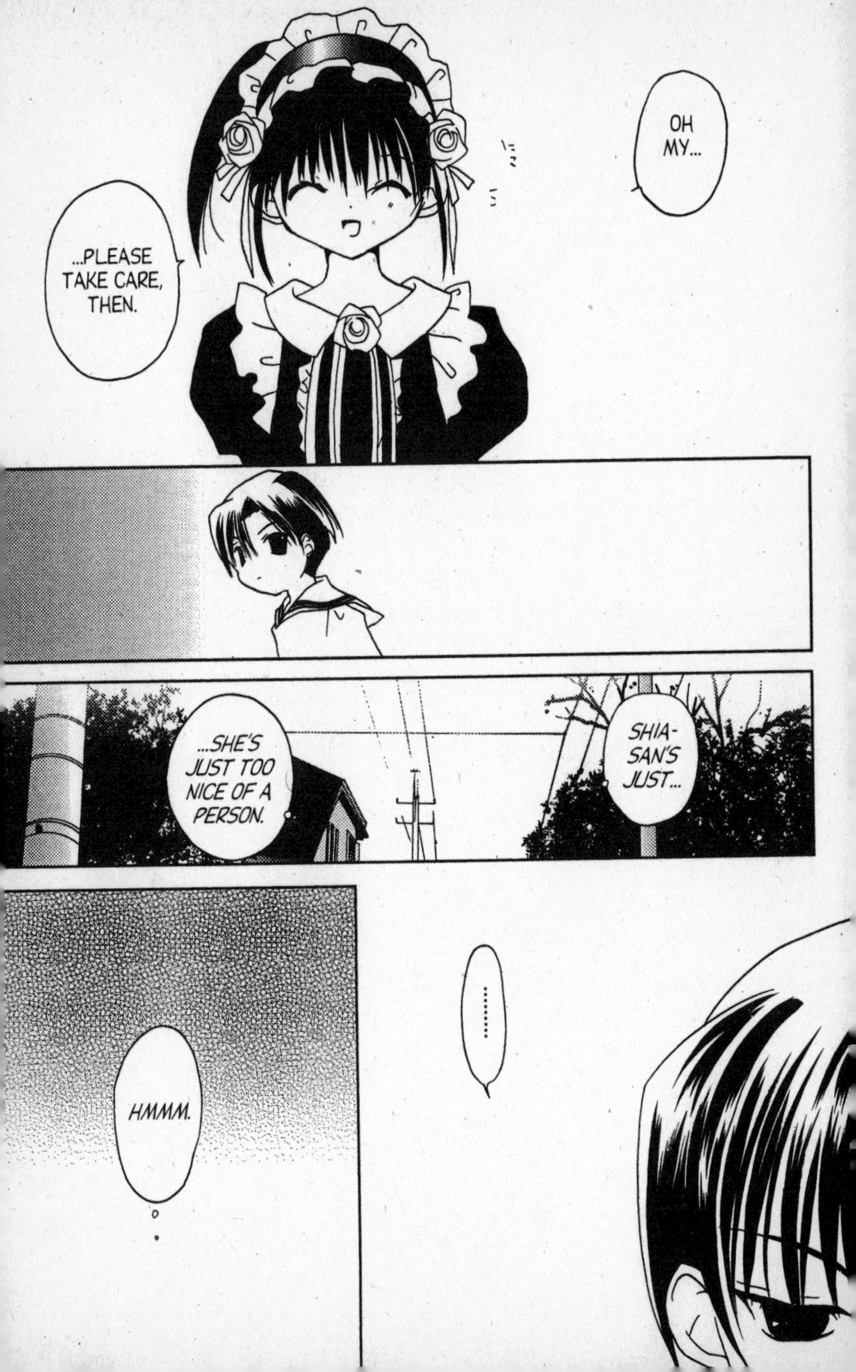
OH MY...
...PLEASE TAKE CARE, THEN.
SHIA-SAN'S JUST...
...SHE'S JUST TOO NICE OF A PERSON.
....
HMMM.

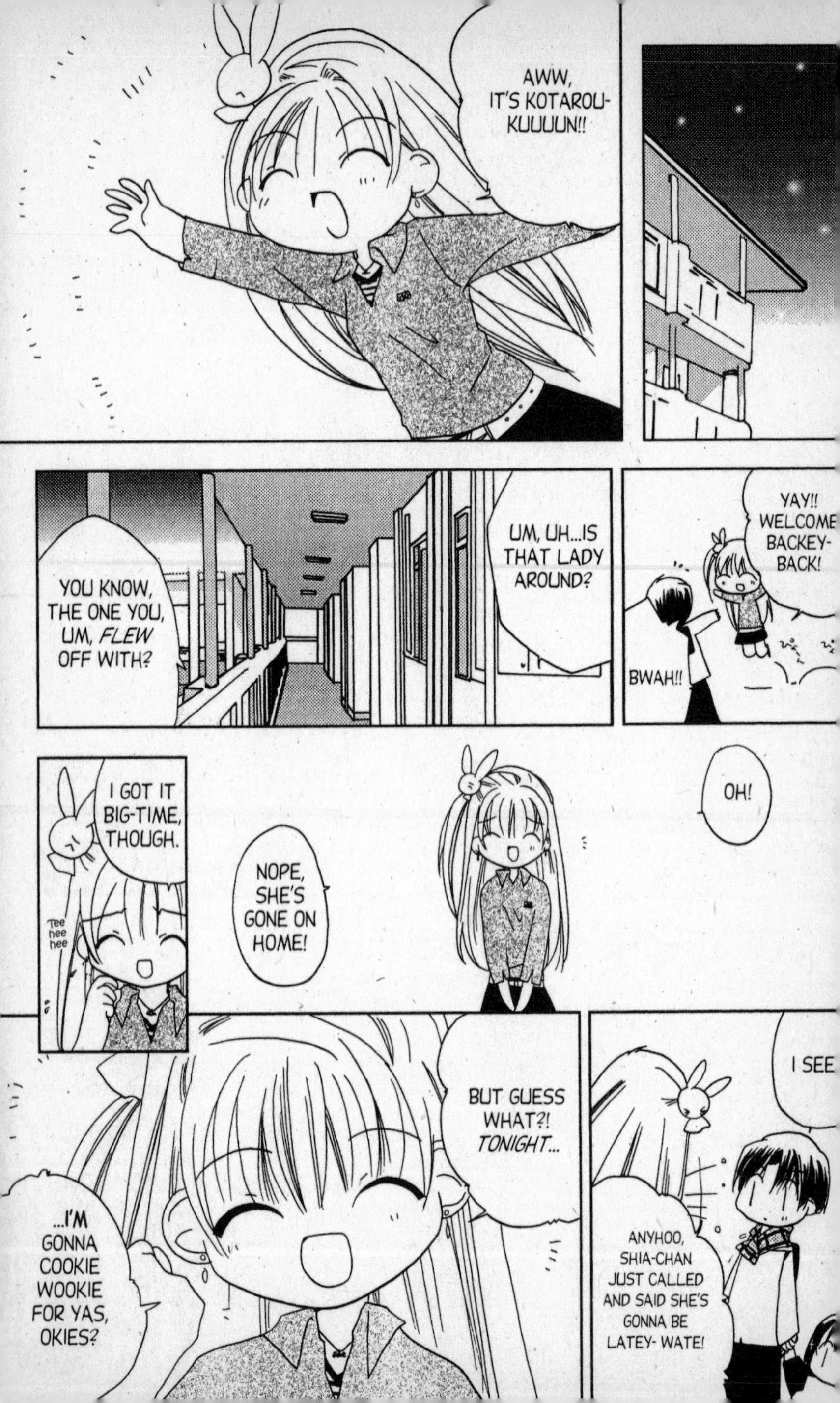
AWW, IT'S KOTAROU-KUUUUN!!
YAY!! WELCOME BACKEY-BACK!
BWAH!!
UM, UH...IS THAT LADY AROUND?
YOU KNOW, THE ONE YOU, UM, *FLEW* OFF WITH?
OH!
NOPE, SHE'S GONE ON HOME!
I GOT IT BIG-TIME, THOUGH.
Tee hee hee
I SEE
ANYHOO, SHIA-CHAN JUST CALLED AND SAID SHE'S GONNA BE LATEY-WATE!
BUT GUESS WHAT?! *TONIGHT*...
...I'M GONNA COOKIE WOOKIE FOR YAS, OKIES?

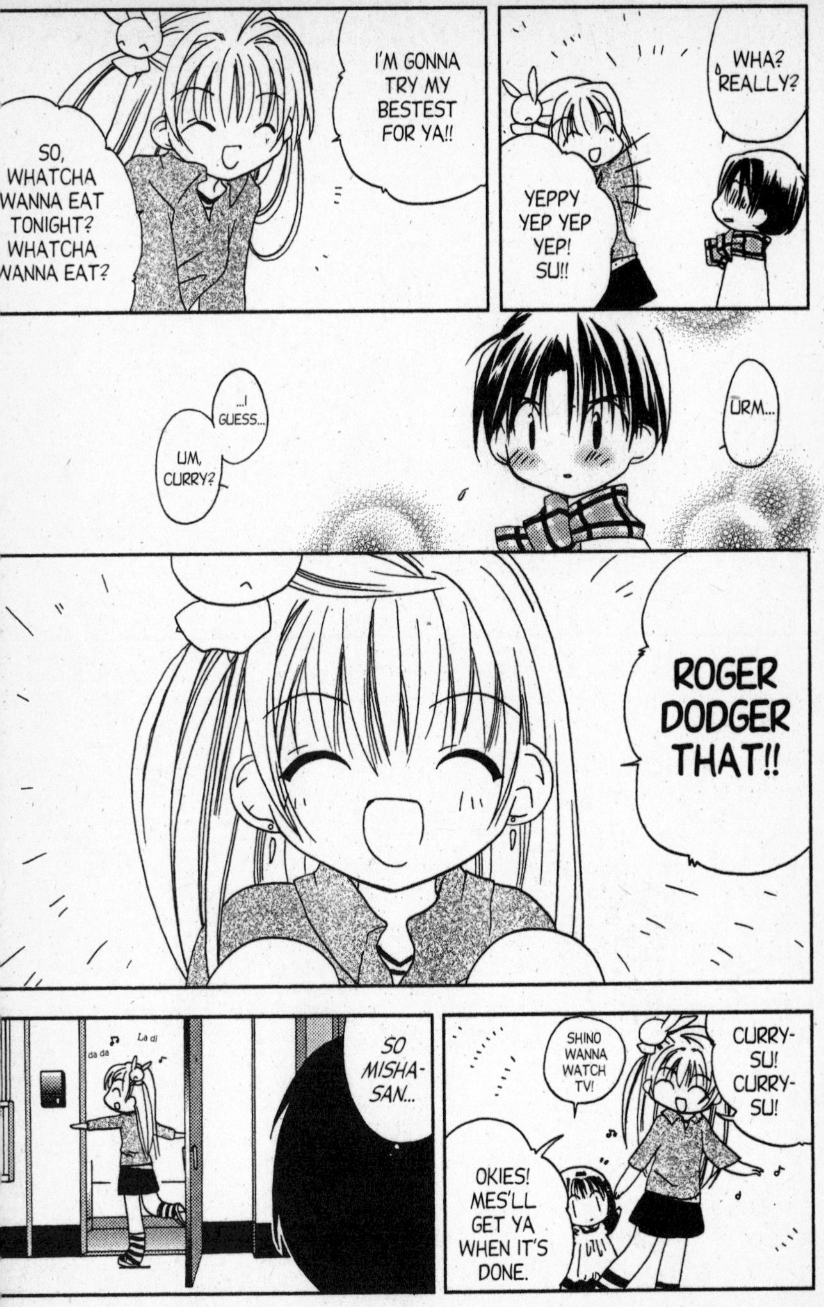
WHA? REALLY?
YEPPY YEP YEP YEP! SU!!
I'M GONNA TRY MY BESTEST FOR YA!!
SO, WHATCHA WANNA EAT TONIGHT? WHATCHA WANNA EAT?
URM...
...I GUESS...
UM, CURRY?
ROGER DODGER THAT!!
CURRY-SU! CURRY-SU!
SHINO WANNA WATCH TV!
OKIES! MES'LL GET YA WHEN IT'S DONE.
SO MISHA-SAN...
La di
da da

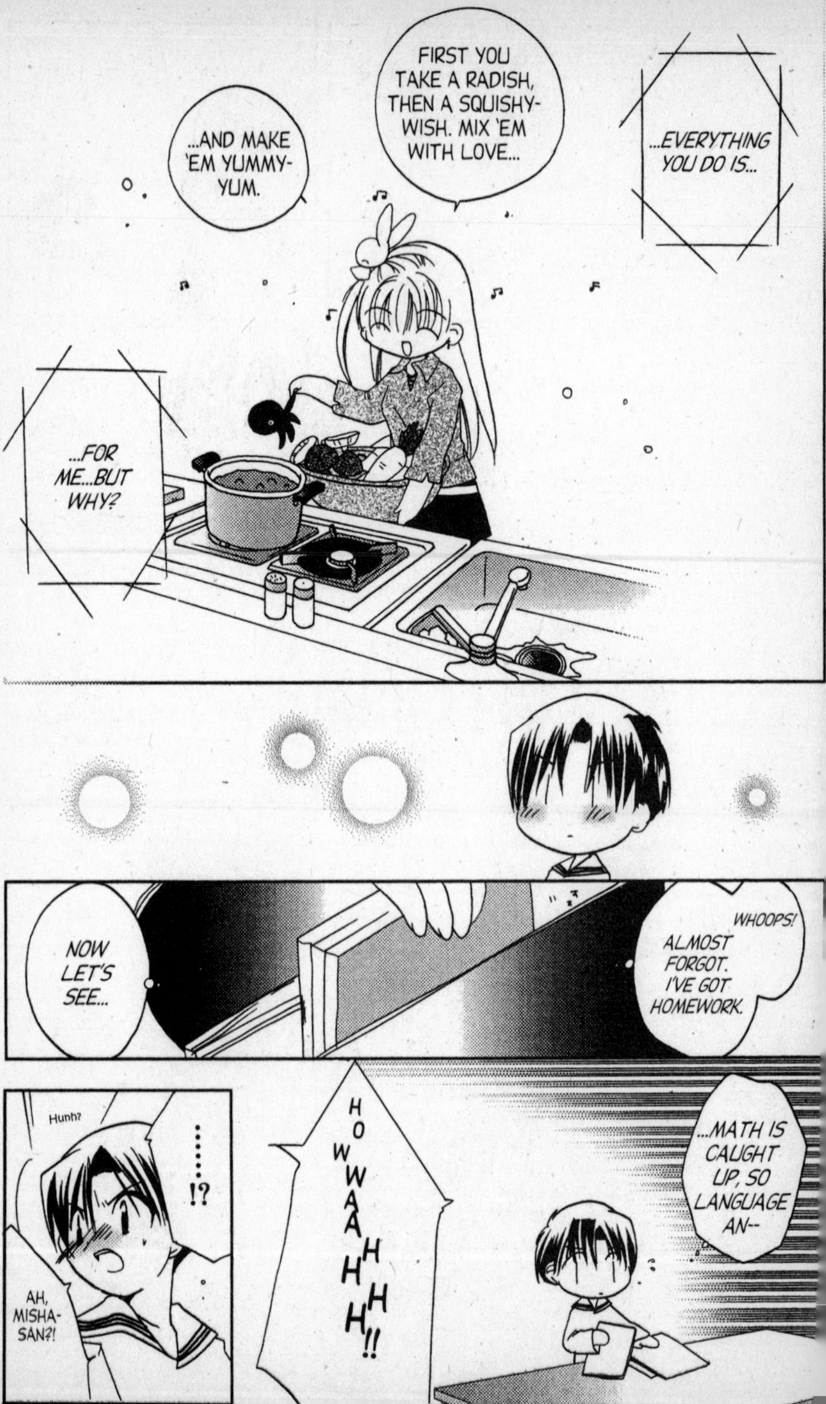
...EVERYTHING YOU DO IS...
FIRST YOU TAKE A RADISH, THEN A SQUISHY-WISH. MIX 'EM WITH LOVE...
...AND MAKE 'EM YUMMY-YUM.
...FOR ME...BUT WHY?
WHOOPS! ALMOST FORGOT. I'VE GOT HOMEWORK.
NOW LET'S SEE...
...MATH IS CAUGHT UP, SO LANGUAGE AN--
HOWWAAAHHHH!!
......!?
Hunh?
AH, MISHA-SAN?!

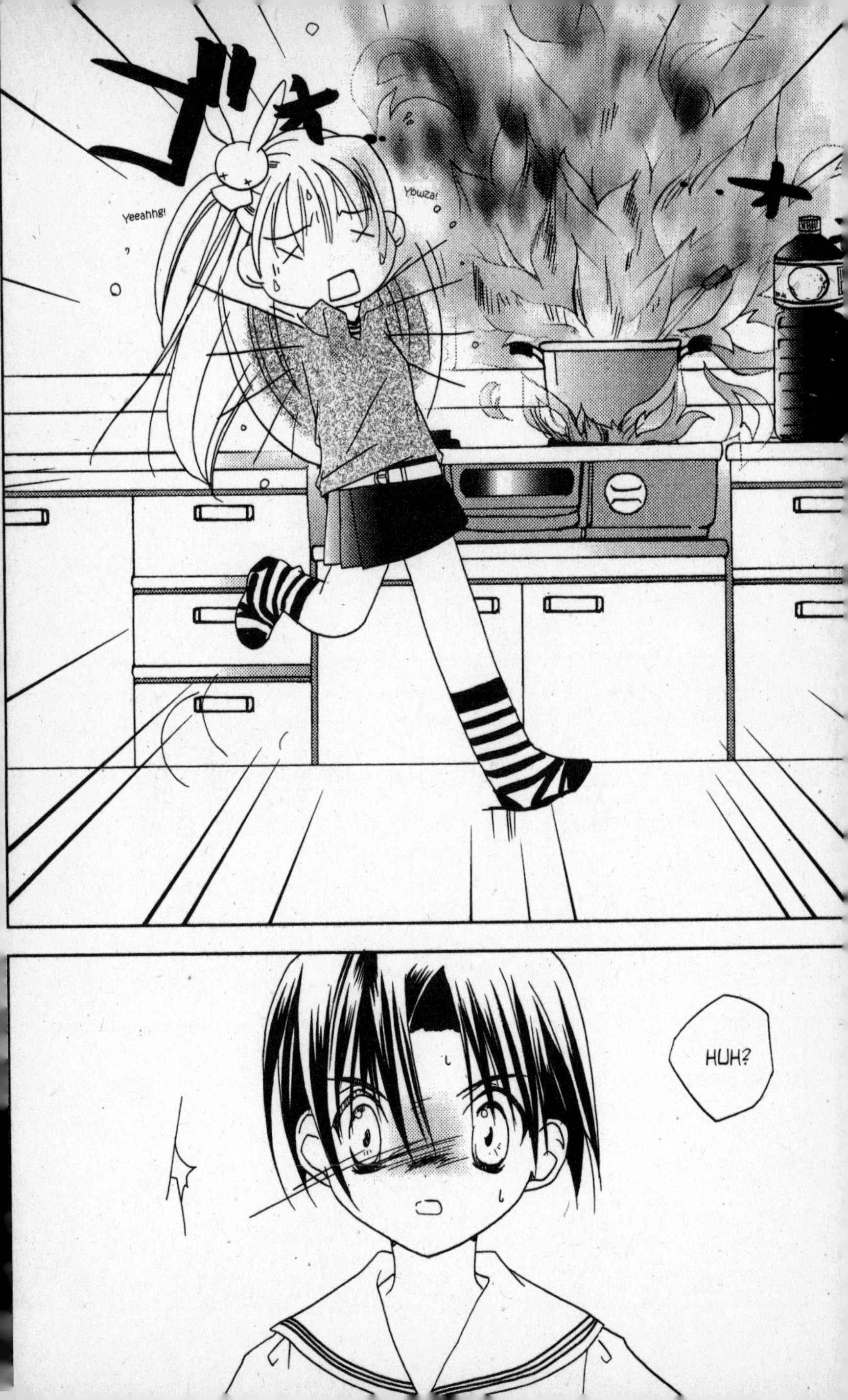
Youza!
Yeeahhg!
HUH?

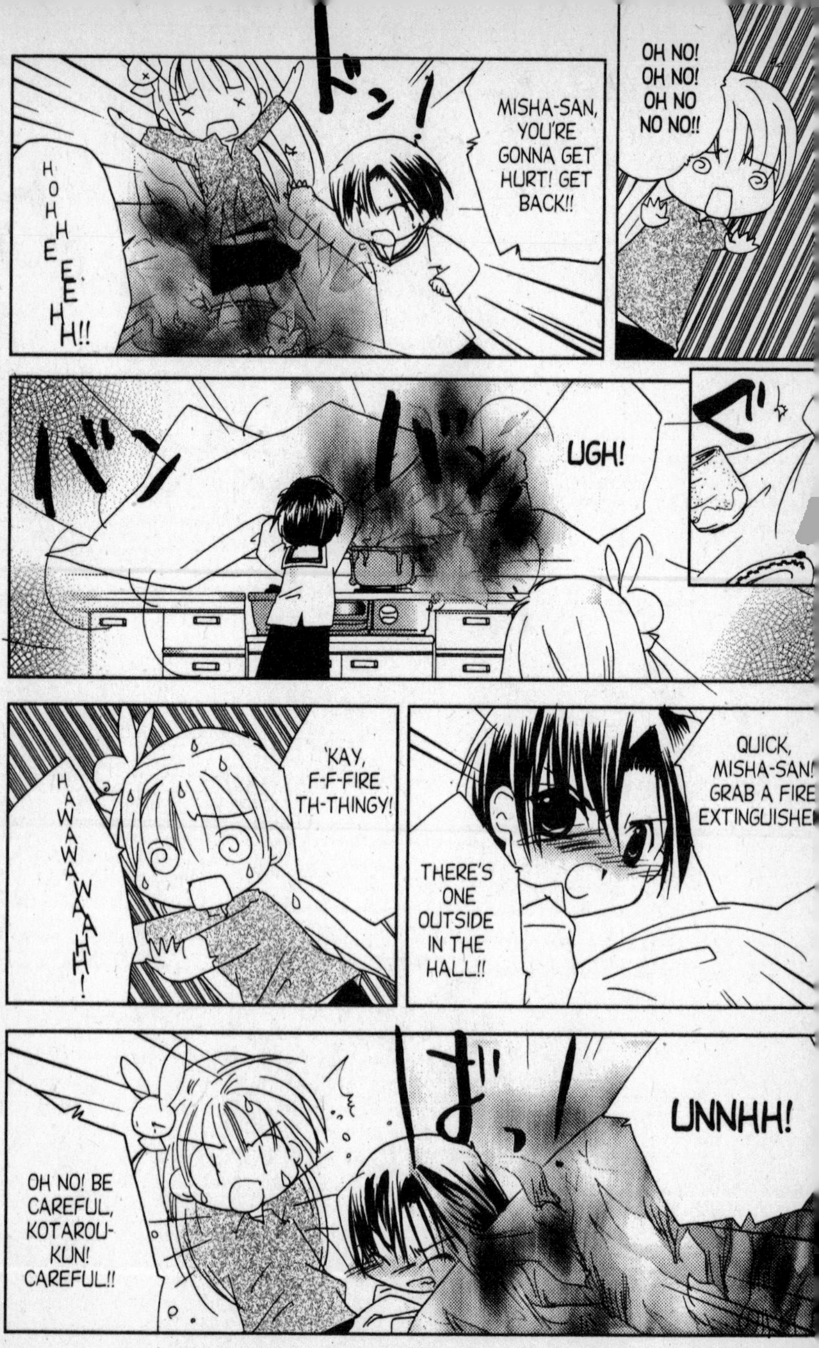
OH NO! OH NO! OH NO NO NO!!
ドン！
MISHA-SAN, YOU'RE GONNA GET HURT! GET BACK!!
HOHHEEEHH!!
UGH!
QUICK, MISHA-SAN! GRAB A FIRE EXTINGUISHE
THERE'S ONE OUTSIDE IN THE HALL!!
'KAY, F-F-FIRE TH-THINGY!
HAWAWAWAAHH!
UNNHH!
OH NO! BE CAREFUL, KOTAROU-KUN! CAREFUL!!

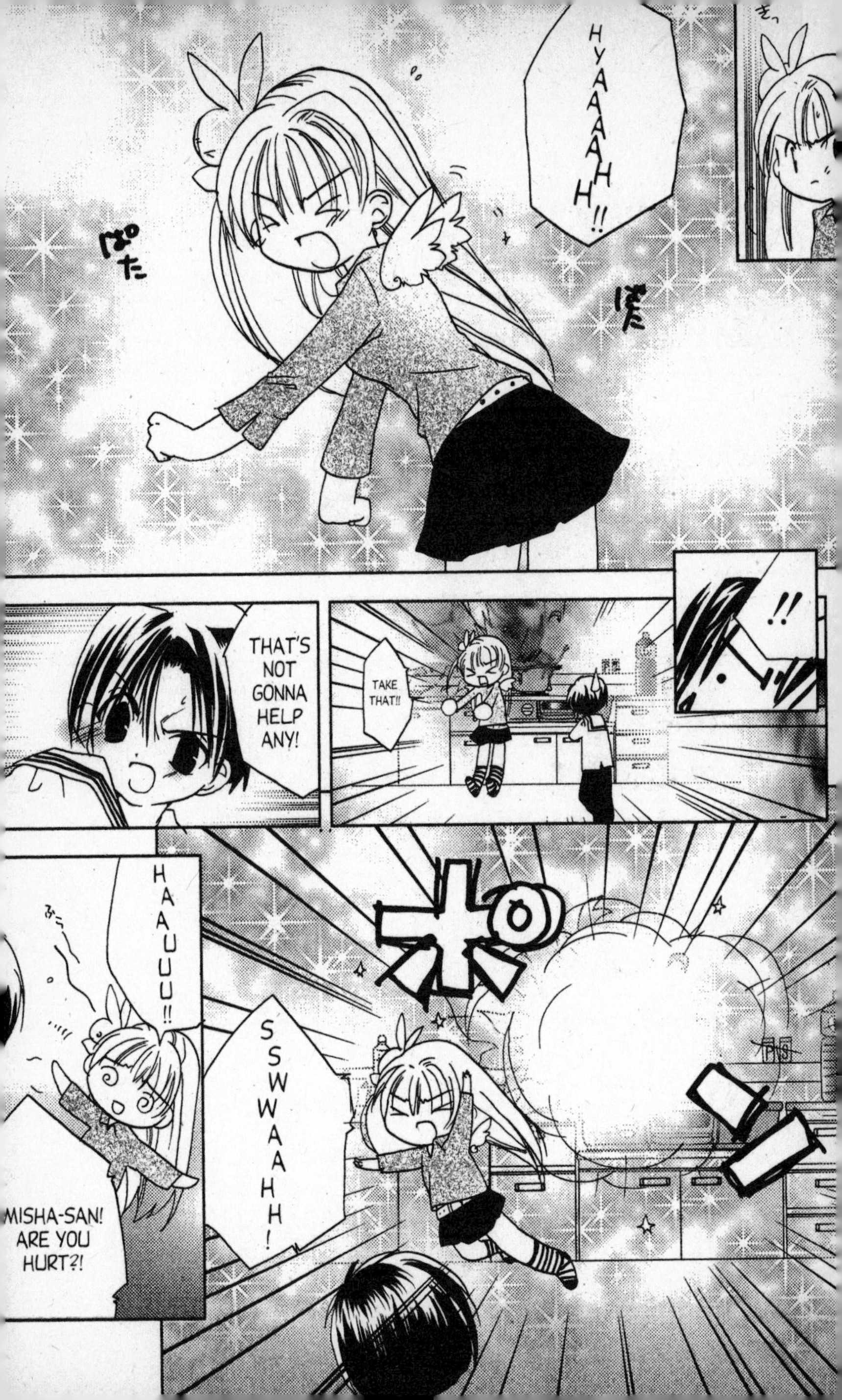
HYAAAAAHH!!
!!
TAKE THAT!!
THAT'S NOT GONNA HELP ANY!
SSWAAAHH!
HAAUUU!!
MISHA-SAN! ARE YOU HURT?!

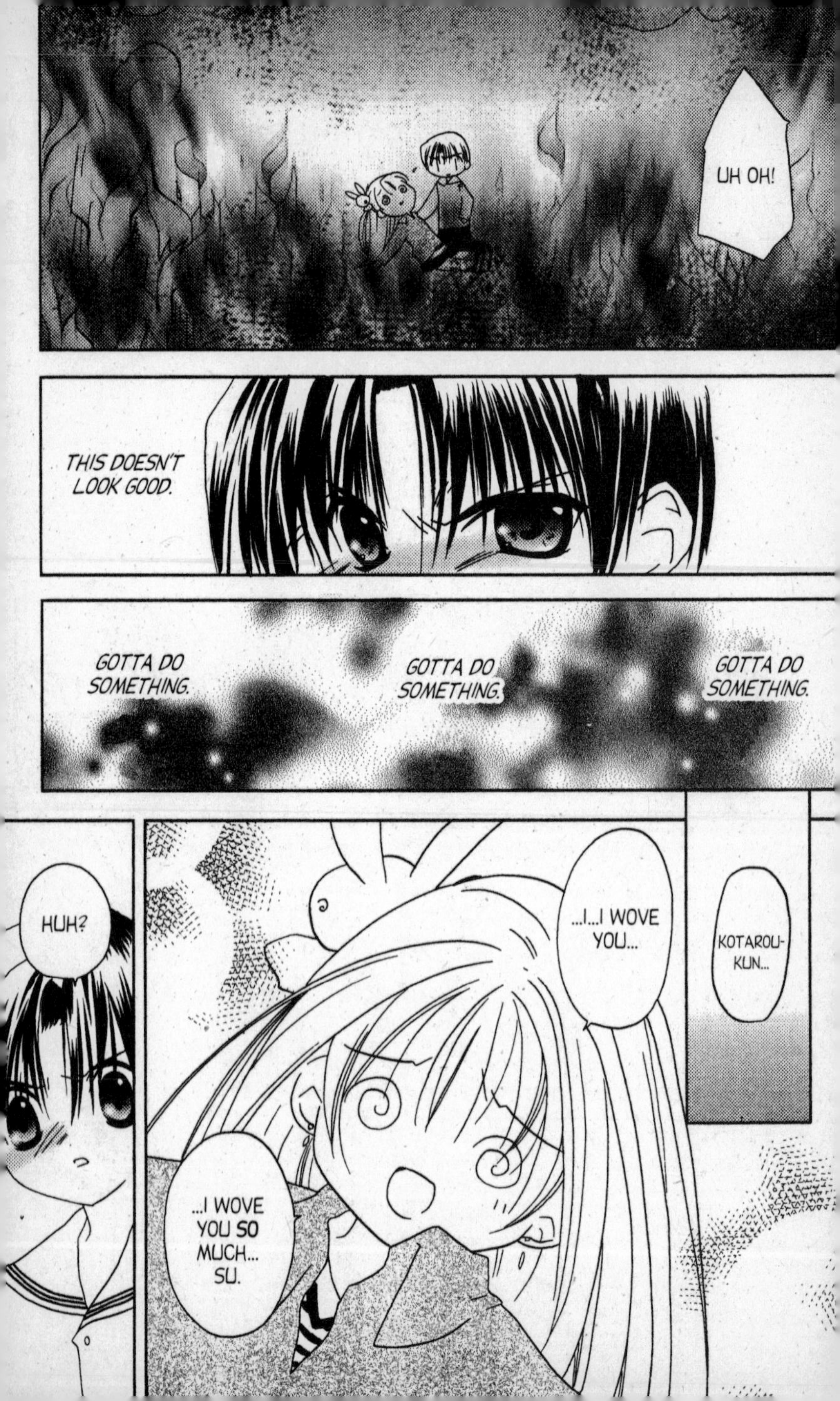
UH OH!
THIS DOESN'T LOOK GOOD.
GOTTA DO SOMETHING.
GOTTA DO SOMETHING.
GOTTA DO SOMETHING.
KOTAROU-KUN...
...I...I WOVE YOU...
...I WOVE YOU SO MUCH... SU.
HUH?

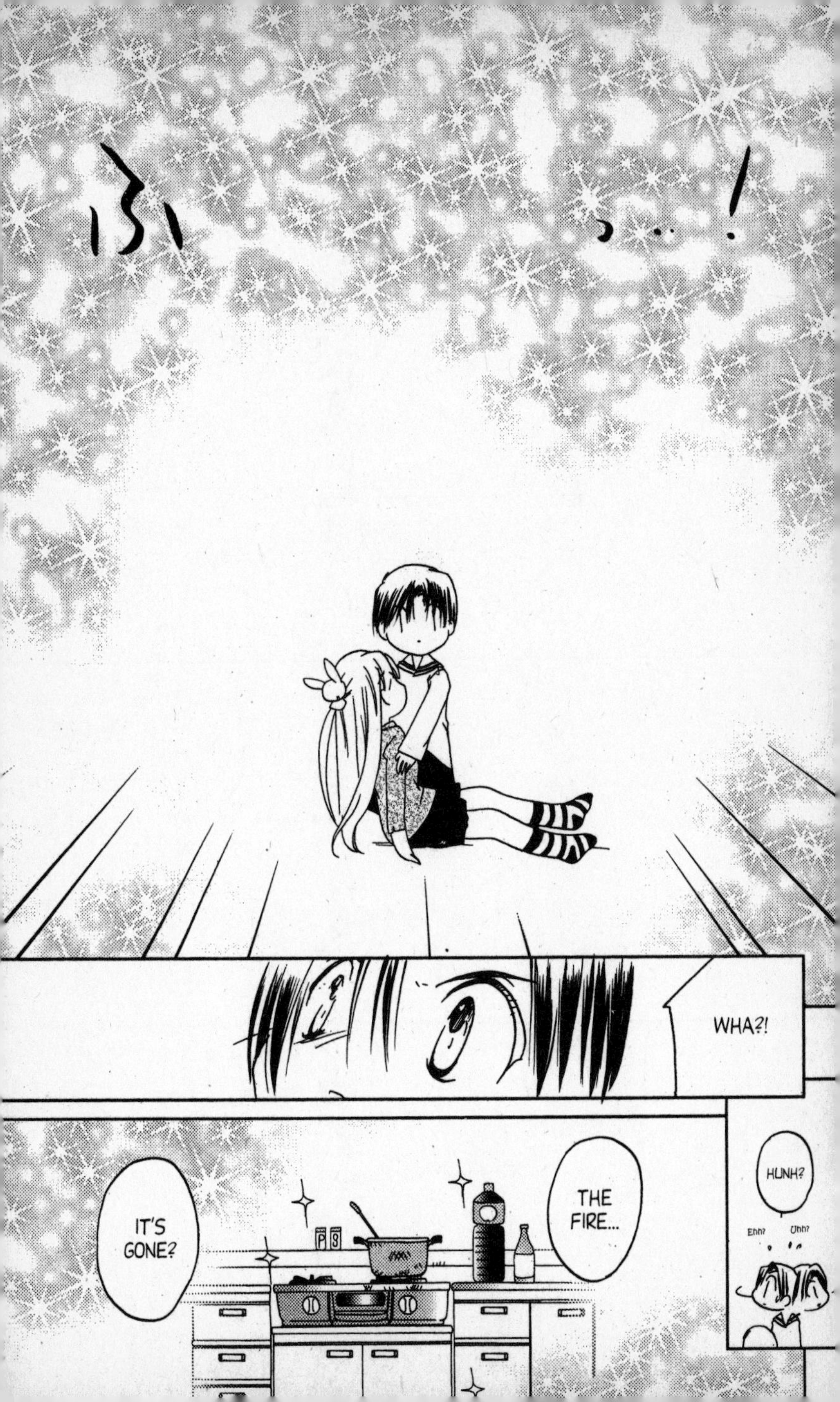
ふっ…!
WHA?!
HUNH?
Uhh?
Ehh?
THE FIRE...
IT'S GONE?

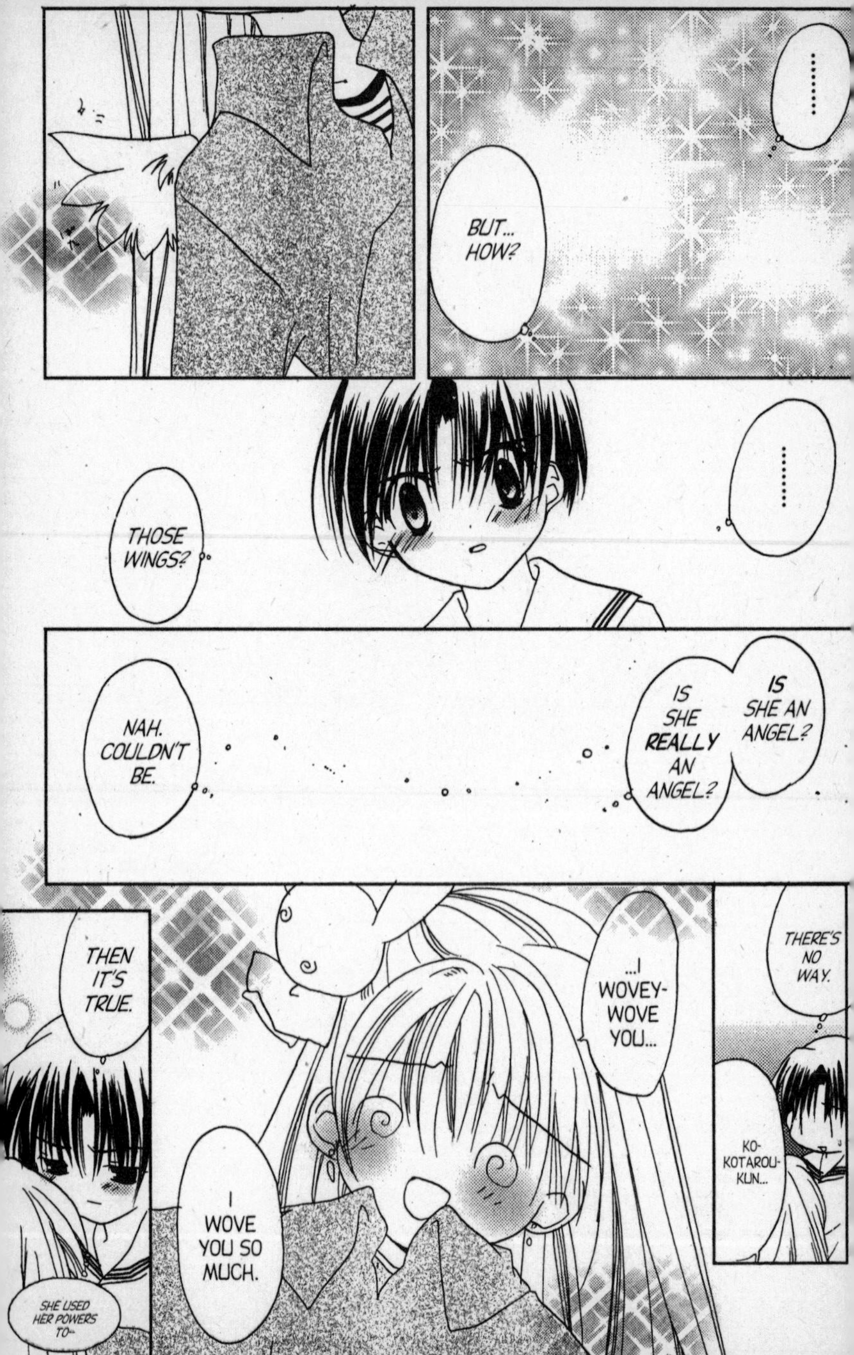
......
BUT... HOW?
......
THOSE WINGS?
IS SHE AN ANGEL?
IS SHE REALLY AN ANGEL?
NAH. COULDN'T BE.
THERE'S NO WAY.
KO-KOTAROU-KUN...
...I WOVEY-WOVE YOU...
I WOVE YOU SO MUCH.
THEN IT'S TRUE.
SHE USED HER POWERS TO--

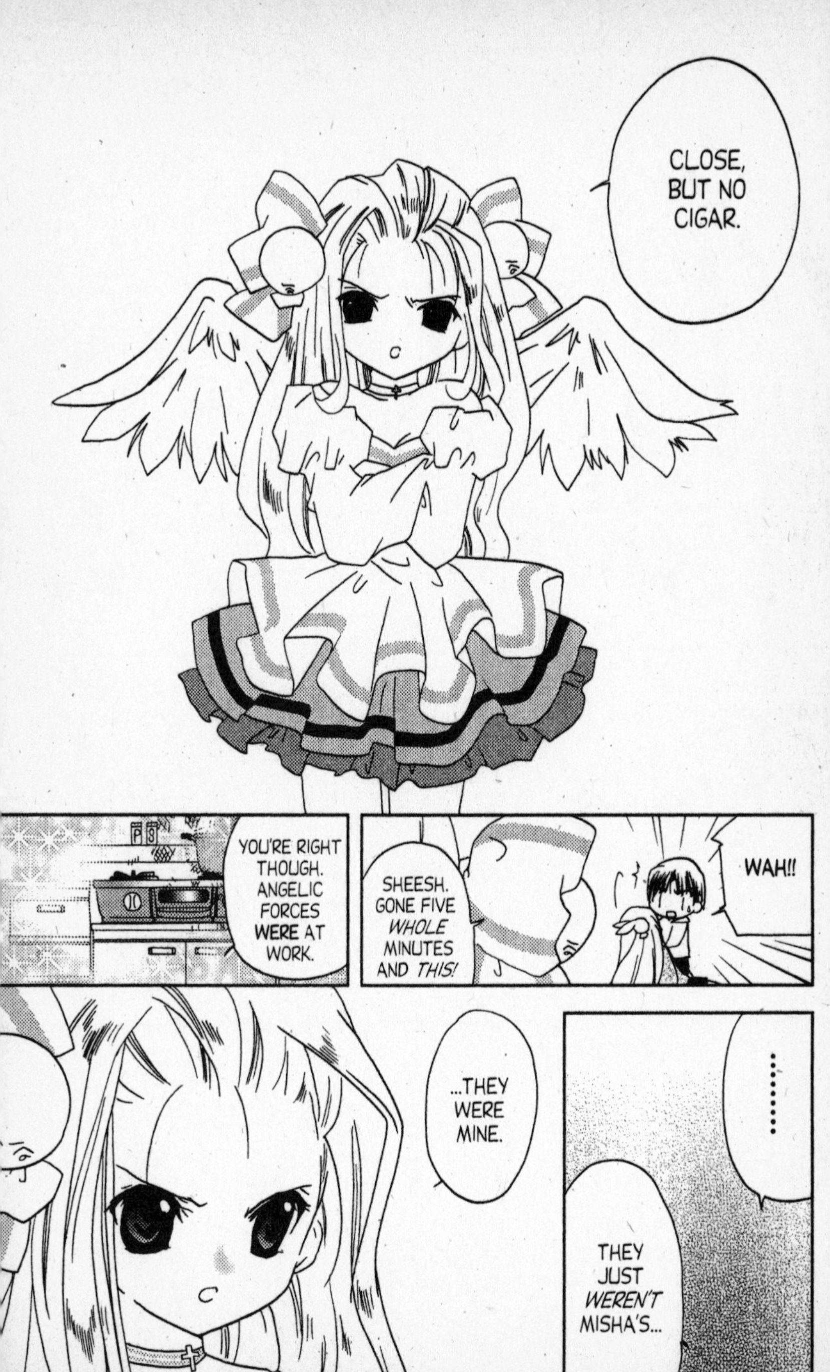
CLOSE, BUT NO CIGAR.
WAH!!
SHEESH. GONE FIVE *WHOLE* MINUTES AND *THIS!*
YOU'RE RIGHT THOUGH. ANGELIC FORCES **WERE** AT WORK.
....
THEY JUST *WEREN'T* MISHA'S...
...THEY WERE MINE.

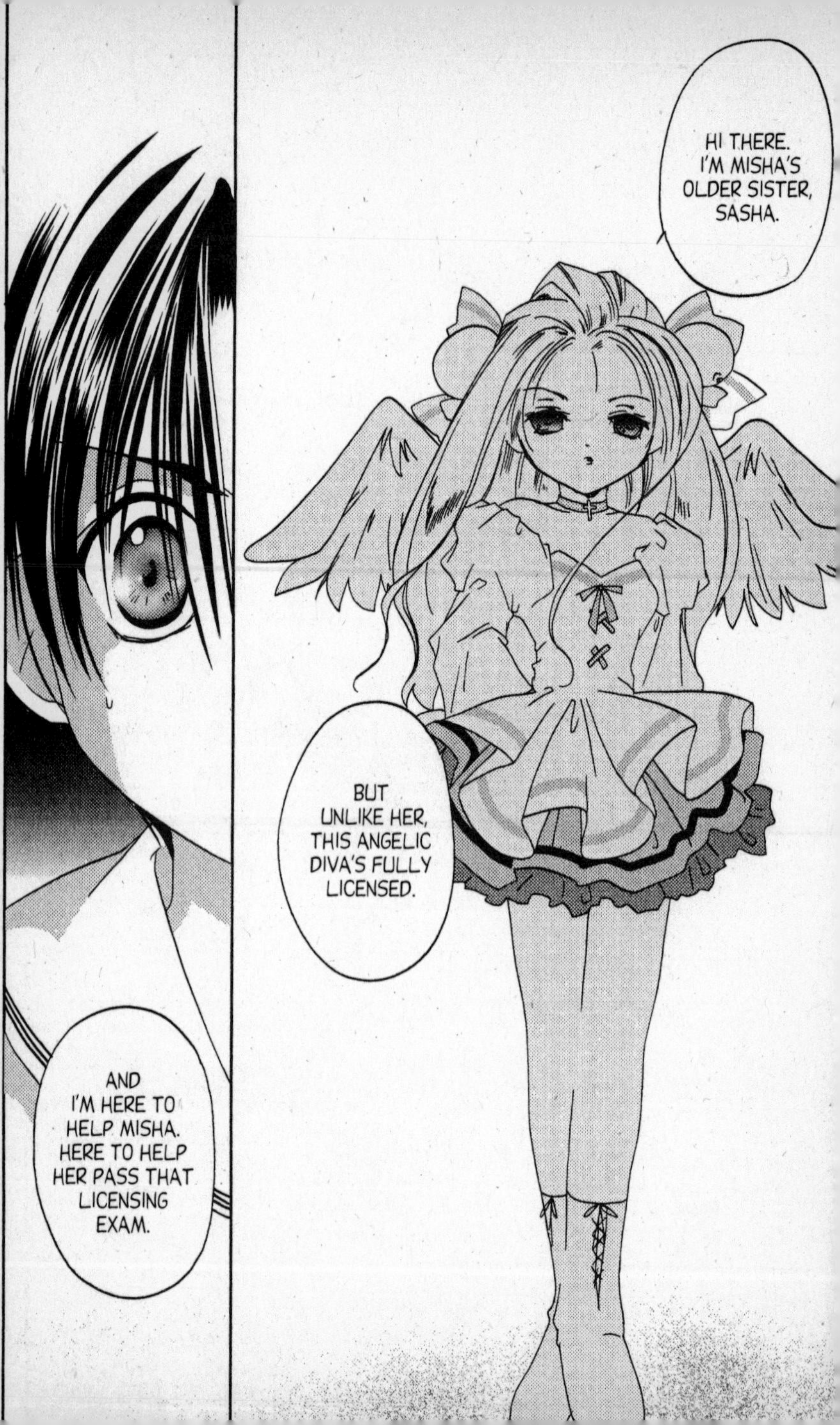
HI THERE. I'M MISHA'S OLDER SISTER, SASHA.
BUT UNLIKE HER, THIS ANGELIC DIVA'S FULLY LICENSED.
AND I'M HERE TO HELP MISHA. HERE TO HELP HER PASS THAT LICENSING EXAM.

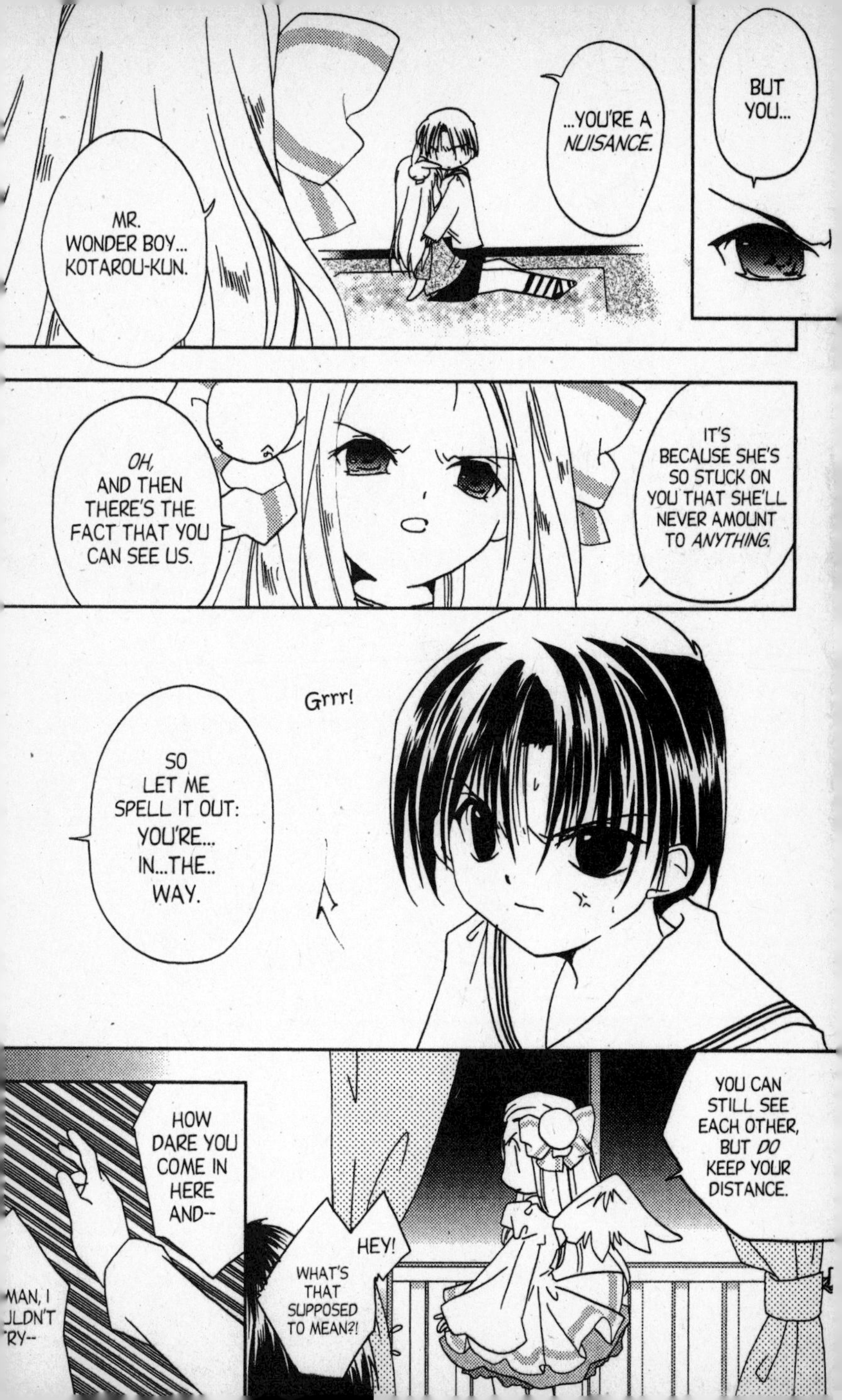
BUT YOU...
...YOU'RE A *NUISANCE.*
MR. WONDER BOY... KOTAROU-KUN.
IT'S BECAUSE SHE'S SO STUCK ON YOU THAT SHE'LL NEVER AMOUNT TO *ANYTHING.*
OH, AND THEN THERE'S THE FACT THAT YOU CAN SEE US.
Grrr!
SO LET ME SPELL IT OUT: YOU'RE... IN...THE.. WAY.
YOU CAN STILL SEE EACH OTHER, BUT *DO* KEEP YOUR DISTANCE.
HEY!
WHAT'S THAT SUPPOSED TO MEAN?!
HOW DARE YOU COME IN HERE AND--
MAN, I
ULDN'T
RY--

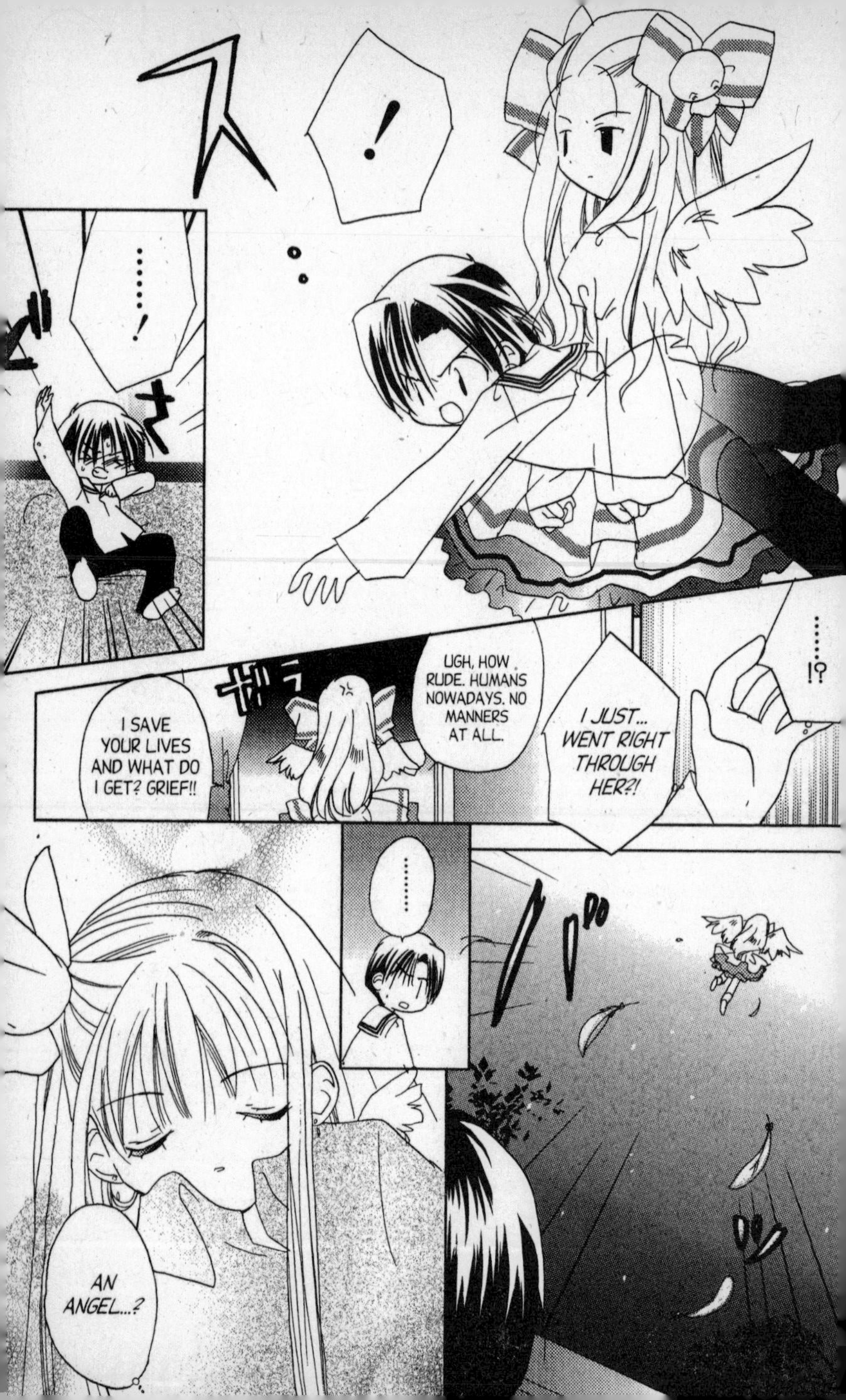
!
......!
......!?
I JUST... WENT RIGHT THROUGH HER?!
UGH, HOW RUDE. HUMANS NOWADAYS. NO MANNERS AT ALL.
I SAVE YOUR LIVES AND WHAT DO I GET? GRIEF!!
......
AN ANGEL...?

Lesson 27

How to Make a Boxed Lunch

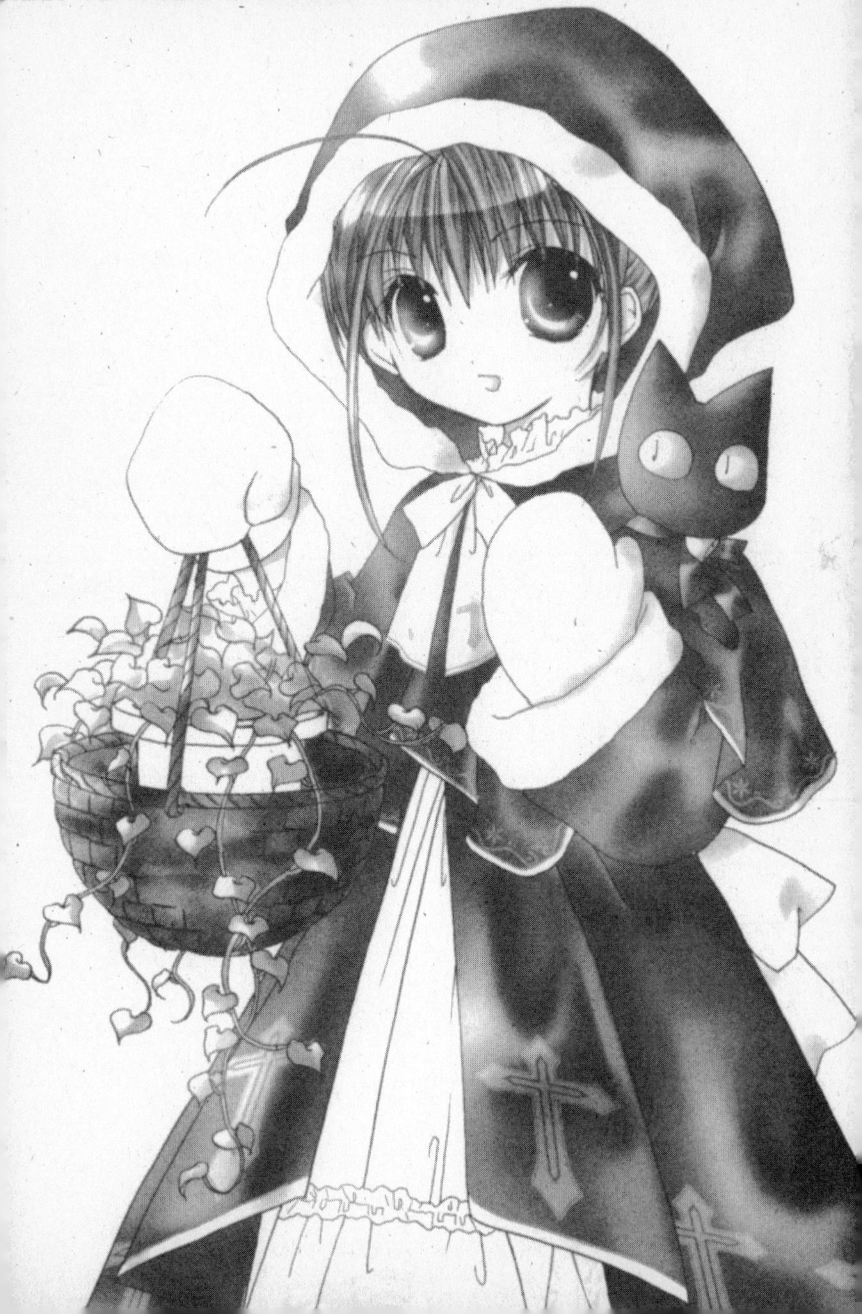

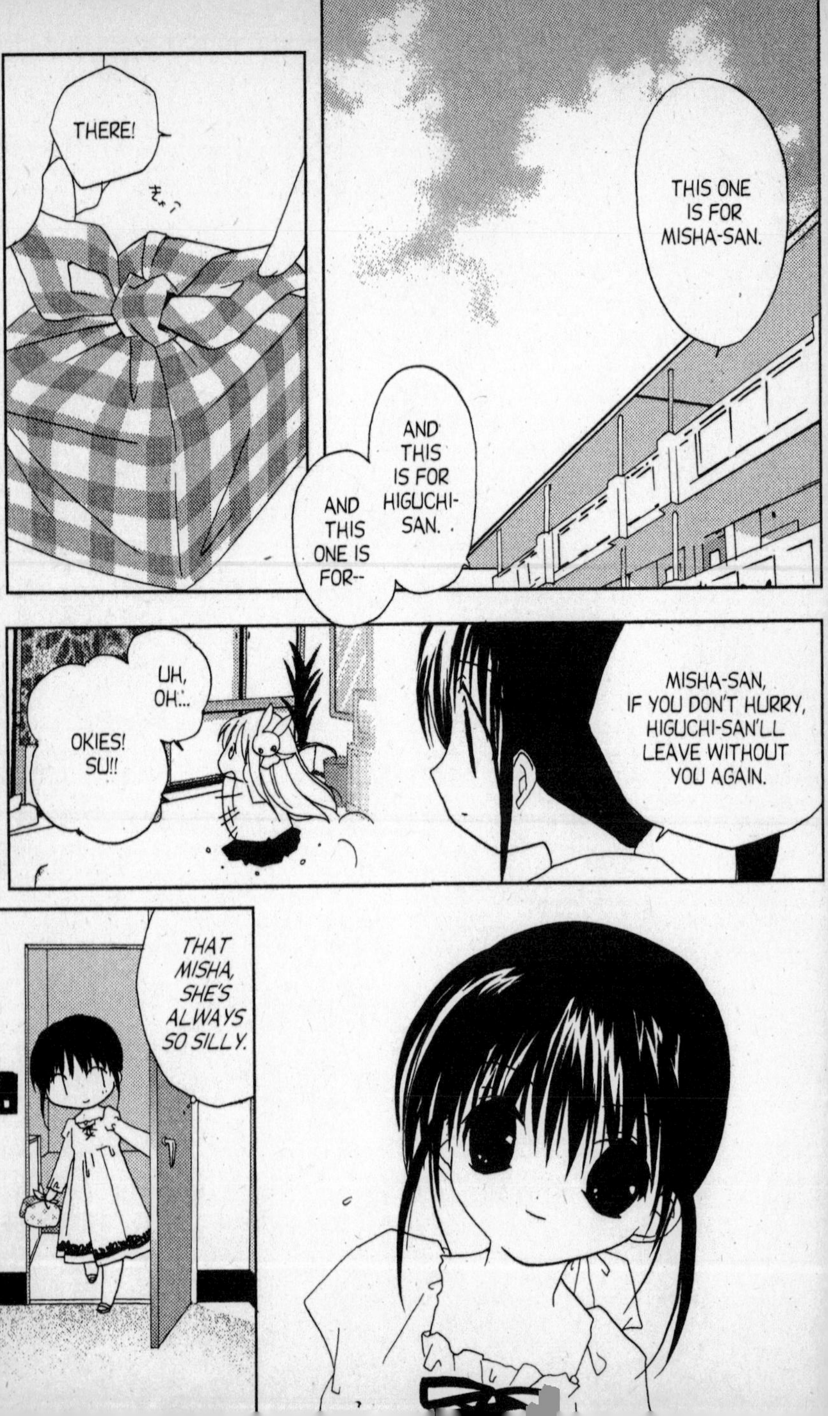
THIS ONE IS FOR MISHA-SAN.
AND THIS IS FOR HIGUCHI-SAN.
AND THIS ONE IS FOR--
THERE!
MISHA-SAN, IF YOU DON'T HURRY, HIGUCHI-SAN'LL LEAVE WITHOUT YOU AGAIN.
UH, OH...
OKIES! SU!!
THAT MISHA, SHE'S ALWAYS SO SILLY.

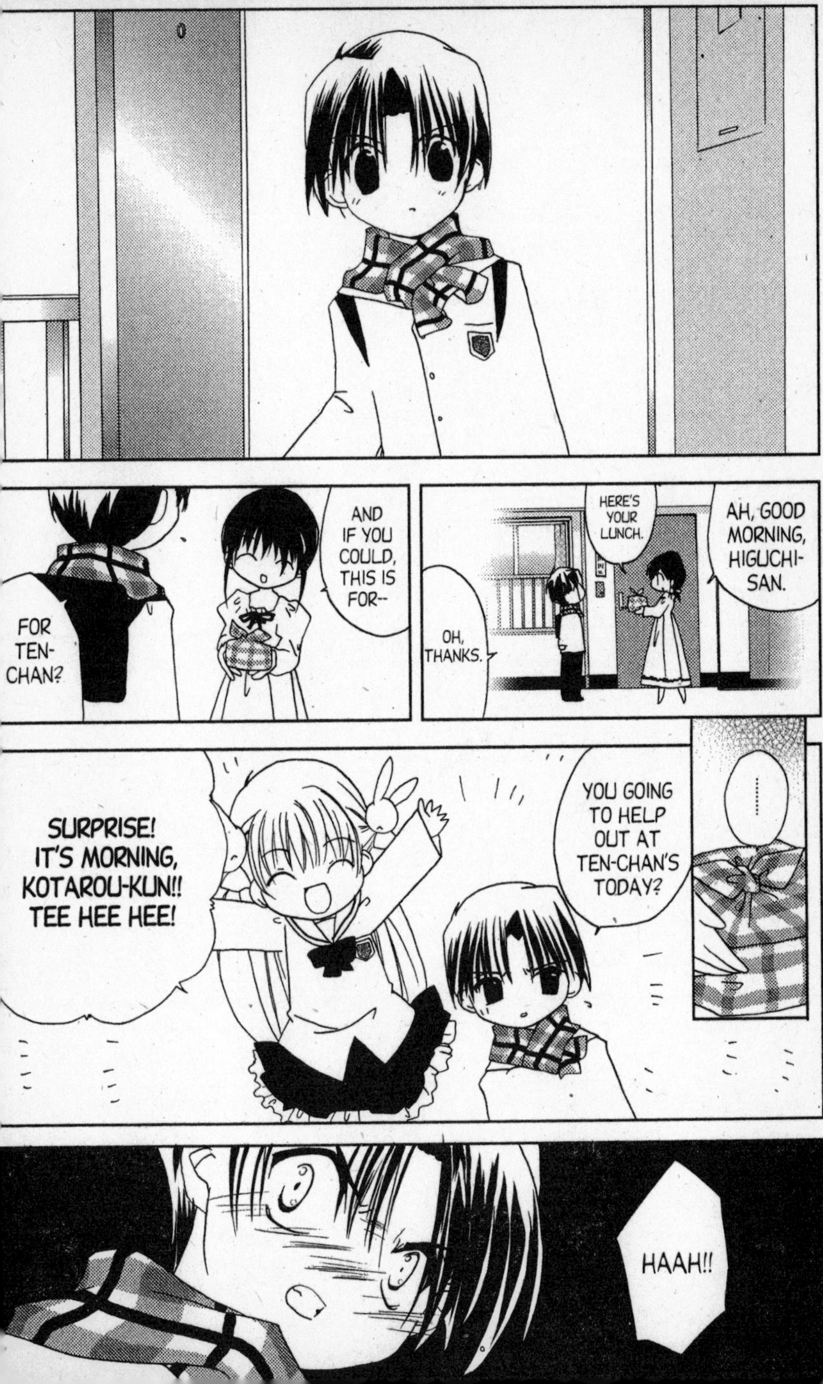
AH, GOOD MORNING, HIGUCHI-SAN.
HERE'S YOUR LUNCH.
OH, THANKS.
AND IF YOU COULD, THIS IS FOR--
FOR TEN-CHAN?
......
YOU GOING TO HELP OUT AT TEN-CHAN'S TODAY?
SURPRISE! IT'S MORNING, KOTAROU-KUN!! TEE HEE HEE!
HAAH!!

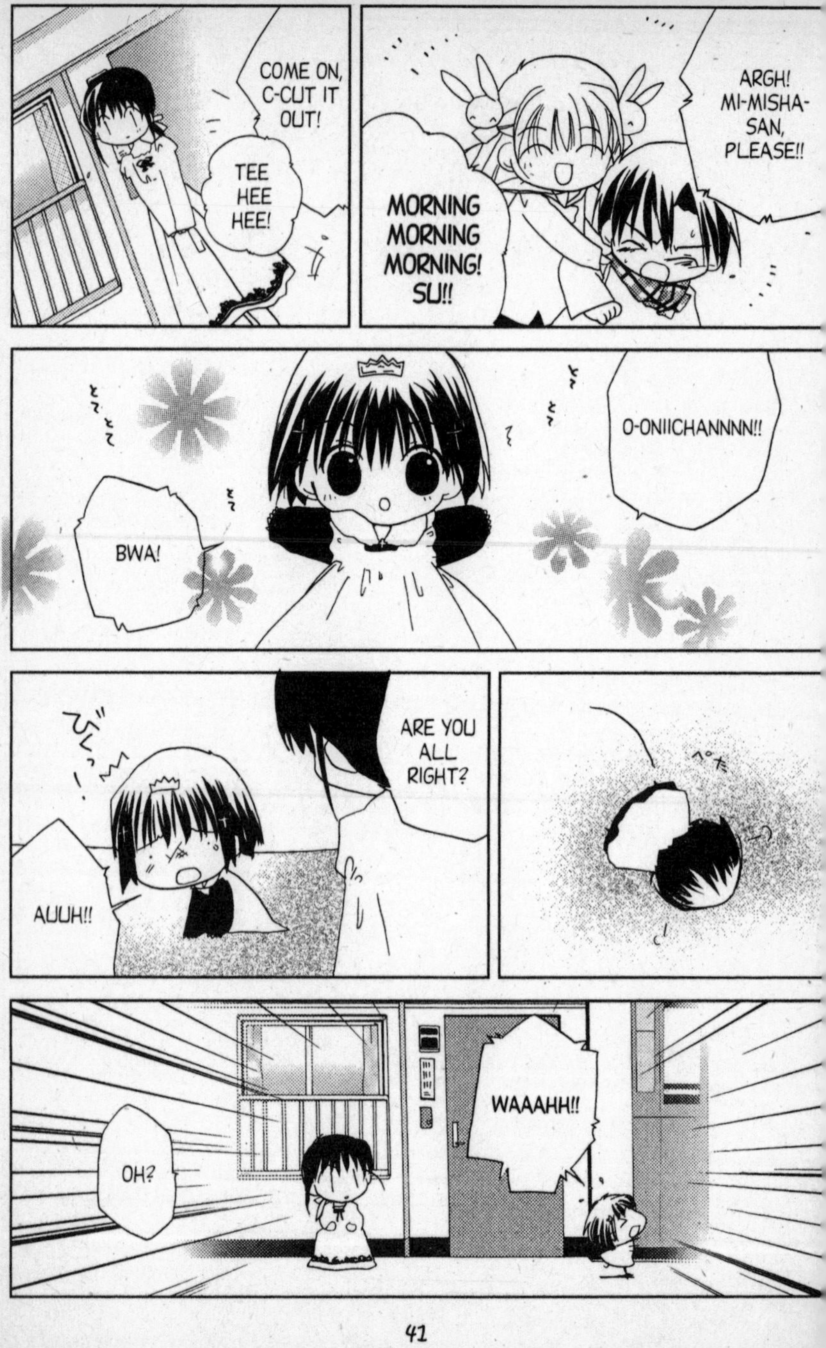
ARGH! MI-MISHA-SAN, PLEASE!!
MORNING MORNING MORNING! SU!!
COME ON, C-CUT IT OUT!
TEE HEE HEE!
O-ONIICHANNNN!!
BWA!
ARE YOU ALL RIGHT?
AUUH!!
WAAAHH!!
OH?

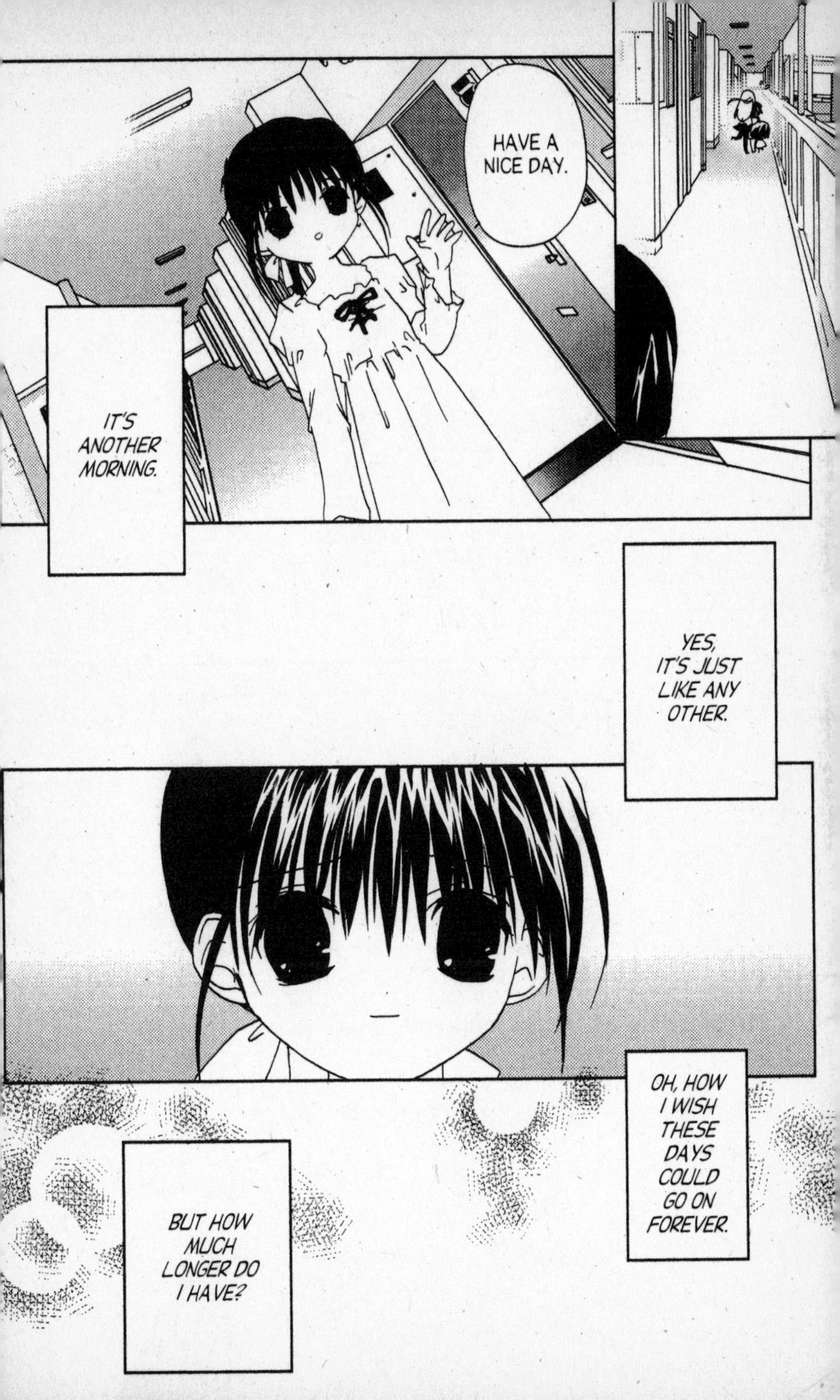
HAVE A NICE DAY.
IT'S ANOTHER MORNING.
YES, IT'S JUST LIKE ANY OTHER.
OH, HOW I WISH THESE DAYS COULD GO ON FOREVER.
BUT HOW MUCH LONGER DO I HAVE?

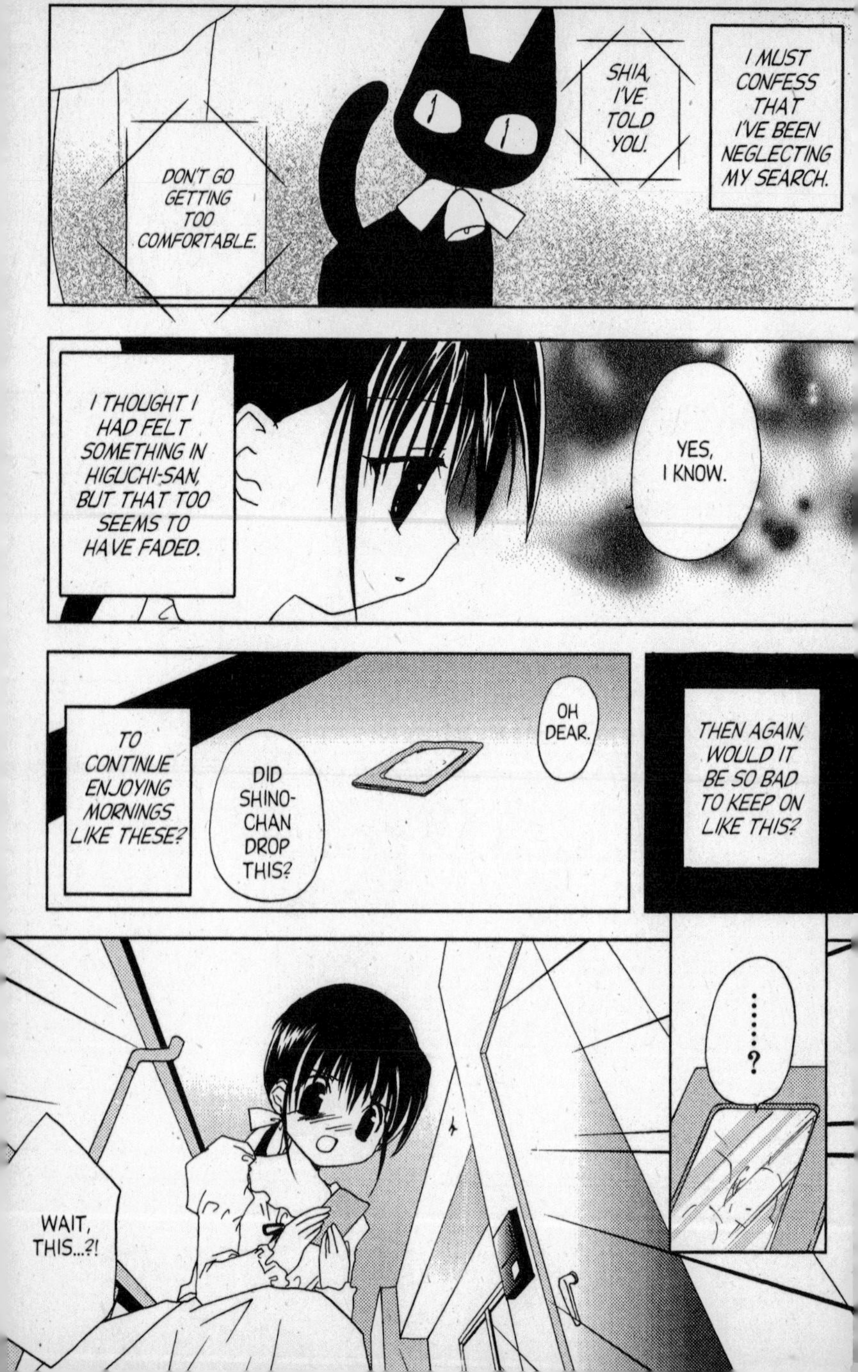
I MUST CONFESS THAT I'VE BEEN NEGLECTING MY SEARCH.
SHIA, I'VE TOLD YOU.
DON'T GO GETTING TOO COMFORTABLE.
YES, I KNOW.
I THOUGHT I HAD FELT SOMETHING IN HIGUCHI-SAN, BUT THAT TOO SEEMS TO HAVE FADED.
THEN AGAIN, WOULD IT BE SO BAD TO KEEP ON LIKE THIS?
OH DEAR.
DID SHINO-CHAN DROP THIS?
TO CONTINUE ENJOYING MORNINGS LIKE THESE?
......?
WAIT, THIS...?!

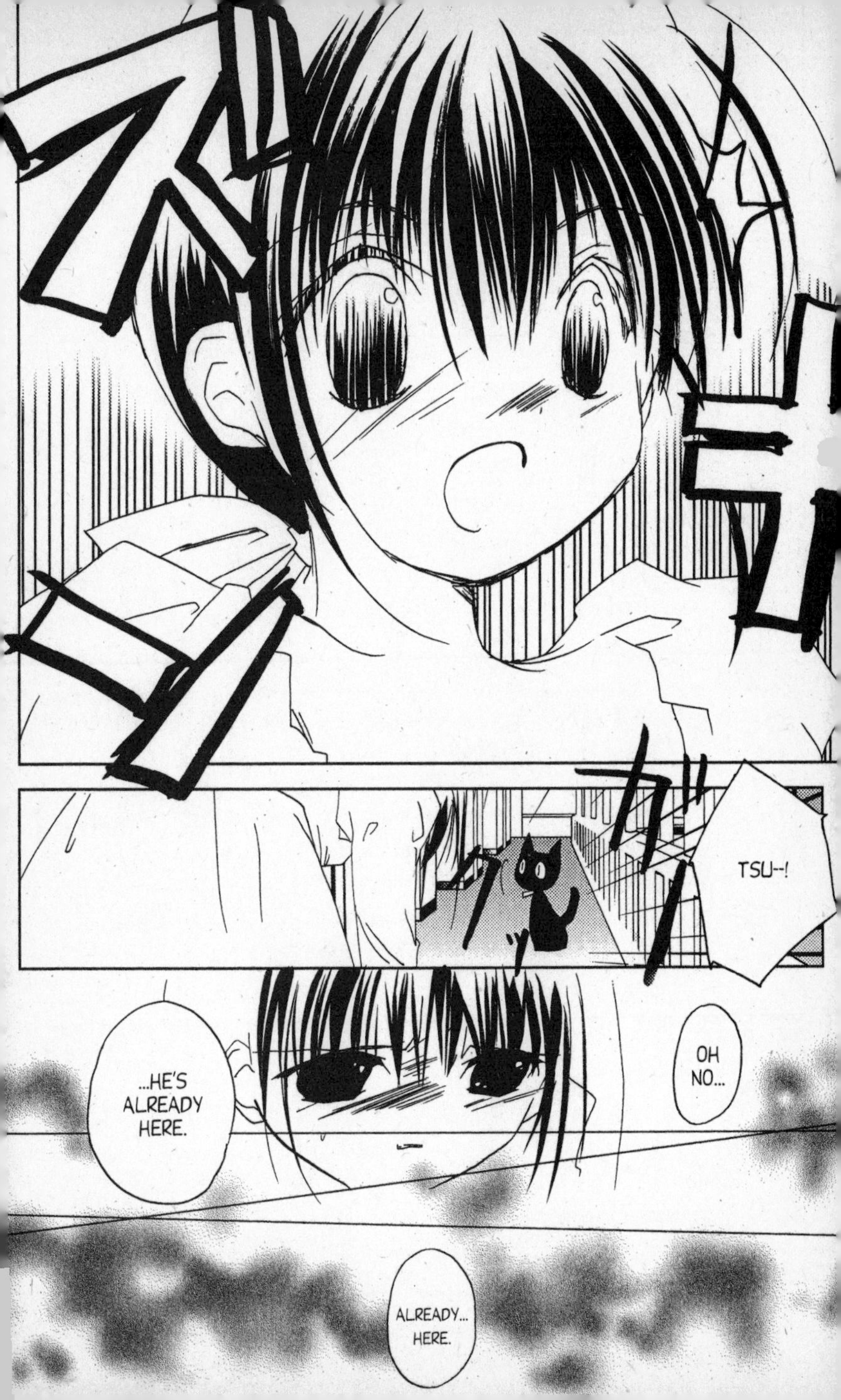
TSU--!
OH NO...
...HE'S ALREADY HERE.
ALREADY... HERE.

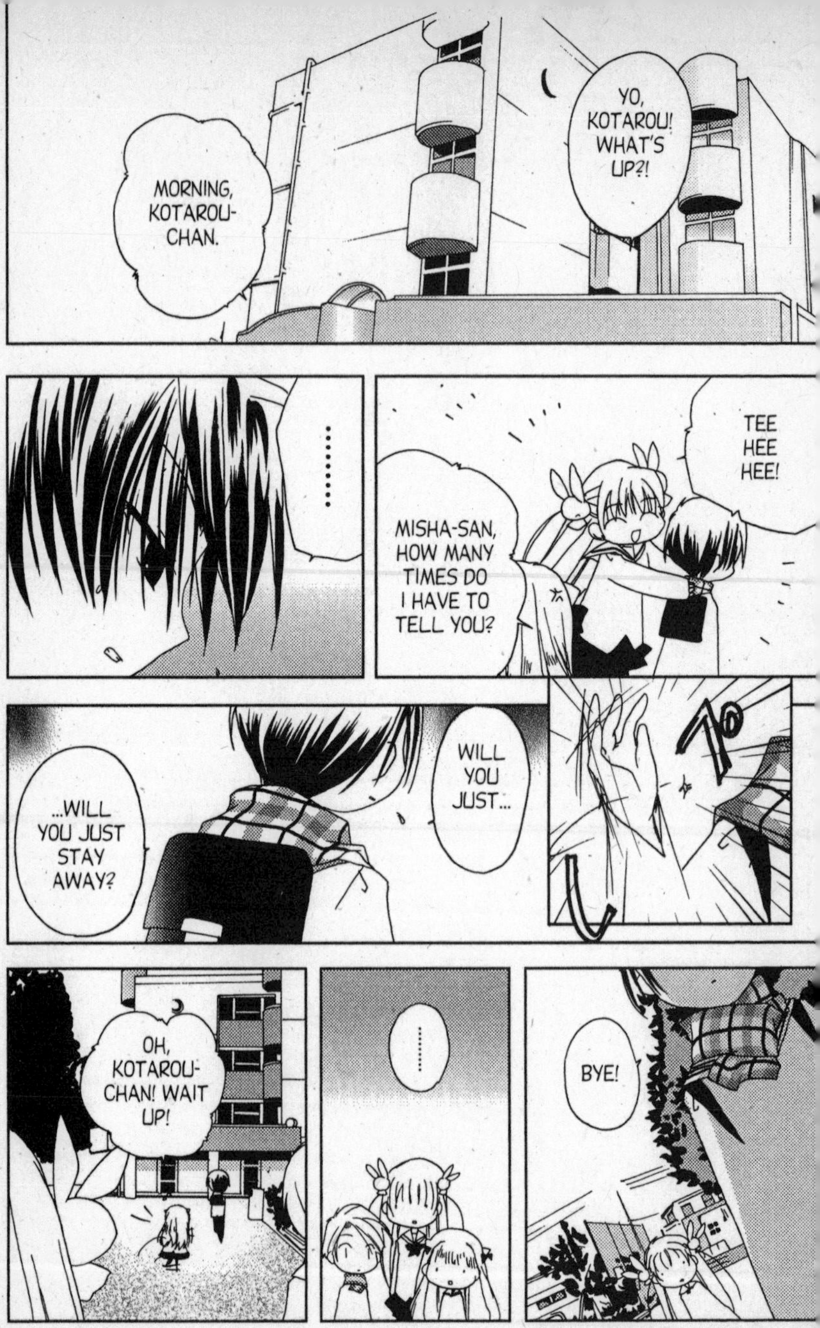
YO, KOTAROU! WHAT'S UP?!
MORNING, KOTAROU-CHAN.
TEE HEE HEE!
MISHA-SAN, HOW MANY TIMES DO I HAVE TO TELL YOU?
......
WILL YOU JUST...
...WILL YOU JUST STAY AWAY?
BYE!
......
OH, KOTAROU-CHAN! WAIT UP!

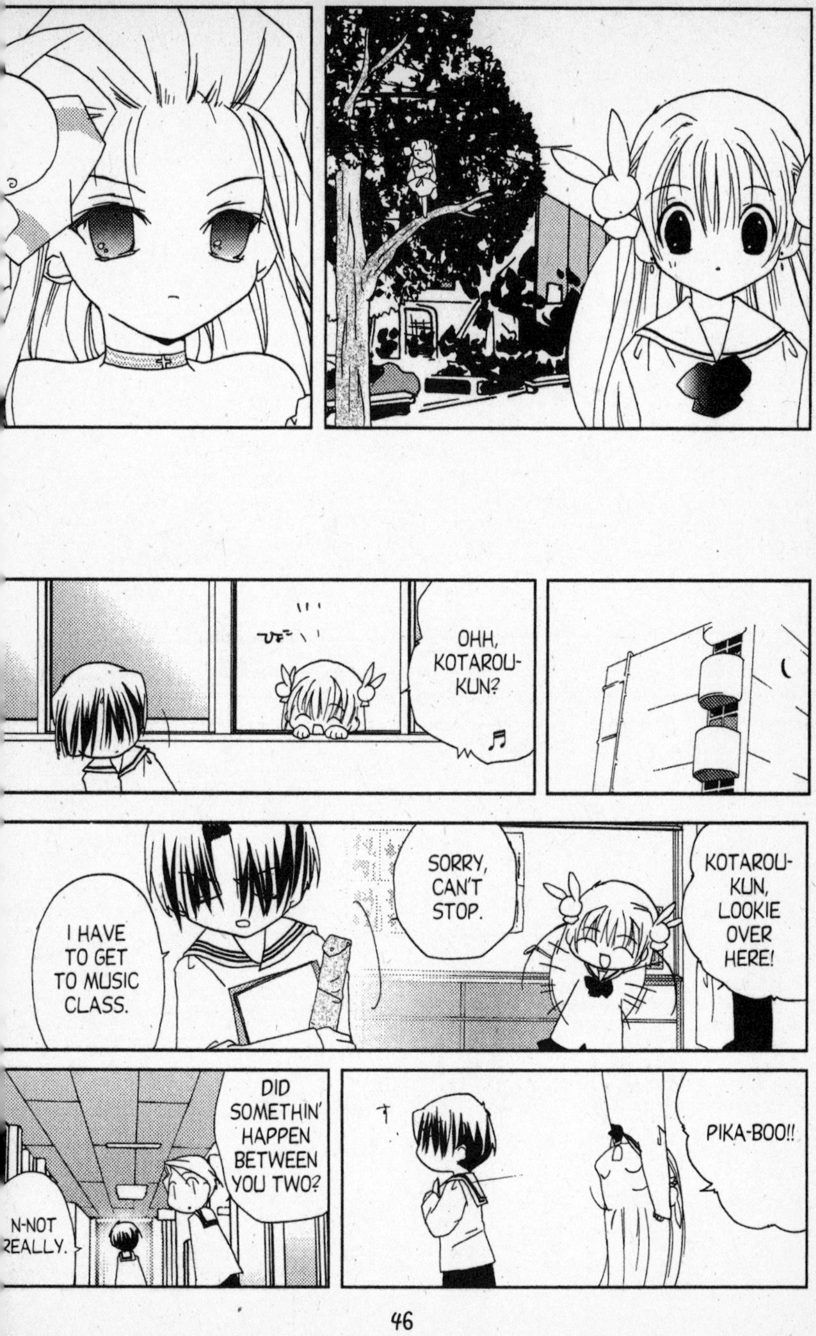
OHH, KOTAROU-KUN?
KOTAROU-KUN, LOOKIE OVER HERE!
SORRY, CAN'T STOP.
I HAVE TO GET TO MUSIC CLASS.
PIKA-BOO!!
DID SOMETHIN' HAPPEN BETWEEN YOU TWO?
N-NOT REALLY.

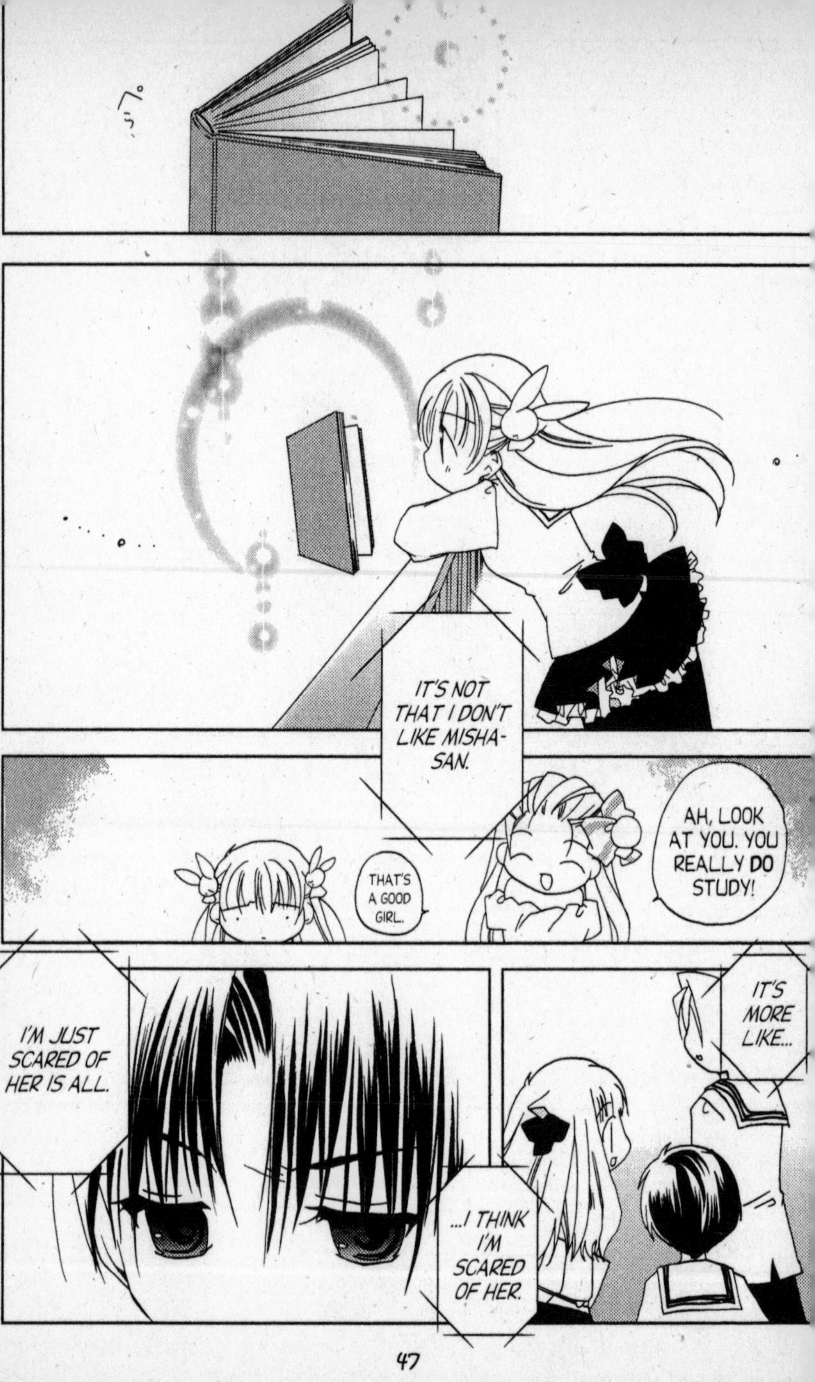
IT'S NOT THAT I DON'T LIKE MISHA-SAN.
AH, LOOK AT YOU. YOU REALLY DO STUDY!
THAT'S A GOOD GIRL.
IT'S MORE LIKE...
...I THINK I'M SCARED OF HER.
I'M JUST SCARED OF HER IS ALL.

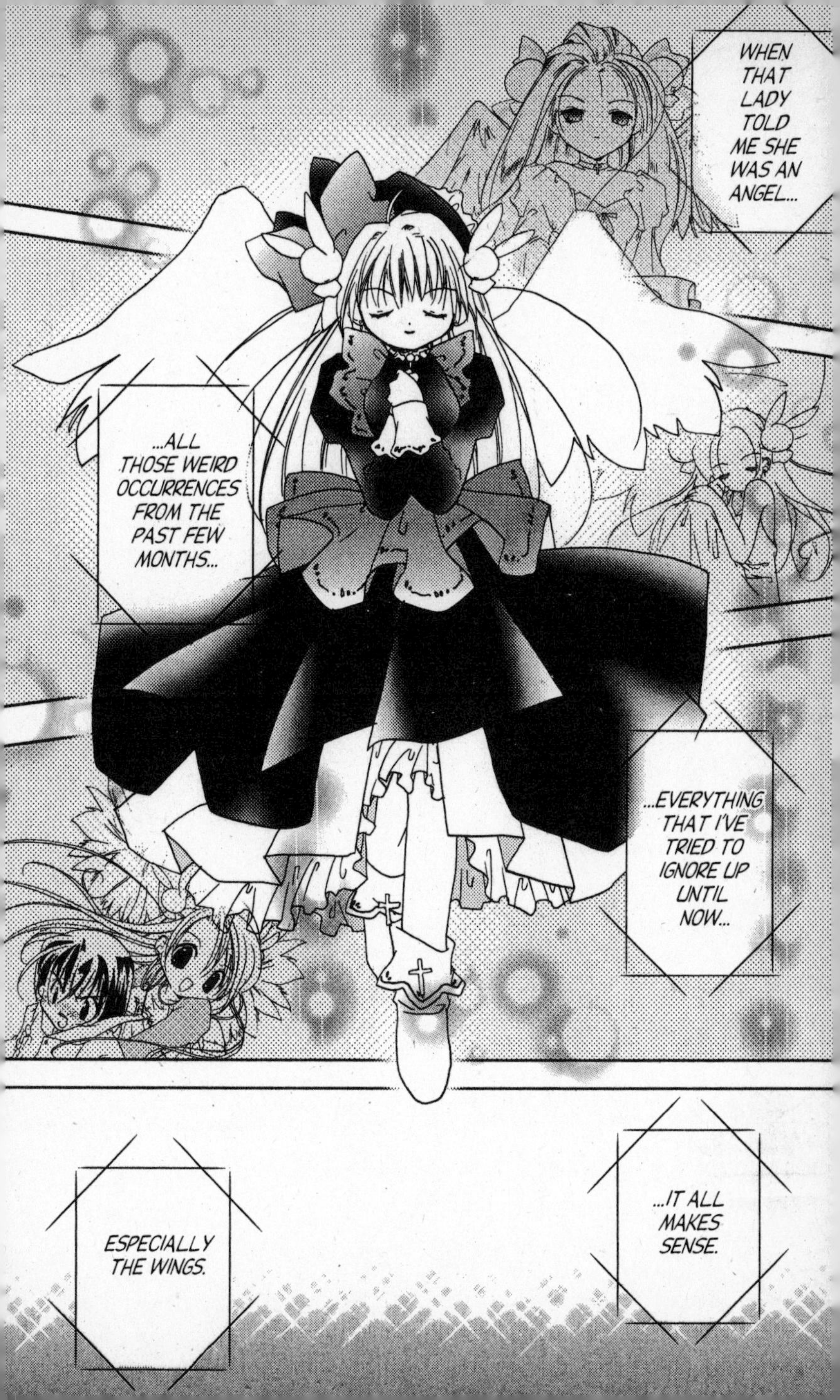
WHEN THAT LADY TOLD ME SHE WAS AN ANGEL...
...ALL THOSE WEIRD OCCURRENCES FROM THE PAST FEW MONTHS...
...EVERYTHING THAT I'VE TRIED TO IGNORE UP UNTIL NOW...
...IT ALL MAKES SENSE.
ESPECIALLY THE WINGS.

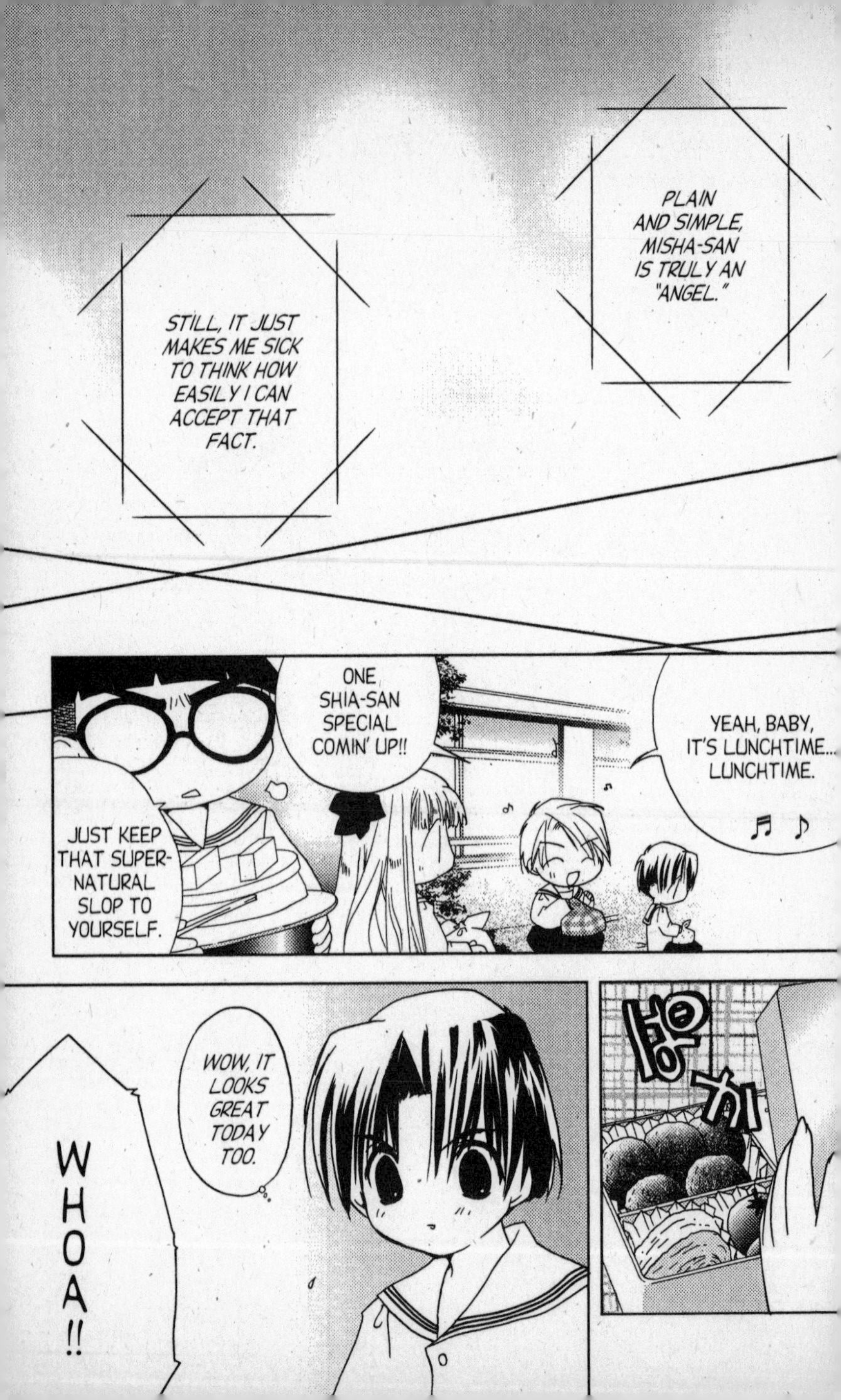
PLAIN AND SIMPLE, MISHA-SAN IS TRULY AN "ANGEL."
STILL, IT JUST MAKES ME SICK TO THINK HOW EASILY I CAN ACCEPT THAT FACT.
YEAH, BABY, IT'S LUNCHTIME... LUNCHTIME. ♬ ♪
ONE SHIA-SAN SPECIAL COMIN' UP!!
JUST KEEP THAT SUPER-NATURAL SLOP TO YOURSELF.
WOW, IT LOOKS GREAT TODAY TOO.
WHOA!!

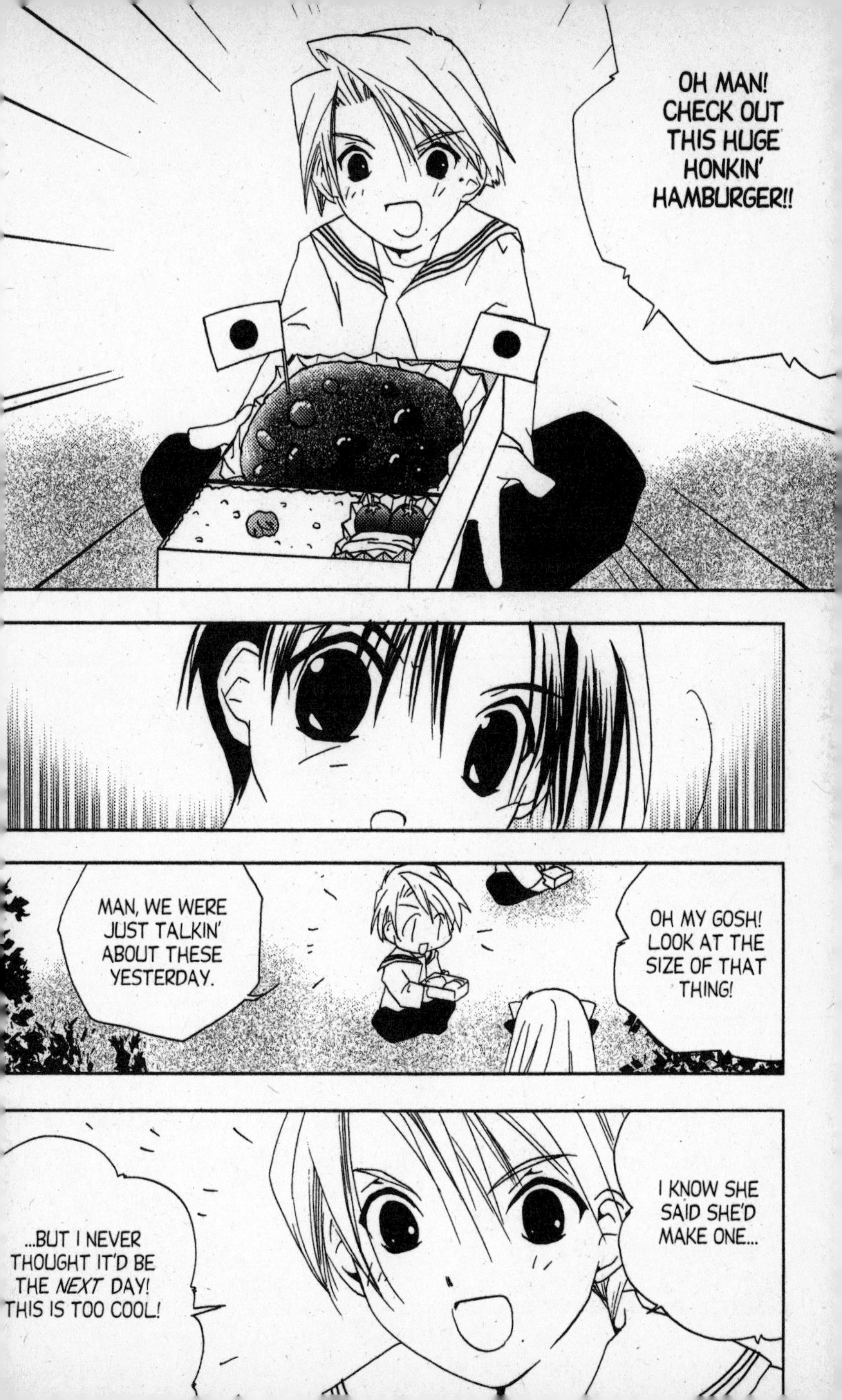
OH MAN! CHECK OUT THIS HUGE HONKIN' HAMBURGER!!
OH MY GOSH! LOOK AT THE SIZE OF THAT THING!
MAN, WE WERE JUST TALKIN' ABOUT THESE YESTERDAY.
I KNOW SHE SAID SHE'D MAKE ONE...
...BUT I NEVER THOUGHT IT'D BE THE *NEXT* DAY! THIS IS TOO COOL!

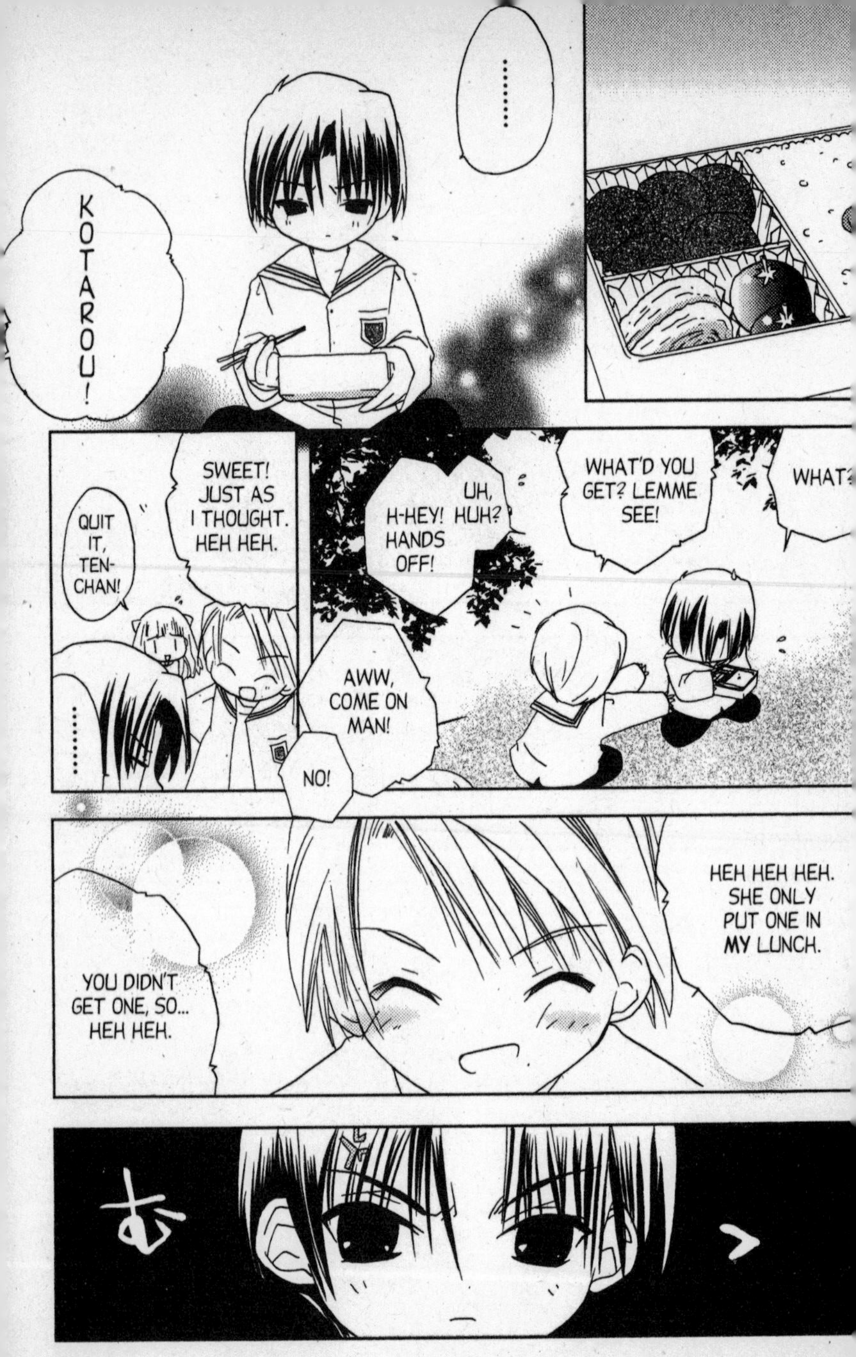
……
KOTAROU!
WHAT?
WHAT'D YOU GET? LEMME SEE!
UH, HUH?
H-HEY! HANDS OFF!
AWW, COME ON MAN!
NO!
SWEET! JUST AS I THOUGHT. HEH HEH.
QUIT IT, TEN-CHAN!
……
HEH HEH HEH. SHE ONLY PUT ONE IN MY LUNCH.
YOU DIDN'T GET ONE, SO... HEH HEH.
む

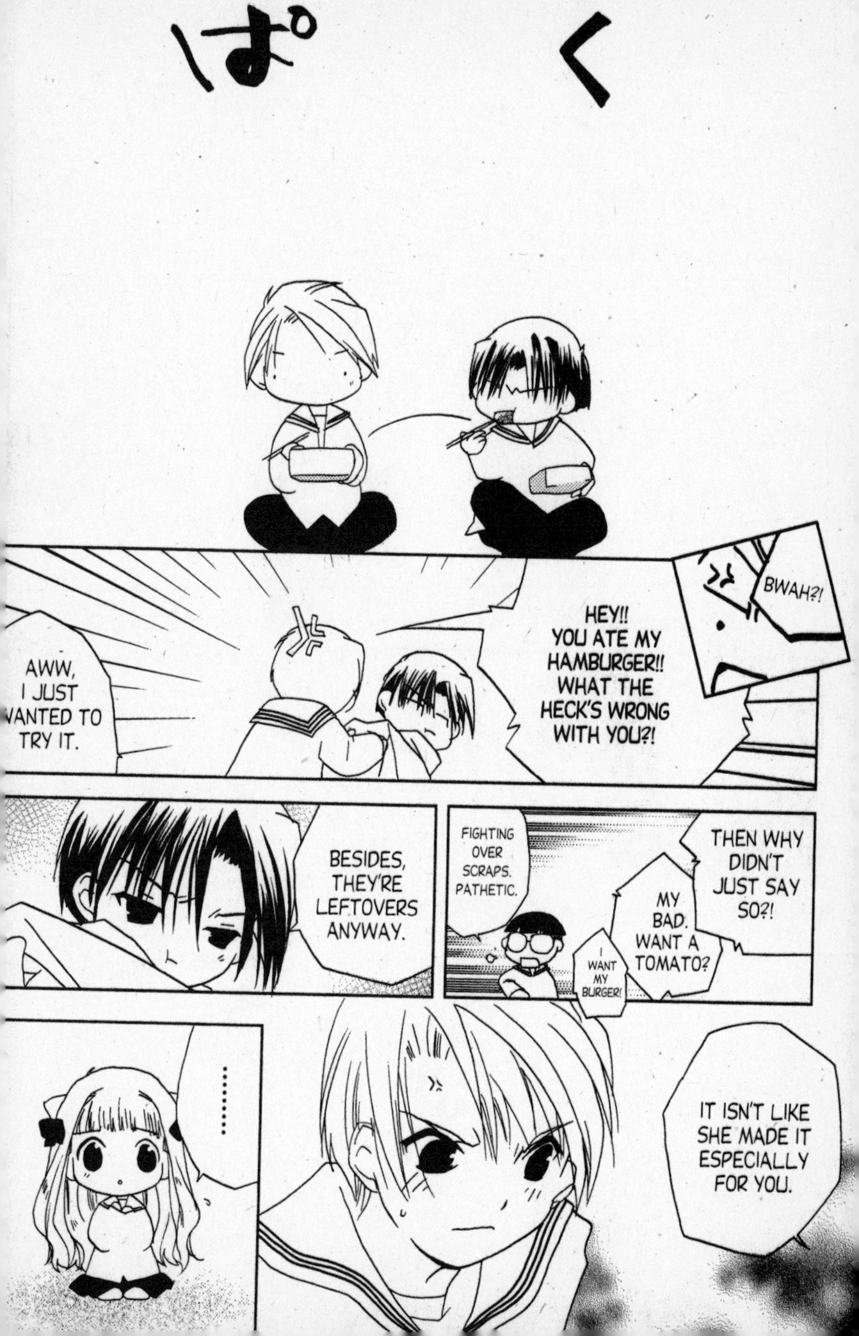
ぱく
BWAH?!
HEY!! YOU ATE MY HAMBURGER!! WHAT THE HECK'S WRONG WITH YOU?!
AWW, I JUST VANTED TO TRY IT.
THEN WHY DIDN'T JUST SAY SO?!
FIGHTING OVER SCRAPS. PATHETIC.
MY BAD. WANT A TOMATO?
I WANT MY BURGER!
BESIDES, THEY'RE LEFTOVERS ANYWAY.
IT ISN'T LIKE SHE MADE IT ESPECIALLY FOR YOU.
......

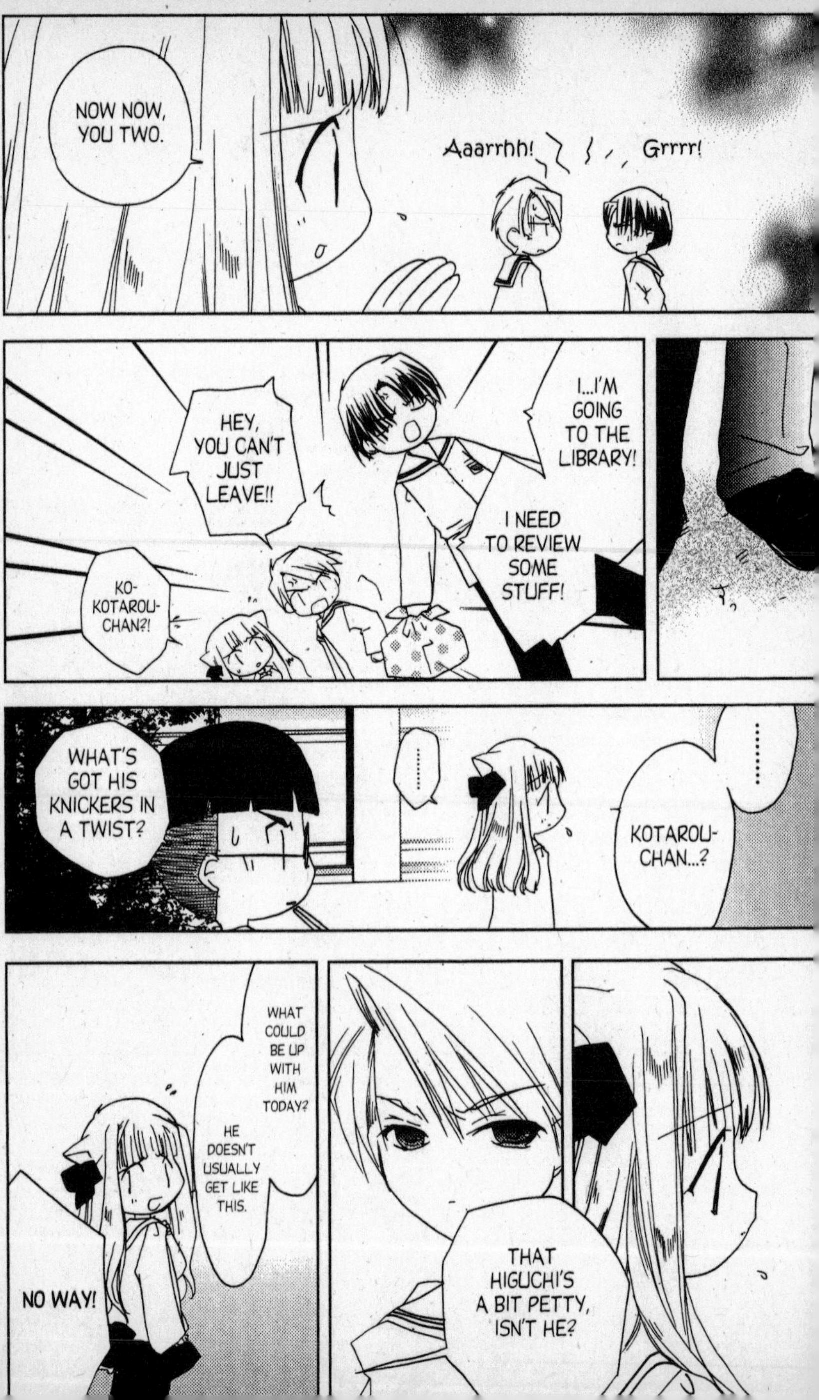
Grrrr!
Aaarrhh!
NOW NOW, YOU TWO.
I...I'M GOING TO THE LIBRARY!
I NEED TO REVIEW SOME STUFF!
HEY, YOU CAN'T JUST LEAVE!!
KO-KOTAROU-CHAN?!
......
KOTAROU-CHAN...?
......
WHAT'S GOT HIS KNICKERS IN A TWIST?
THAT HIGUCHI'S A BIT PETTY, ISN'T HE?
WHAT COULD BE UP WITH HIM TODAY?
HE DOESN'T USUALLY GET LIKE THIS.
NO WAY!

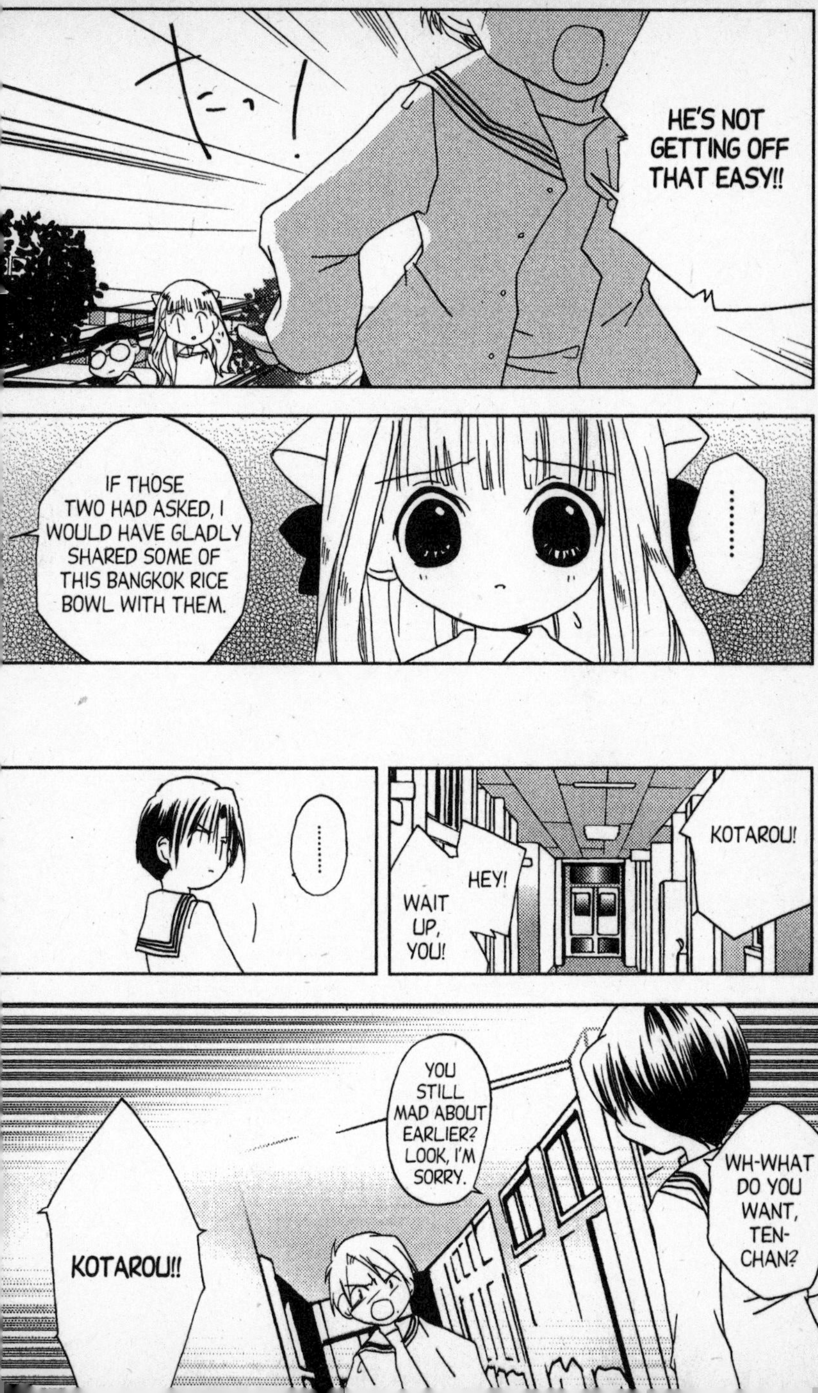
HE'S NOT GETTING OFF THAT EASY!!
....
IF THOSE TWO HAD ASKED, I WOULD HAVE GLADLY SHARED SOME OF THIS BANGKOK RICE BOWL WITH THEM.
KOTAROU!
HEY!
WAIT UP, YOU!
....
WH-WHAT DO YOU WANT, TEN-CHAN?
YOU STILL MAD ABOUT EARLIER? LOOK, I'M SORRY.
KOTAROU!!

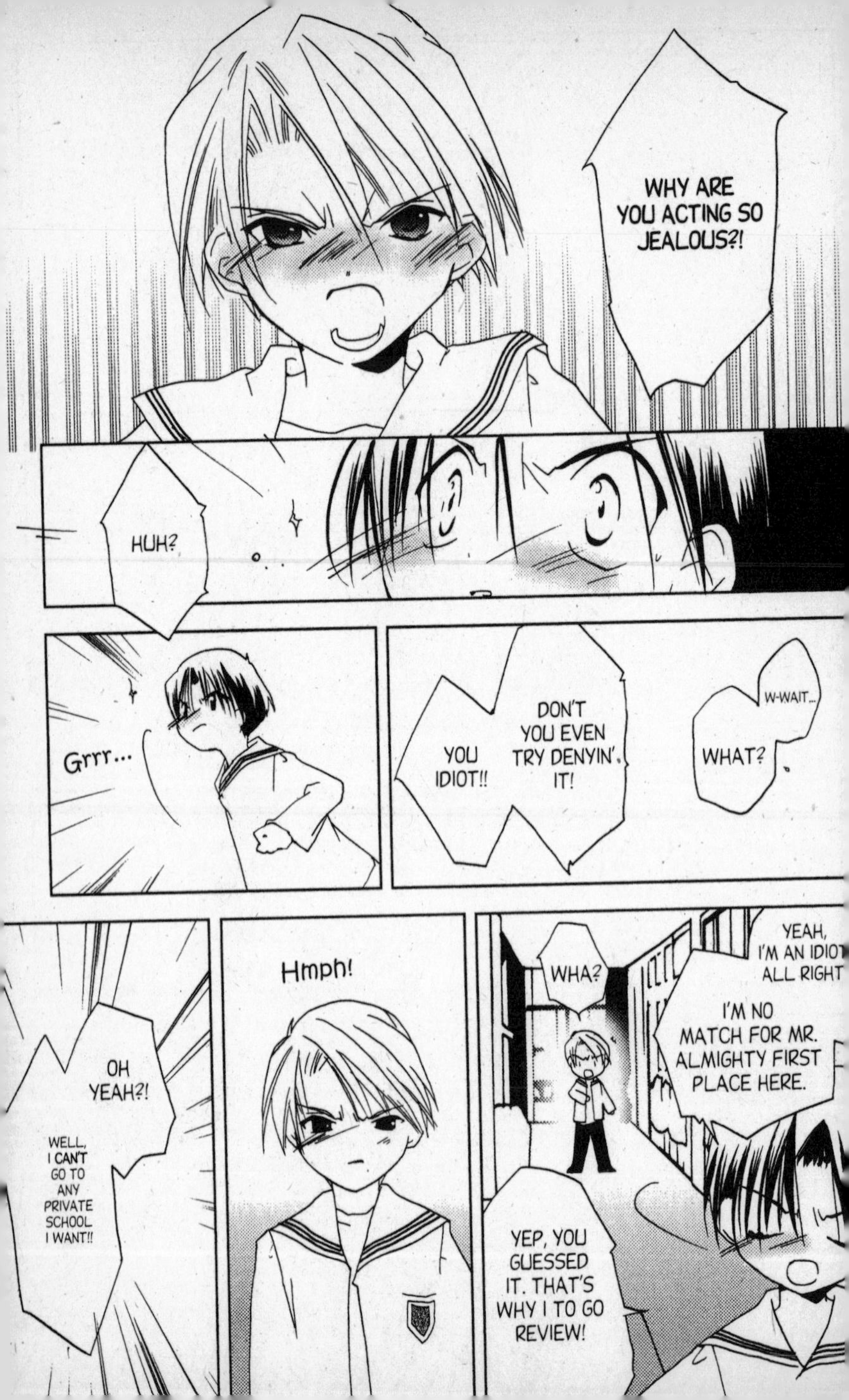
WHY ARE YOU ACTING SO JEALOUS?!
HUH?
W-WAIT...
WHAT?
DON'T YOU EVEN TRY DENYIN' IT!
YOU IDIOT!!
Grrr...
YEAH, I'M AN IDIOT ALL RIGHT
I'M NO MATCH FOR MR. ALMIGHTY FIRST PLACE HERE.
WHA?
YEP, YOU GUESSED IT. THAT'S WHY I TO GO REVIEW!
Hmph!
OH YEAH?!
WELL, I CAN'T GO TO ANY PRIVATE SCHOOL I WANT!!

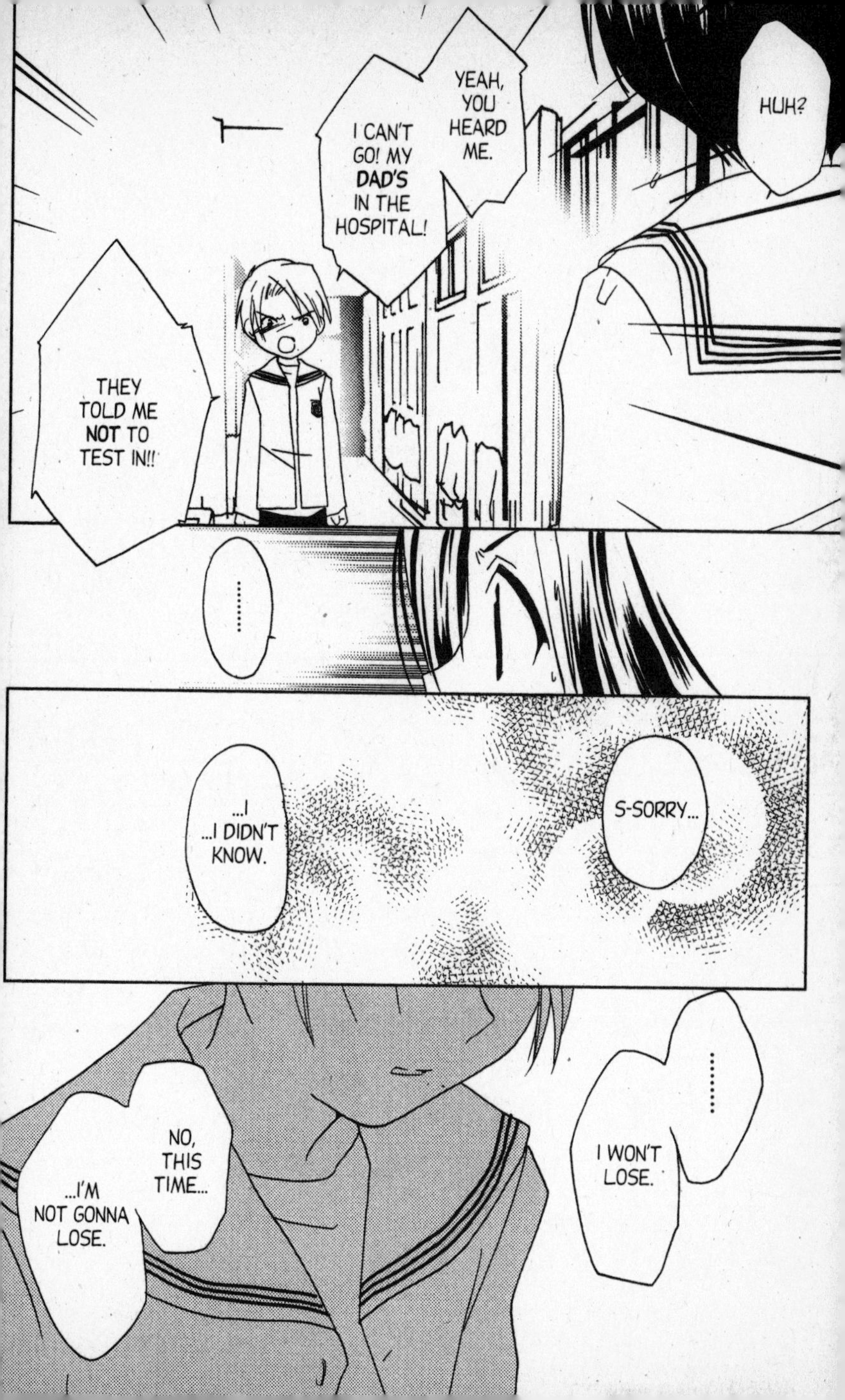
HUH?
YEAH, YOU HEARD ME.
I CAN'T GO! MY **DAD'S** IN THE HOSPITAL!
THEY TOLD ME **NOT** TO TEST IN!!
......
S-SORRY...
...I ...I DIDN'T KNOW.
......
I WON'T LOSE.
NO, THIS TIME...
...I'M NOT GONNA LOSE.

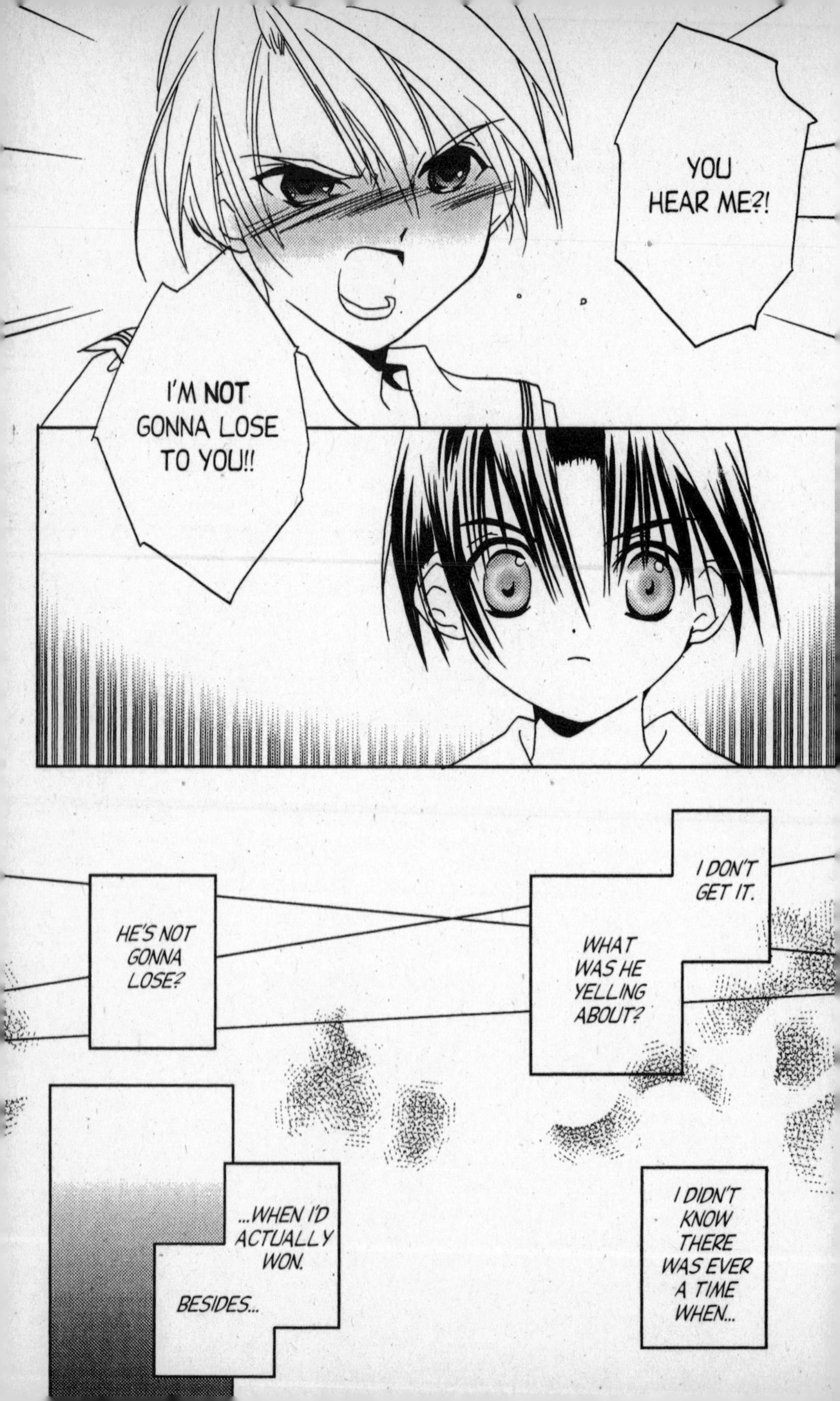
YOU HEAR ME?!
I'M NOT GONNA LOSE TO YOU!!
I DON'T GET IT.
WHAT WAS HE YELLING ABOUT?
HE'S NOT GONNA LOSE?
I DIDN'T KNOW THERE WAS EVER A TIME WHEN...
...WHEN I'D ACTUALLY WON.
BESIDES...

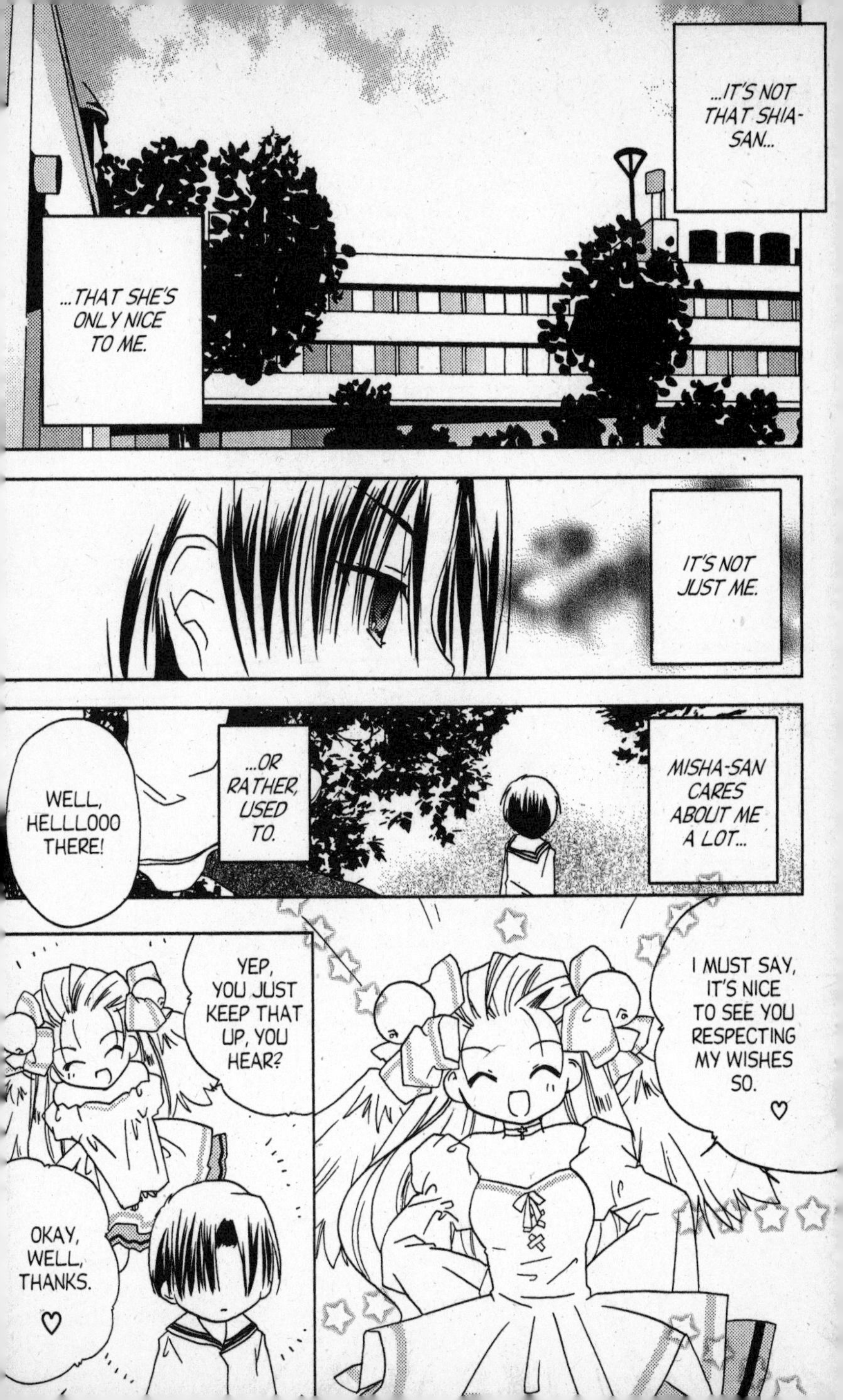
...IT'S NOT THAT SHIA-SAN...
...THAT SHE'S ONLY NICE TO ME.
IT'S NOT JUST ME.
MISHA-SAN CARES ABOUT ME A LOT...
...OR RATHER, USED TO.
WELL, HELLLOOO THERE!
I MUST SAY, IT'S NICE TO SEE YOU RESPECTING MY WISHES SO. ♡
YEP, YOU JUST KEEP THAT UP, YOU HEAR?
OKAY, WELL, THANKS. ♡

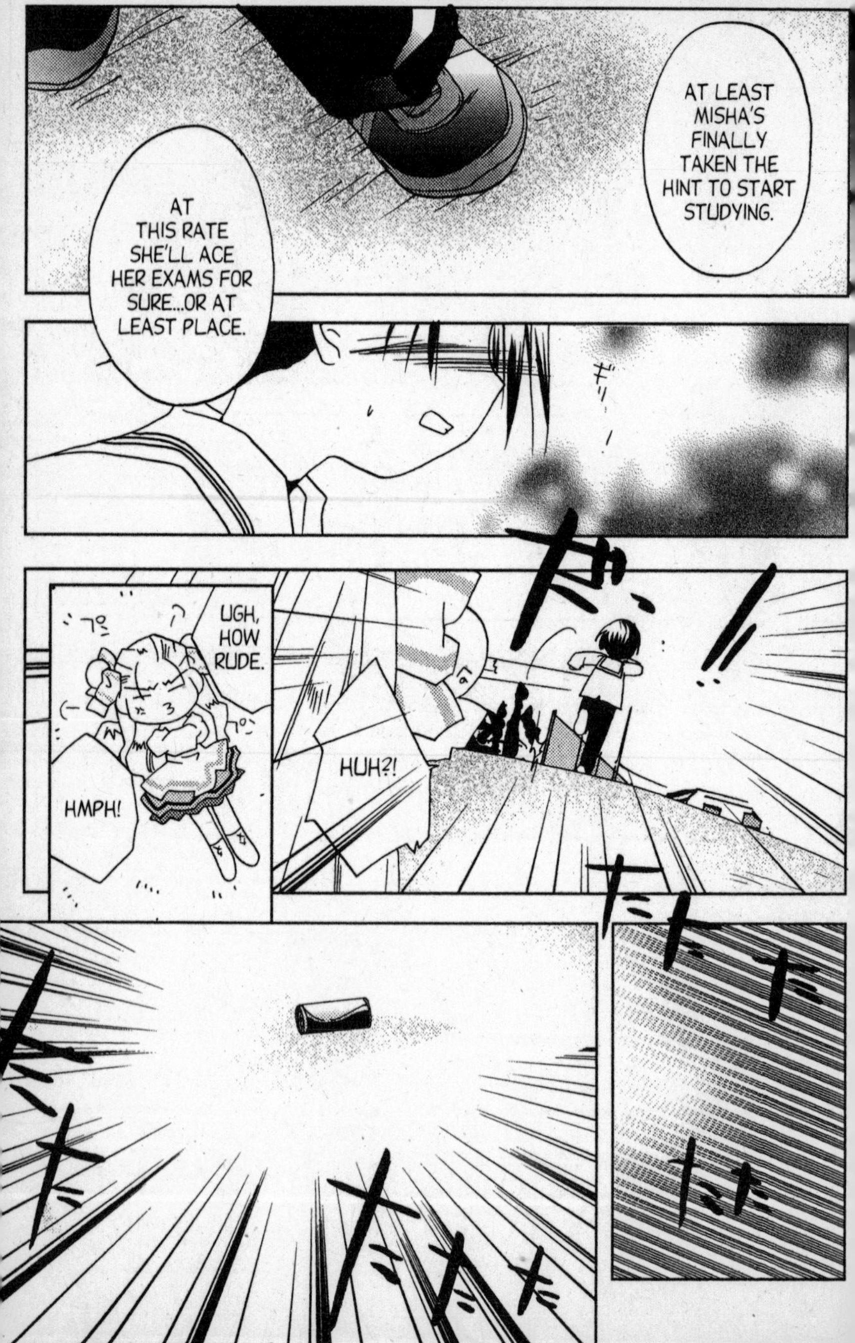
AT LEAST MISHA'S FINALLY TAKEN THE HINT TO START STUDYING.
AT THIS RATE SHE'LL ACE HER EXAMS FOR SURE...OR AT LEAST PLACE.
HUH?!
UGH, HOW RUDE.
HMPH!

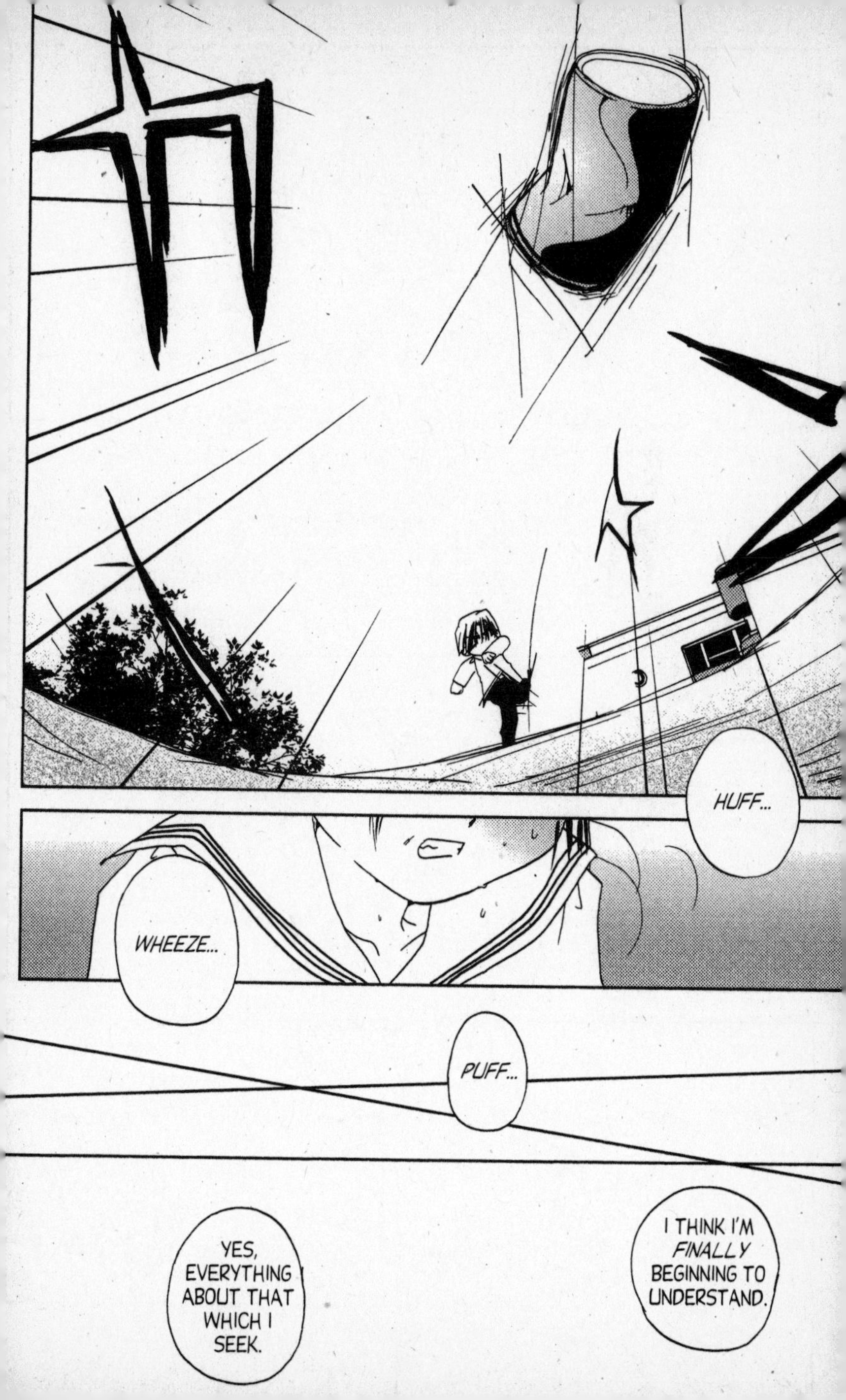
HUFF...
WHEEZE...
PUFF...
I THINK I'M *FINALLY* BEGINNING TO UNDERSTAND.
YES, EVERYTHING ABOUT THAT WHICH I SEEK.

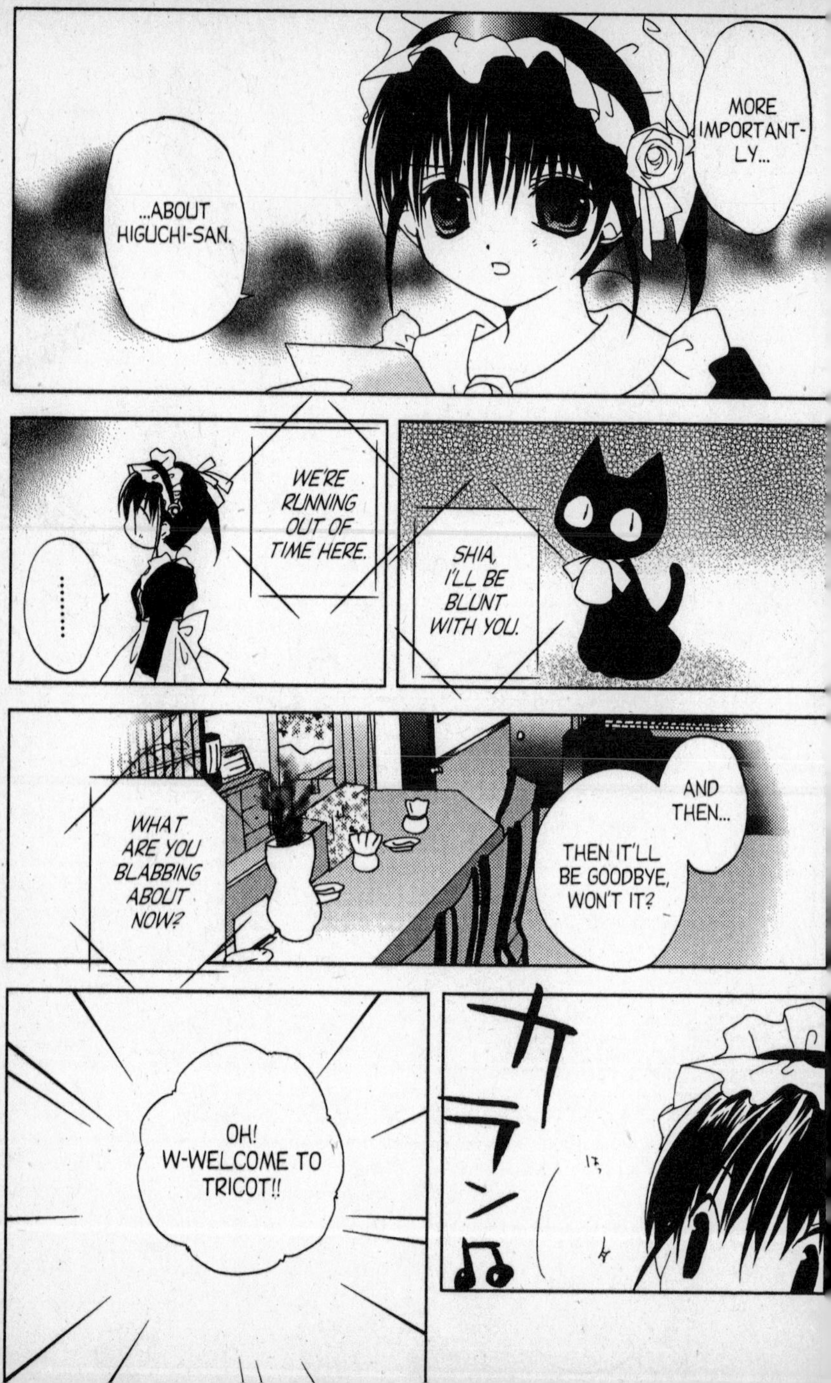
MORE IMPORTANT-LY...
...ABOUT HIGUCHI-SAN.
SHIA, I'LL BE BLUNT WITH YOU.
WE'RE RUNNING OUT OF TIME HERE.
......
AND THEN...
THEN IT'LL BE GOODBYE, WON'T IT?
WHAT ARE YOU BLABBING ABOUT NOW?
カラン
OH! W-WELCOME TO TRICOT!!

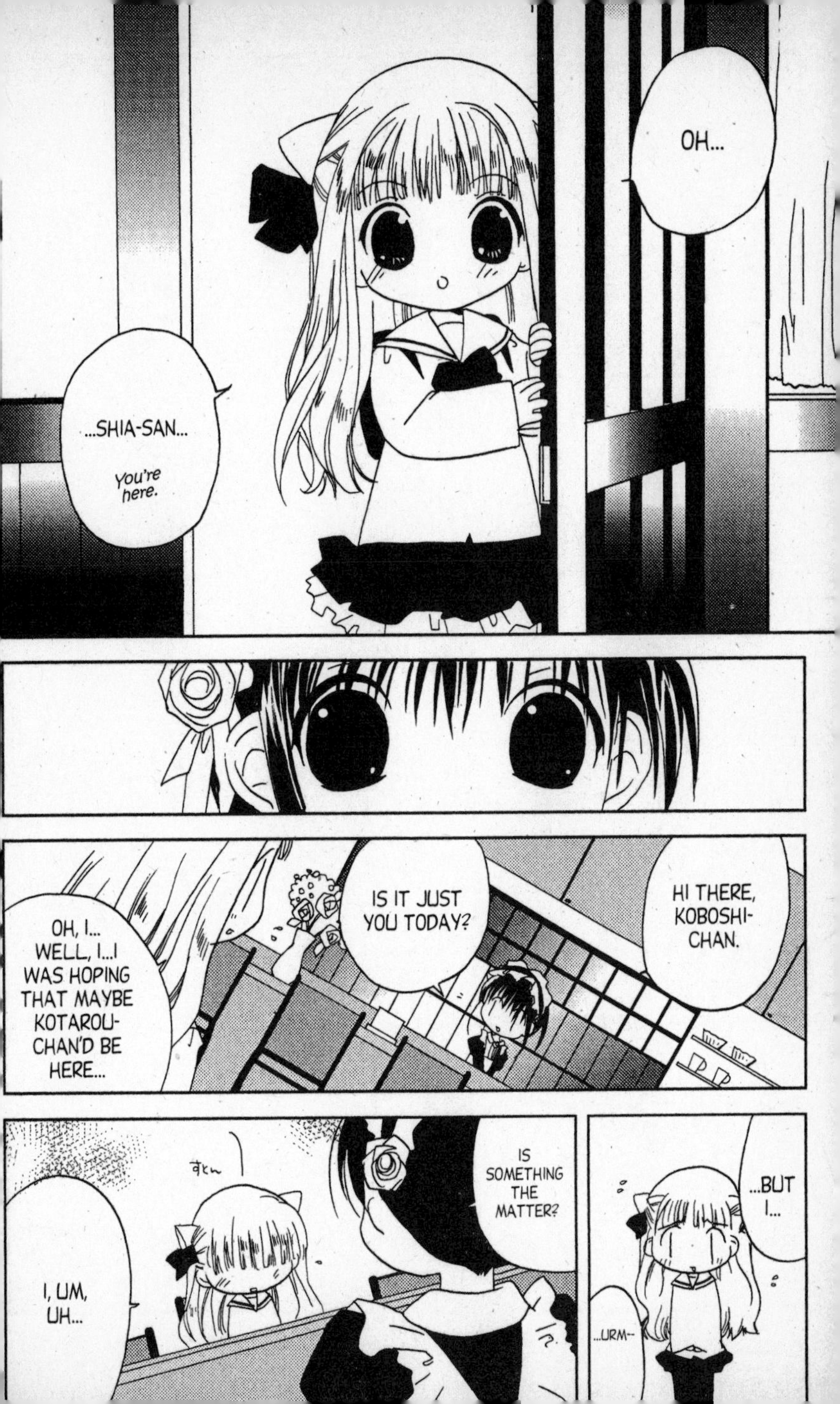
OH...
...SHIA-SAN... You're here.
HI THERE, KOBOSHI-CHAN.
IS IT JUST YOU TODAY?
OH, I... WELL, I...I WAS HOPING THAT MAYBE KOTAROU-CHAN'D BE HERE...
...BUT I...
...URM--
IS SOMETHING THE MATTER?
すとん
I, UM, UH...

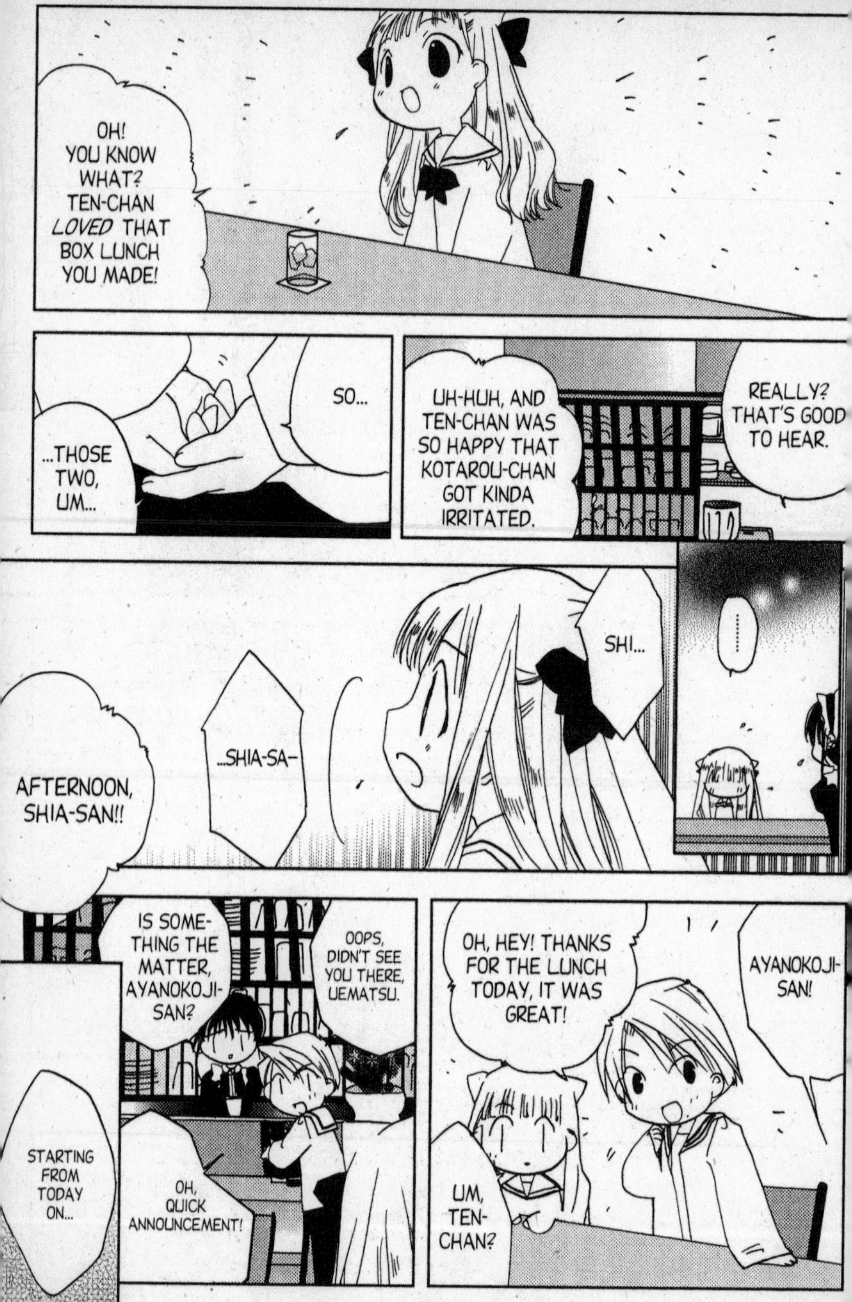
OH! YOU KNOW WHAT? TEN-CHAN *LOVED* THAT BOX LUNCH YOU MADE!
REALLY? THAT'S GOOD TO HEAR.
UH-HUH, AND TEN-CHAN WAS SO HAPPY THAT KOTAROU-CHAN GOT KINDA IRRITATED.
SO...
...THOSE TWO, UM...
......
SHI...
...SHIA-SA-
AFTERNOON, SHIA-SAN!!
AYANOKOJI-SAN!
OH, HEY! THANKS FOR THE LUNCH TODAY, IT WAS GREAT!
UM, TEN-CHAN?
OOPS, DIDN'T SEE YOU THERE, UEMATSU.
IS SOMETHING THE MATTER, AYANOKOJI-SAN?
OH, QUICK ANNOUNCEMENT!
STARTING FROM TODAY ON...

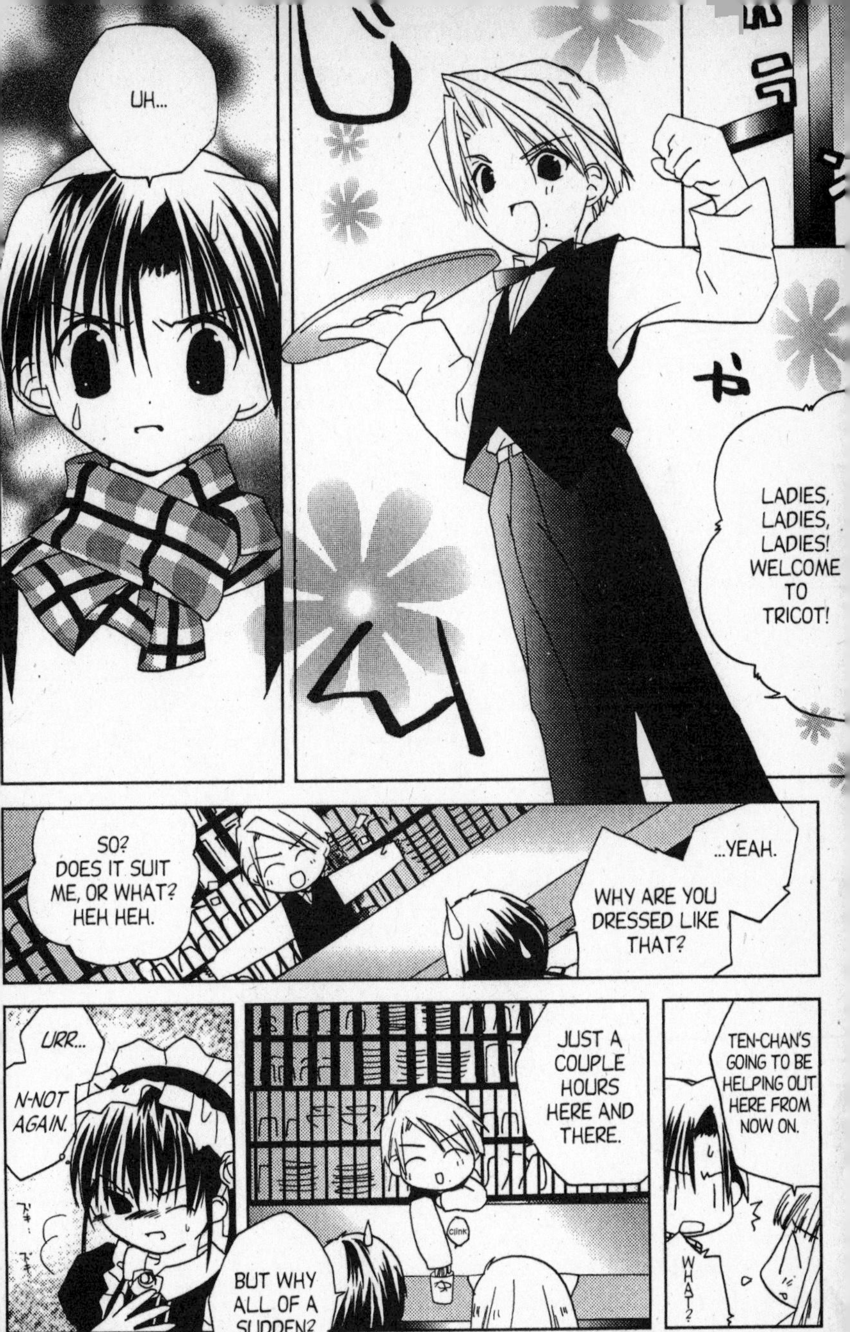
LADIES, LADIES, LADIES! WELCOME TO TRICOT!
UH...
...YEAH.
WHY ARE YOU DRESSED LIKE THAT?
SO? DOES IT SUIT ME, OR WHAT? HEH HEH.
TEN-CHAN'S GOING TO BE HELPING OUT HERE FROM NOW ON.
WHAT?
JUST A COUPLE HOURS HERE AND THERE.
CLINK
BUT WHY ALL OF A SUDDEN?
URR...
N-NOT AGAIN.

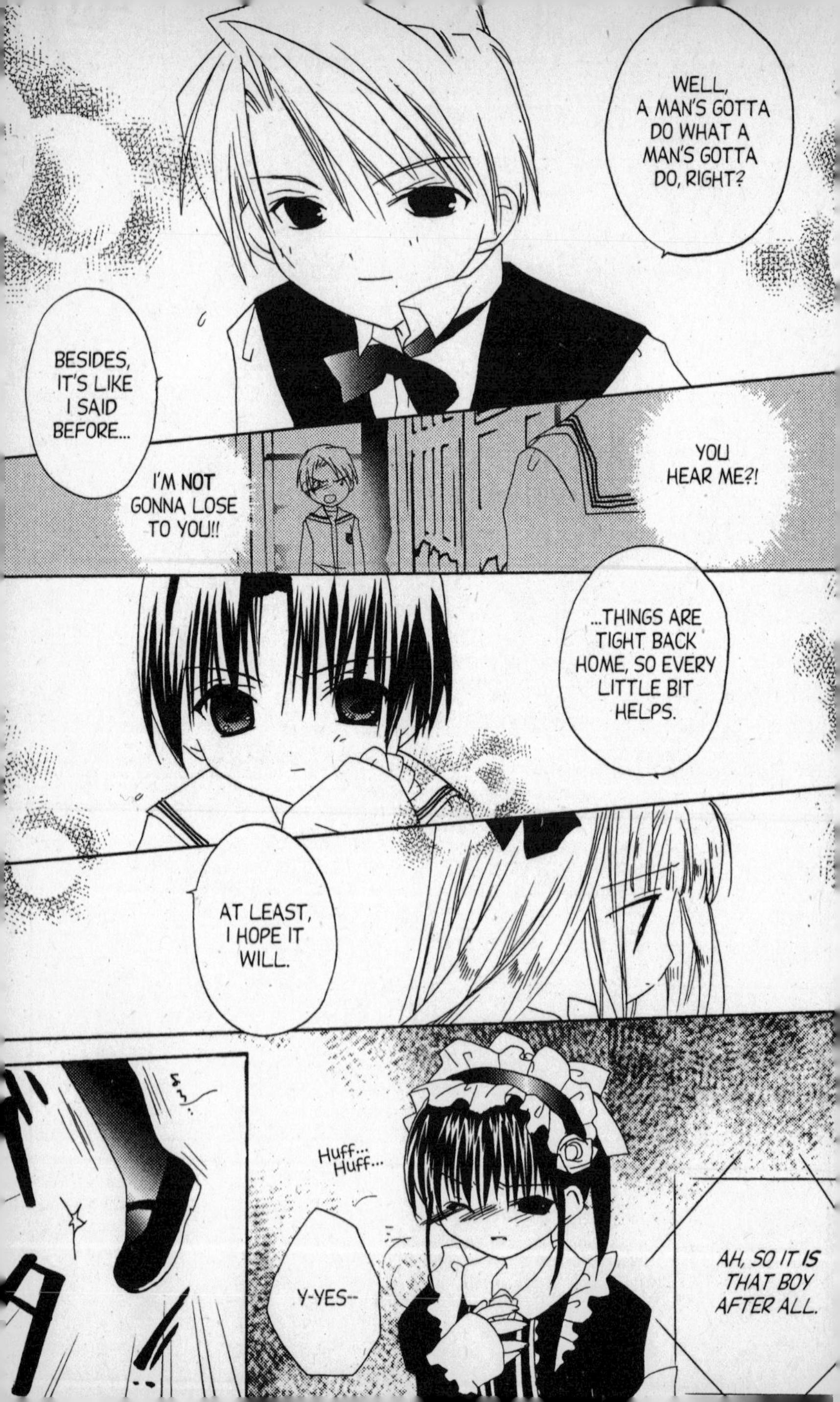
WELL, A MAN'S GOTTA DO WHAT A MAN'S GOTTA DO, RIGHT?
BESIDES, IT'S LIKE I SAID BEFORE...
YOU HEAR ME?!
I'M **NOT** GONNA LOSE TO YOU!!
...THINGS ARE TIGHT BACK HOME, SO EVERY LITTLE BIT HELPS.
AT LEAST, I HOPE IT WILL.
Huff... Huff...
AH, SO IT IS THAT BOY AFTER ALL.
Y-YES--

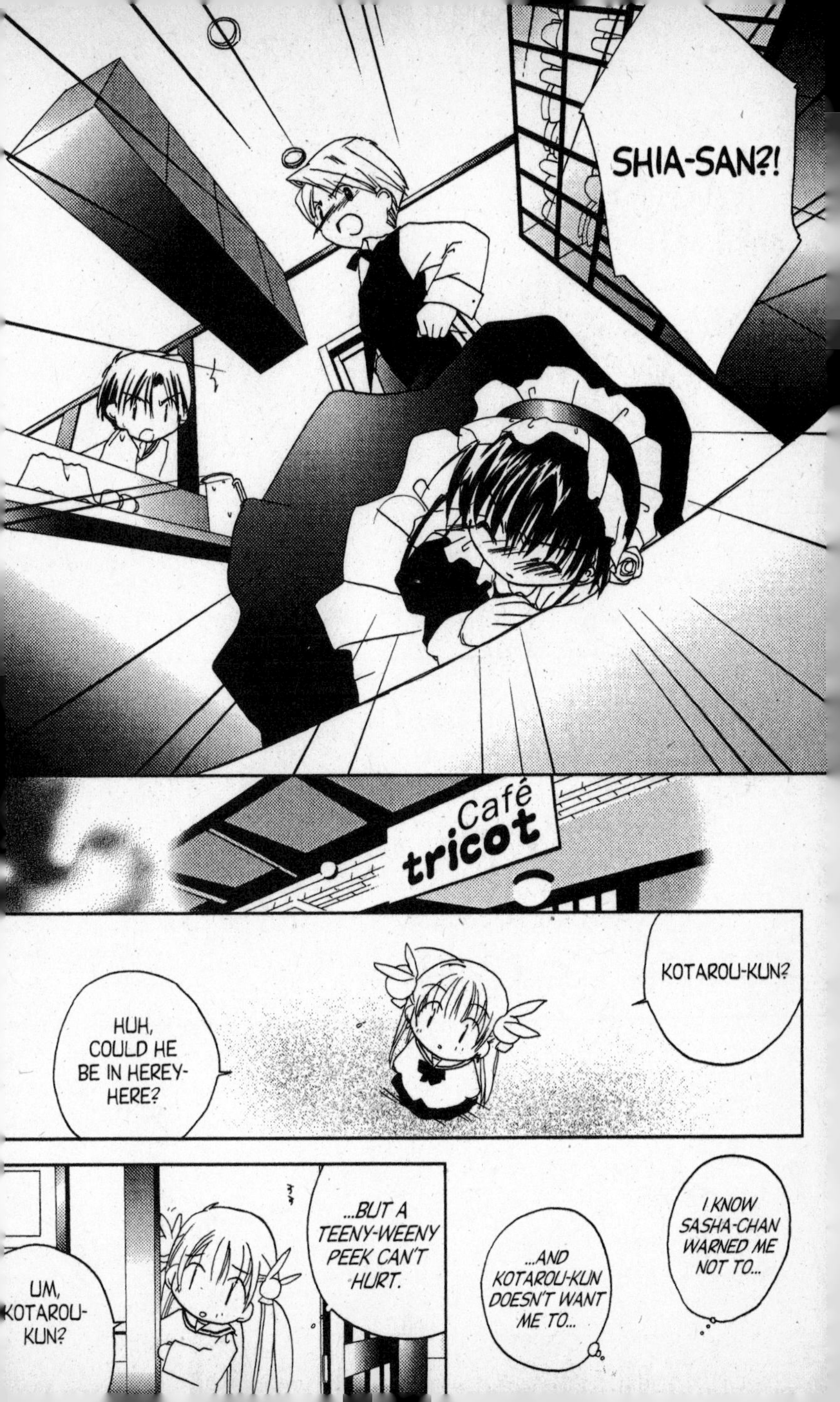
SHIA-SAN?!
Café tricot
KOTAROU-KUN?
HUH, COULD HE BE IN HEREY-HERE?
I KNOW SASHA-CHAN WARNED ME NOT TO...
...AND KOTAROU-KUN DOESN'T WANT ME TO...
...BUT A TEENY-WEENY PEEK CAN'T HURT.
UM, KOTAROU-KUN?

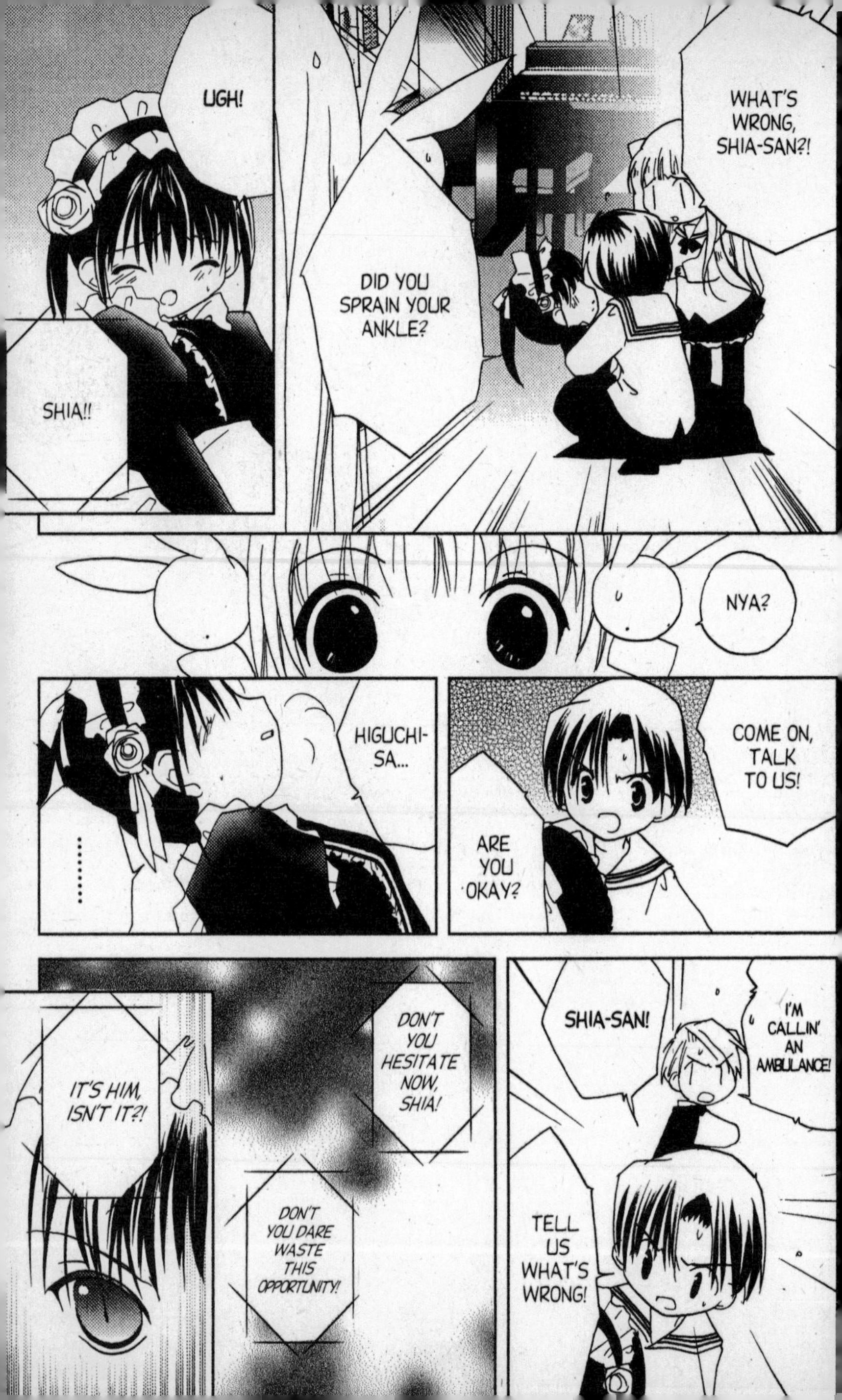

WHAT'S WRONG, SHIA-SAN?!
DID YOU SPRAIN YOUR ANKLE?
UGH!
SHIA!!
NYA?
COME ON, TALK TO US!
ARE YOU OKAY?
HIGUCHI-SA...
....
I'M CALLIN' AN AMBULANCE!
SHIA-SAN!
TELL US WHAT'S WRONG!
DON'T YOU HESITATE NOW, SHIA!
DON'T YOU DARE WASTE THIS OPPORTUNITY!
IT'S HIM, ISN'T IT?!

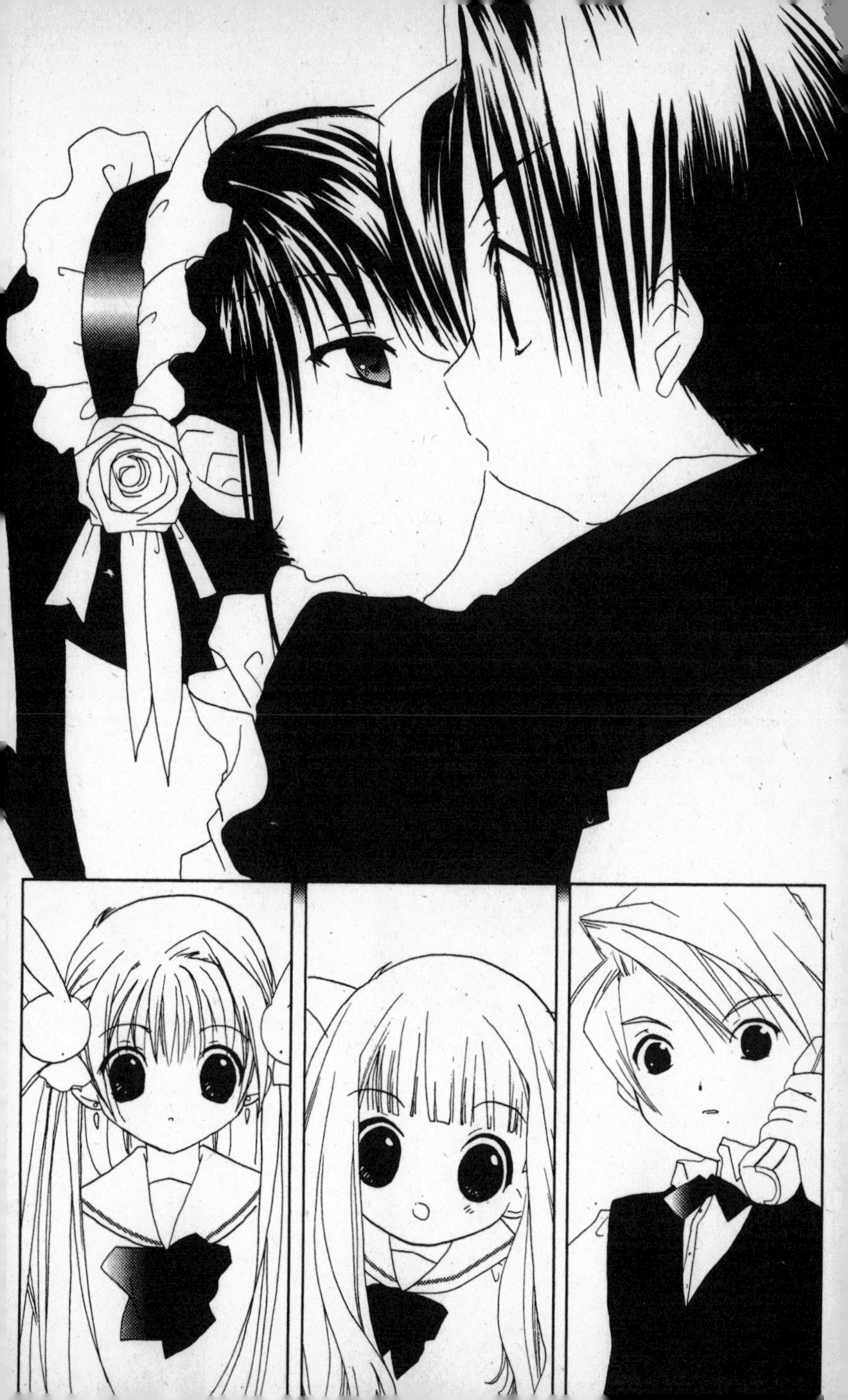

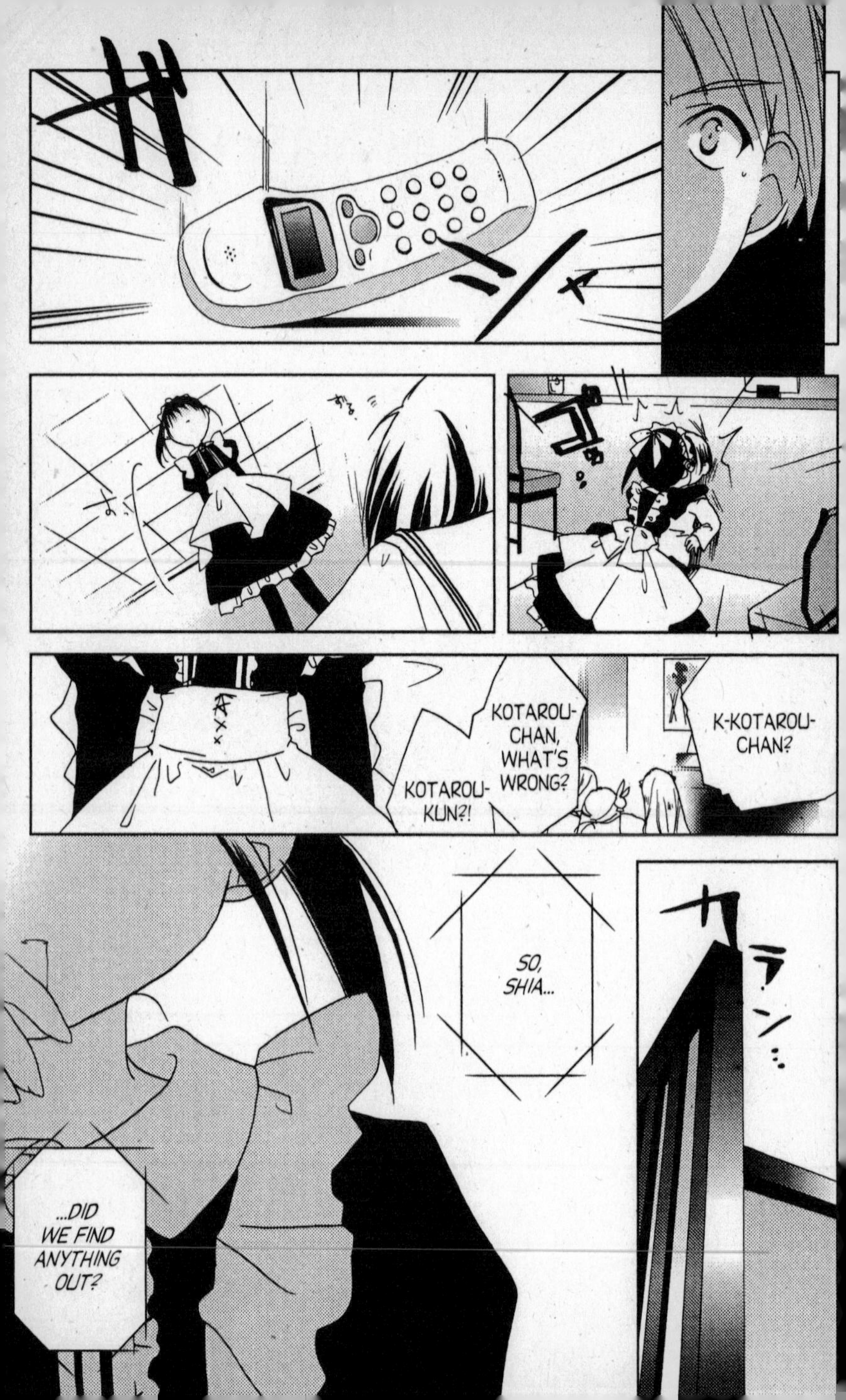
K-KOTAROU-CHAN?
KOTAROU-CHAN, WHAT'S WRONG?
KOTAROU-KUN?!
SO, SHIA...
...DID WE FIND ANYTHING OUT?

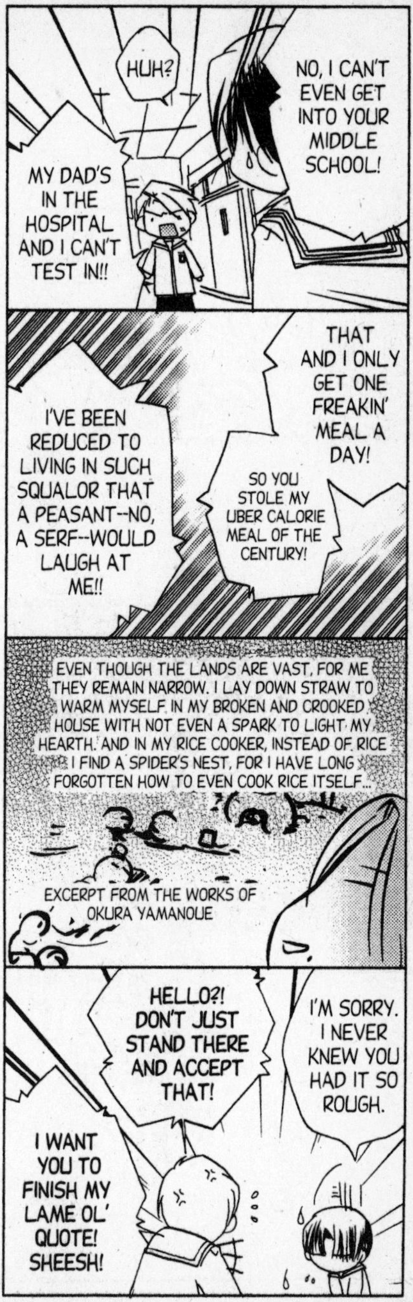
NO, I CAN'T EVEN GET INTO YOUR MIDDLE SCHOOL!
HUH?
MY DAD'S IN THE HOSPITAL AND I CAN'T TEST IN!!
THAT AND I ONLY GET ONE FREAKIN' MEAL A DAY!
SO YOU STOLE MY UBER CALORIE MEAL OF THE CENTURY!
I'VE BEEN REDUCED TO LIVING IN SUCH SQUALOR THAT A PEASANT--NO, A SERF--WOULD LAUGH AT ME!!
EVEN THOUGH THE LANDS ARE VAST, FOR ME THEY REMAIN NARROW. I LAY DOWN STRAW TO WARM MYSELF IN MY BROKEN AND CROOKED HOUSE WITH NOT EVEN A SPARK TO LIGHT MY HEARTH. AND IN MY RICE COOKER, INSTEAD OF RICE I FIND A SPIDER'S NEST, FOR I HAVE LONG FORGOTTEN HOW TO EVEN COOK RICE ITSELF...
EXCERPT FROM THE WORKS OF OKURA YAMANOUE
I'M SORRY. I NEVER KNEW YOU HAD IT SO ROUGH.
HELLO?! DON'T JUST STAND THERE AND ACCEPT THAT!
I WANT YOU TO FINISH MY LAME OL' QUOTE! SHEESH!

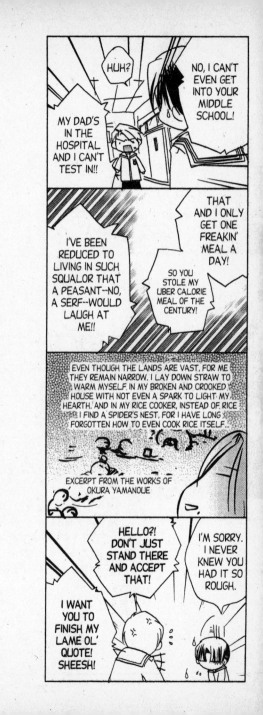

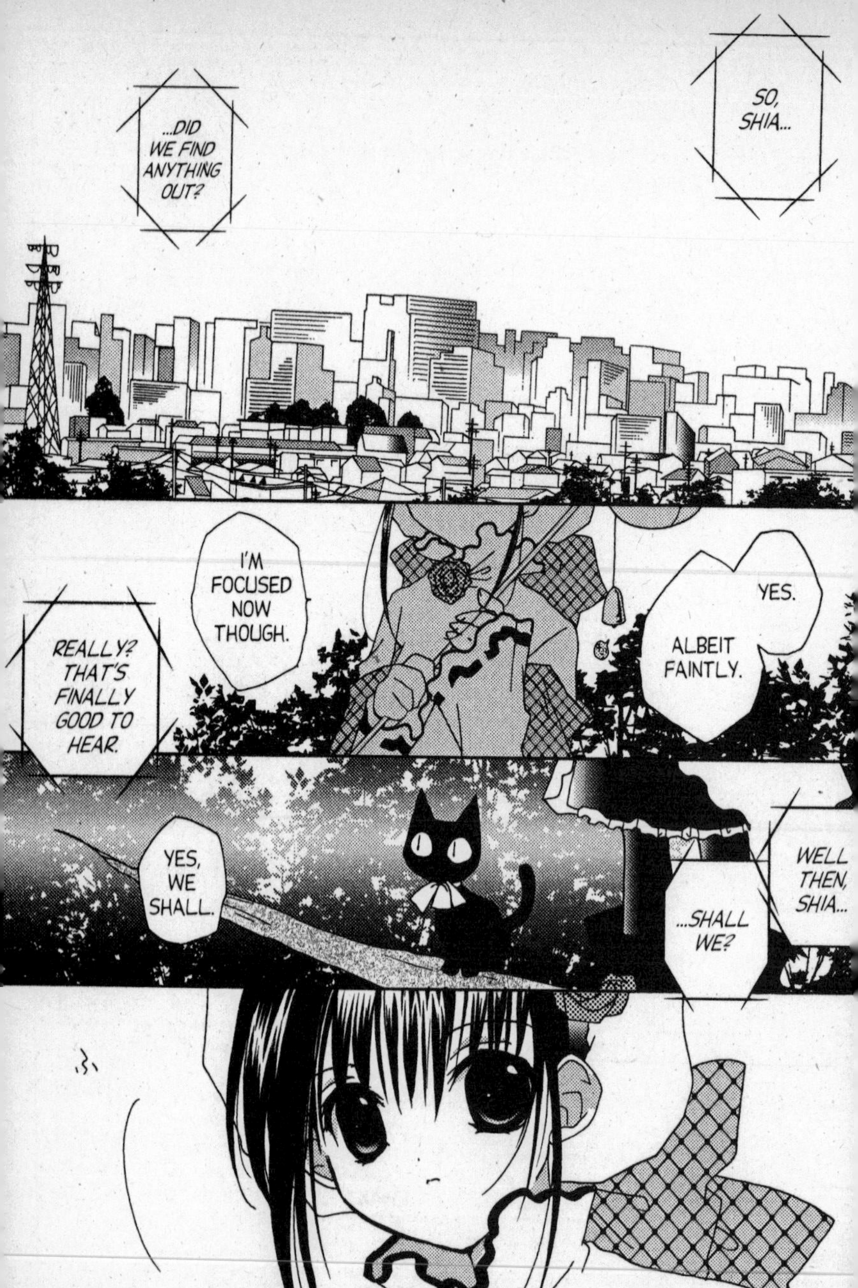
SO, SHIA...
...DID WE FIND ANYTHING OUT?
YES.
ALBEIT FAINTLY.
I'M FOCUSED NOW THOUGH.
REALLY? THAT'S FINALLY GOOD TO HEAR.
WELL THEN, SHIA...
...SHALL WE?
YES, WE SHALL.

Lesson 29
How to Discover One's Loneliness

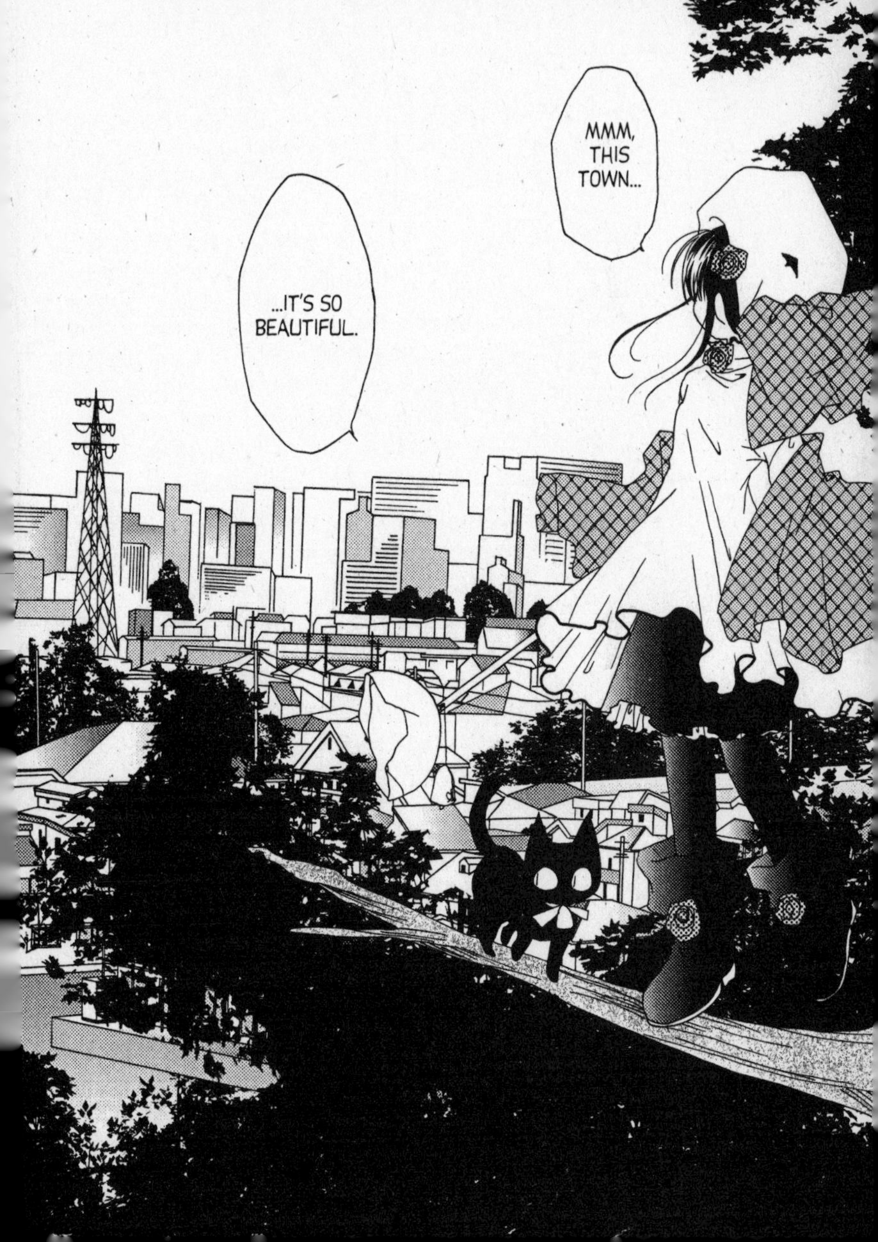
MMM, THIS TOWN...
...IT'S SO BEAUTIFUL.

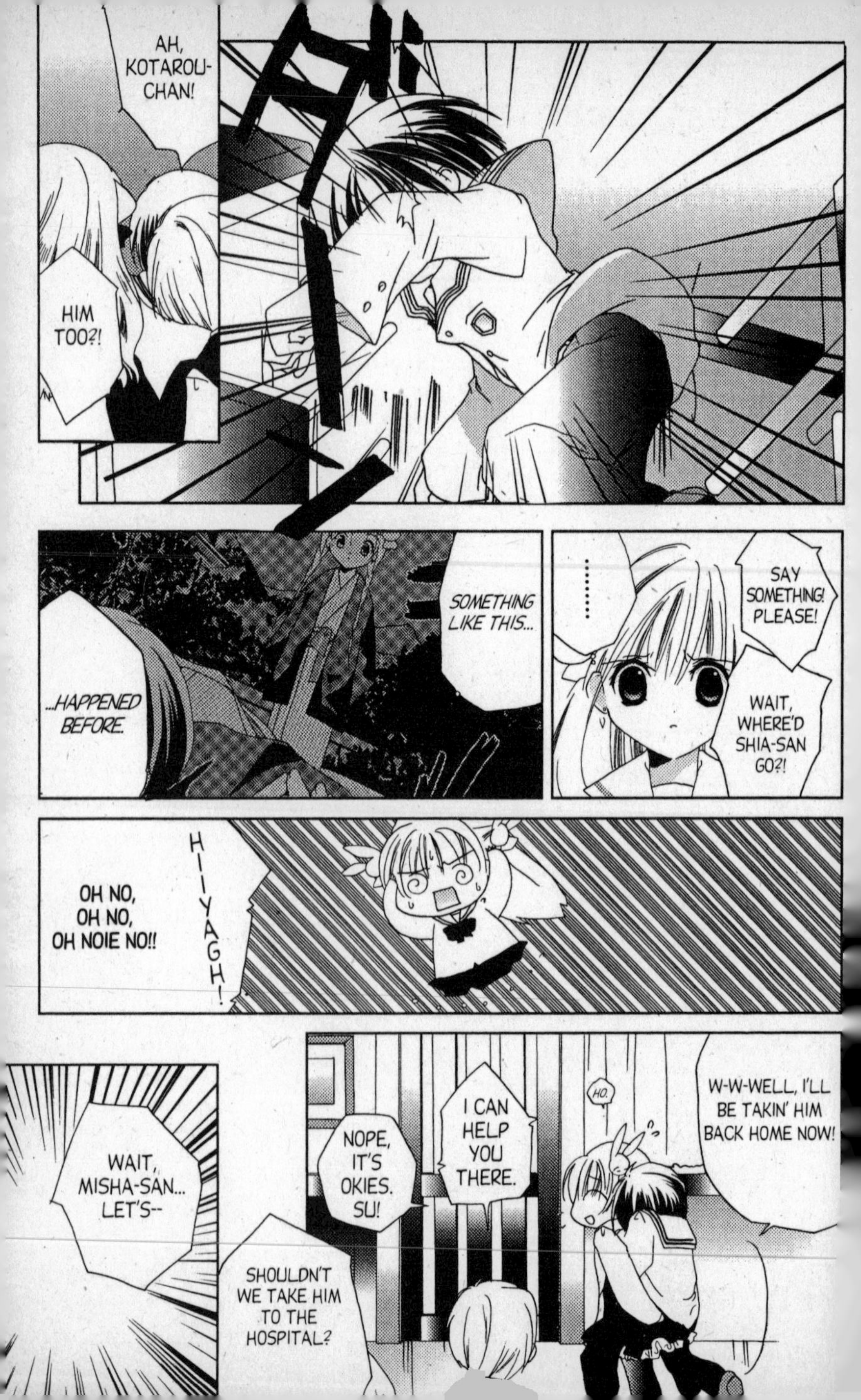
AH, KOTAROU-CHAN!
HIM TOO?!
SAY SOMETHING! PLEASE!
......
WAIT, WHERE'D SHIA-SAN GO?!
SOMETHING LIKE THIS...
...HAPPENED BEFORE.
HIIYAGH!
OH NO, OH NO, OH NOIE NO!!
W-W-WELL, I'LL BE TAKIN' HIM BACK HOME NOW!
HO.
I CAN HELP YOU THERE.
NOPE, IT'S OKIES. SU!
WAIT, MISHA-SAN... LET'S--
SHOULDN'T WE TAKE HIM TO THE HOSPITAL?

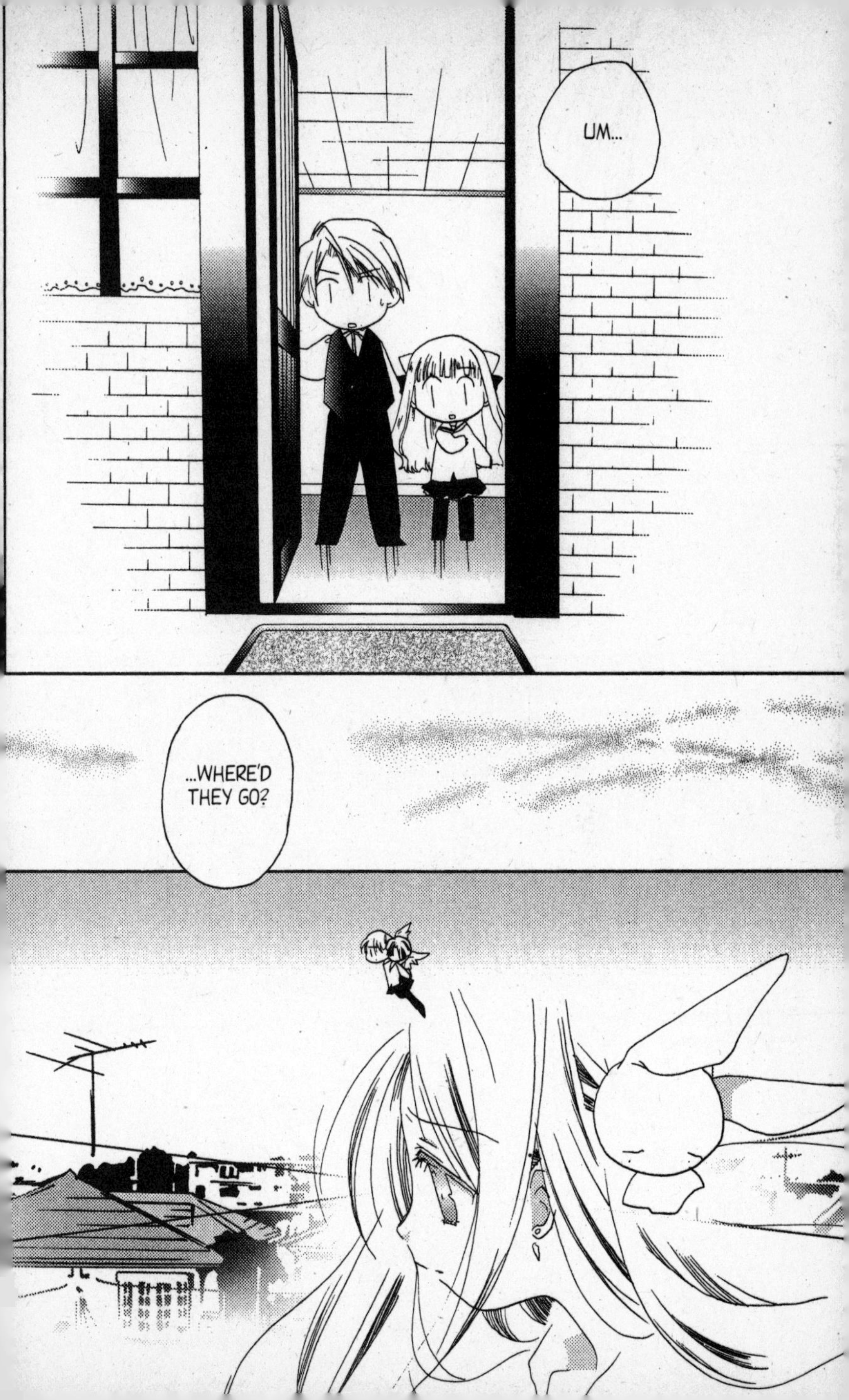
UM...
...WHERE'D THEY GO?

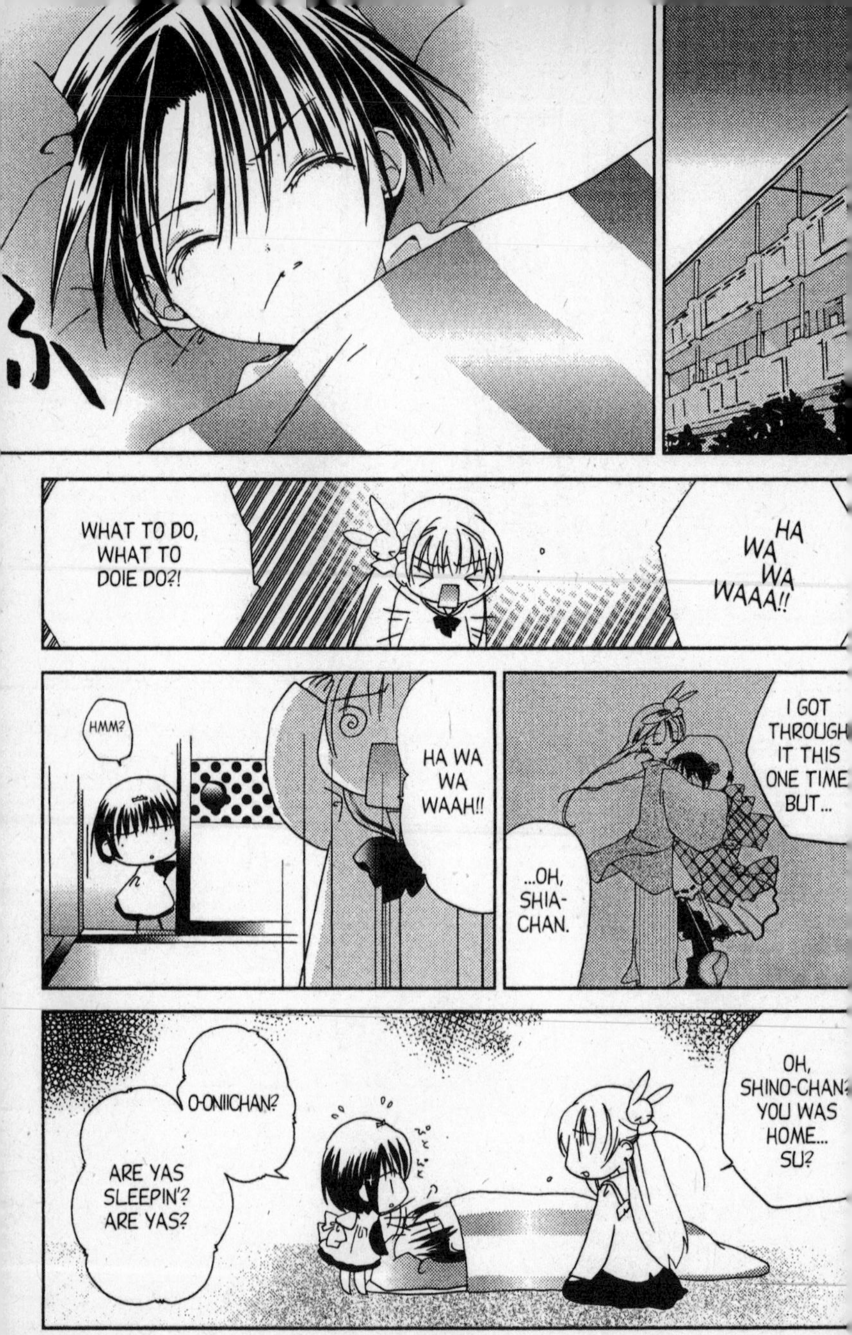

ふ
HA WA WA WAAA!!
WHAT TO DO, WHAT TO DOIE DO?!
I GOT THROUGH IT THIS ONE TIME BUT...
...OH, SHIA-CHAN.
HA WA WA WAAH!!
HMM?
OH, SHINO-CHAN? YOU WAS HOME... SU?
O-ONIICHAN?
ARE YAS SLEEPIN'? ARE YAS?

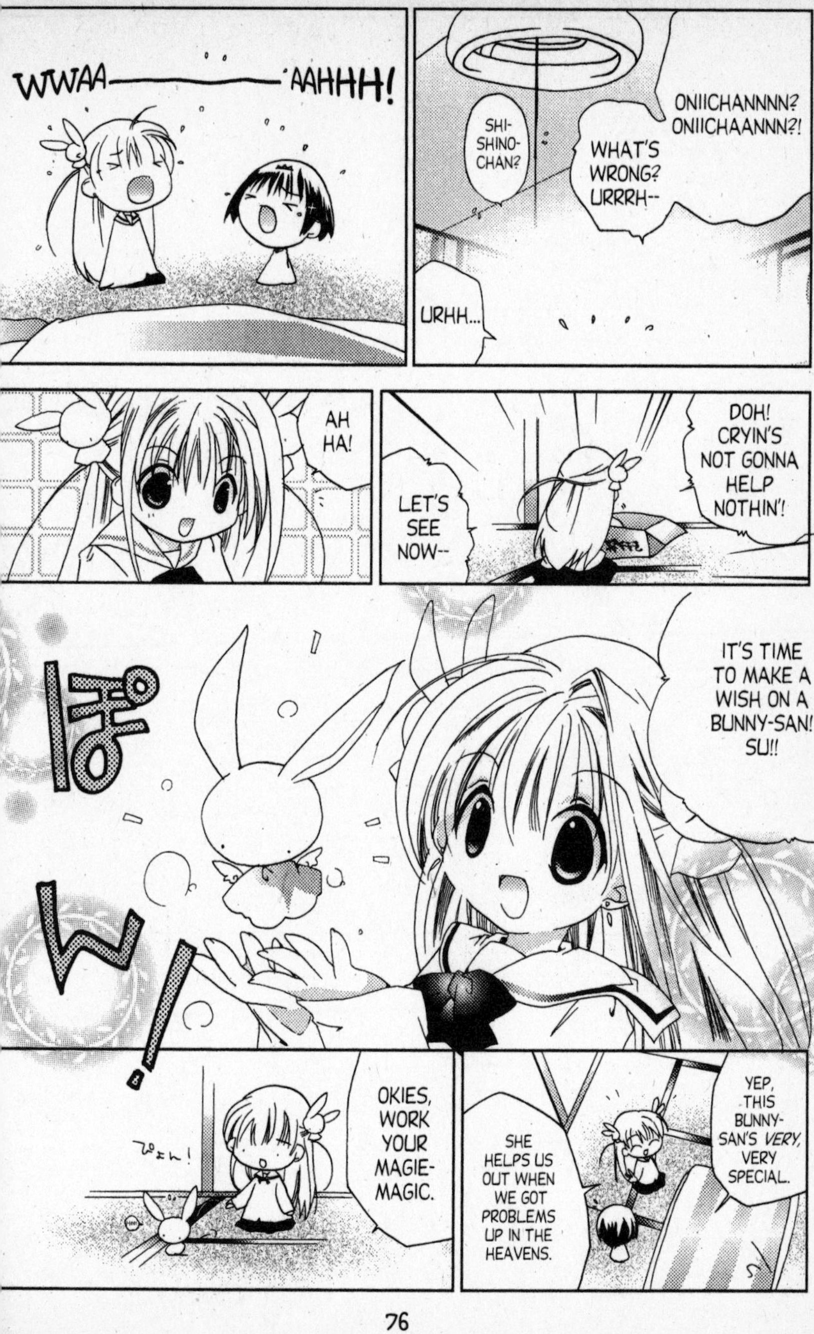
ONIICHANNNN? ONIICHAANNN?!
WHAT'S WRONG? URRRH--
SHI-SHINO-CHAN?
URHH...
WWAA————AAHHH!
DOH! CRYIN'S NOT GONNA HELP NOTHIN'!
LET'S SEE NOW--
AH HA!
IT'S TIME TO MAKE A WISH ON A BUNNY-SAN! SU!!
ぽん!
YEP, THIS BUNNY-SAN'S *VERY,* VERY SPECIAL.
SHE HELPS US OUT WHEN WE GOT PROBLEMS UP IN THE HEAVENS.
OKIES, WORK YOUR MAGIE-MAGIC.
ぴょん!

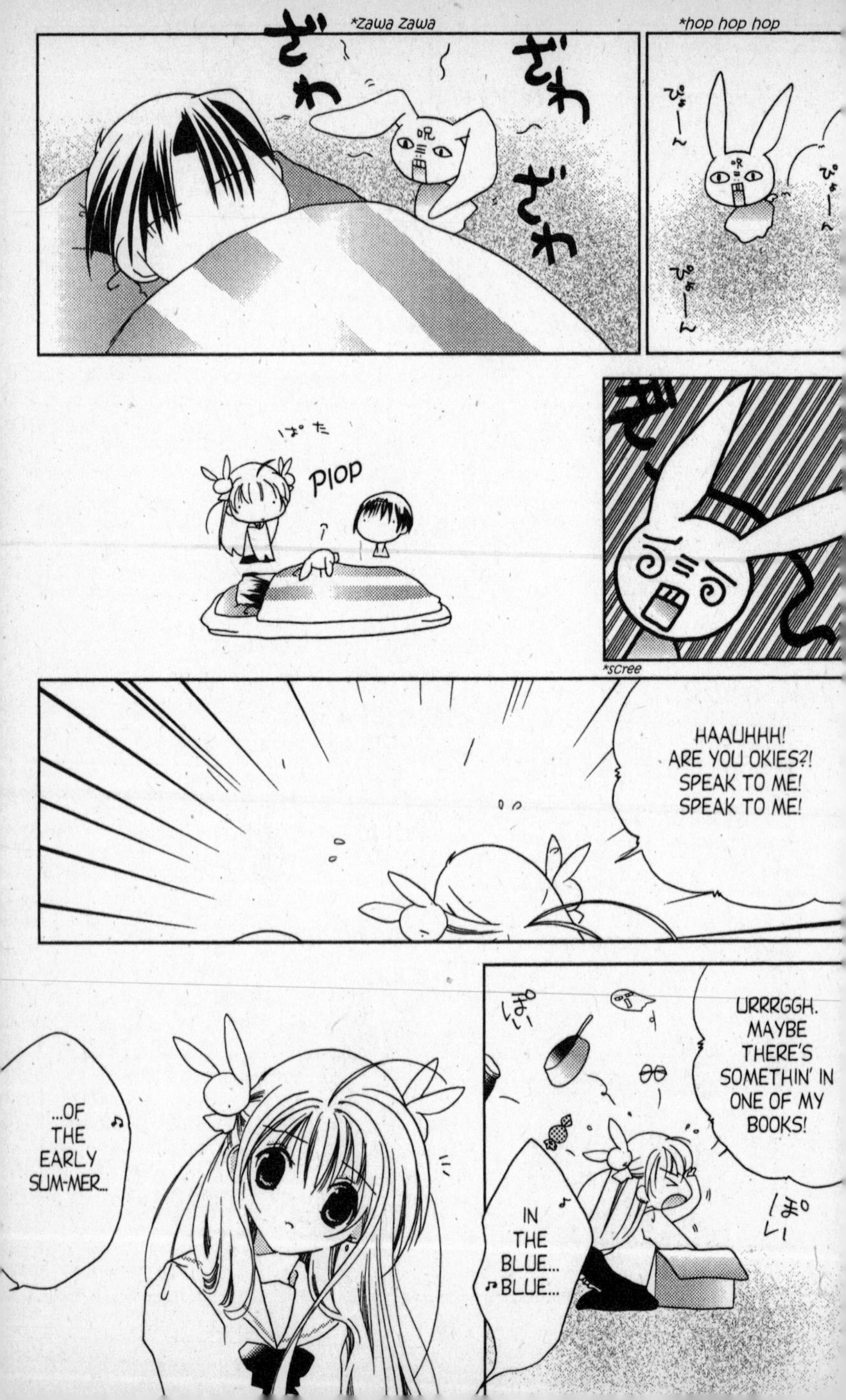
*hop hop hop
ぴょーん
ぴょーん
ぴょーん
*Zawa Zawa
ざわ~
ざわ~
ざわ~
*scree
ぱた
PLOP
HAAUHHH! ARE YOU OKIES?! SPEAK TO ME! SPEAK TO ME!
URRRGGH. MAYBE THERE'S SOMETHIN' IN ONE OF MY BOOKS!
ぽい
ぽい
IN THE BLUE... ♪BLUE...
...OF THE EARLY SUM-MER... ♪

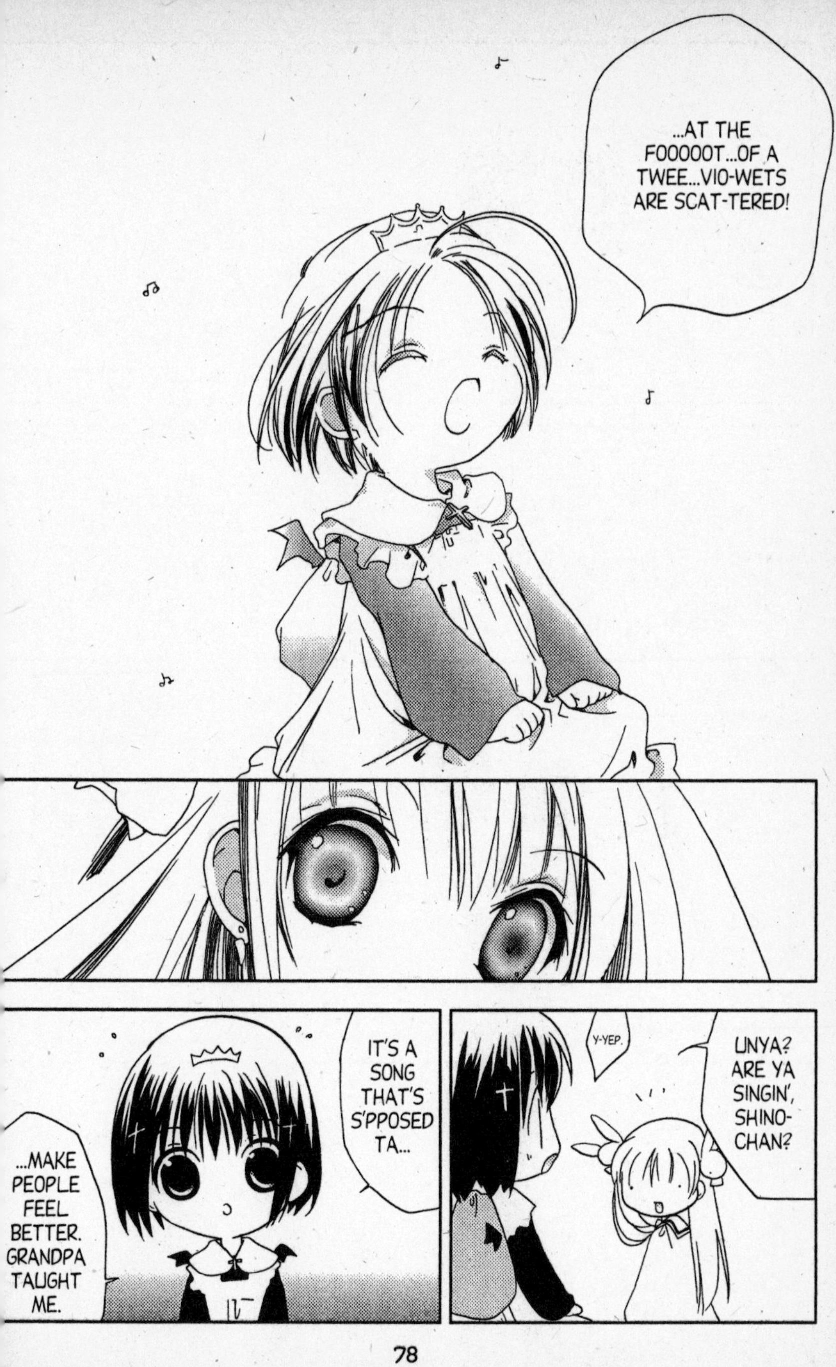

...AT THE FOOOOOT...OF A TWEE...VIO-WETS ARE SCAT-TERED!
UNYA? ARE YA SINGIN', SHINO-CHAN?
Y-YEP.
IT'S A SONG THAT'S S'PPOSED TA...
...MAKE PEOPLE FEEL BETTER. GRANDPA TAUGHT ME.

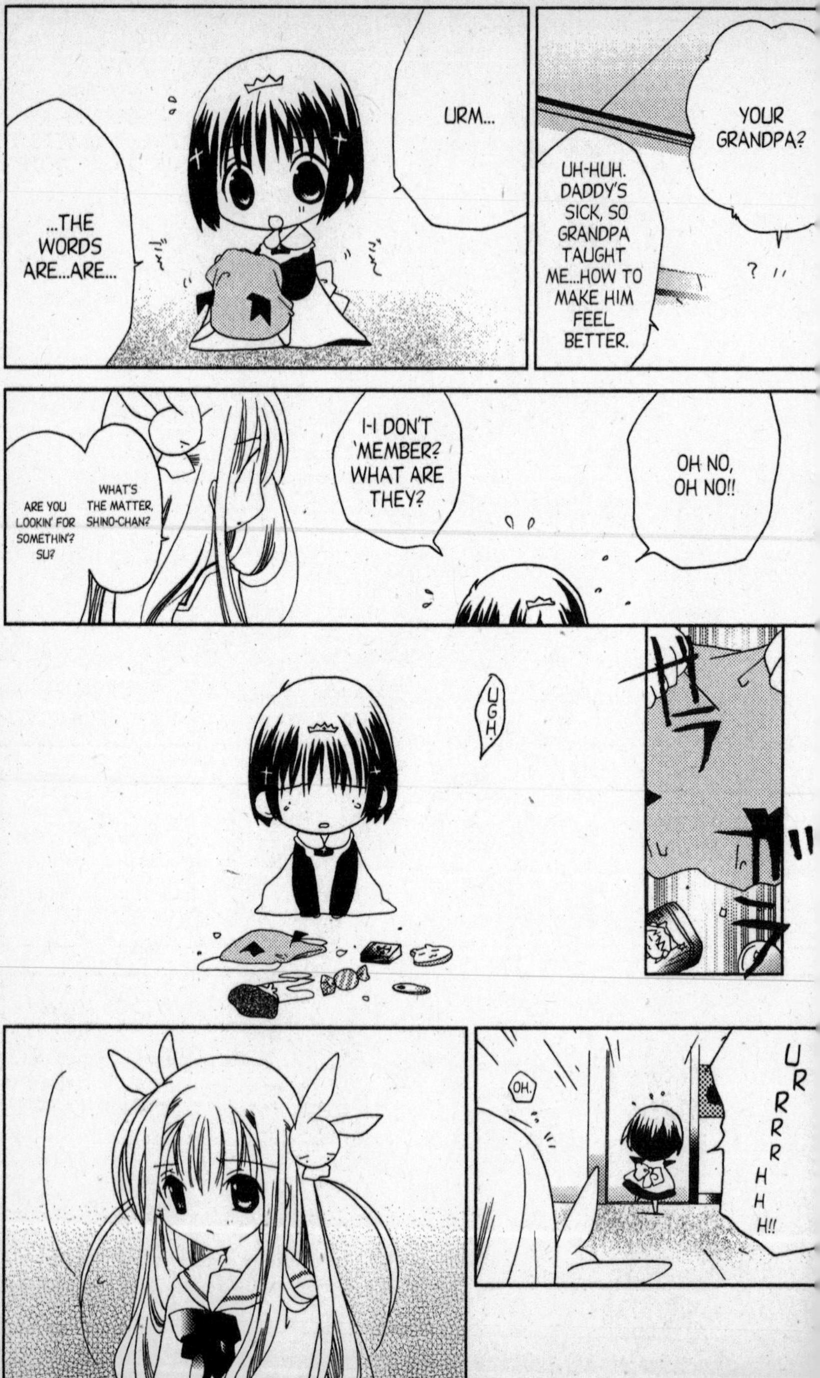
YOUR GRANDPA?
UH-HUH. DADDY'S SICK, SO GRANDPA TAUGHT ME...HOW TO MAKE HIM FEEL BETTER.
URM...
...THE WORDS ARE...ARE...
OH NO, OH NO!!
I-I DON'T 'MEMBER? WHAT ARE THEY?
WHAT'S THE MATTER, SHINO-CHAN?
ARE YOU LOOKIN' FOR SOMETHIN'? SU?
UGH.
URRRRHHHH!!
OH.

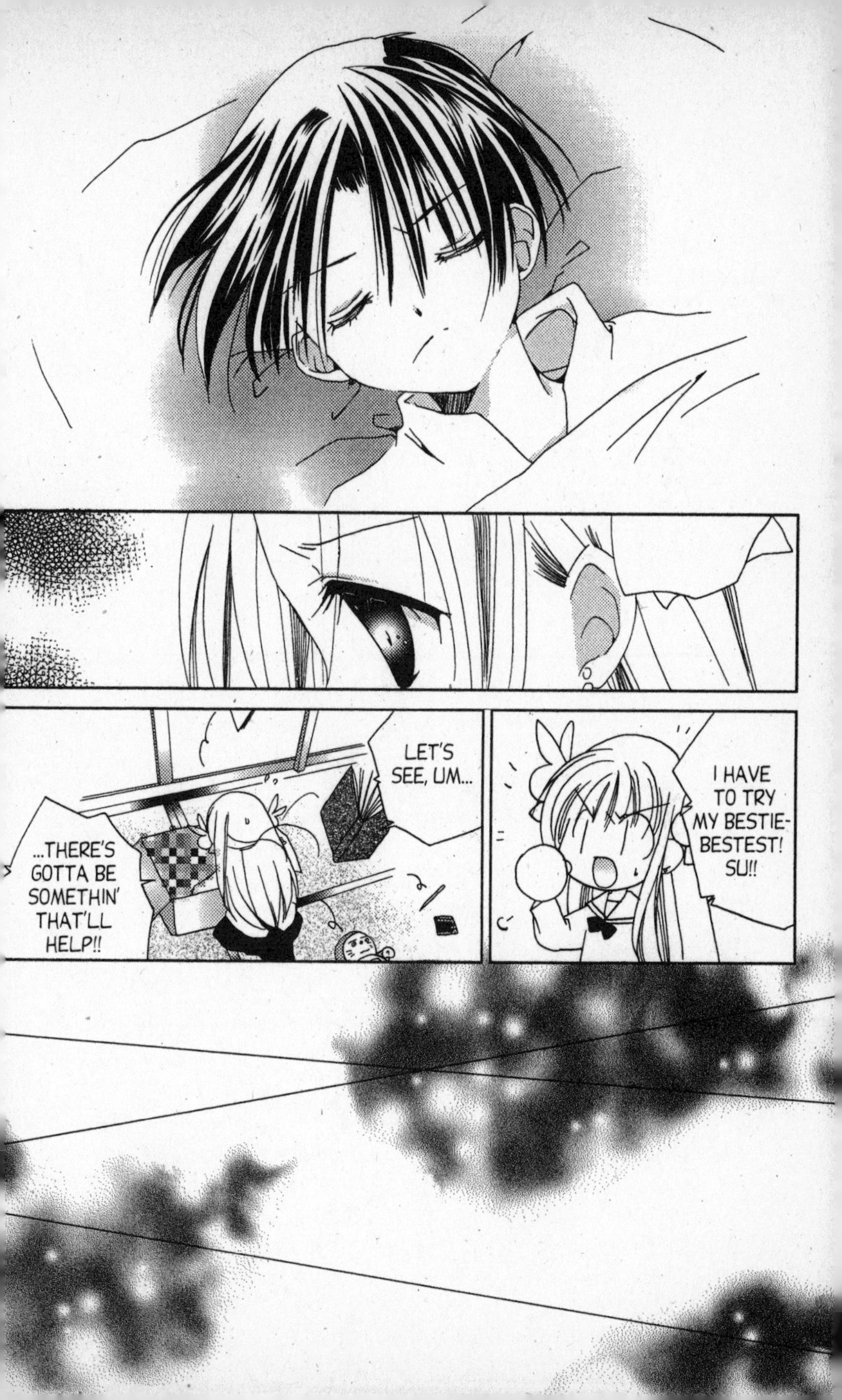
I HAVE TO TRY MY BESTIE-BESTEST! SU!!
LET'S SEE, UM...
...THERE'S GOTTA BE SOMETHIN' THAT'LL HELP!!

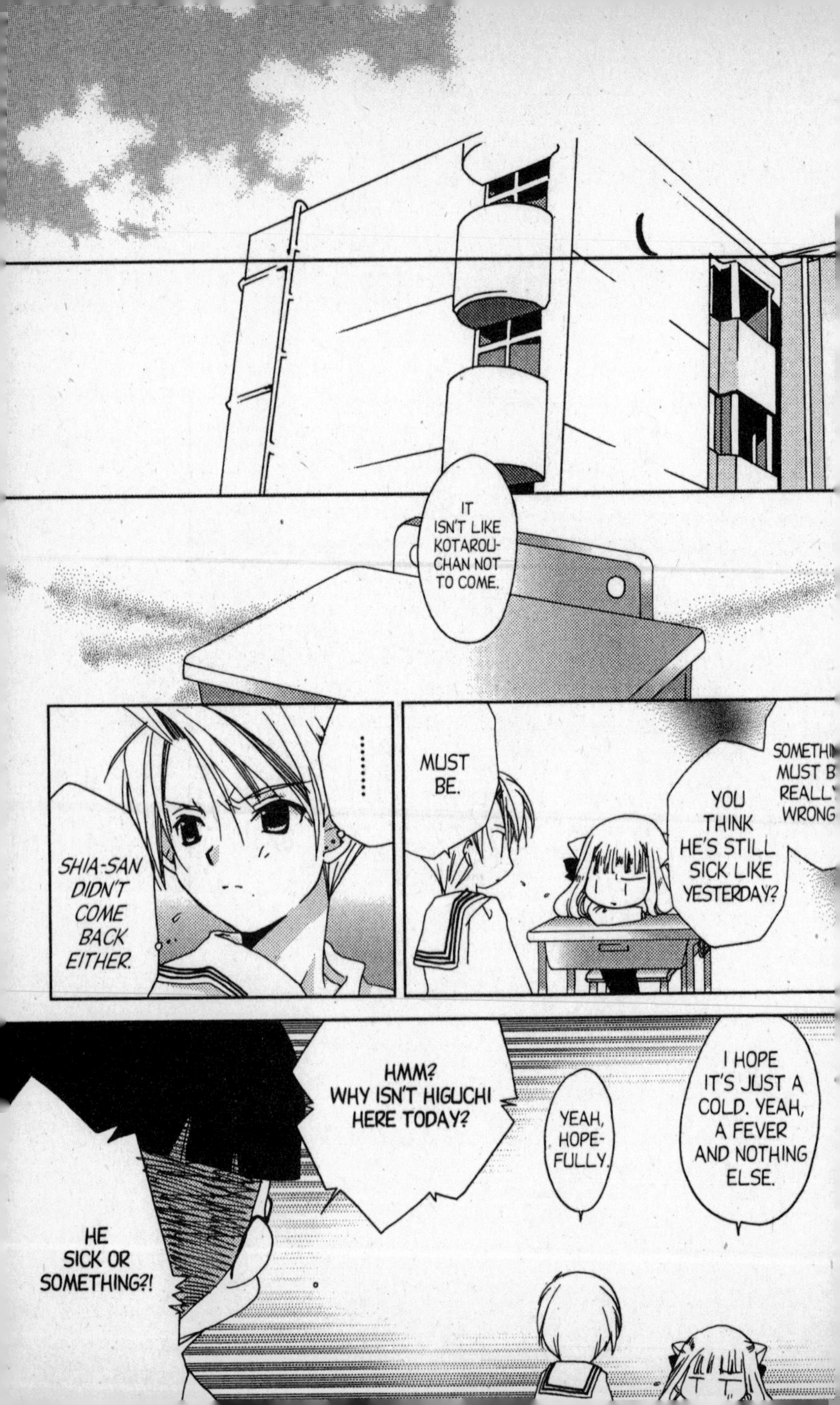
IT ISN'T LIKE KOTAROU-CHAN NOT TO COME.
SOMETHI MUST B REALL WRONG
YOU THINK HE'S STILL SICK LIKE YESTERDAY?
MUST BE.
......
SHIA-SAN DIDN'T COME BACK EITHER.
I HOPE IT'S JUST A COLD. YEAH, A FEVER AND NOTHING ELSE.
YEAH, HOPE-FULLY.
HMM? WHY ISN'T HIGUCHI HERE TODAY?
HE SICK OR SOMETHING?!

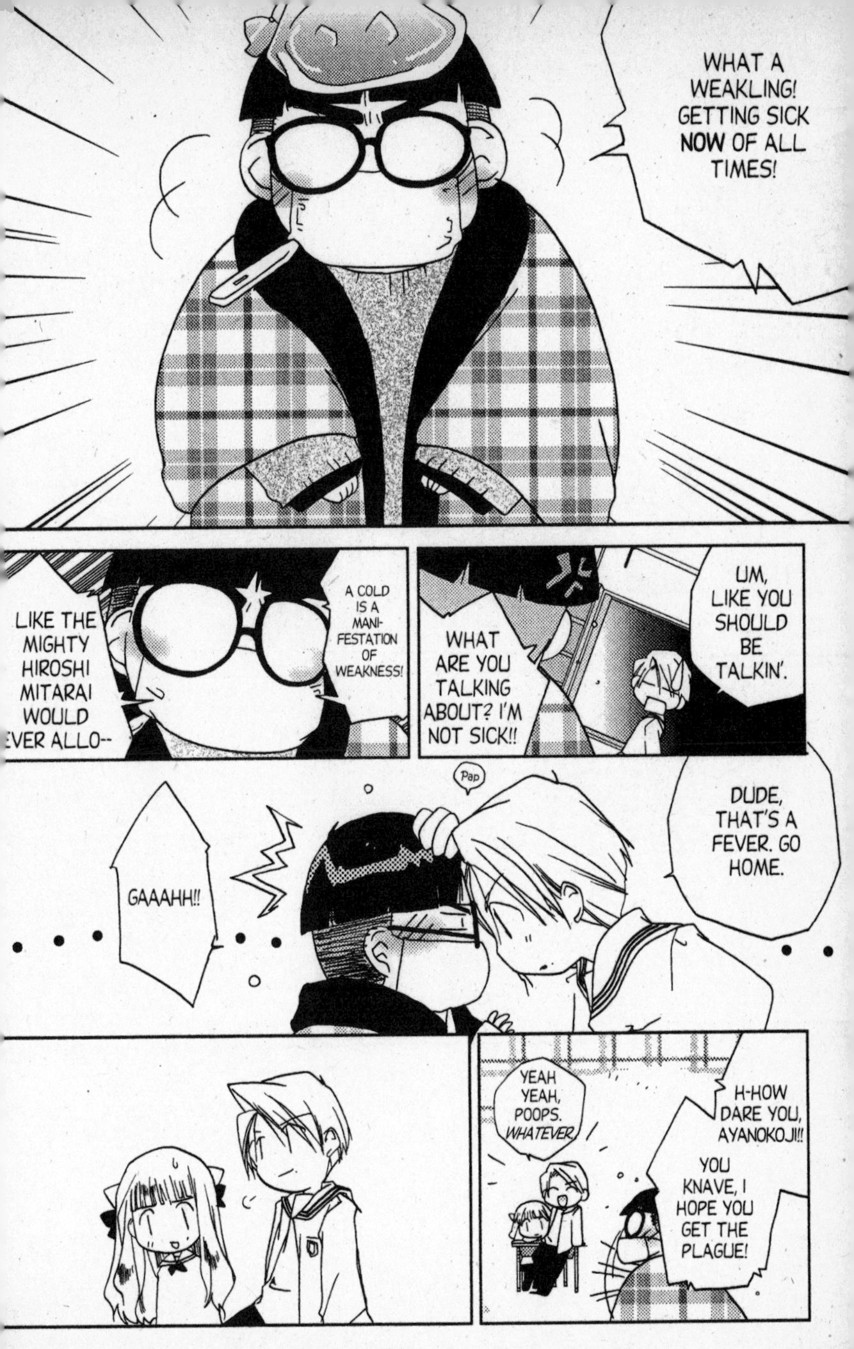
WHAT A WEAKLING! GETTING SICK NOW OF ALL TIMES!
UM, LIKE YOU SHOULD BE TALKIN'.
WHAT ARE YOU TALKING ABOUT? I'M NOT SICK!!
A COLD IS A MANI-FESTATION OF WEAKNESS!
LIKE THE MIGHTY HIROSHI MITARAI WOULD EVER ALLO--
Pap
DUDE, THAT'S A FEVER. GO HOME.
GAAAHH!!
H-HOW DARE YOU, AYANOKOJI!!
YOU KNAVE, I HOPE YOU GET THE PLAGUE!
YEAH YEAH, POOPS. *WHATEVER.*

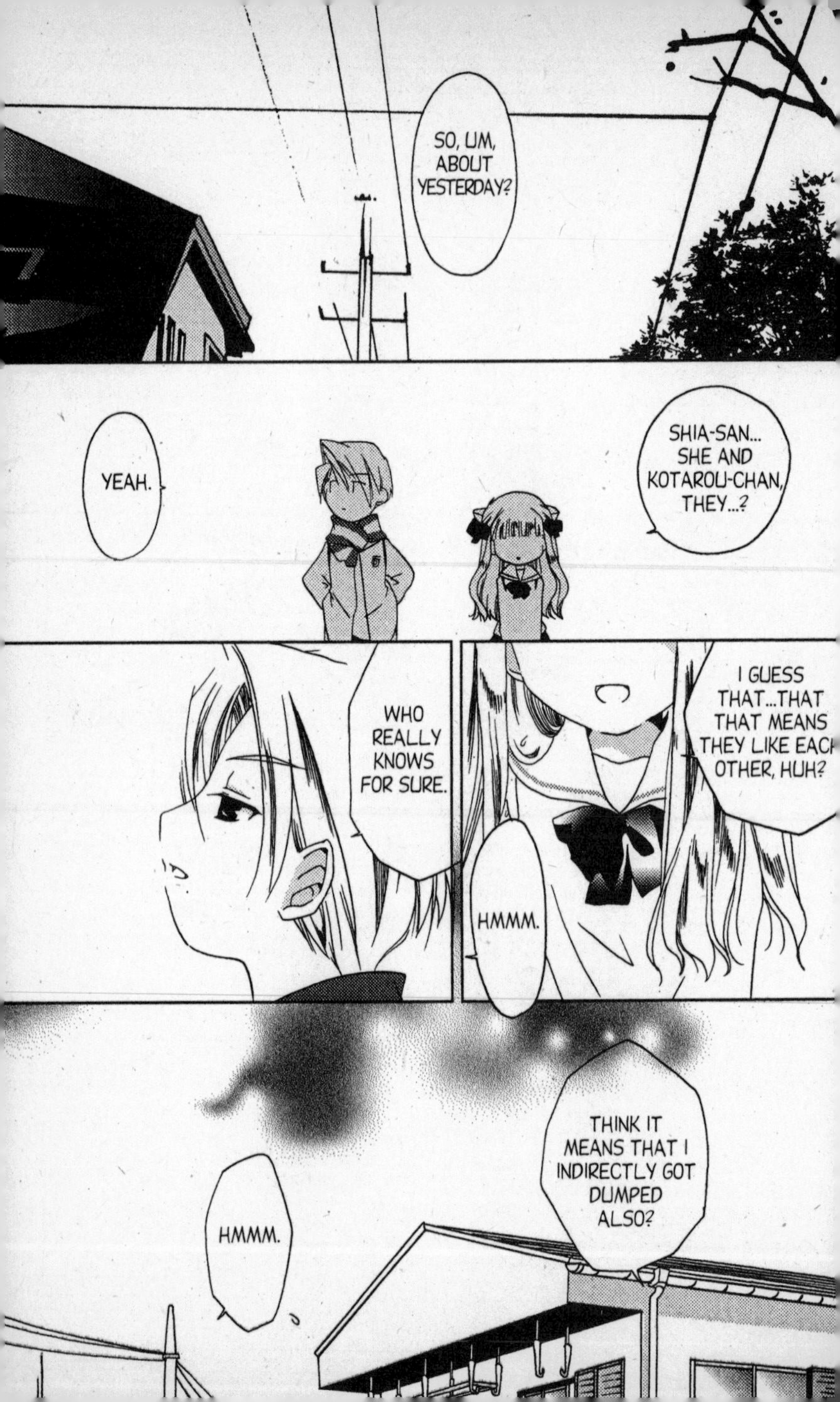
SO, UM, ABOUT YESTERDAY?
SHIA-SAN... SHE AND KOTAROU-CHAN, THEY...?
YEAH.
I GUESS THAT...THAT THAT MEANS THEY LIKE EACH OTHER, HUH?
HMMM.
WHO REALLY KNOWS FOR SURE.
THINK IT MEANS THAT I INDIRECTLY GOT DUMPED ALSO?
HMMM.

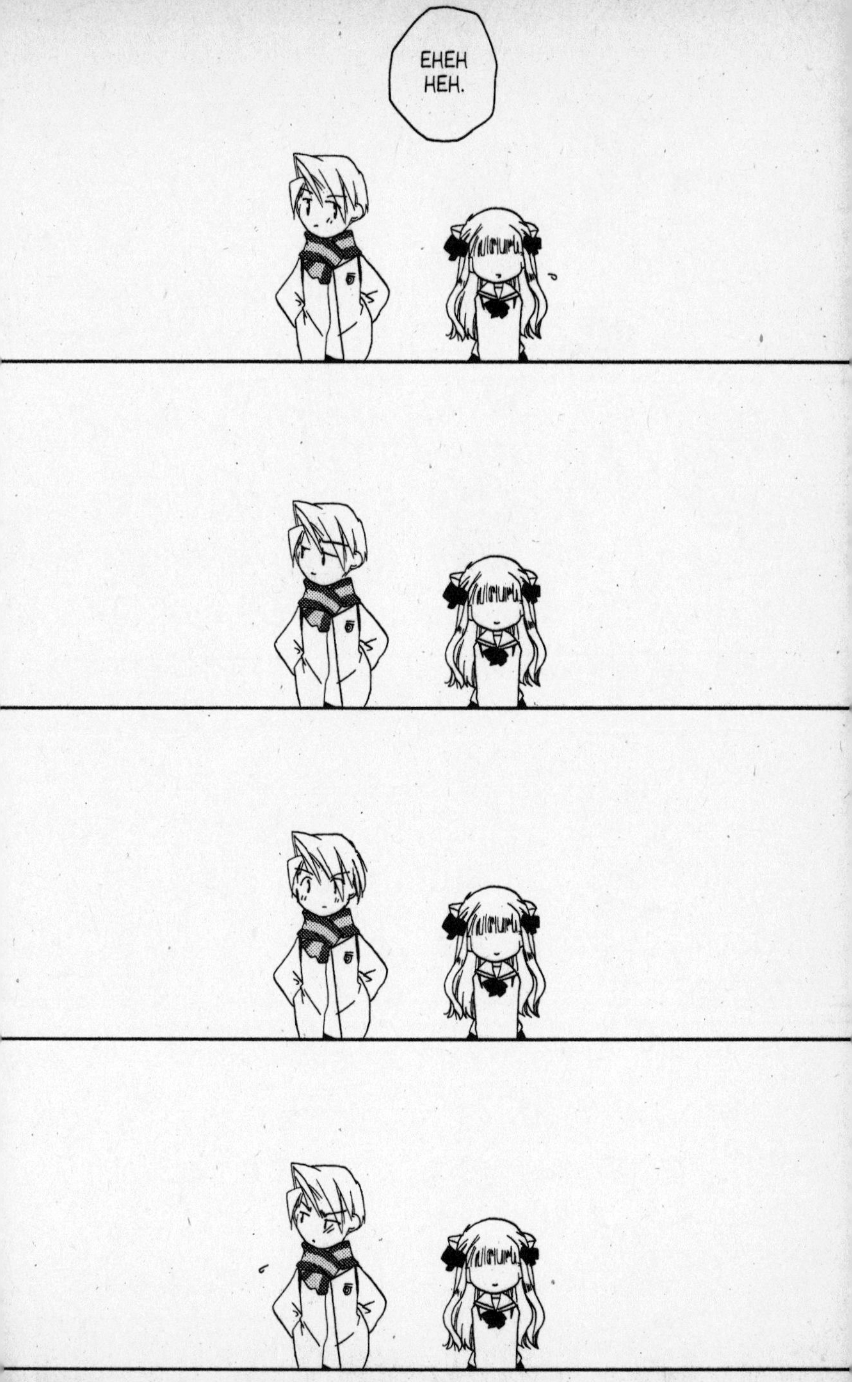
EHEH HEH.

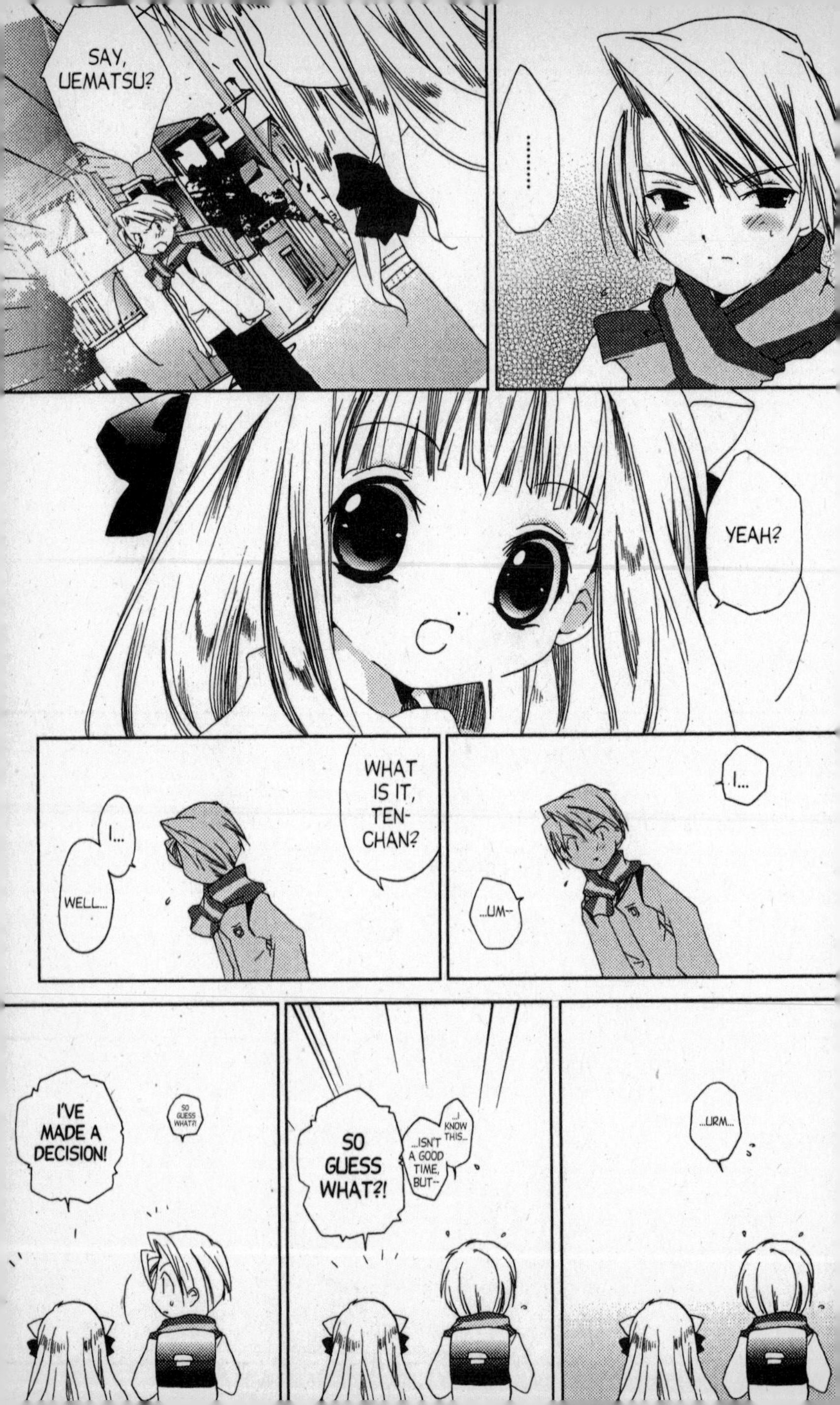
......
SAY, UEMATSU?
YEAH?
...I...
...UM--
WHAT IS IT, TEN-CHAN?
I...
WELL...
...URM...
...I KNOW THIS...
...ISN'T A GOOD TIME, BUT--
SO GUESS WHAT?!
SO GUESS WHAT?!
I'VE MADE A DECISION!

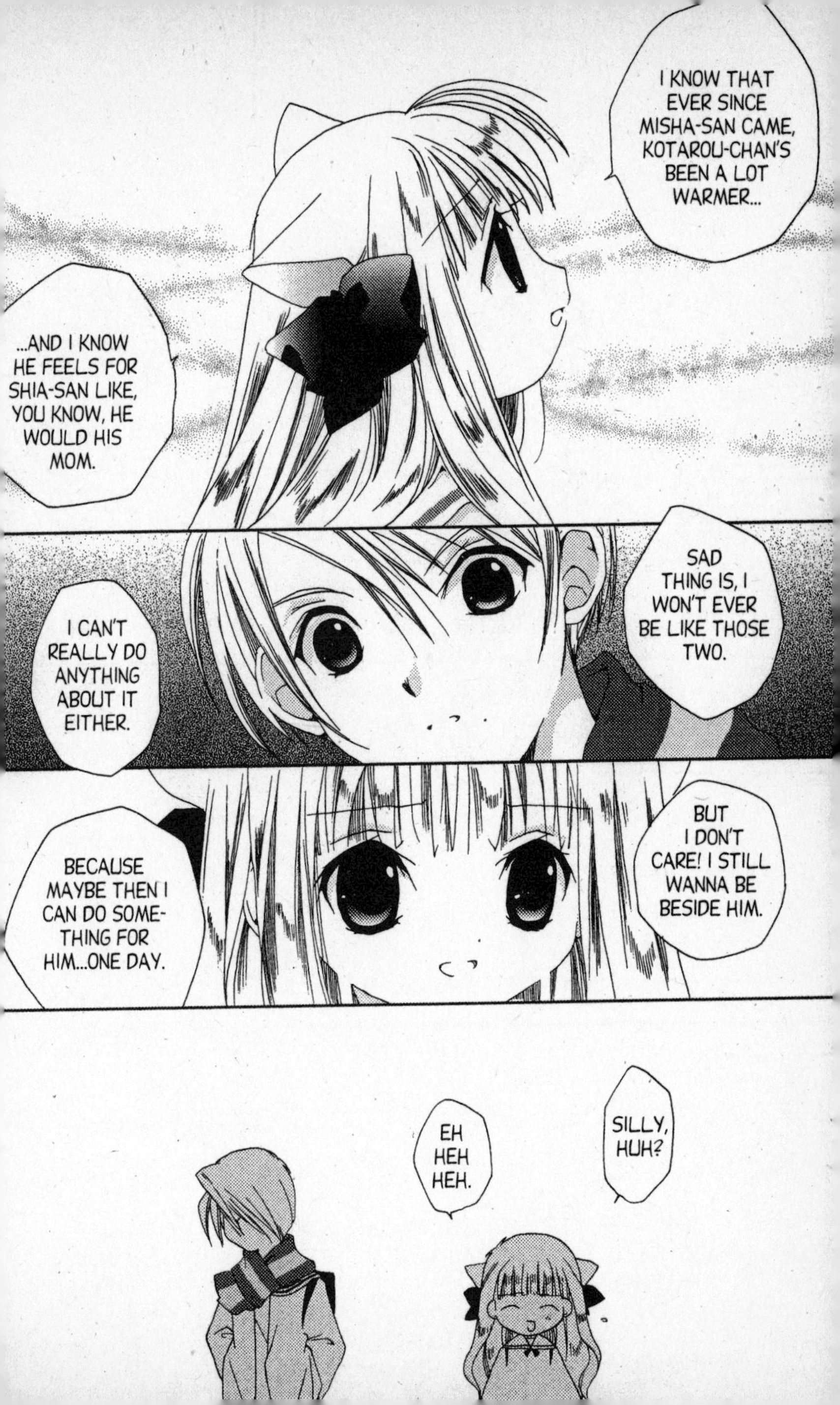
I KNOW THAT EVER SINCE MISHA-SAN CAME, KOTAROU-CHAN'S BEEN A LOT WARMER...
...AND I KNOW HE FEELS FOR SHIA-SAN LIKE, YOU KNOW, HE WOULD HIS MOM.
SAD THING IS, I WON'T EVER BE LIKE THOSE TWO.
I CAN'T REALLY DO ANYTHING ABOUT IT EITHER.
BUT I DON'T CARE! I STILL WANNA BE BESIDE HIM.
BECAUSE MAYBE THEN I CAN DO SOME-THING FOR HIM...ONE DAY.
SILLY, HUH?
EH HEH HEH.

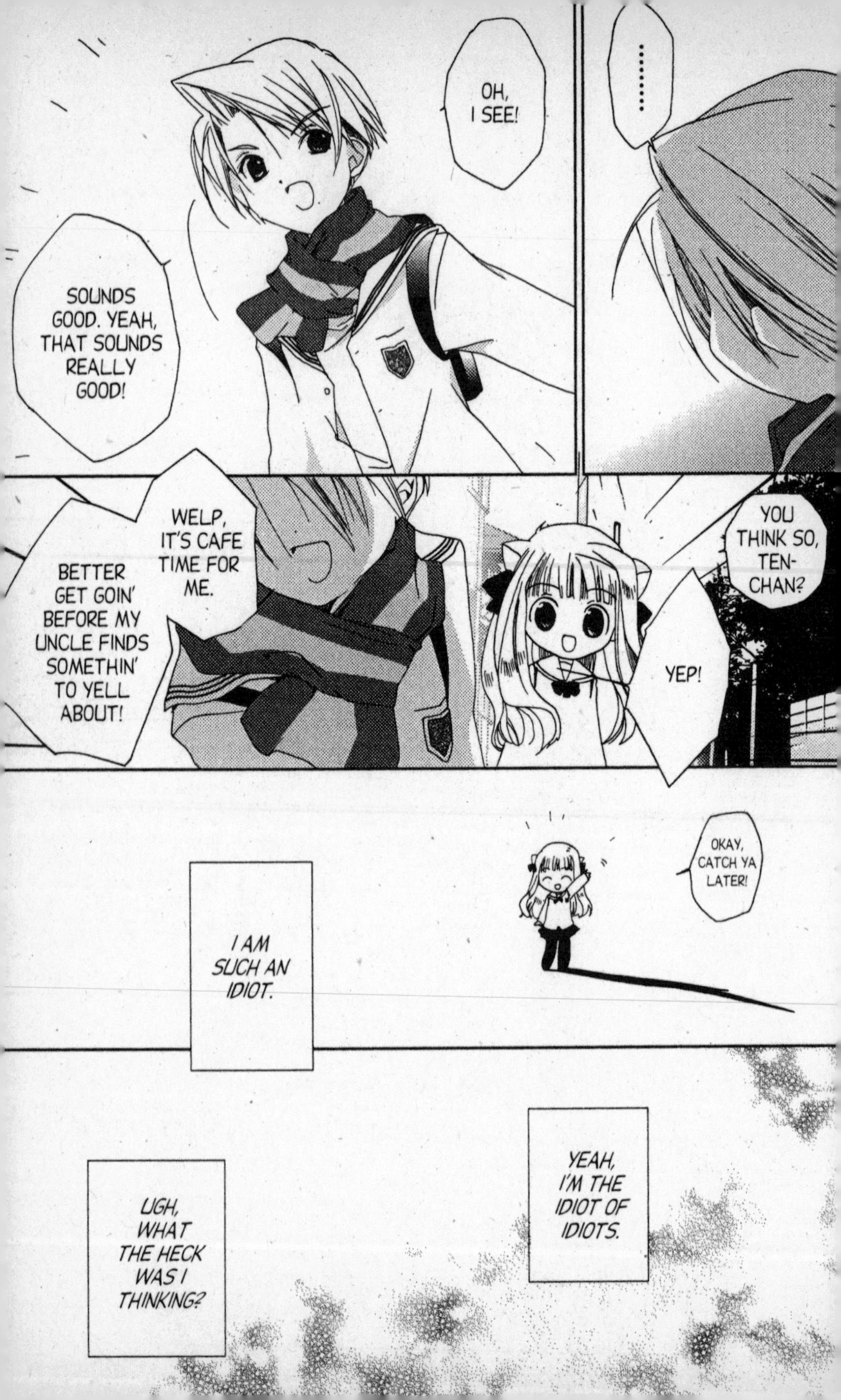
……
OH, I SEE!
SOUNDS GOOD. YEAH, THAT SOUNDS REALLY GOOD!
YOU THINK SO, TEN-CHAN?
YEP!
WELP, IT'S CAFE TIME FOR ME.
BETTER GET GOIN' BEFORE MY UNCLE FINDS SOMETHIN' TO YELL ABOUT!
OKAY, CATCH YA LATER!
I AM SUCH AN IDIOT.
YEAH, I'M THE IDIOT OF IDIOTS.
UGH, WHAT THE HECK WAS I THINKING?

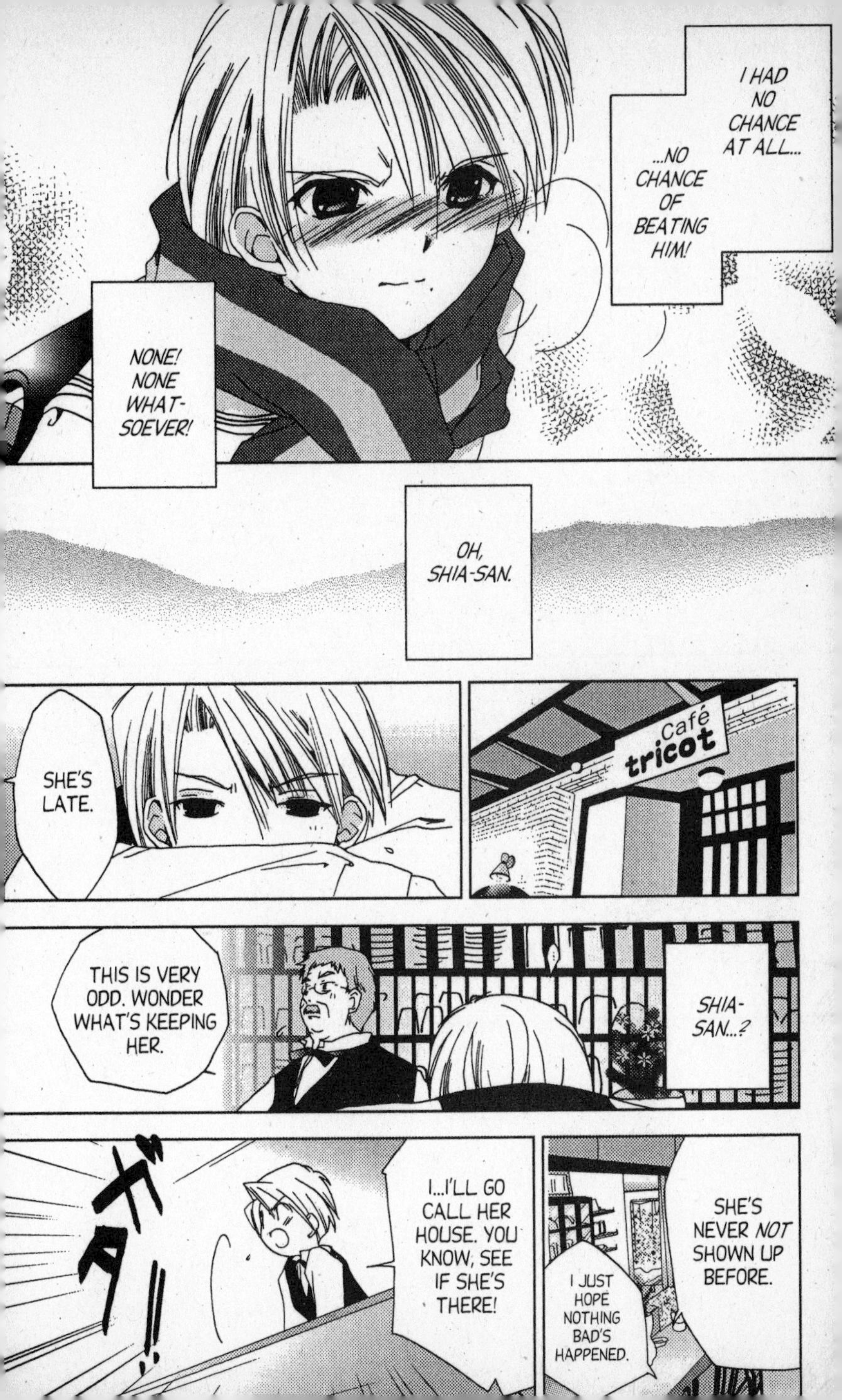
I HAD NO CHANCE AT ALL...
...NO CHANCE OF BEATING HIM!
NONE! NONE WHAT-SOEVER!
OH, SHIA-SAN.
Café tricot
SHE'S LATE.
SHIA-SAN...?
THIS IS VERY ODD. WONDER WHAT'S KEEPING HER.
SHE'S NEVER *NOT* SHOWN UP BEFORE.
I JUST HOPE NOTHING BAD'S HAPPENED.
I...I'LL GO CALL HER HOUSE. YOU KNOW, SEE IF SHE'S THERE!
ガタ!!

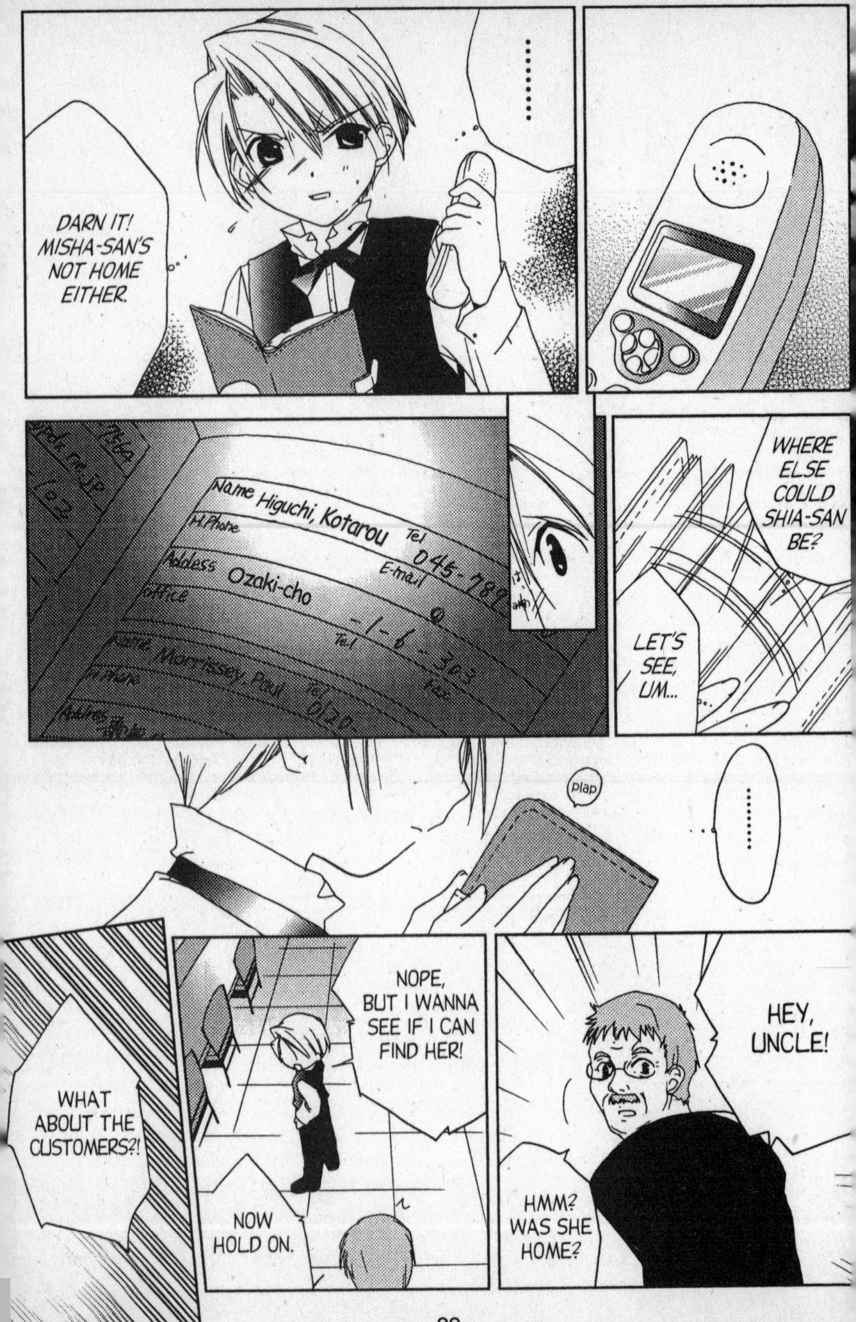
......
DARN IT! MISHA-SAN'S NOT HOME EITHER.
WHERE ELSE COULD SHIA-SAN BE?
LET'S SEE, UM...
Name Higuchi, Kotarou
Tel 045-789
H.Phone
E-mail
Address Ozaki-cho
Office
-1-6-303
Tel
Name Morrissey, Paul
Tel 0120-
Fax
......
plap
HEY, UNCLE!
HMM? WAS SHE HOME?
NOPE, BUT I WANNA SEE IF I CAN FIND HER!
NOW HOLD ON.
WHAT ABOUT THE CUSTOMERS?!

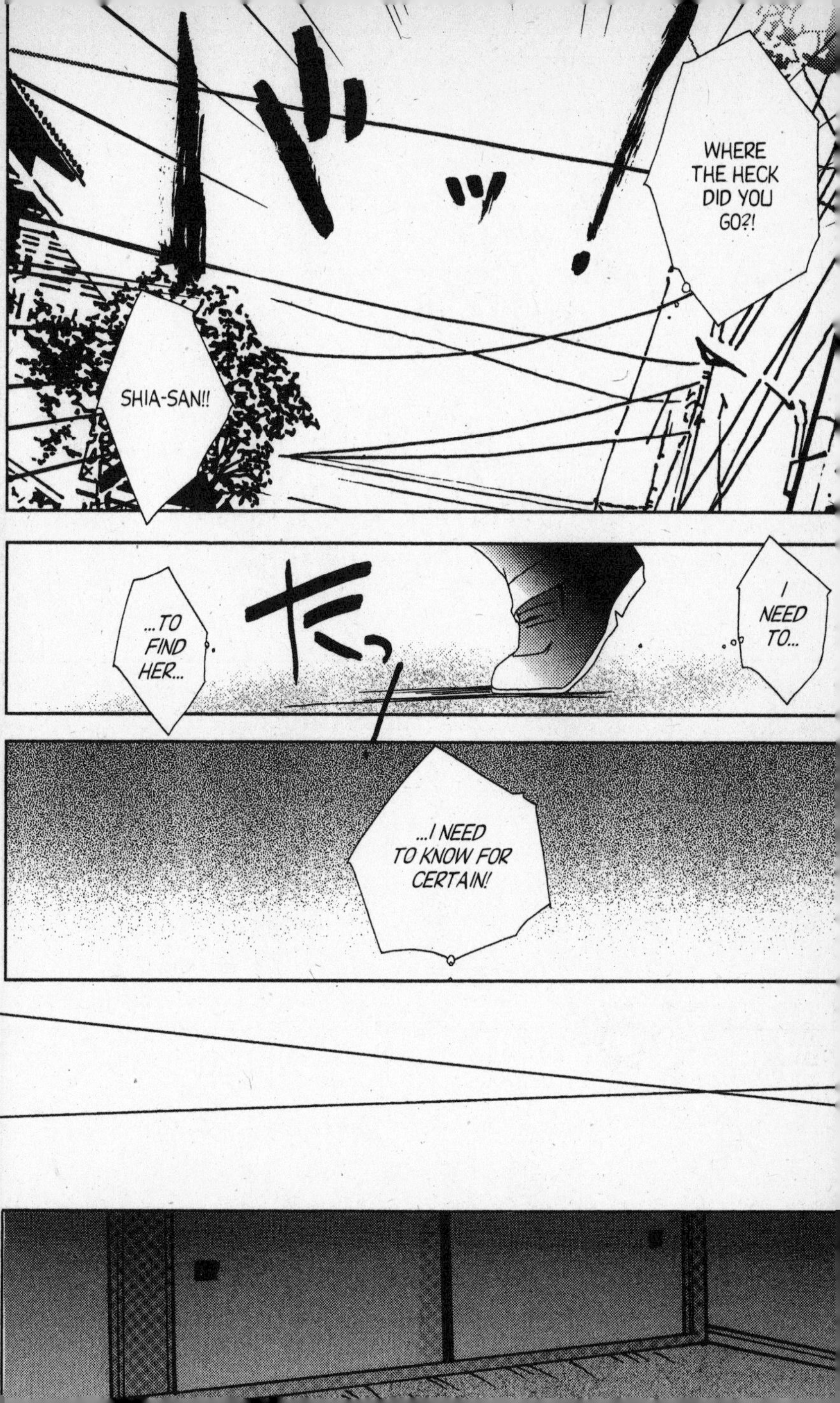
WHERE THE HECK DID YOU GO?!
ドッ!
SHIA-SAN!!
I NEED TO...
たっ
...TO FIND HER...
...I NEED TO KNOW FOR CERTAIN!

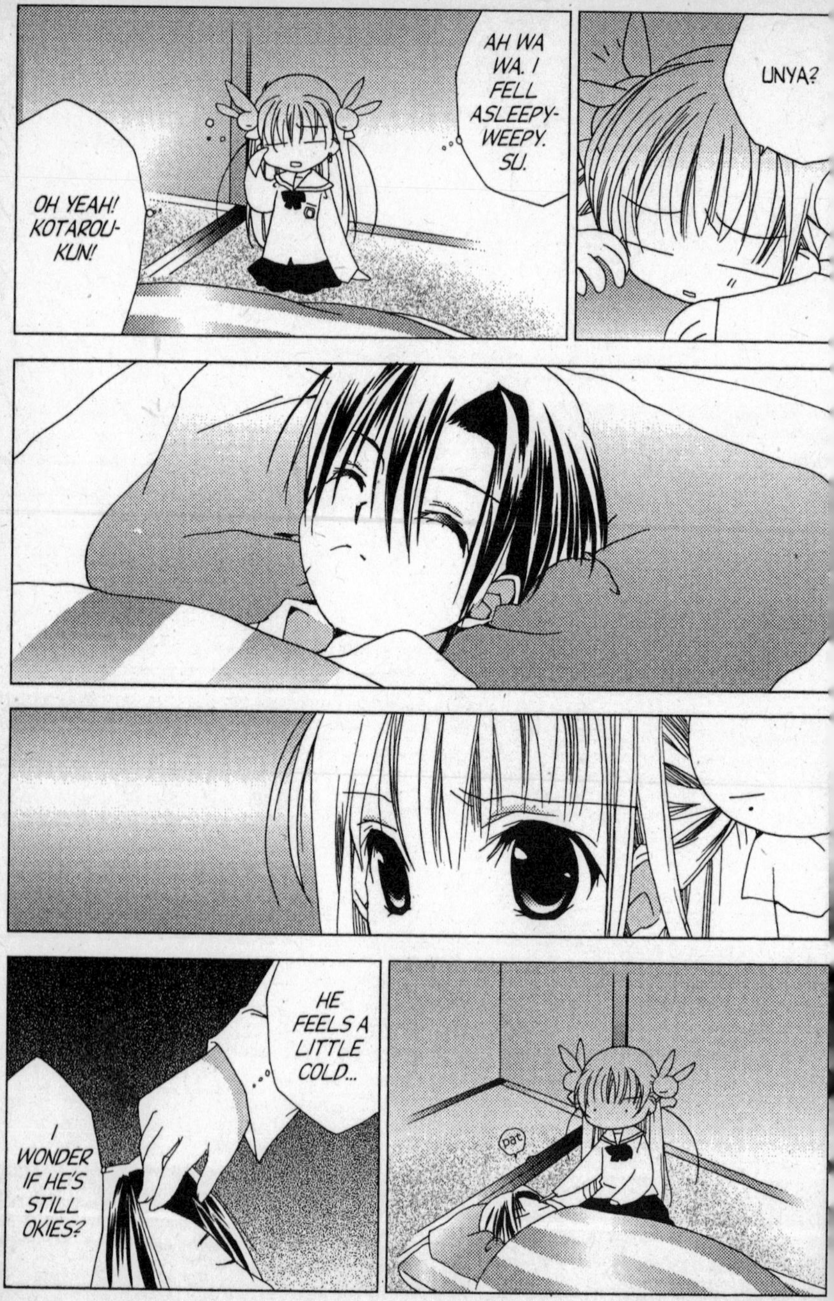
UNYA?
AH WA WA. I FELL ASLEEPY-WEEPY. SU.
OH YEAH! KOTAROU-KUN!
pat
HE FEELS A LITTLE COLD...
I WONDER IF HE'S STILL OKIES?

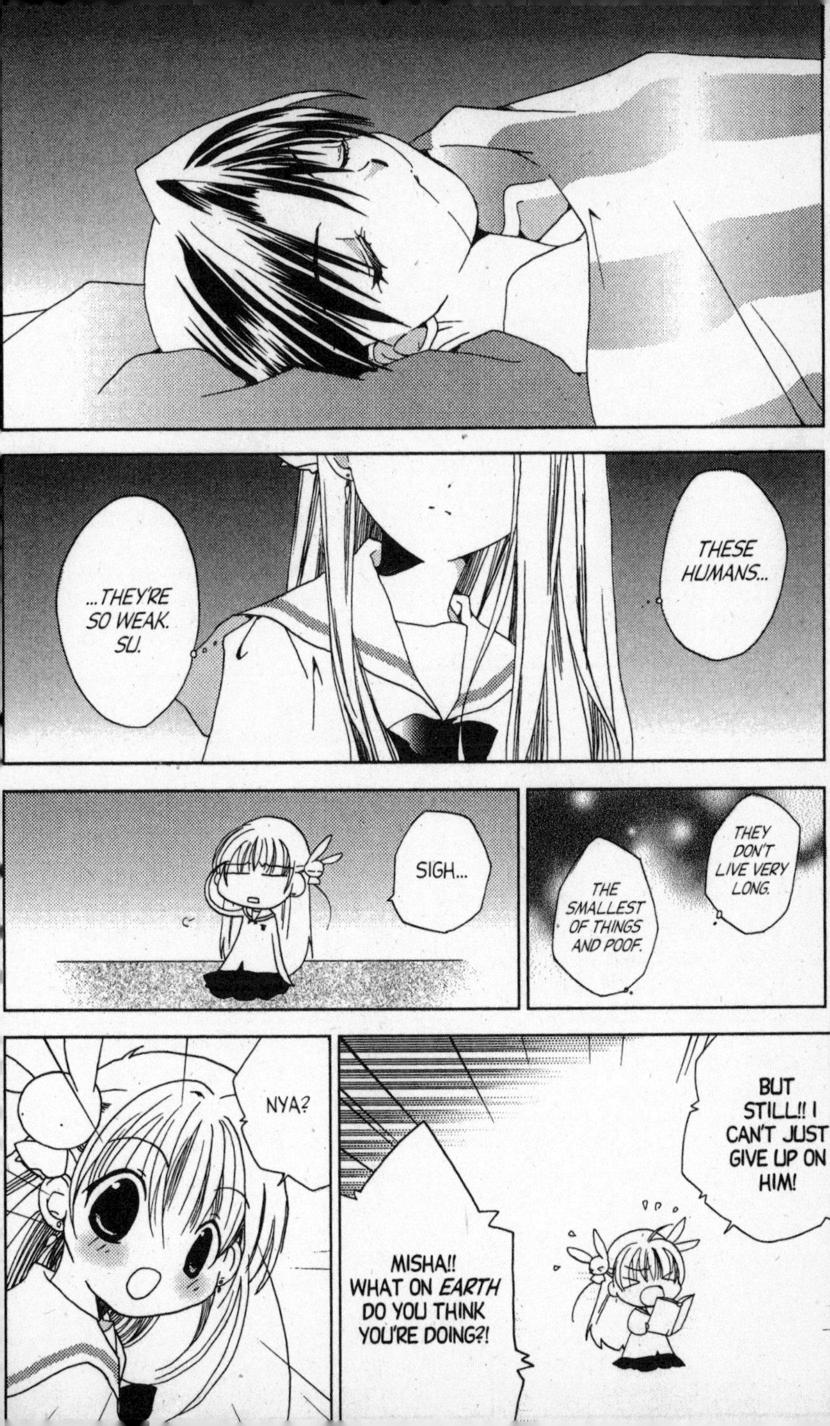
THESE HUMANS...
...THEY'RE SO WEAK. SU.
THEY DON'T LIVE VERY LONG.
THE SMALLEST OF THINGS AND POOF.
SIGH...
BUT STILL!! I CAN'T JUST GIVE UP ON HIM!
MISHA!! WHAT ON *EARTH* DO YOU THINK YOU'RE DOING?!
NYA?

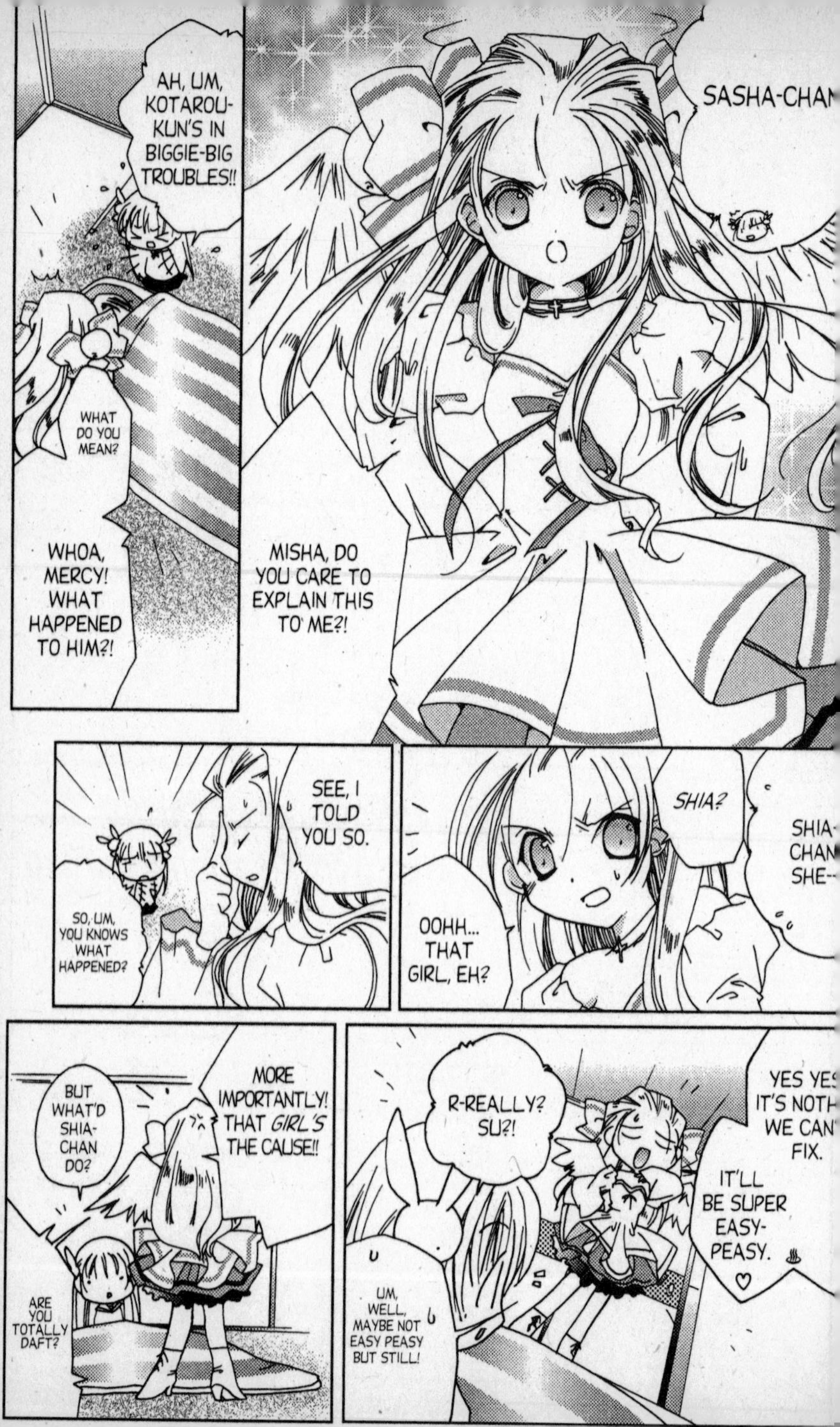
SASHA-CHAN
MISHA, DO YOU CARE TO EXPLAIN THIS TO ME?!
AH, UM, KOTAROU-KUN'S IN BIGGIE-BIG TROUBLES!!
WHAT DO YOU MEAN?
WHOA, MERCY! WHAT HAPPENED TO HIM?!
SHIA-CHAN SHE--
SHIA?
OOHH... THAT GIRL, EH?
SEE, I TOLD YOU SO.
SO, UM, YOU KNOWS WHAT HAPPENED?
YES YES IT'S NOTH WE CAN FIX.
R-REALLY? SU?!
IT'LL BE SUPER EASY-PEASY. ♡
UM, WELL, MAYBE NOT EASY PEASY BUT STILL!
MORE IMPORTANTLY! THAT *GIRL'S* THE CAUSE!!
BUT WHAT'D SHIA-CHAN DO?
ARE YOU TOTALLY DAFT?

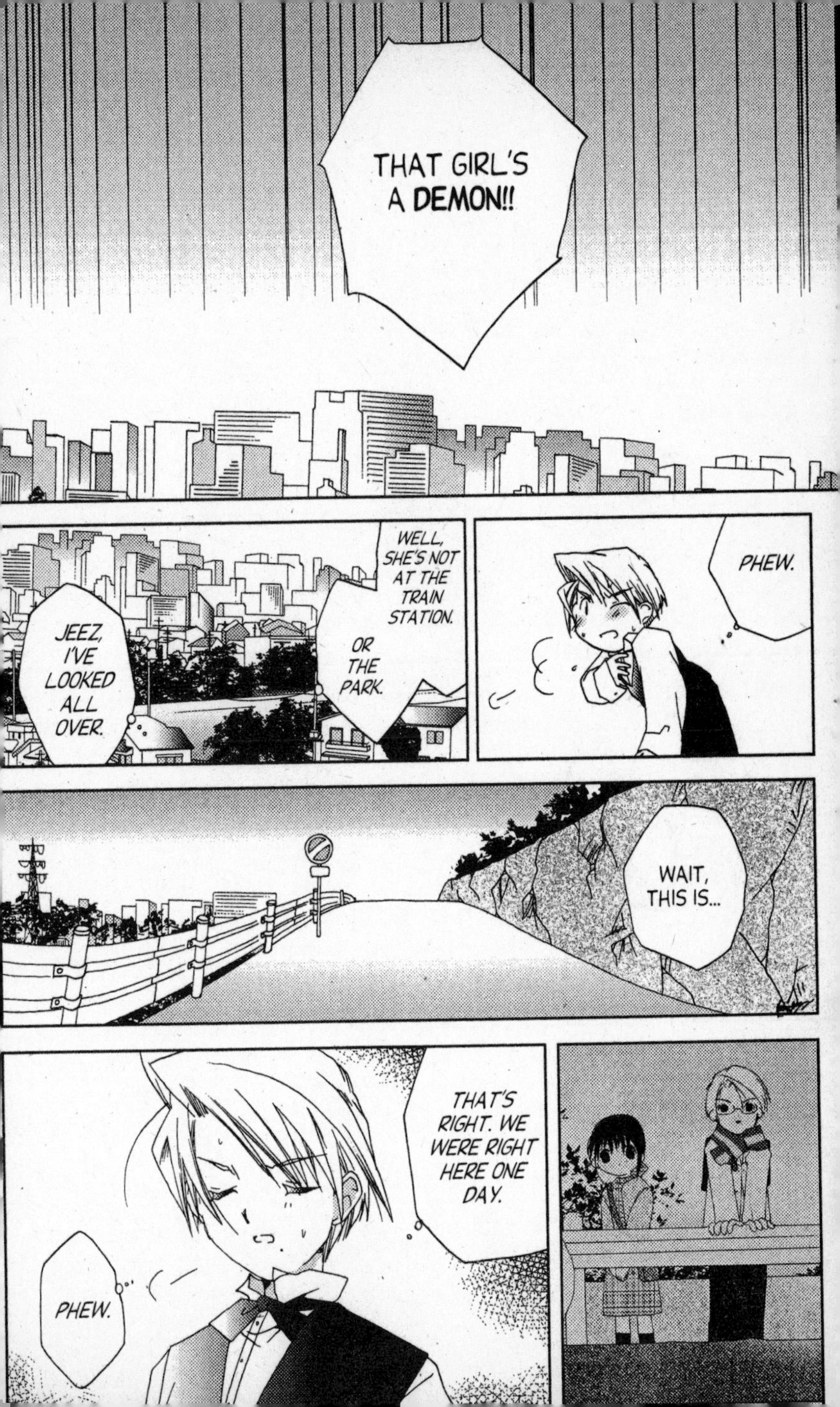
THAT GIRL'S A DEMON!!
PHEW.
WELL, SHE'S NOT AT THE TRAIN STATION.
OR THE PARK.
JEEZ, I'VE LOOKED ALL OVER.
WAIT, THIS IS...
THAT'S RIGHT. WE WERE RIGHT HERE ONE DAY.
PHEW.

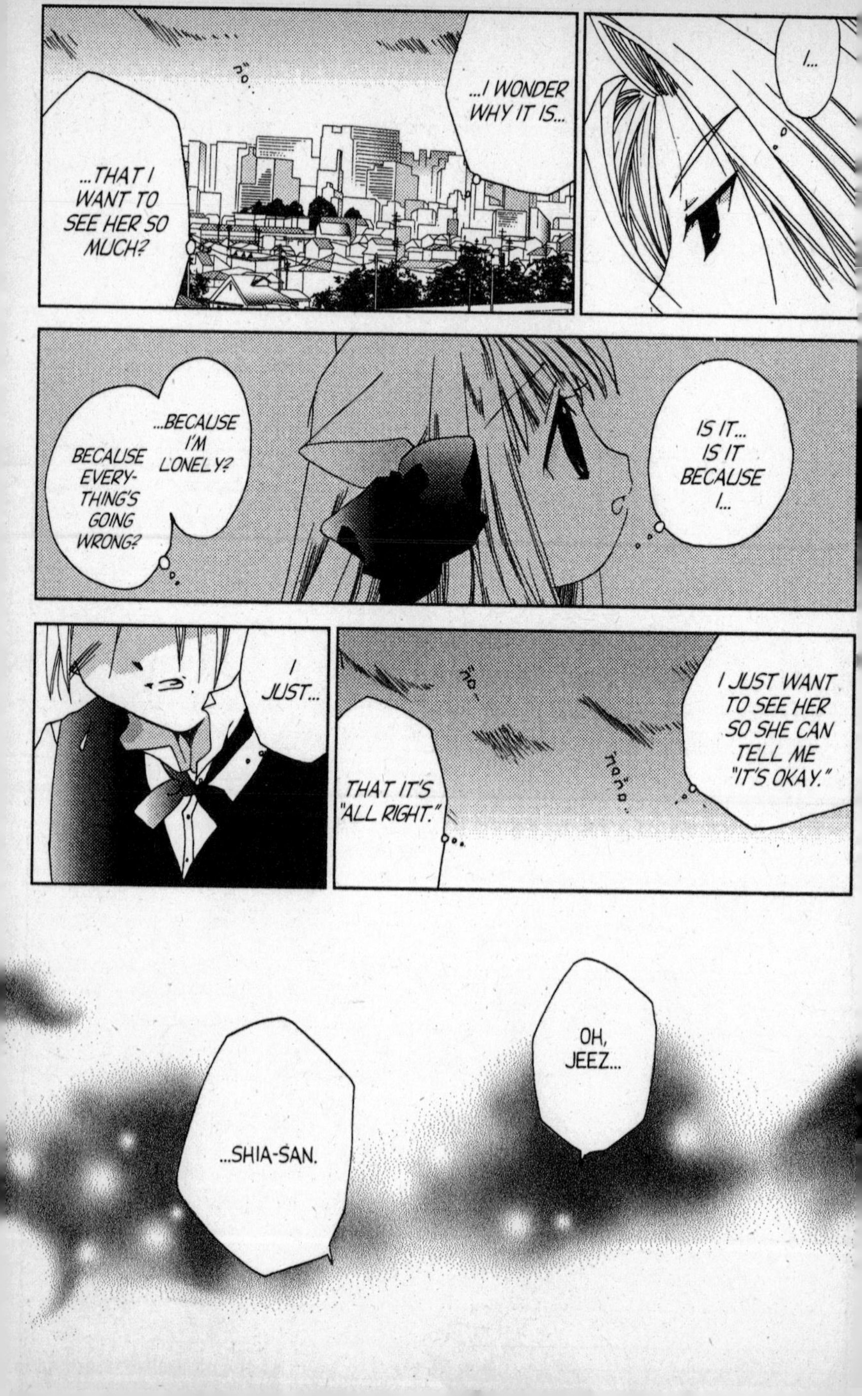
I...
...I WONDER WHY IT IS...
...THAT I WANT TO SEE HER SO MUCH?
IS IT... IS IT BECAUSE I...
...BECAUSE I'M LONELY?
BECAUSE EVERY-THING'S GOING WRONG?
I JUST WANT TO SEE HER SO SHE CAN TELL ME "IT'S OKAY."
THAT IT'S "ALL RIGHT."
I JUST...
OH, JEEZ...
...SHIA-SAN.

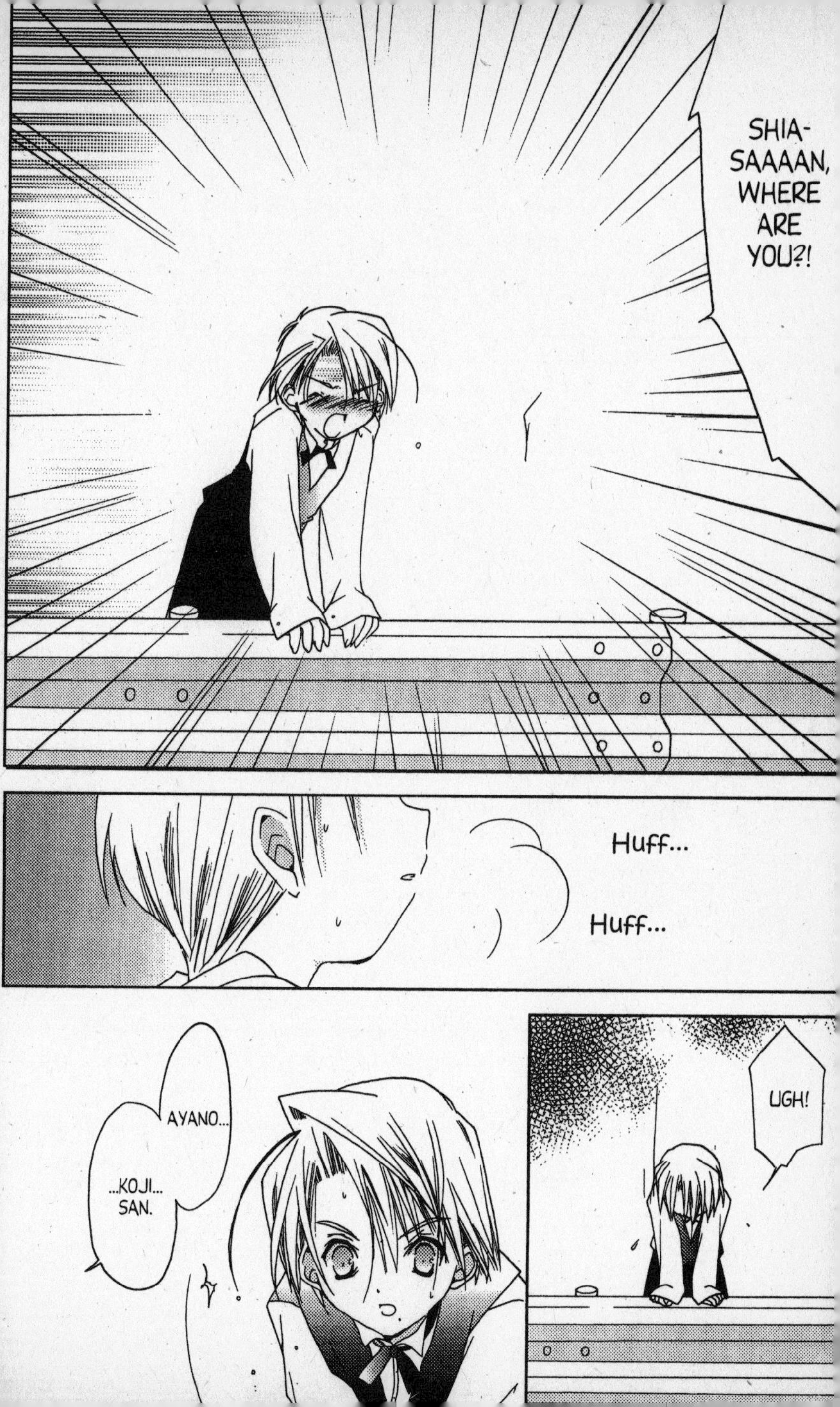
SHIA-SAAAAN, WHERE ARE YOU?!
Huff...
Huff...
UGH!
AYANO...
...KOJI... SAN.

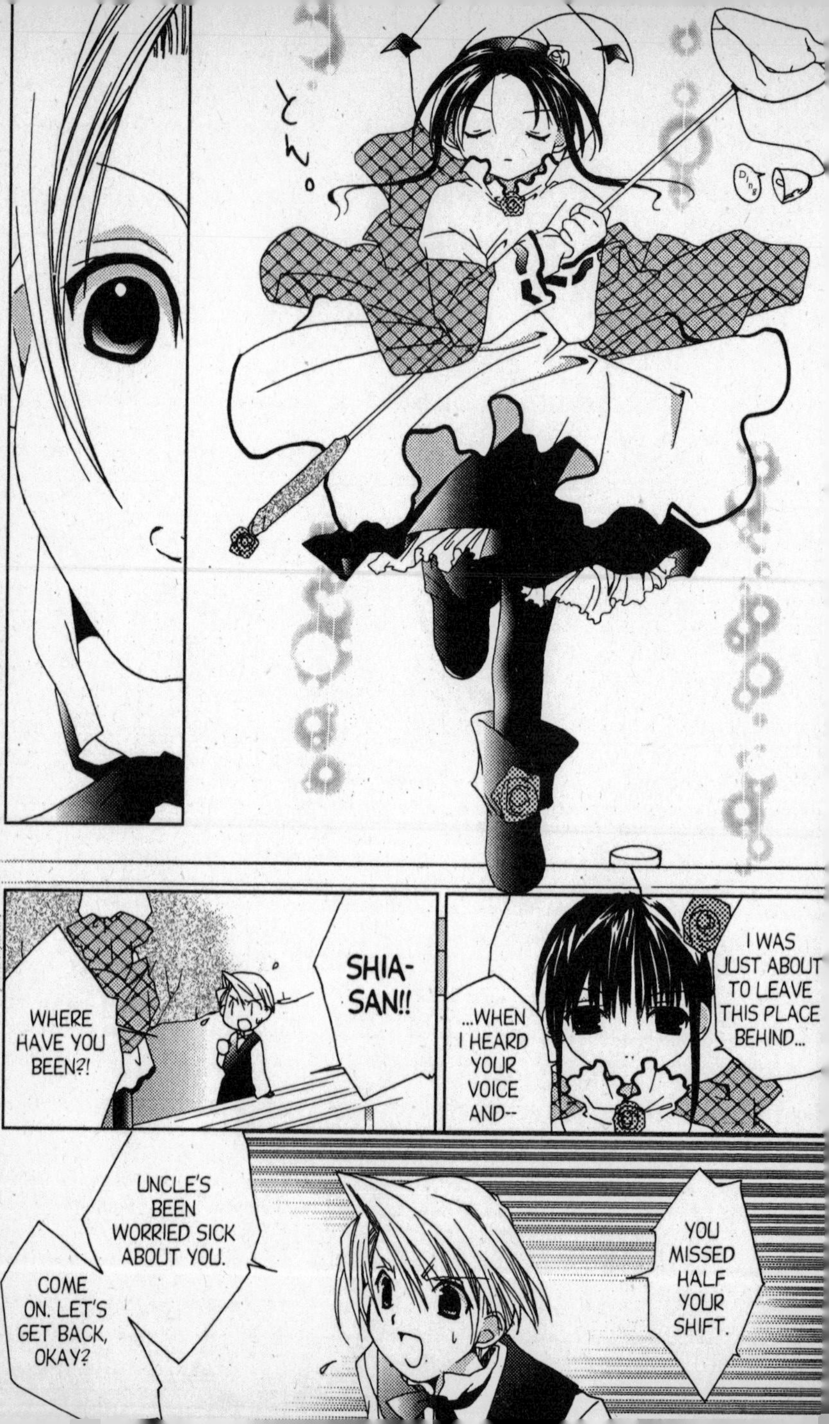
とん。
Ding
I WAS JUST ABOUT TO LEAVE THIS PLACE BEHIND...
...WHEN I HEARD YOUR VOICE AND--
SHIA-SAN!!
WHERE HAVE YOU BEEN?!
YOU MISSED HALF YOUR SHIFT.
UNCLE'S BEEN WORRIED SICK ABOUT YOU.
COME ON. LET'S GET BACK, OKAY?

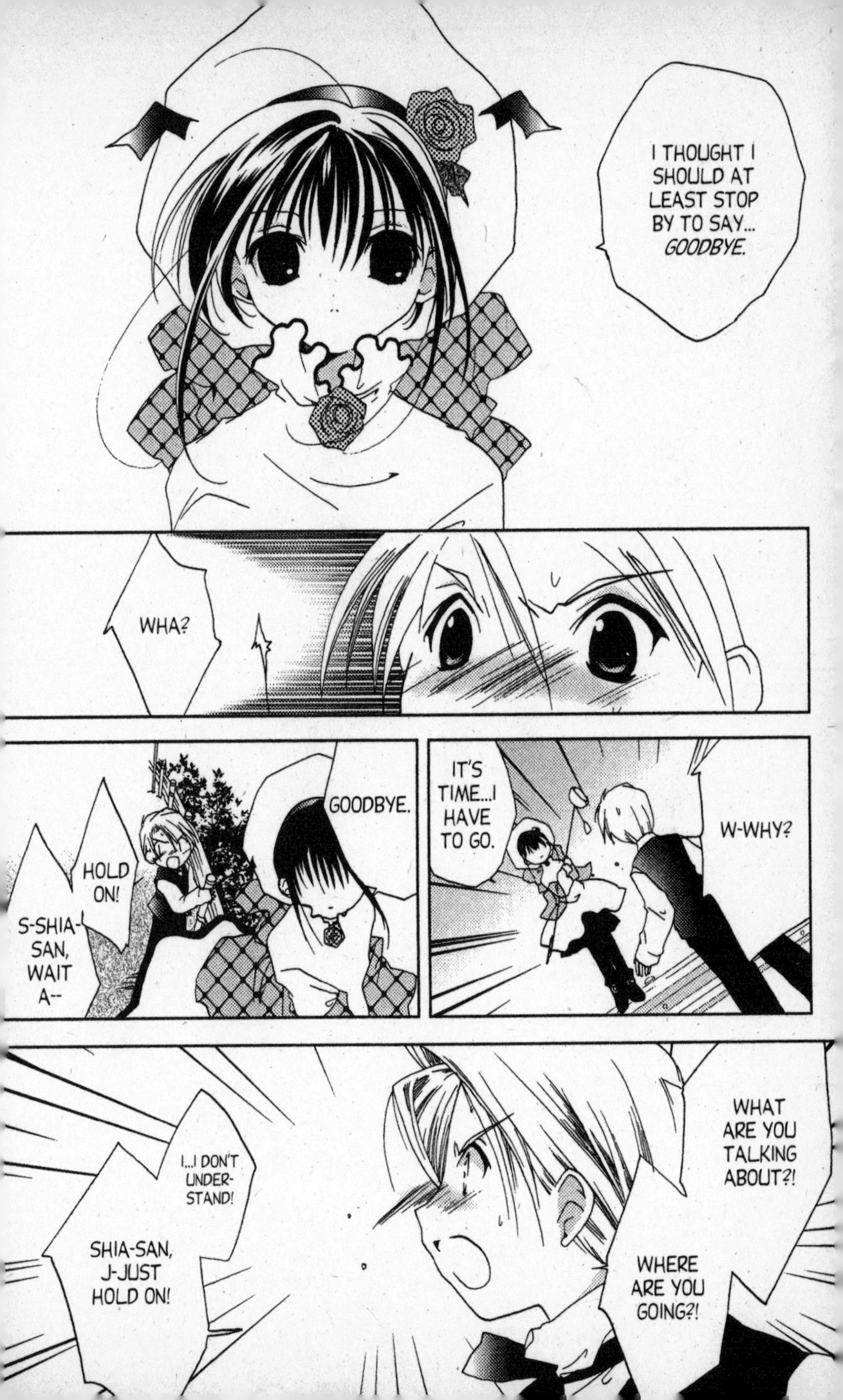
I THOUGHT I SHOULD AT LEAST STOP BY TO SAY... *GOODBYE.*
WHA?
W-WHY?
IT'S TIME...I HAVE TO GO.
GOODBYE.
HOLD ON!
S-SHIA-SAN, WAIT A--
WHAT ARE YOU TALKING ABOUT?!
WHERE ARE YOU GOING?!
I...I DON'T UNDER-STAND!
SHIA-SAN, J-JUST HOLD ON!

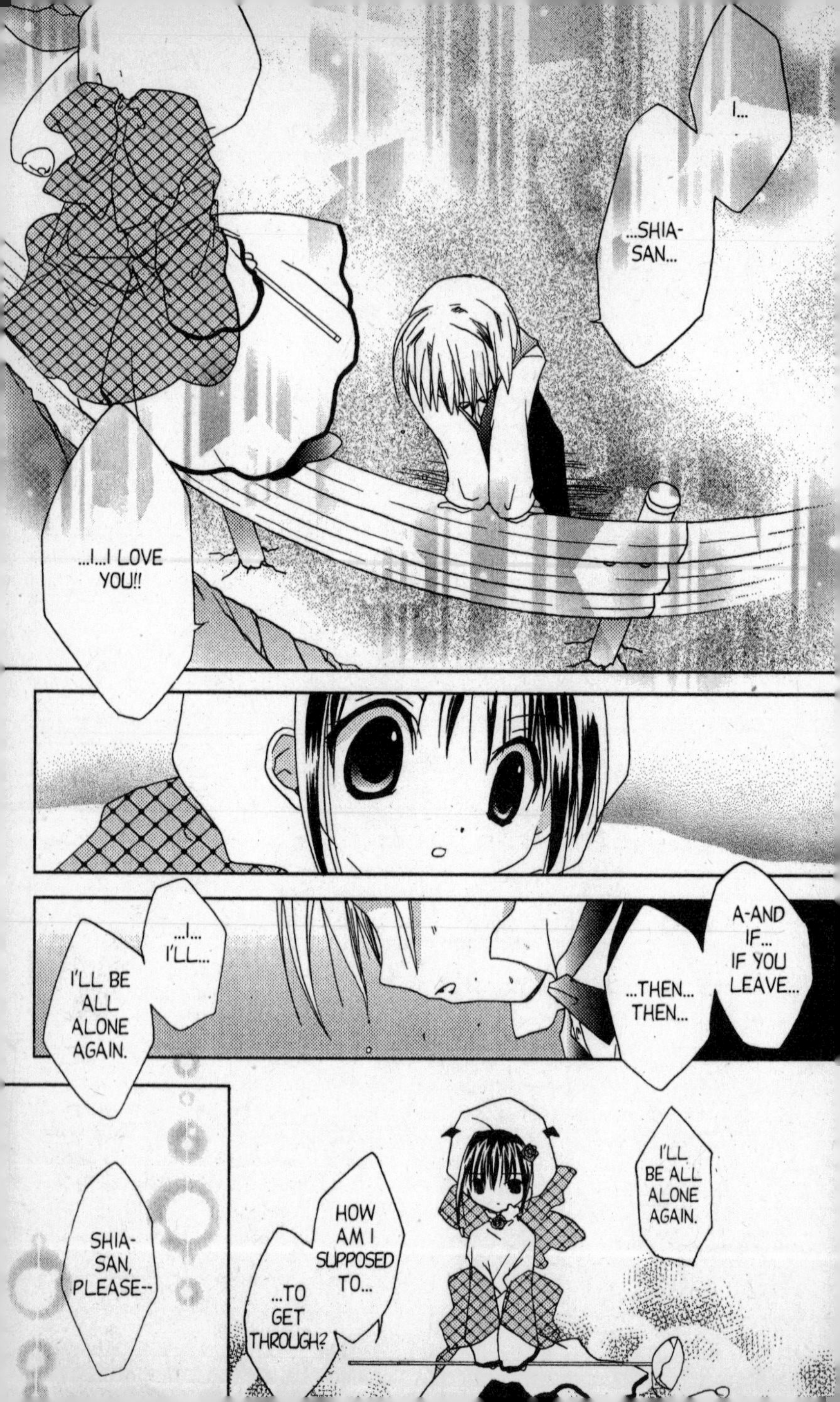

I...
...SHIA-SAN...
...I...I LOVE YOU!!
A-AND IF... IF YOU LEAVE...
...THEN... THEN...
...I... I'LL...
I'LL BE ALL ALONE AGAIN.
I'LL BE ALL ALONE AGAIN.
HOW AM I SUPPOSED TO...
...TO GET THROUGH?
SHIA-SAN, PLEASE--

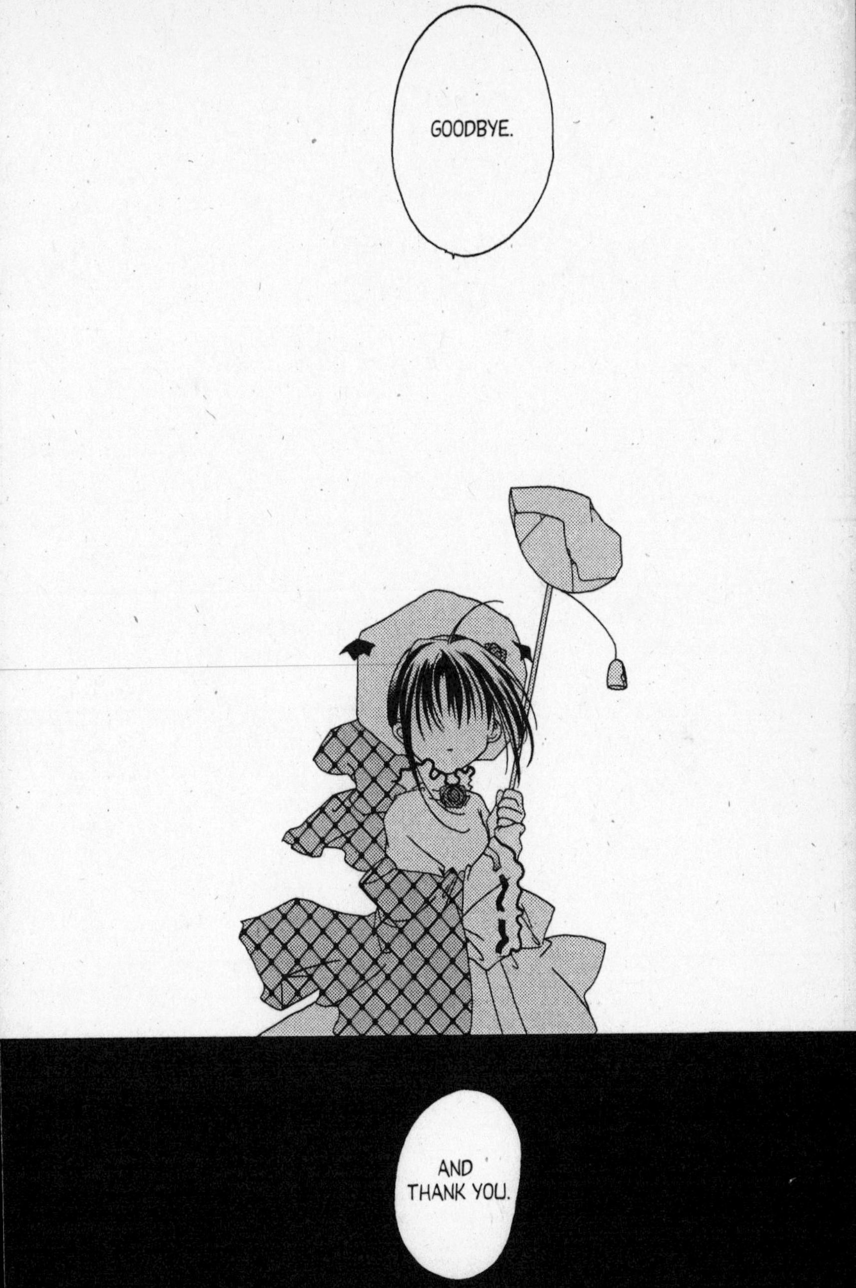
GOODBYE.
AND THANK YOU.

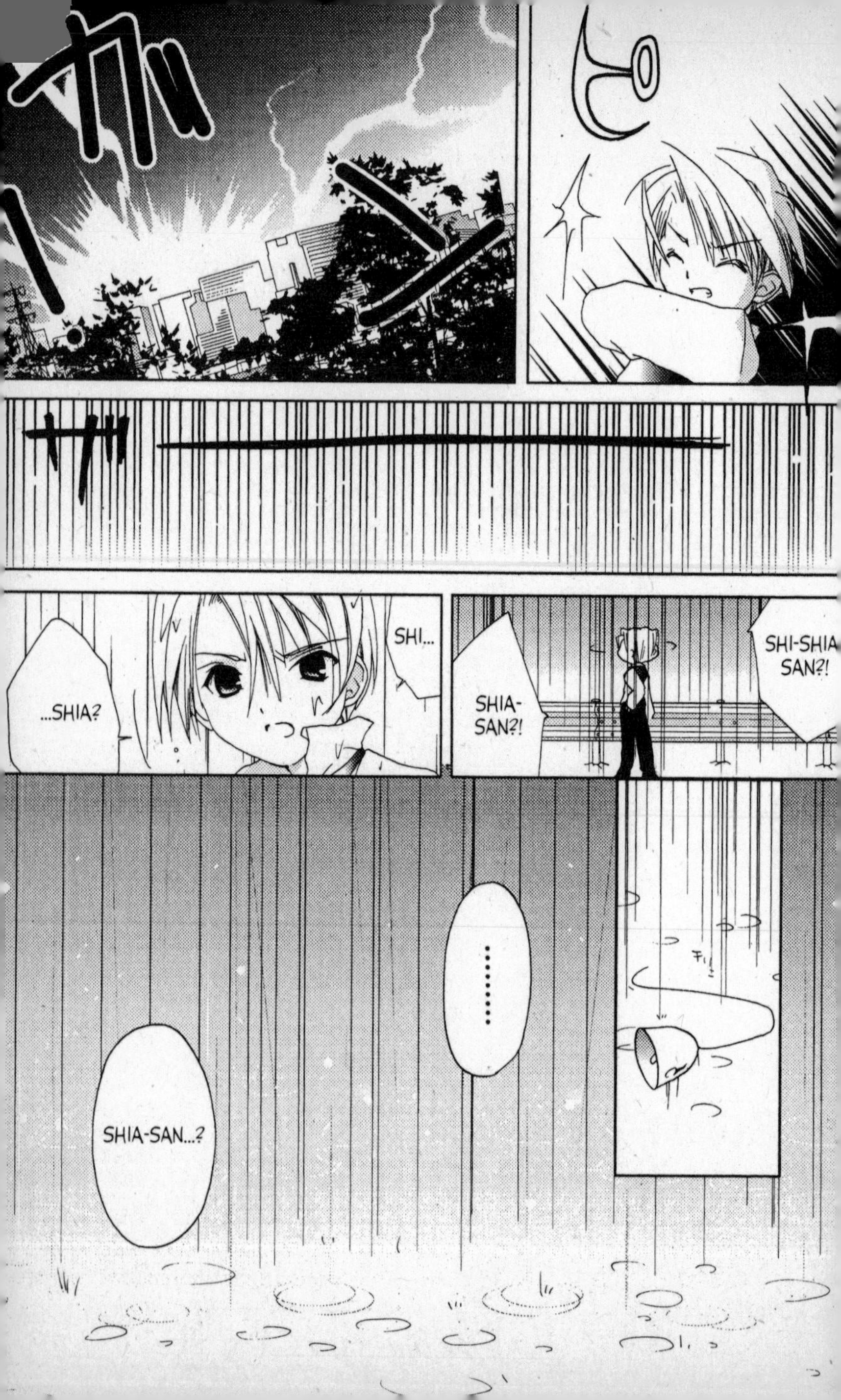
SHI-SHIA SAN?!
SHIA-SAN?!
SHI...
...SHIA?
....
SHIA-SAN...?

Lesson 29

How to Find One's Way Back

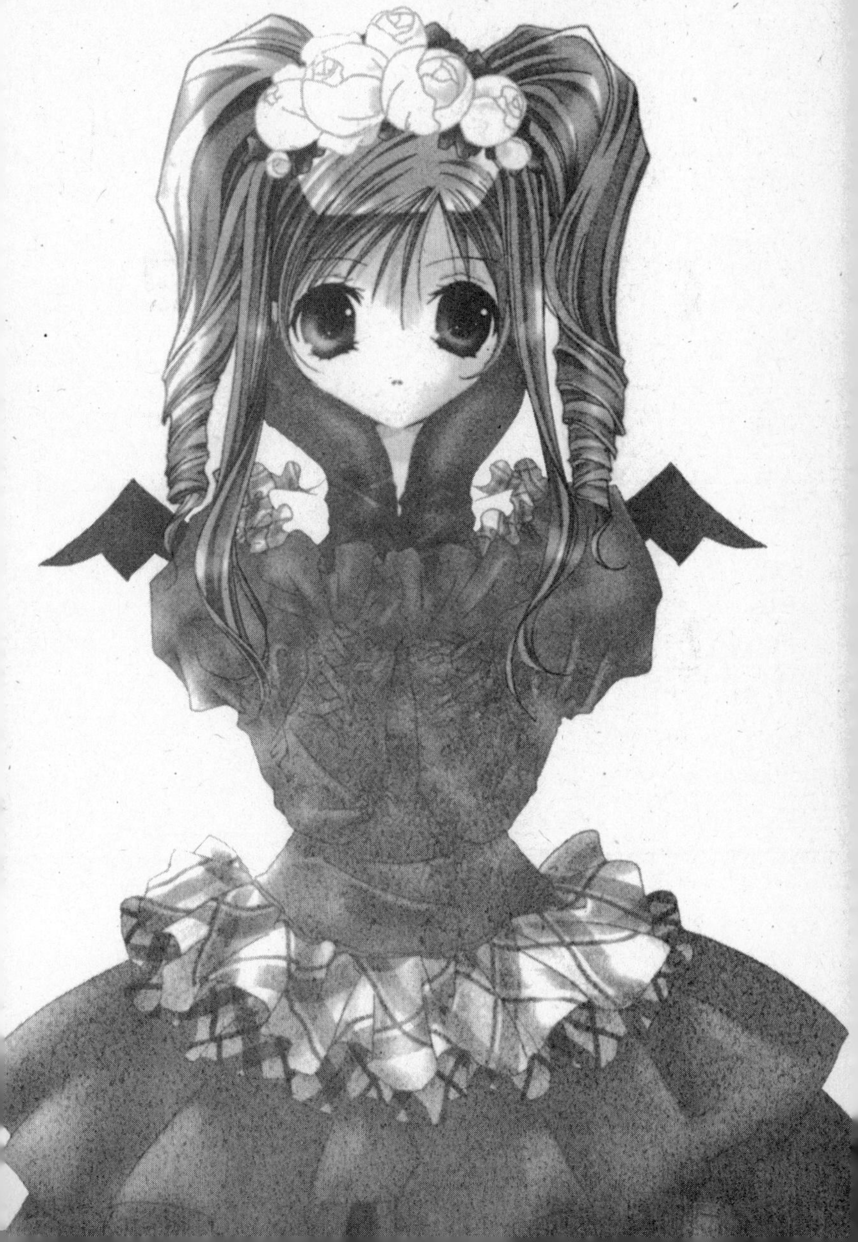

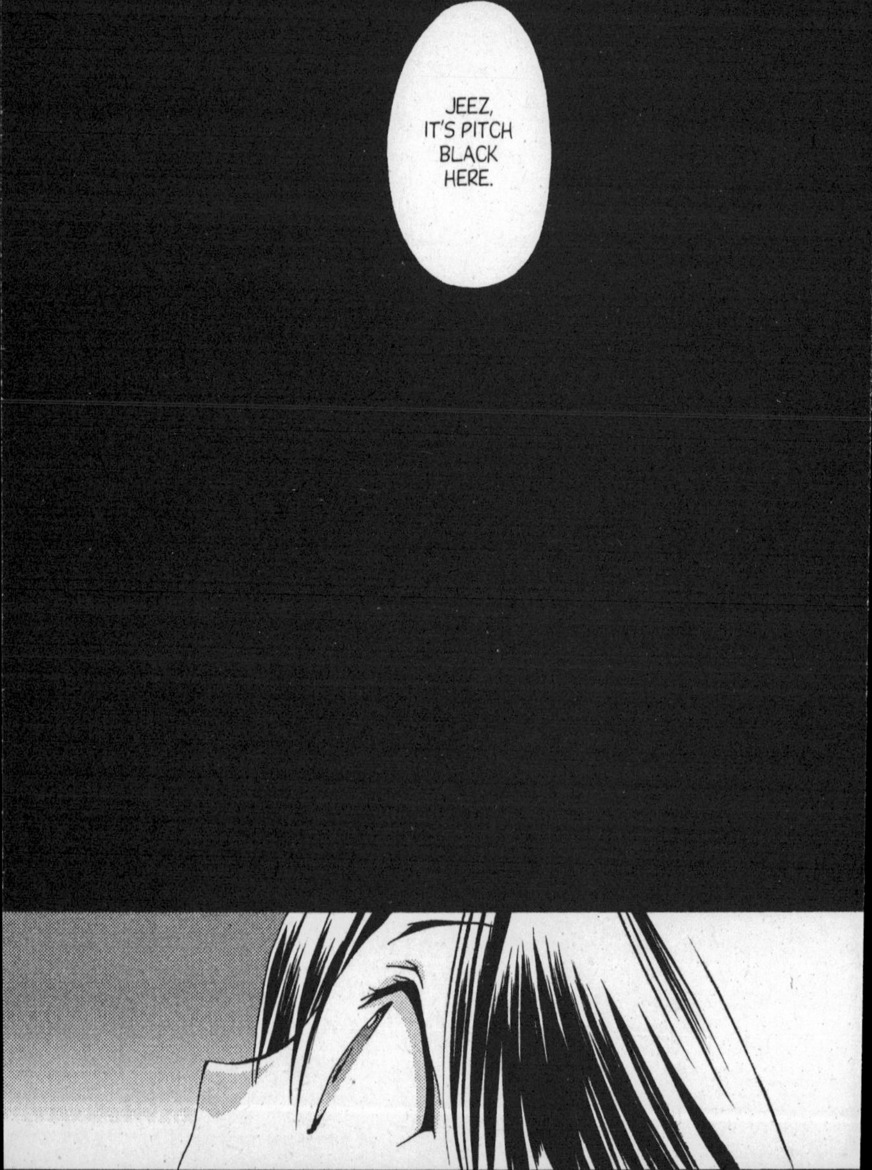
JEEZ, IT'S PITCH BLACK HERE.

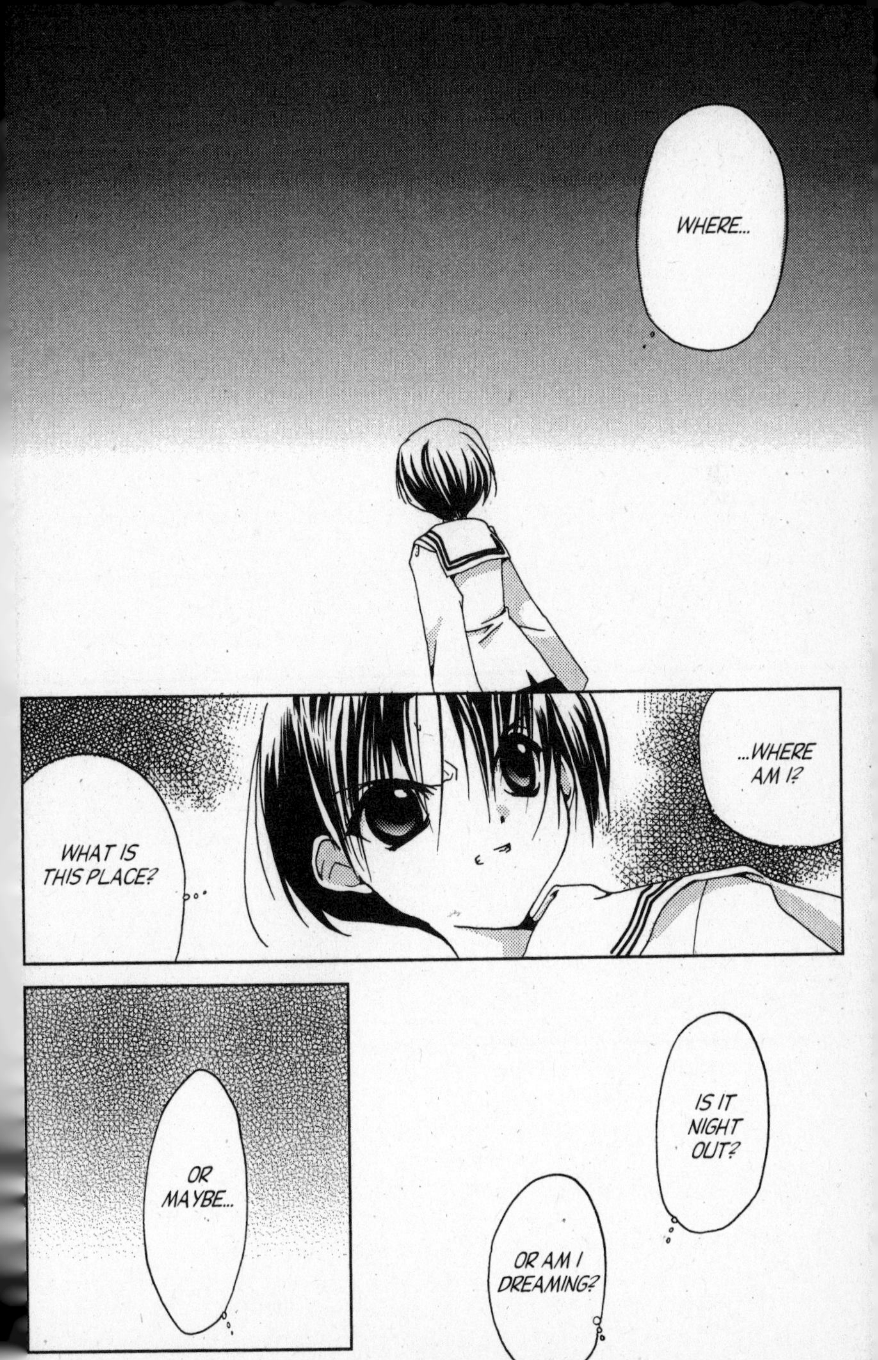
WHERE...
...WHERE AM I?
WHAT IS THIS PLACE?
IS IT NIGHT OUT?
OR AM I DREAMING?
OR MAYBE...

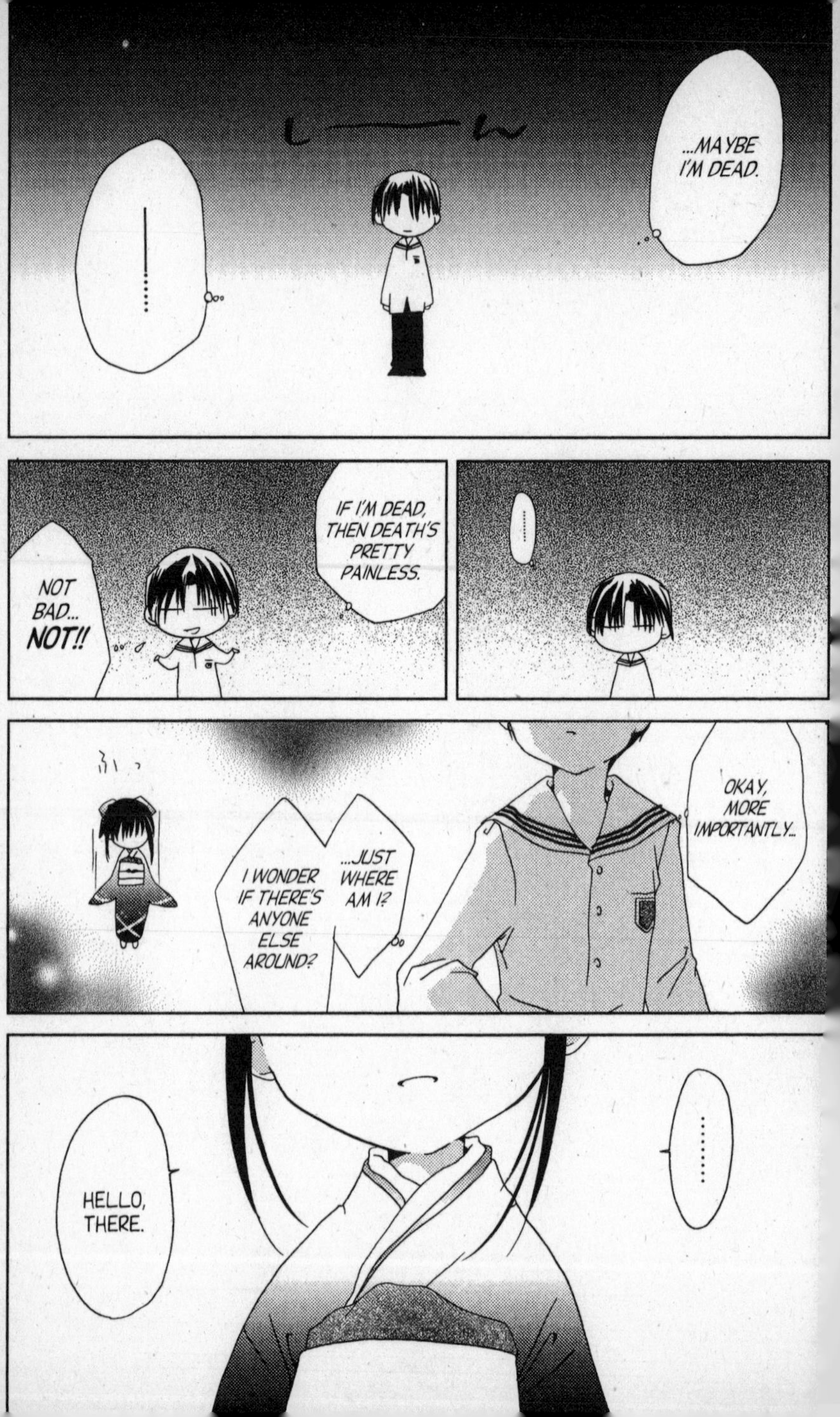
...MAYBE I'M DEAD.
しーーん
......
......
IF I'M DEAD, THEN DEATH'S PRETTY PAINLESS.
NOT BAD... **NOT!!**
OKAY, MORE IMPORTANTLY...
...JUST WHERE AM I?
I WONDER IF THERE'S ANYONE ELSE AROUND?
ふっ
......
HELLO, THERE.

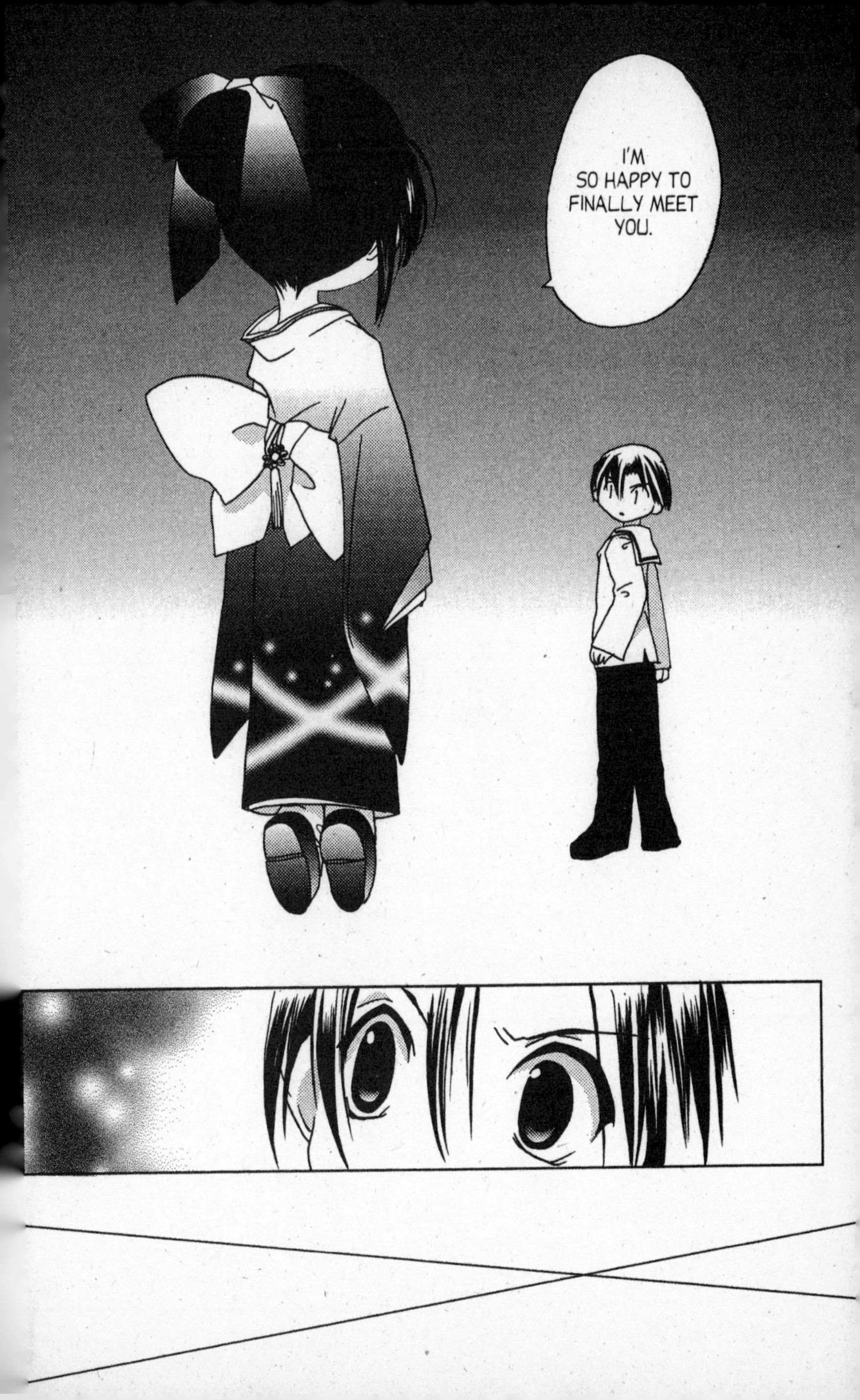
I'M SO HAPPY TO FINALLY MEET YOU.

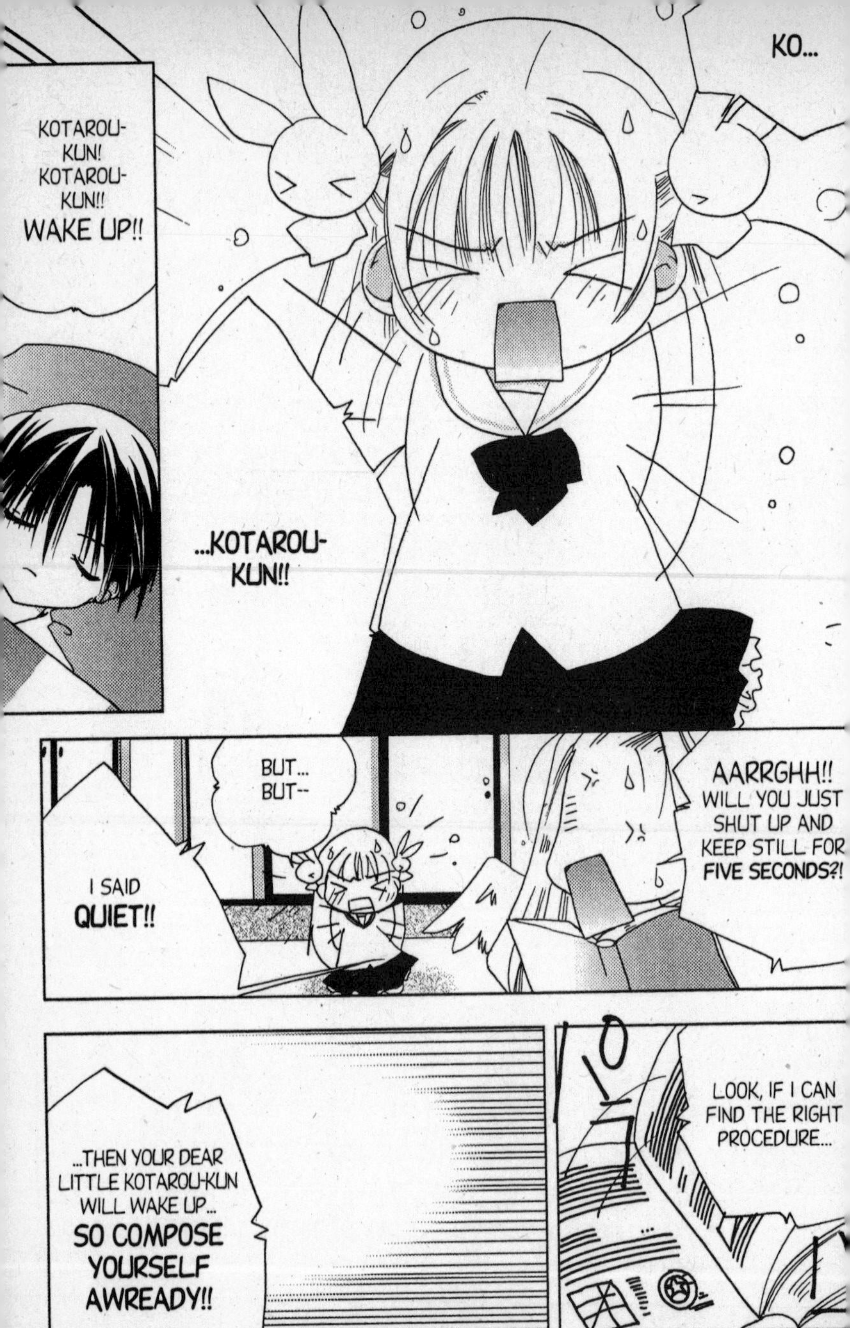
KO...
...KOTAROU-KUN!!
KOTAROU-KUN! KOTAROU-KUN!! WAKE UP!!
AARRGHH!! WILL YOU JUST SHUT UP AND KEEP STILL FOR FIVE SECONDS?!
BUT... BUT--
I SAID QUIET!!
LOOK, IF I CAN FIND THE RIGHT PROCEDURE...
...THEN YOUR DEAR LITTLE KOTAROU-KUN WILL WAKE UP... SO COMPOSE YOURSELF AWREADY!!

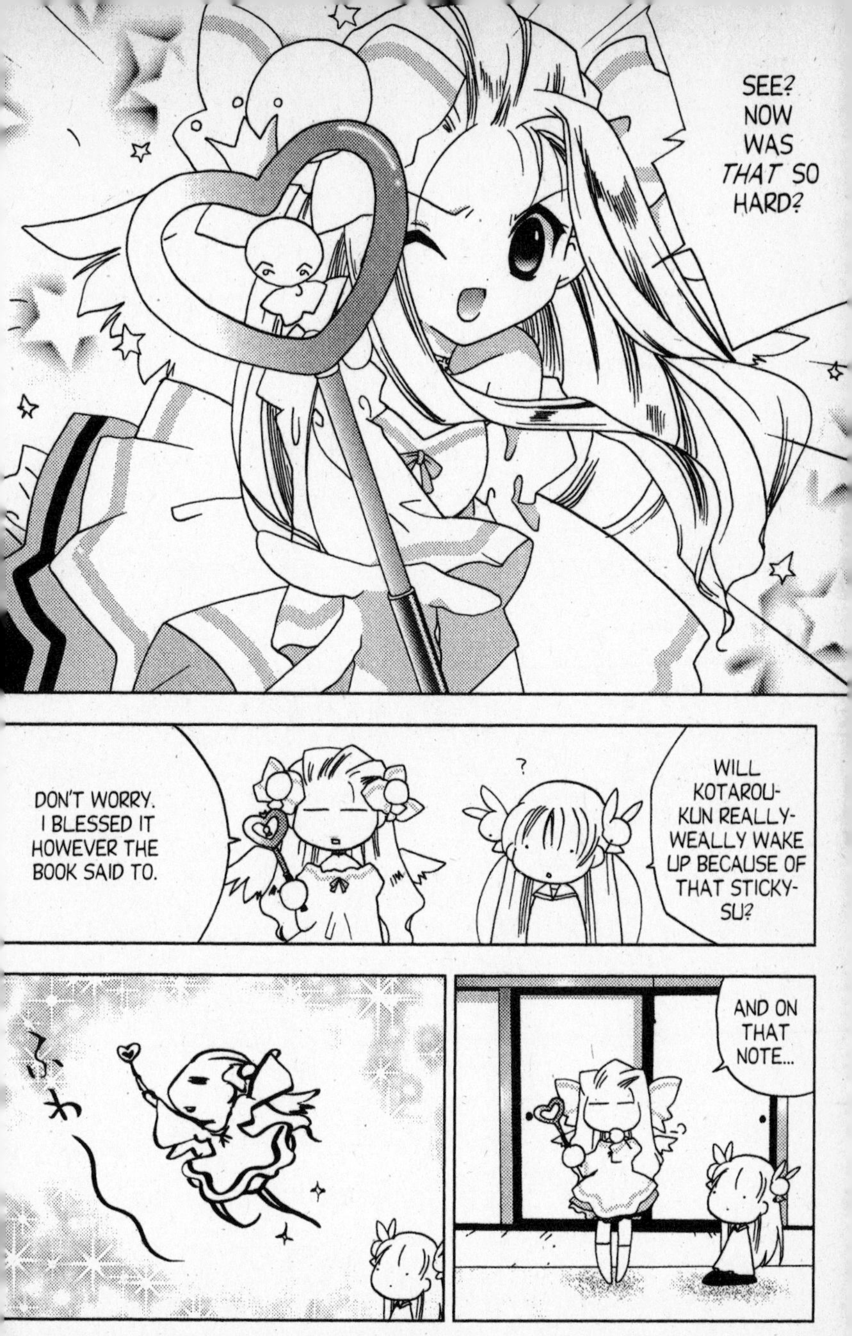
SEE? NOW WAS *THAT* SO HARD?
WILL KOTAROU-KUN REALLY-WEALLY WAKE UP BECAUSE OF THAT STICKY-SU?
DON'T WORRY. I BLESSED IT HOWEVER THE BOOK SAID TO.
AND ON THAT NOTE...
ふわ

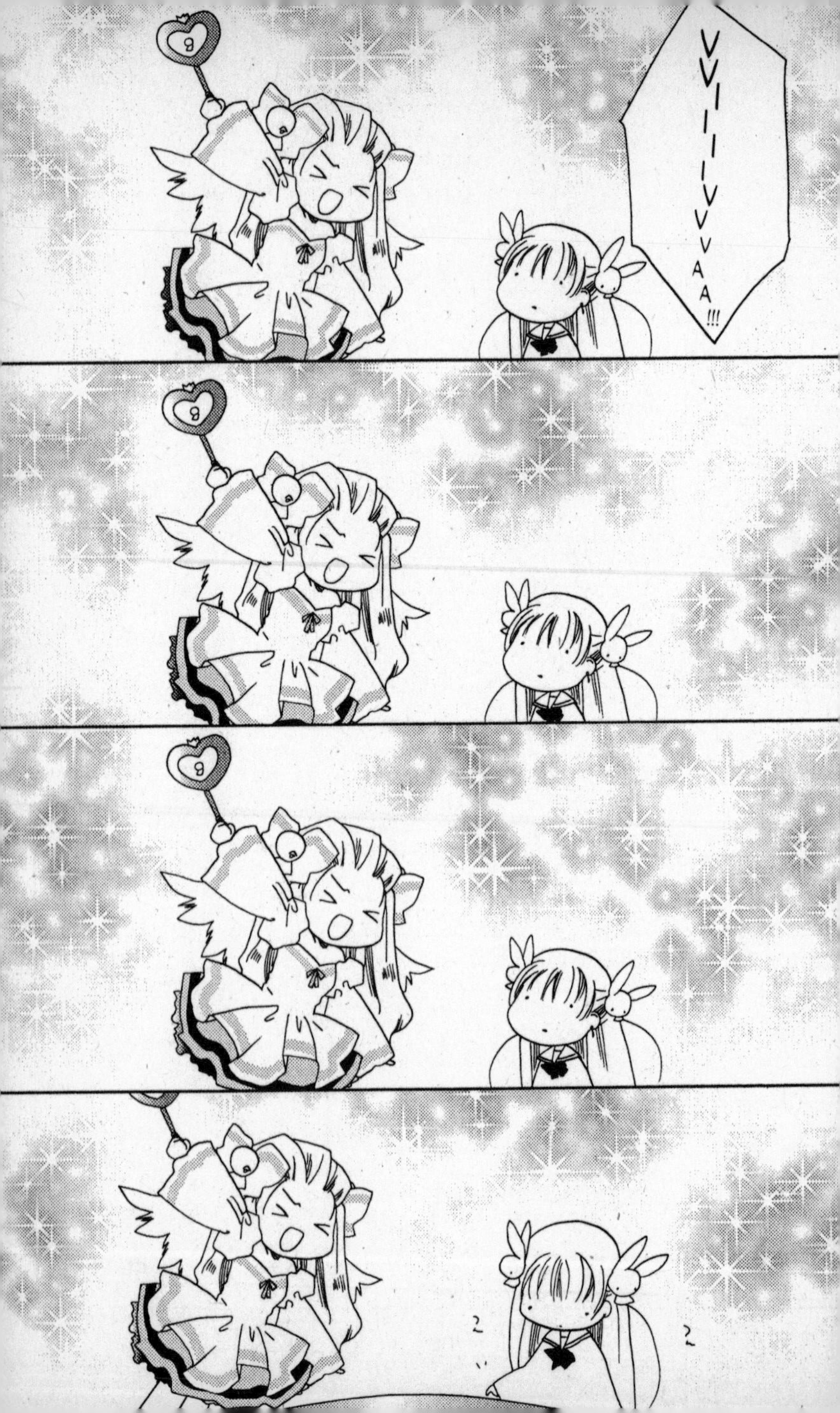
VVIIIIVVVAA!!!

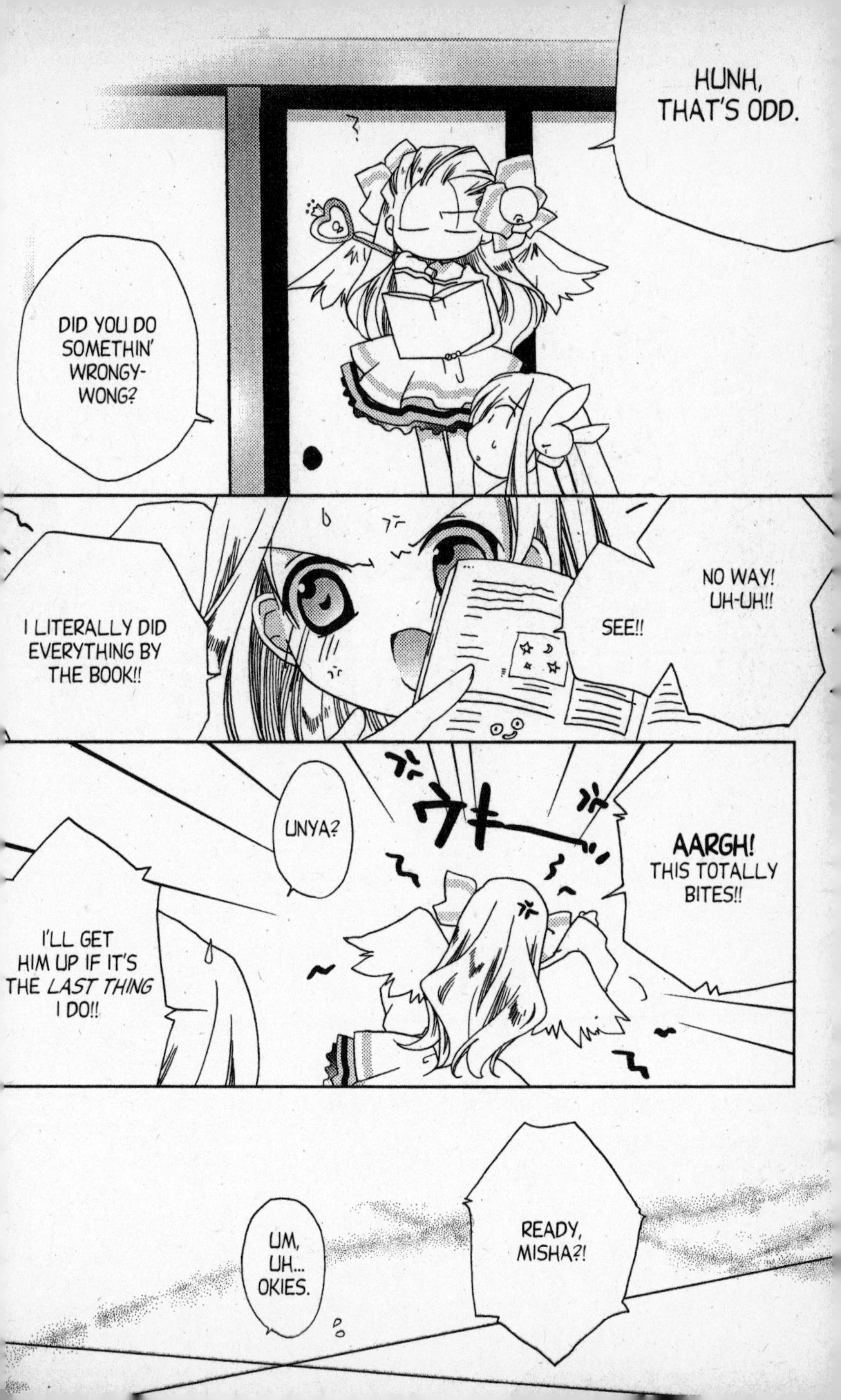
HUNH, THAT'S ODD.
DID YOU DO SOMETHIN' WRONGY-WONG?
NO WAY! UH-UH!!
SEE!!
I LITERALLY DID EVERYTHING BY THE BOOK!!
AARGH! THIS TOTALLY BITES!!
ウキー
UNYA?
I'LL GET HIM UP IF IT'S THE *LAST THING* I DO!!
READY, MISHA?!
UM, UH... OKIES.

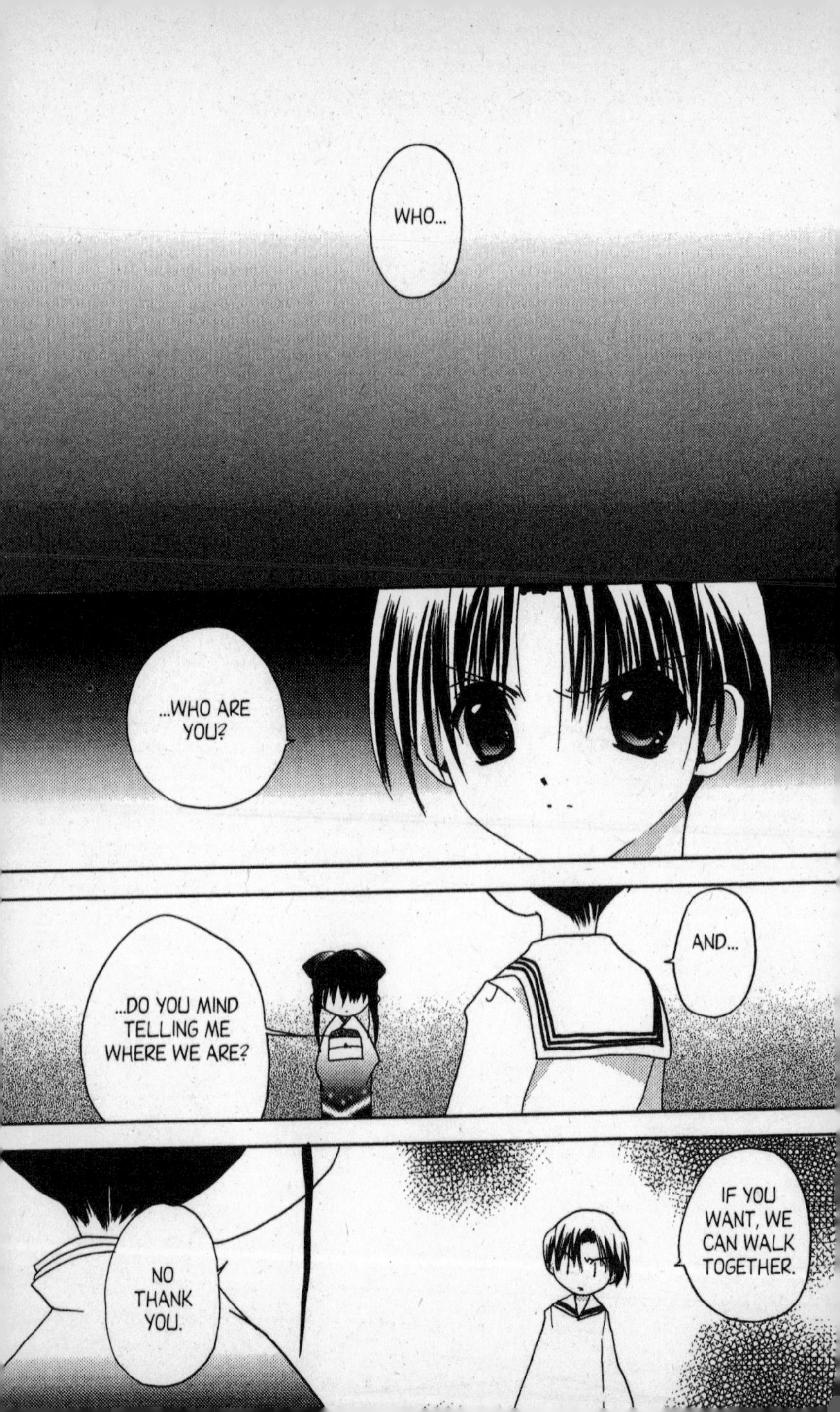
WHO...
...WHO ARE YOU?
AND...
...DO YOU MIND TELLING ME WHERE WE ARE?
IF YOU WANT, WE CAN WALK TOGETHER.
NO THANK YOU.

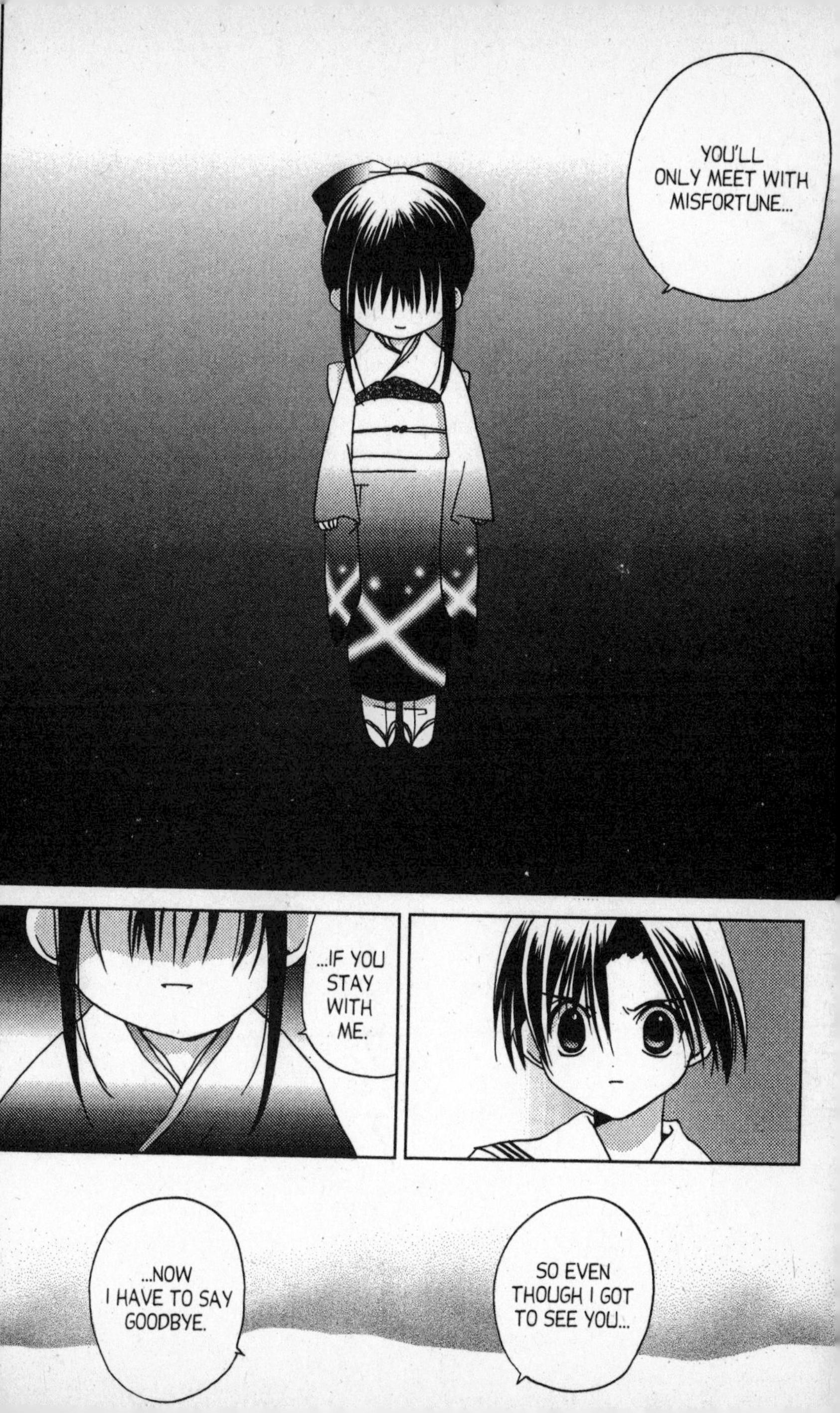
YOU'LL ONLY MEET WITH MISFORTUNE...
...IF YOU STAY WITH ME.
SO EVEN THOUGH I GOT TO SEE YOU...
...NOW I HAVE TO SAY GOODBYE.

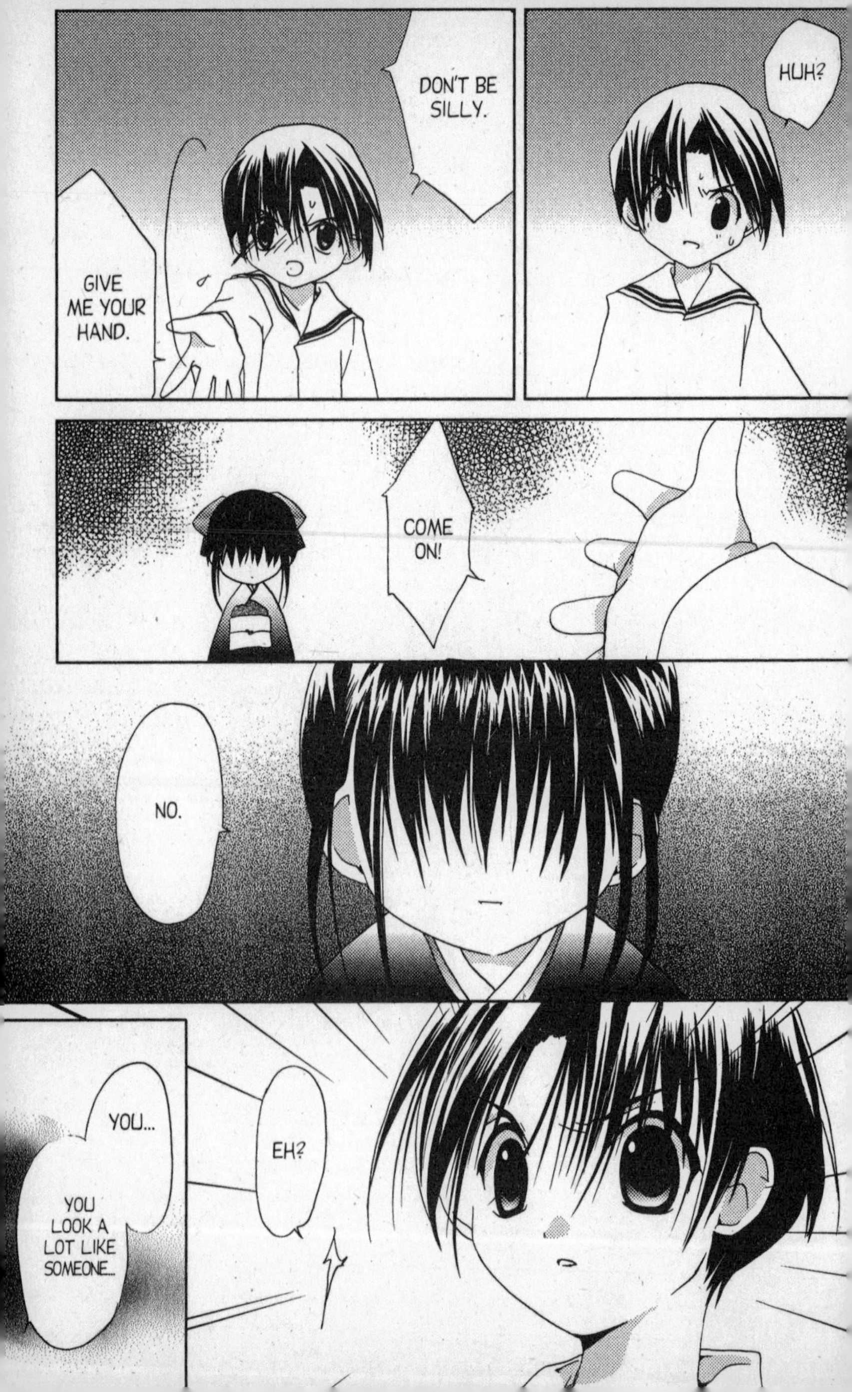
HUH?
DON'T BE SILLY.
GIVE ME YOUR HAND.
COME ON!
NO.
EH?
YOU...
YOU LOOK A LOT LIKE SOMEONE...

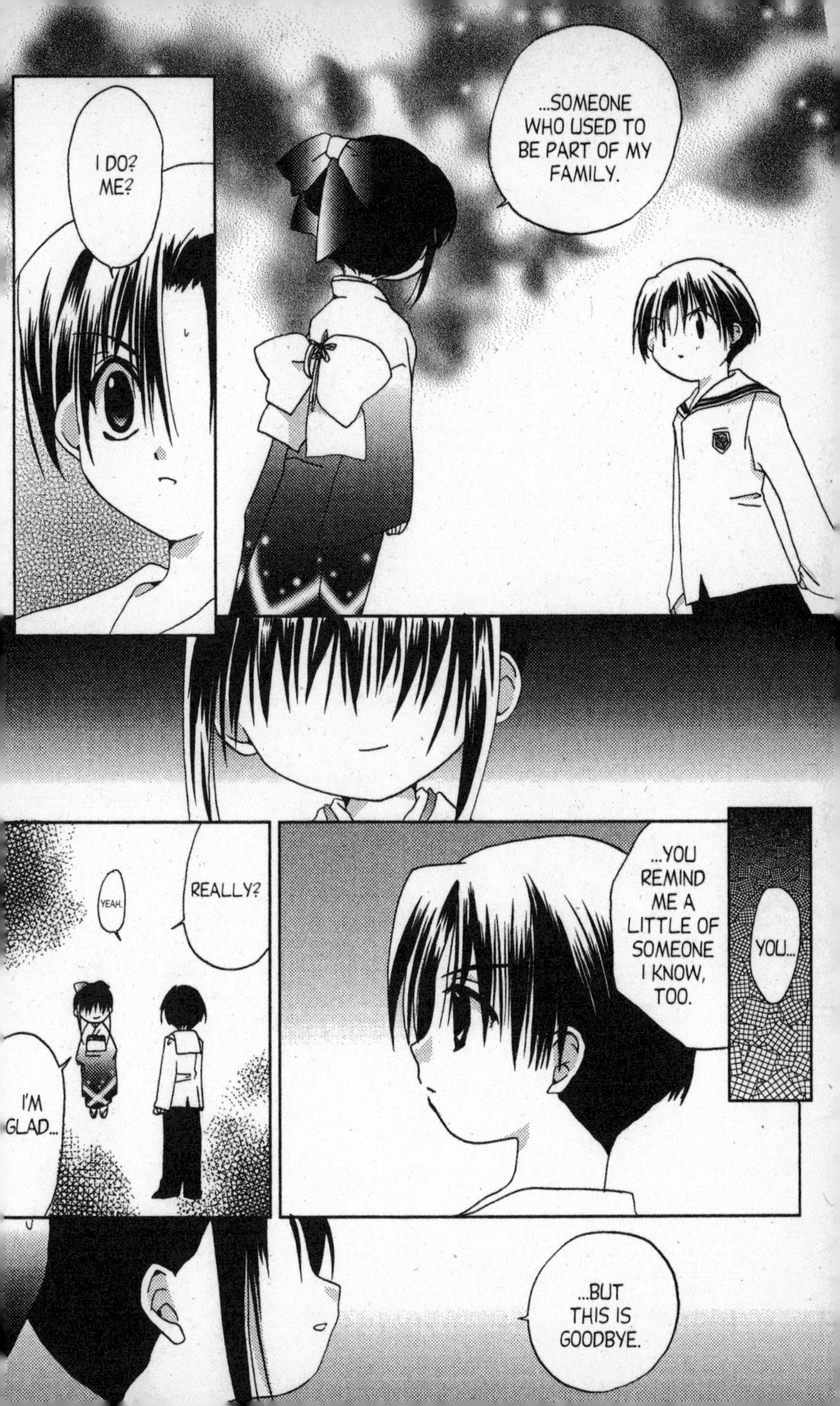
...SOMEONE WHO USED TO BE PART OF MY FAMILY.
I DO? ME?
YOU...
...YOU REMIND ME A LITTLE OF SOMEONE I KNOW, TOO.
REALLY?
YEAH.
I'M GLAD...
...BUT THIS IS GOODBYE.

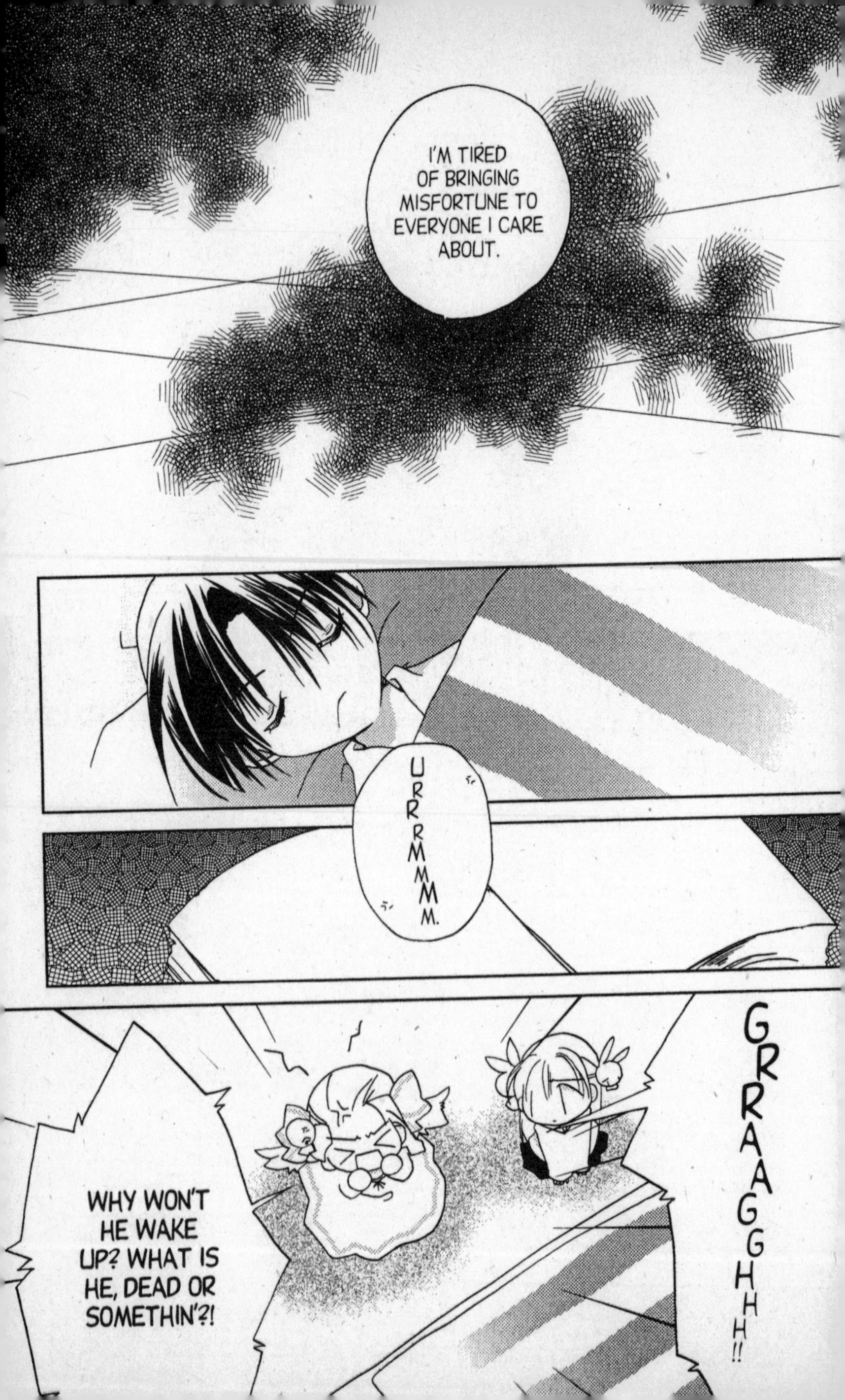
I'M TIRED OF BRINGING MISFORTUNE TO EVERYONE I CARE ABOUT.
URRRMMMM.
GRRAAGGHHH!!
WHY WON'T HE WAKE UP? WHAT IS HE, DEAD OR SOMETHIN'?!

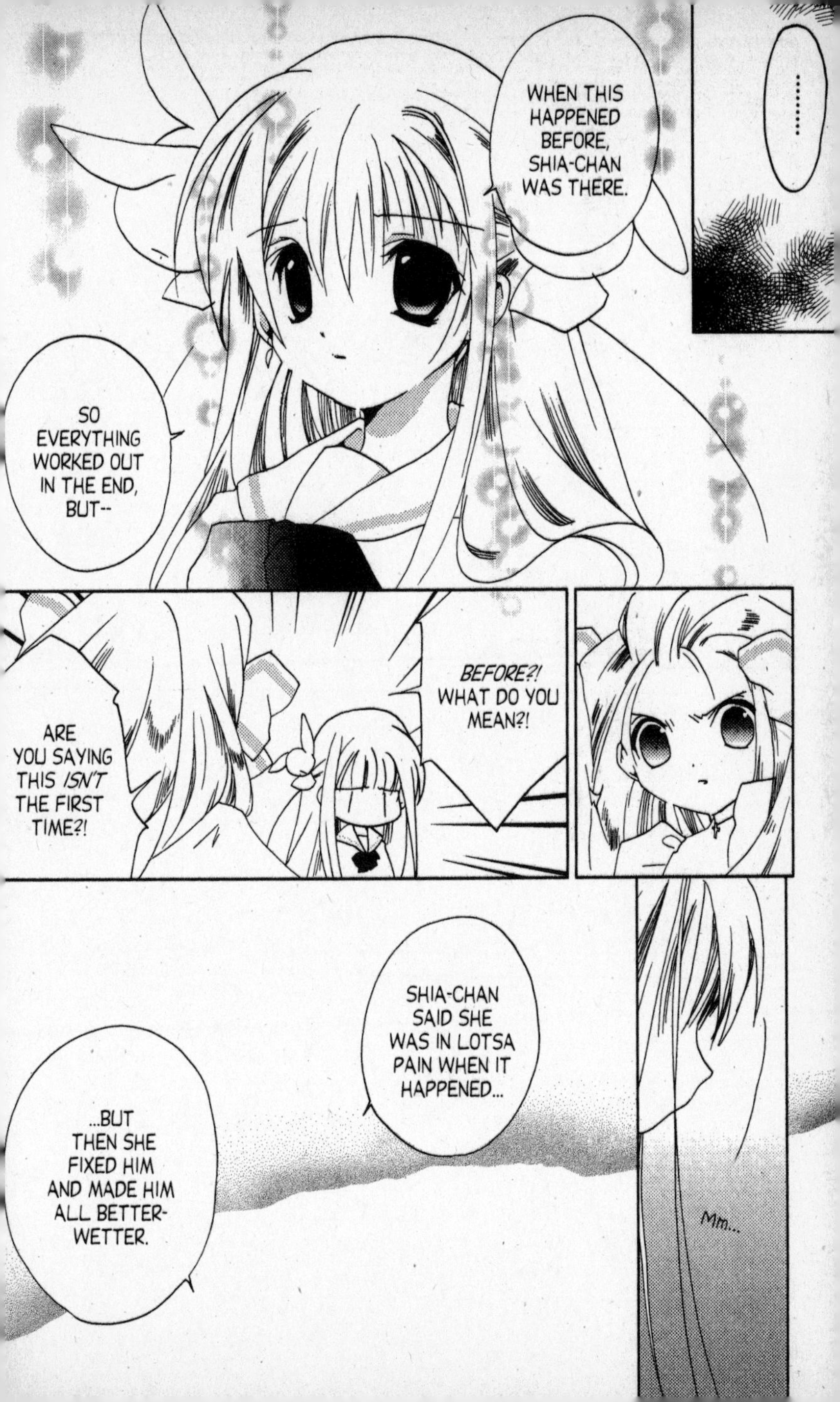
......
WHEN THIS HAPPENED BEFORE, SHIA-CHAN WAS THERE.
SO EVERYTHING WORKED OUT IN THE END, BUT--
BEFORE?! WHAT DO YOU MEAN?!
ARE YOU SAYING THIS *ISN'T* THE FIRST TIME?!
Mm...
SHIA-CHAN SAID SHE WAS IN LOTSA PAIN WHEN IT HAPPENED...
...BUT THEN SHE FIXED HIM AND MADE HIM ALL BETTER-WETTER.

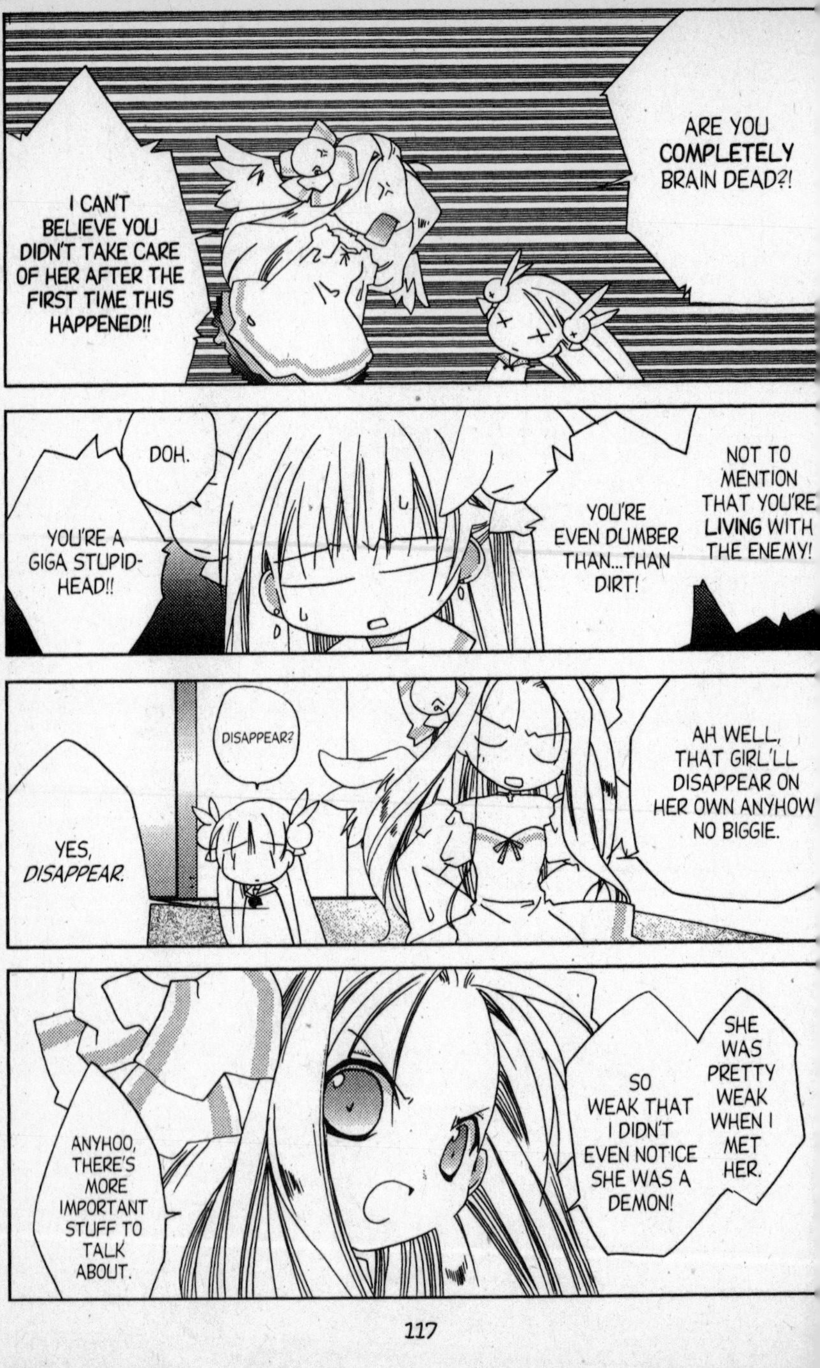
ARE YOU **COMPLETELY** BRAIN DEAD?!
I CAN'T BELIEVE YOU DIDN'T TAKE CARE OF HER AFTER THE FIRST TIME THIS HAPPENED!!
NOT TO MENTION THAT YOU'RE **LIVING** WITH THE ENEMY!
YOU'RE EVEN DUMBER THAN...THAN DIRT!
DOH.
YOU'RE A GIGA STUPID-HEAD!!
AH WELL, THAT GIRL'LL DISAPPEAR ON HER OWN ANYHOW NO BIGGIE.
DISAPPEAR?
YES, *DISAPPEAR*.
SHE WAS PRETTY WEAK WHEN I MET HER.
SO WEAK THAT I DIDN'T EVEN NOTICE SHE WAS A DEMON!
ANYHOO, THERE'S MORE IMPORTANT STUFF TO TALK ABOUT.

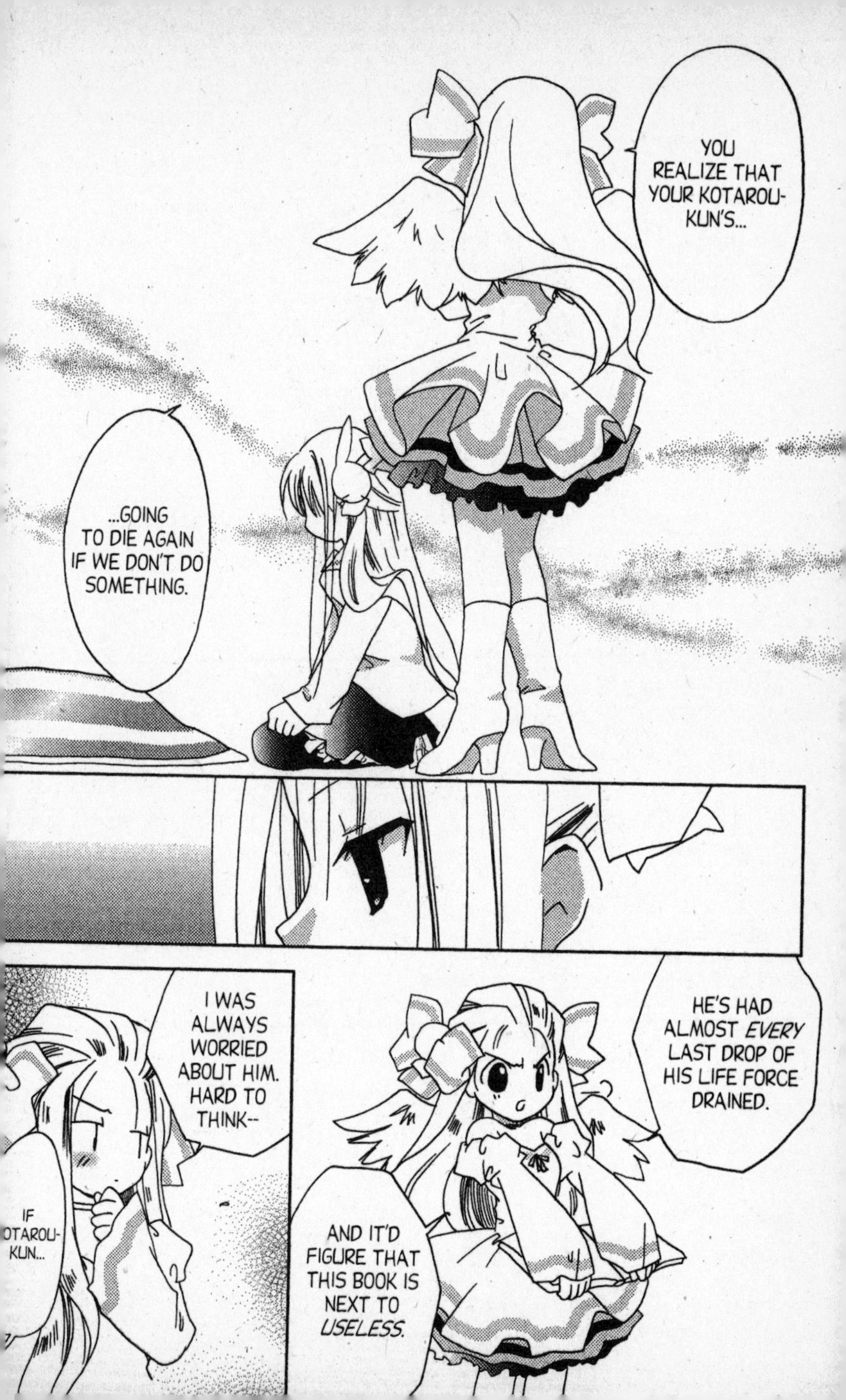
YOU REALIZE THAT YOUR KOTAROU-KUN'S...
...GOING TO DIE AGAIN IF WE DON'T DO SOMETHING.
HE'S HAD ALMOST *EVERY* LAST DROP OF HIS LIFE FORCE DRAINED.
AND IT'D FIGURE THAT THIS BOOK IS NEXT TO *USELESS.*
I WAS ALWAYS WORRIED ABOUT HIM. HARD TO THINK--
IF OTAROU-KUN...

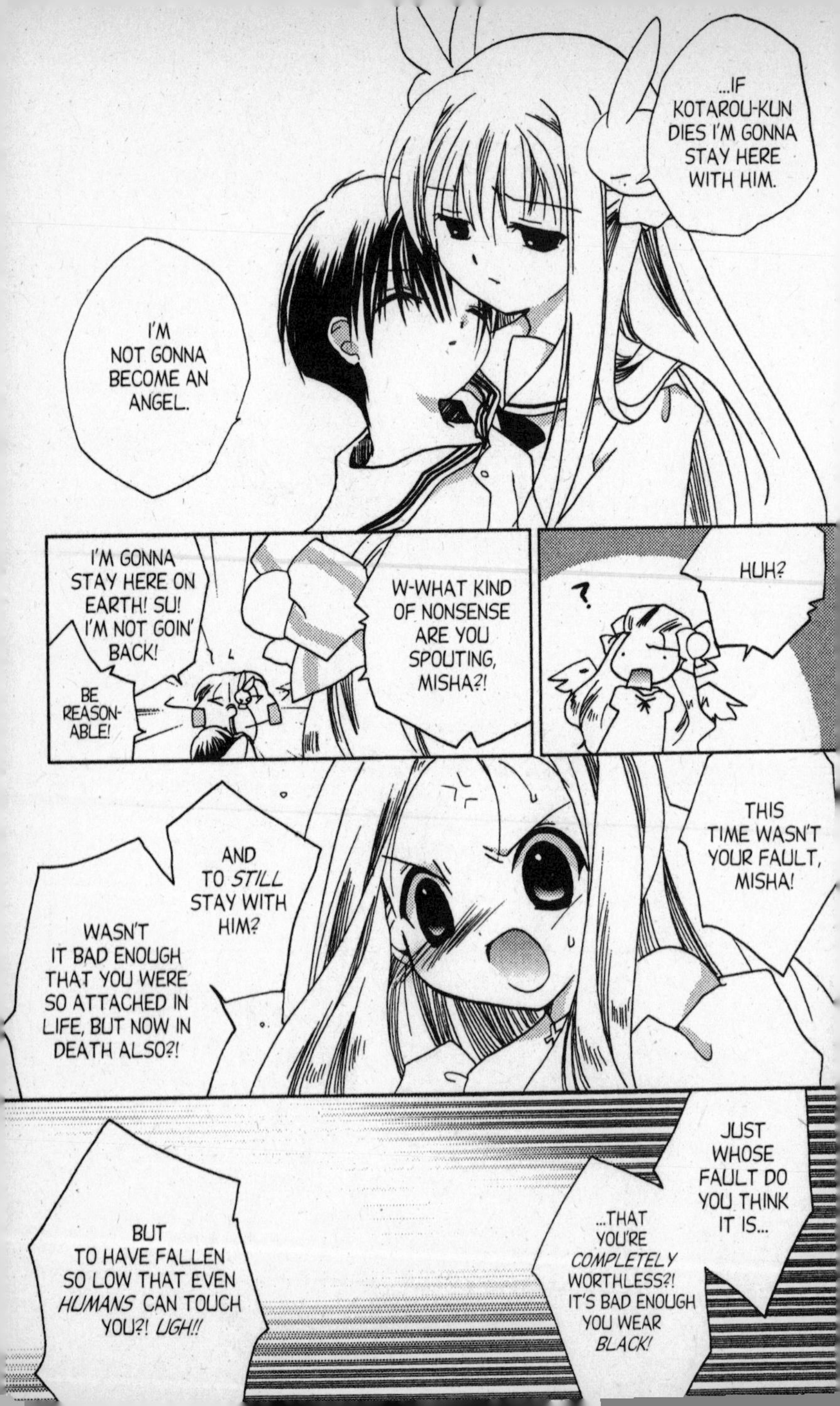
...IF KOTAROU-KUN DIES I'M GONNA STAY HERE WITH HIM.
I'M NOT GONNA BECOME AN ANGEL.
HUH?
W-WHAT KIND OF NONSENSE ARE YOU SPOUTING, MISHA?!
I'M GONNA STAY HERE ON EARTH! SU! I'M NOT GOIN' BACK!
BE REASONABLE!
THIS TIME WASN'T YOUR FAULT, MISHA!
AND TO *STILL* STAY WITH HIM?
WASN'T IT BAD ENOUGH THAT YOU WERE SO ATTACHED IN LIFE, BUT NOW IN DEATH ALSO?!
JUST WHOSE FAULT DO YOU THINK IT IS...
...THAT YOU'RE *COMPLETELY* WORTHLESS?! IT'S BAD ENOUGH YOU WEAR *BLACK!*
BUT TO HAVE FALLEN SO LOW THAT EVEN *HUMANS* CAN TOUCH YOU?! *UGH!!*

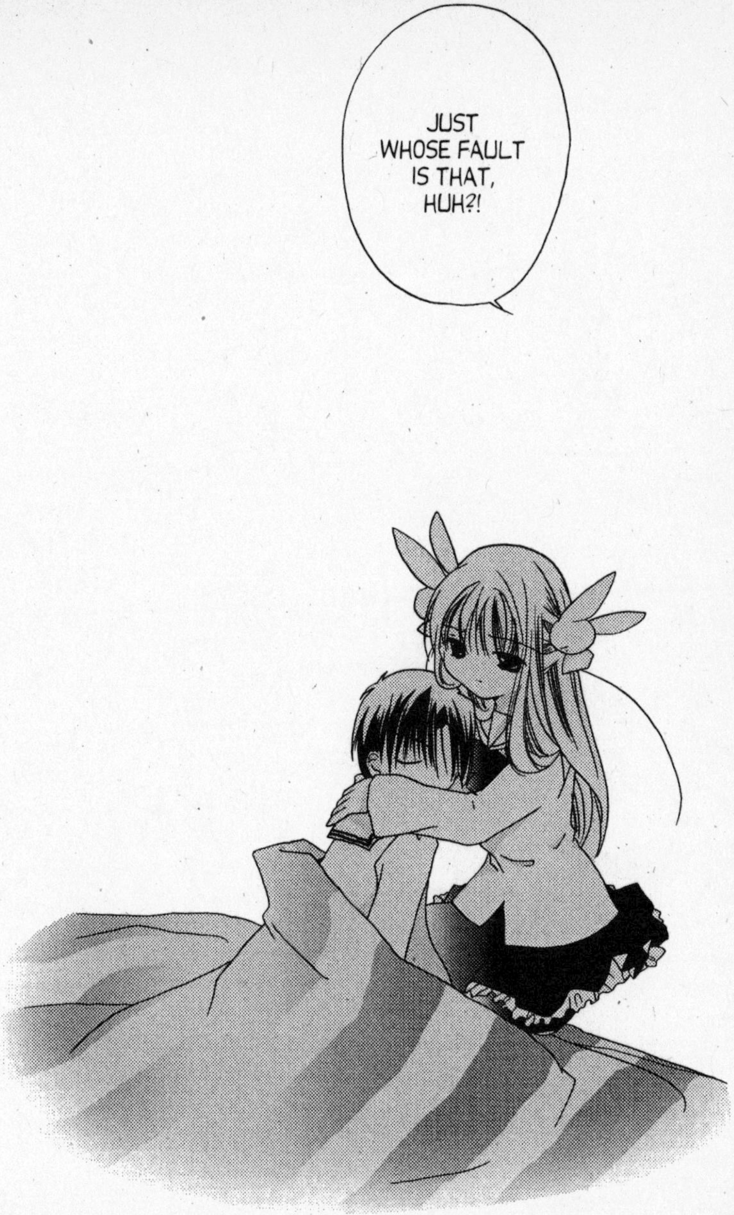
JUST WHOSE FAULT IS THAT, HUH?!

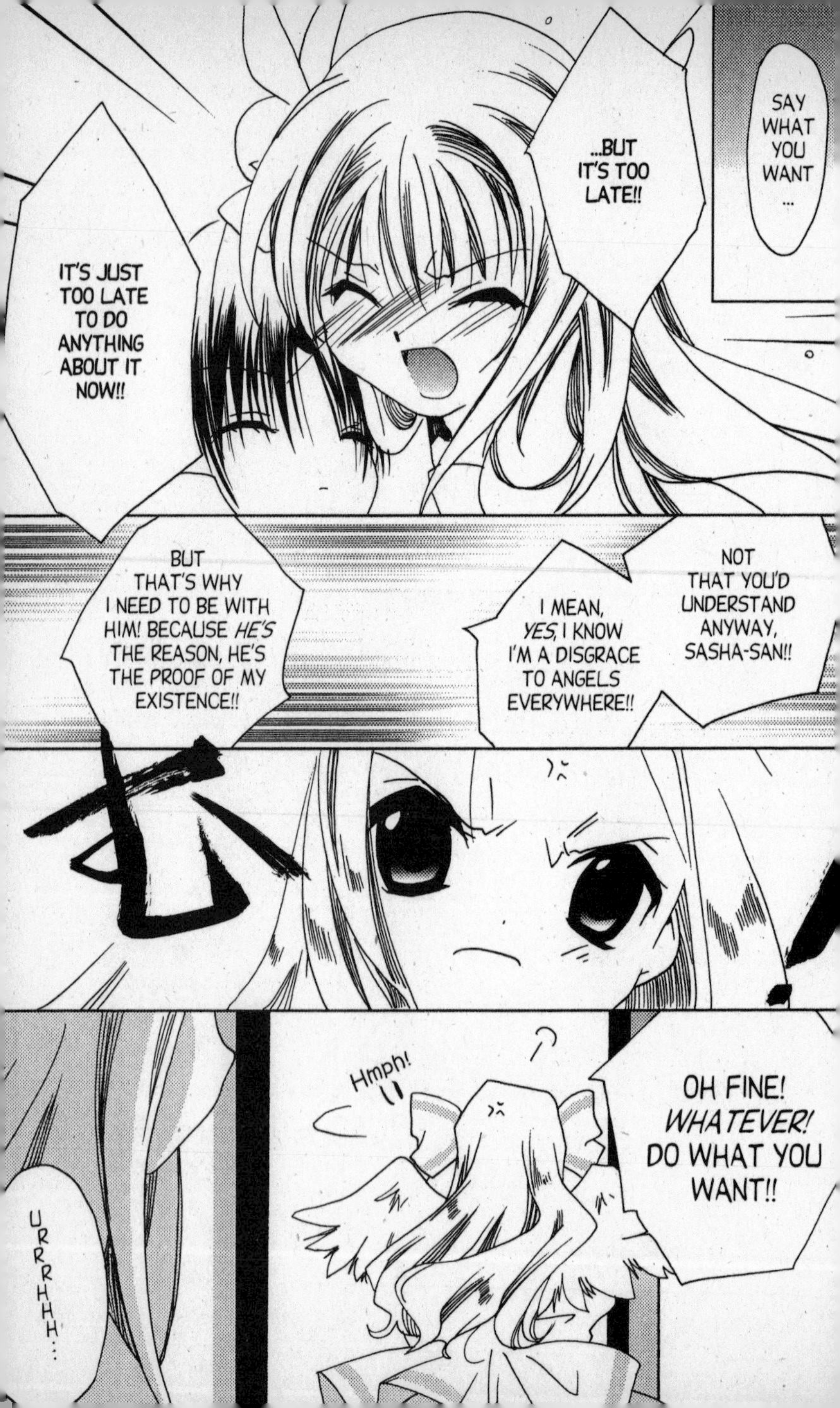
SAY WHAT YOU WANT...
...BUT IT'S TOO LATE!!
IT'S JUST TOO LATE TO DO ANYTHING ABOUT IT NOW!!
NOT THAT YOU'D UNDERSTAND ANYWAY, SASHA-SAN!!
I MEAN, *YES,* I KNOW I'M A DISGRACE TO ANGELS EVERYWHERE!!
BUT THAT'S WHY I NEED TO BE WITH HIM! BECAUSE *HE'S* THE REASON, HE'S THE *PROOF* OF MY EXISTENCE!!
む
OH FINE! *WHATEVER!* DO WHAT YOU WANT!!
Hmph!
URRRHHH...

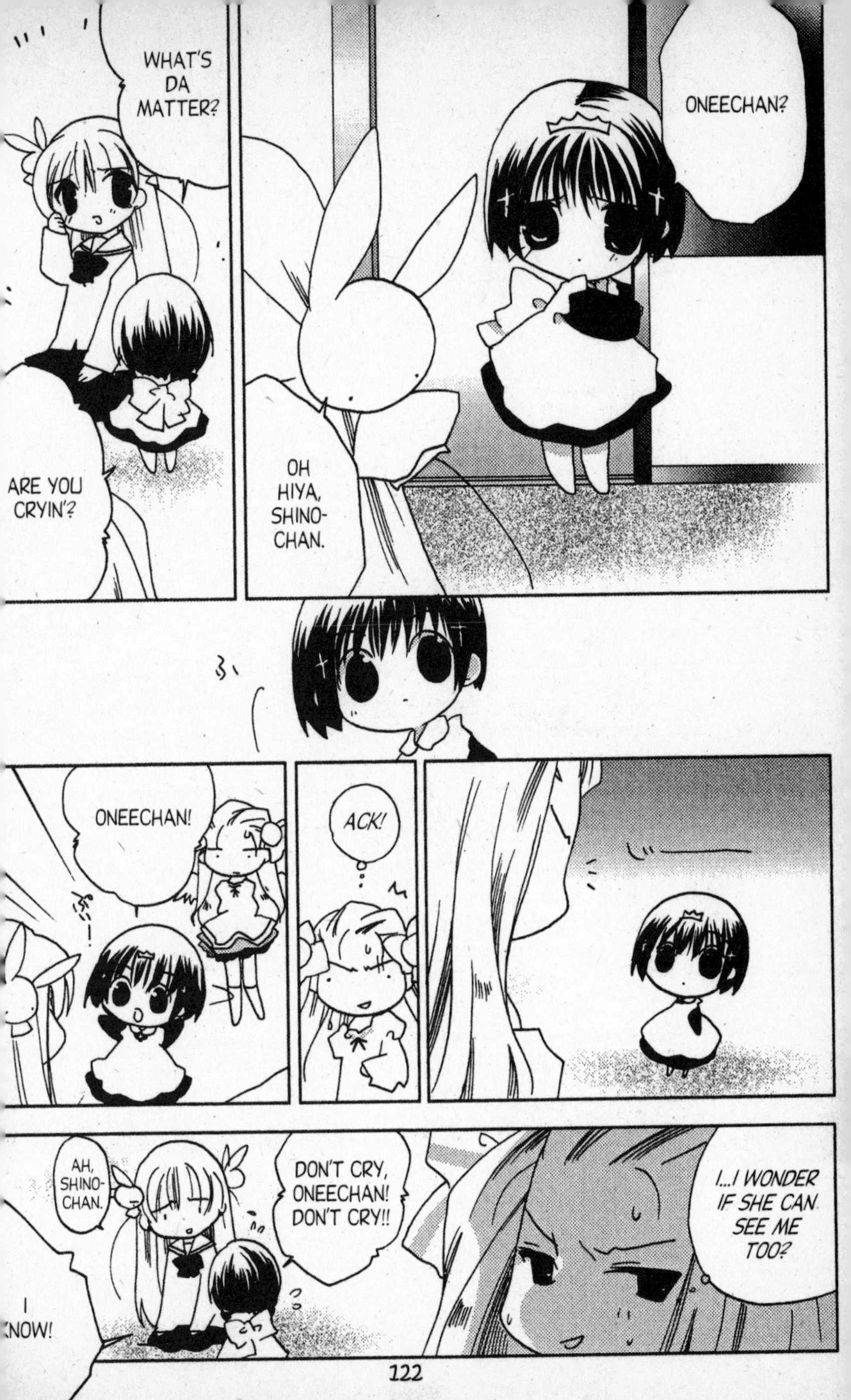
ONEECHAN?
OH HIYA, SHINO-CHAN.
WHAT'S DA MATTER?
ARE YOU CRYIN'?
ACK!
ONEECHAN!
I...I WONDER IF SHE CAN SEE ME TOO?
DON'T CRY, ONEECHAN! DON'T CRY!!
AH, SHINO-CHAN.
I KNOW!

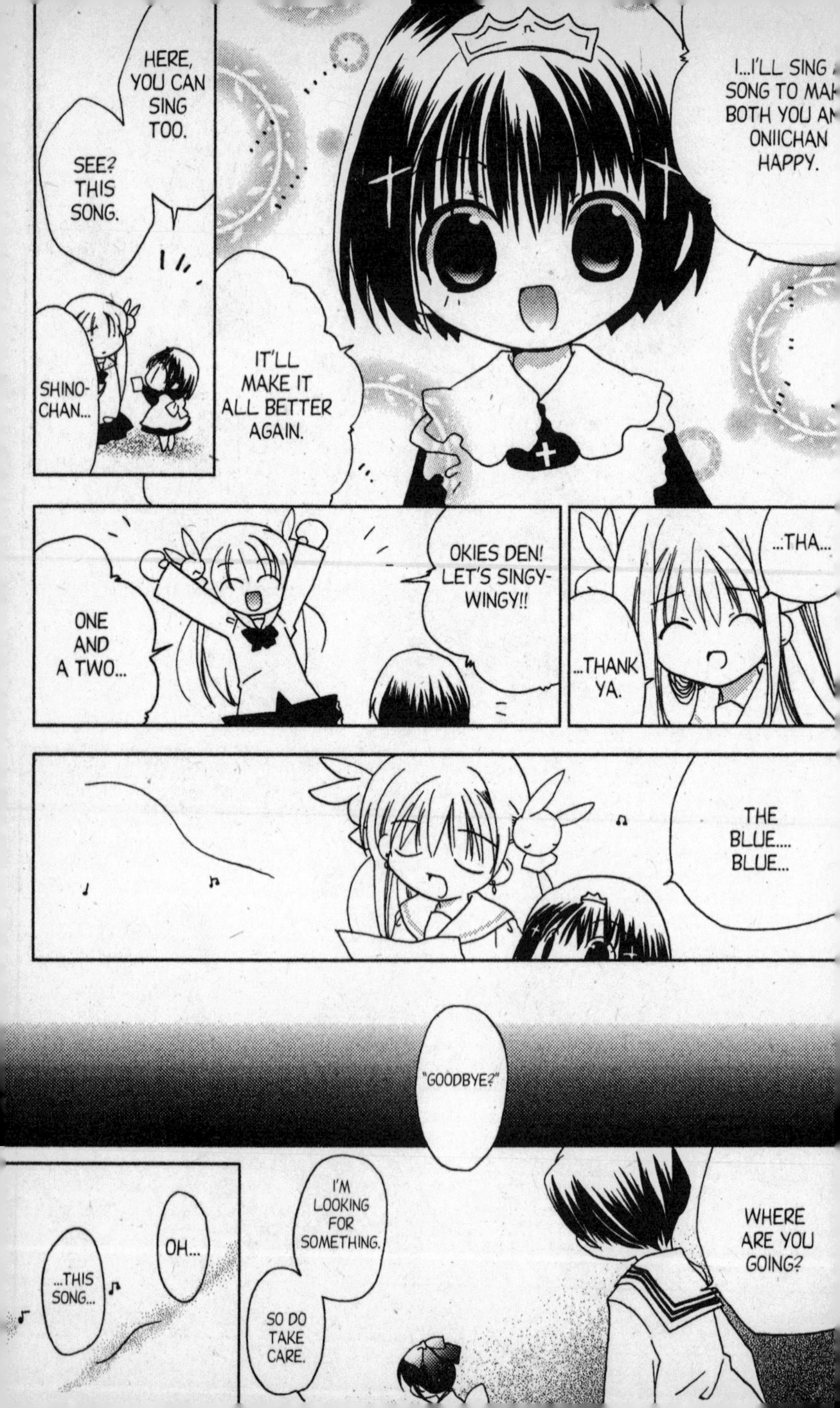
I...I'LL SING A SONG TO MAK BOTH YOU AN ONIICHAN HAPPY.
IT'LL MAKE IT ALL BETTER AGAIN.
HERE, YOU CAN SING TOO.
SEE? THIS SONG.
SHINO-CHAN...
...THA...
...THANK YA.
OKIES DEN! LET'S SINGY-WINGY!!
ONE AND A TWO...
THE BLUE.... BLUE...
"GOODBYE?"
WHERE ARE YOU GOING?
I'M LOOKING FOR SOMETHING.
SO DO TAKE CARE.
OH...
...THIS SONG...

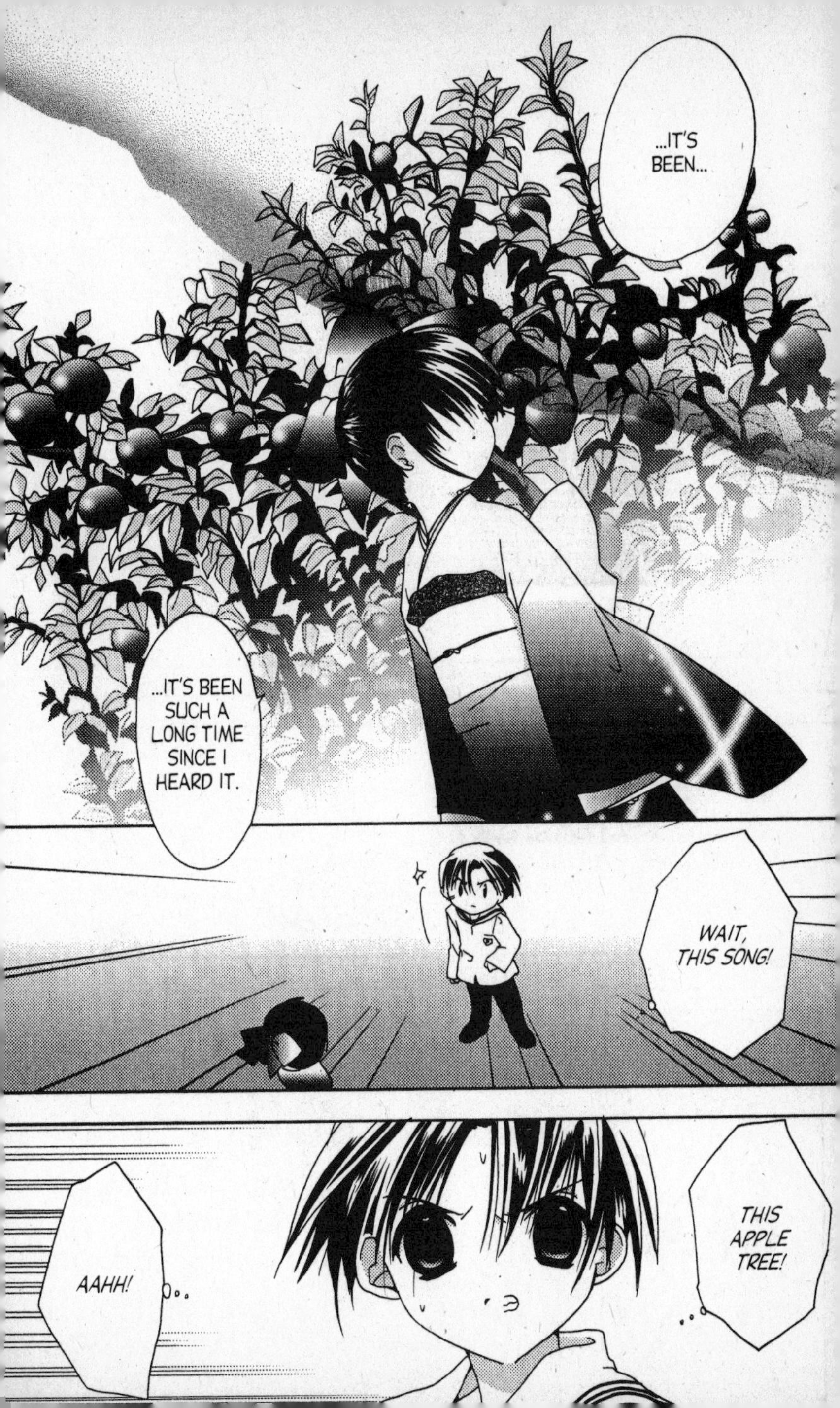

...IT'S BEEN...
...IT'S BEEN SUCH A LONG TIME SINCE I HEARD IT.
WAIT, THIS SONG!
THIS APPLE TREE!
AAHH!

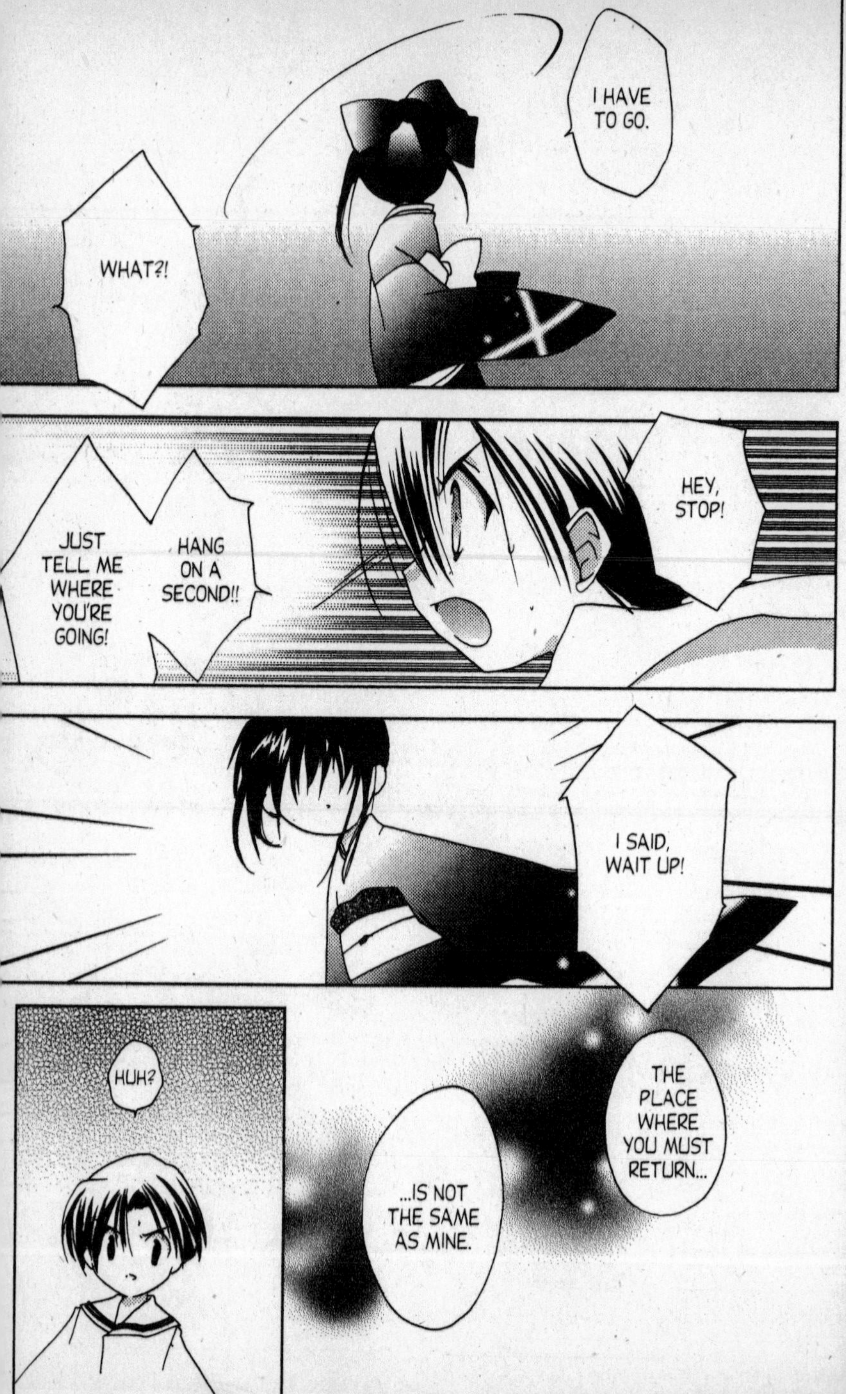
I HAVE TO GO.
WHAT?!
HEY, STOP!
HANG ON A SECOND!!
JUST TELL ME WHERE YOU'RE GOING!
I SAID, WAIT UP!
THE PLACE WHERE YOU MUST RETURN...
...IS NOT THE SAME AS MINE.
HUH?

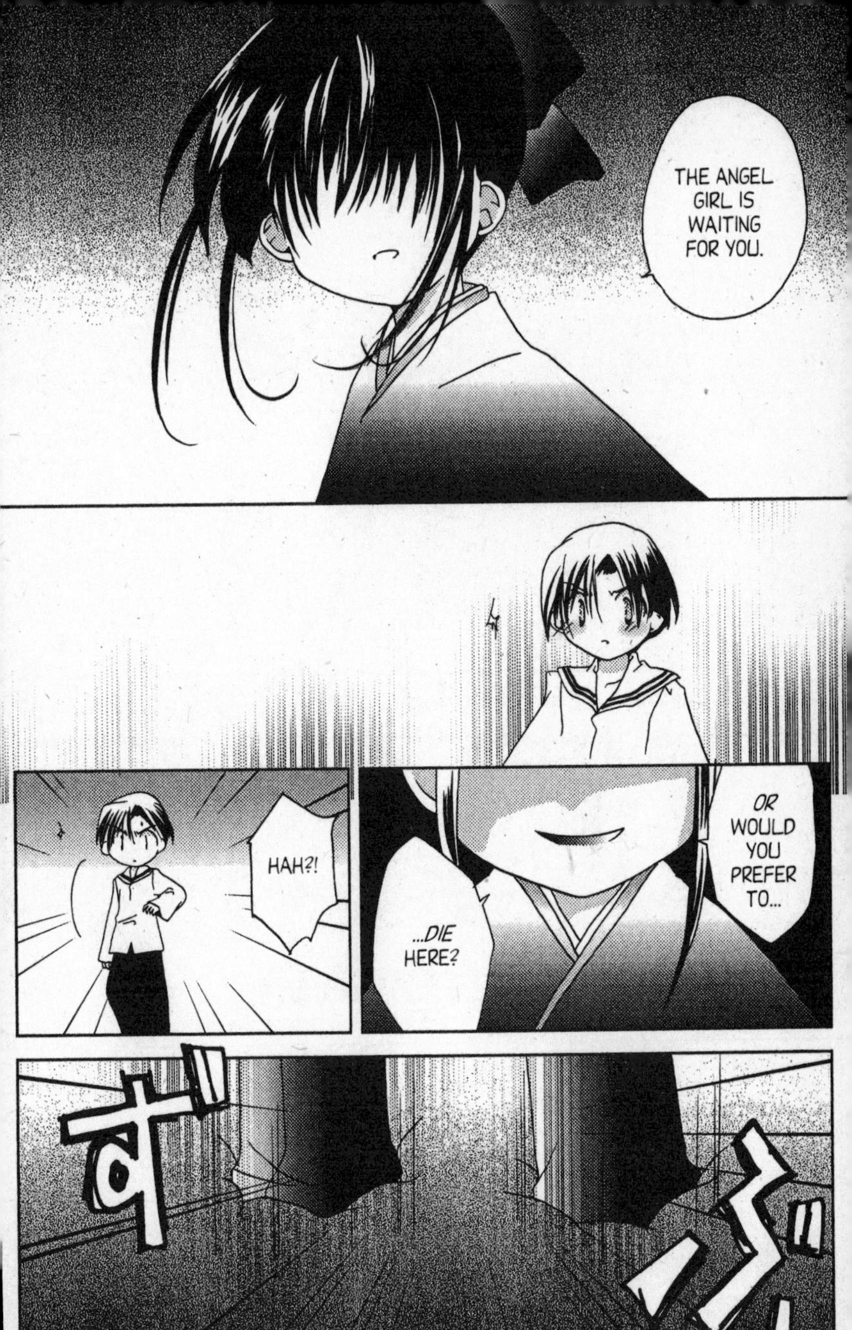
THE ANGEL GIRL IS WAITING FOR YOU.
OR WOULD YOU PREFER TO...
...DIE HERE?
HAH?!

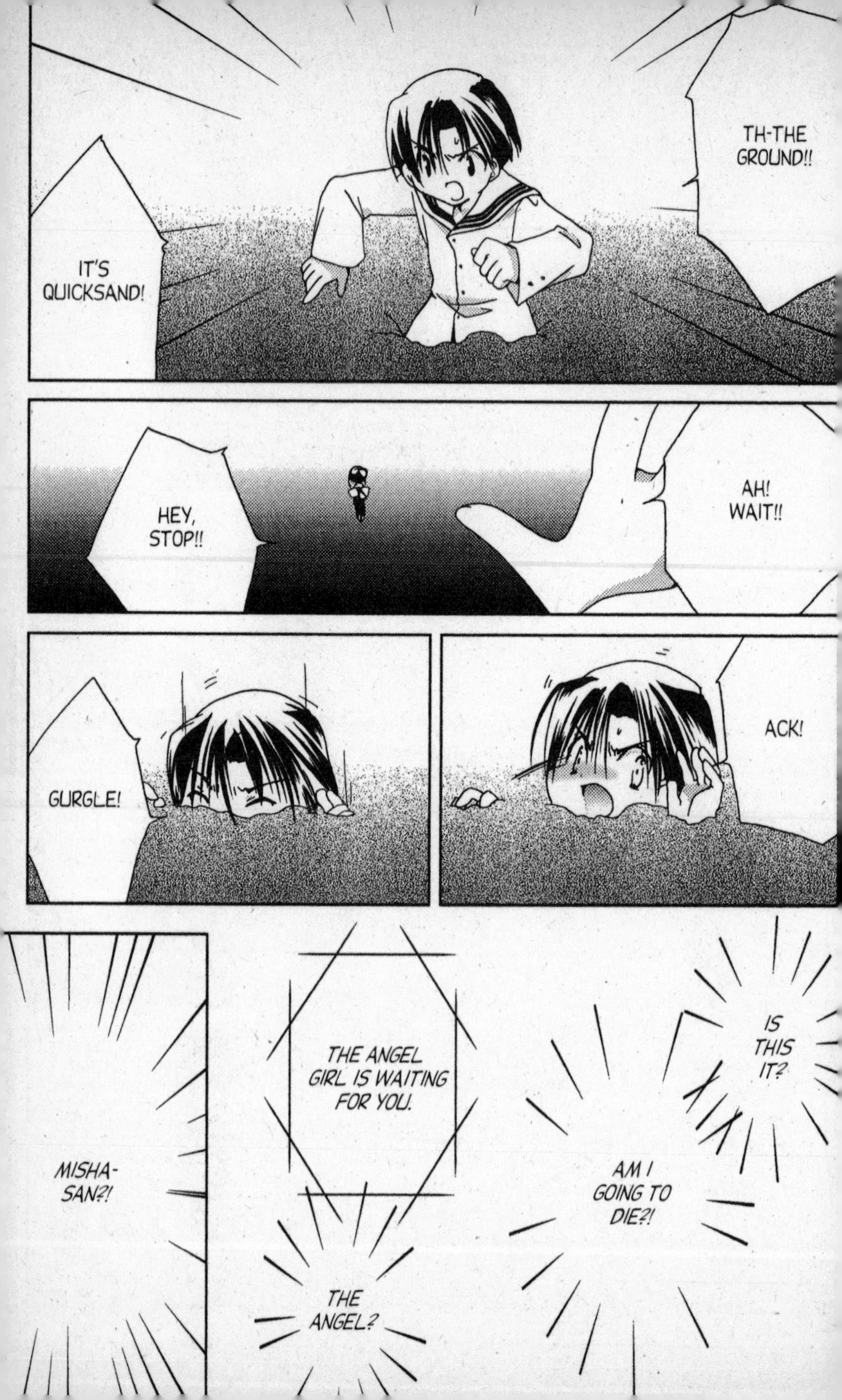
TH-THE GROUND!!
IT'S QUICKSAND!
AH! WAIT!!
HEY, STOP!!
ACK!
GURGLE!
IS THIS IT?
AM I GOING TO DIE?!
THE ANGEL GIRL IS WAITING FOR YOU.
THE ANGEL?
MISHA-SAN?!

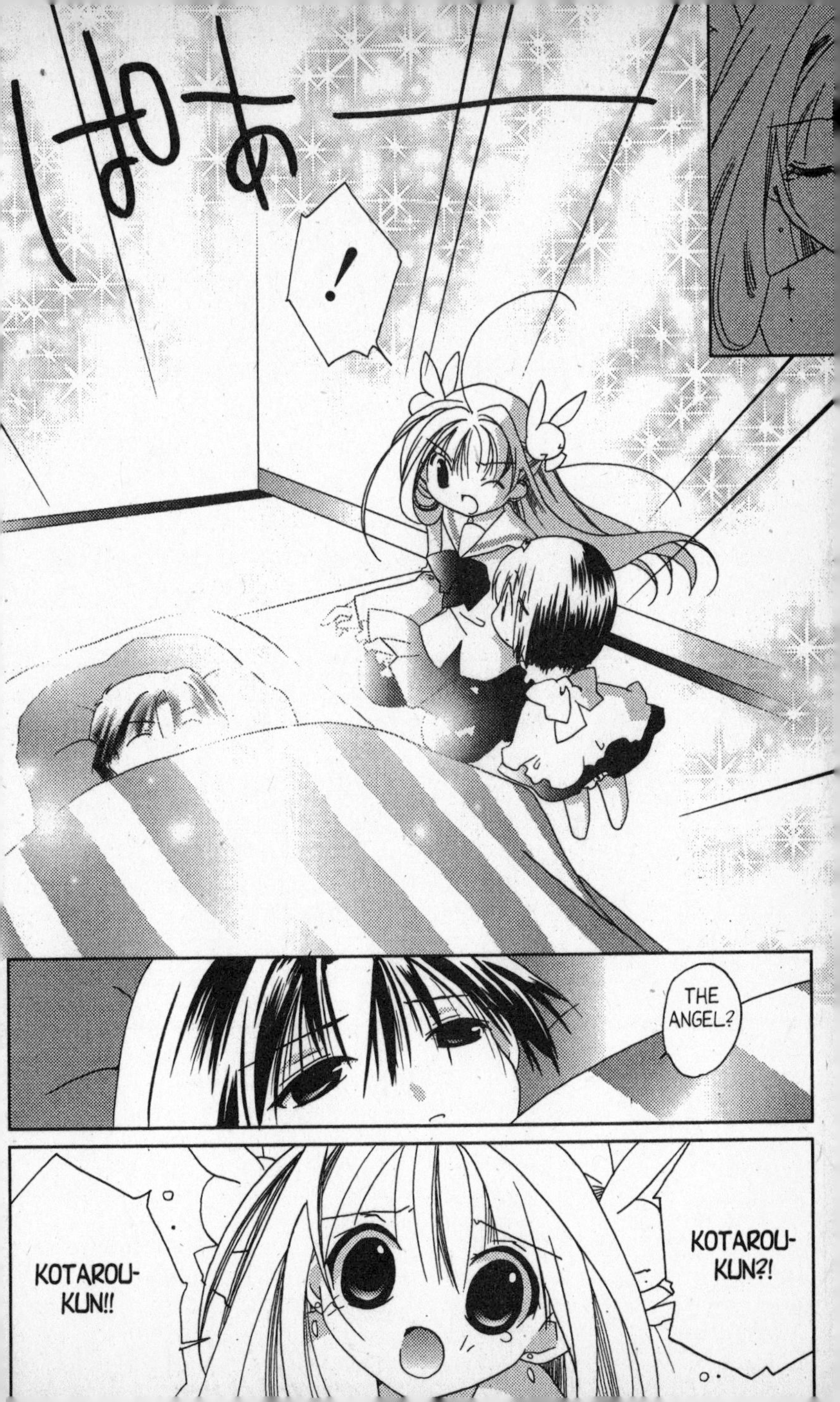
ぱあー
!
THE ANGEL?
KOTAROU-KUN?!
KOTAROU-KUN!!

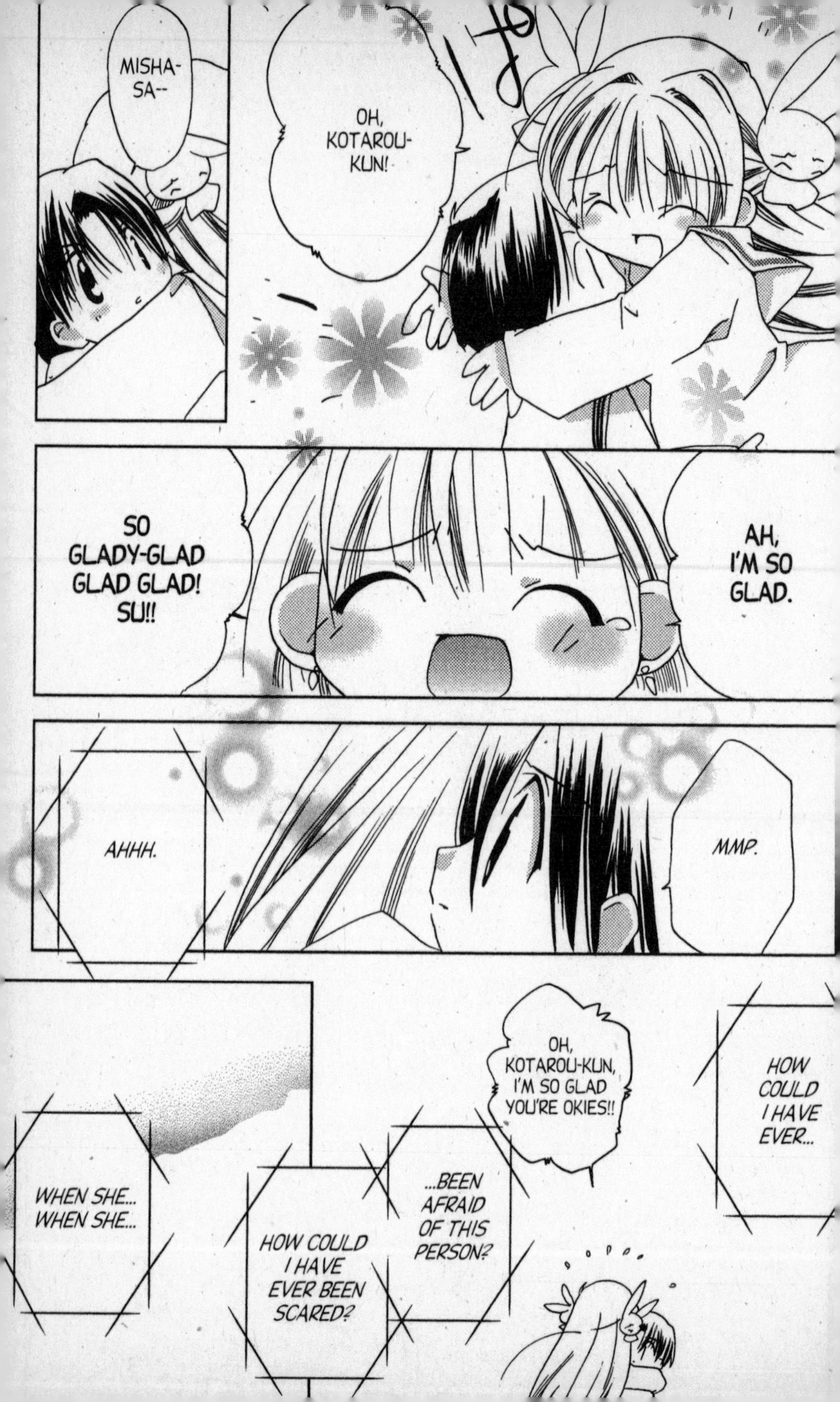
OH, KOTAROU-KUN!
MISHA-SA--
AH, I'M SO GLAD.
SO GLADY-GLAD GLAD GLAD! SU!!
MMP.
AHHH.
HOW COULD I HAVE EVER...
OH, KOTAROU-KUN, I'M SO GLAD YOU'RE OKIES!!
...BEEN AFRAID OF THIS PERSON?
HOW COULD I HAVE EVER BEEN SCARED?
WHEN SHE... WHEN SHE...

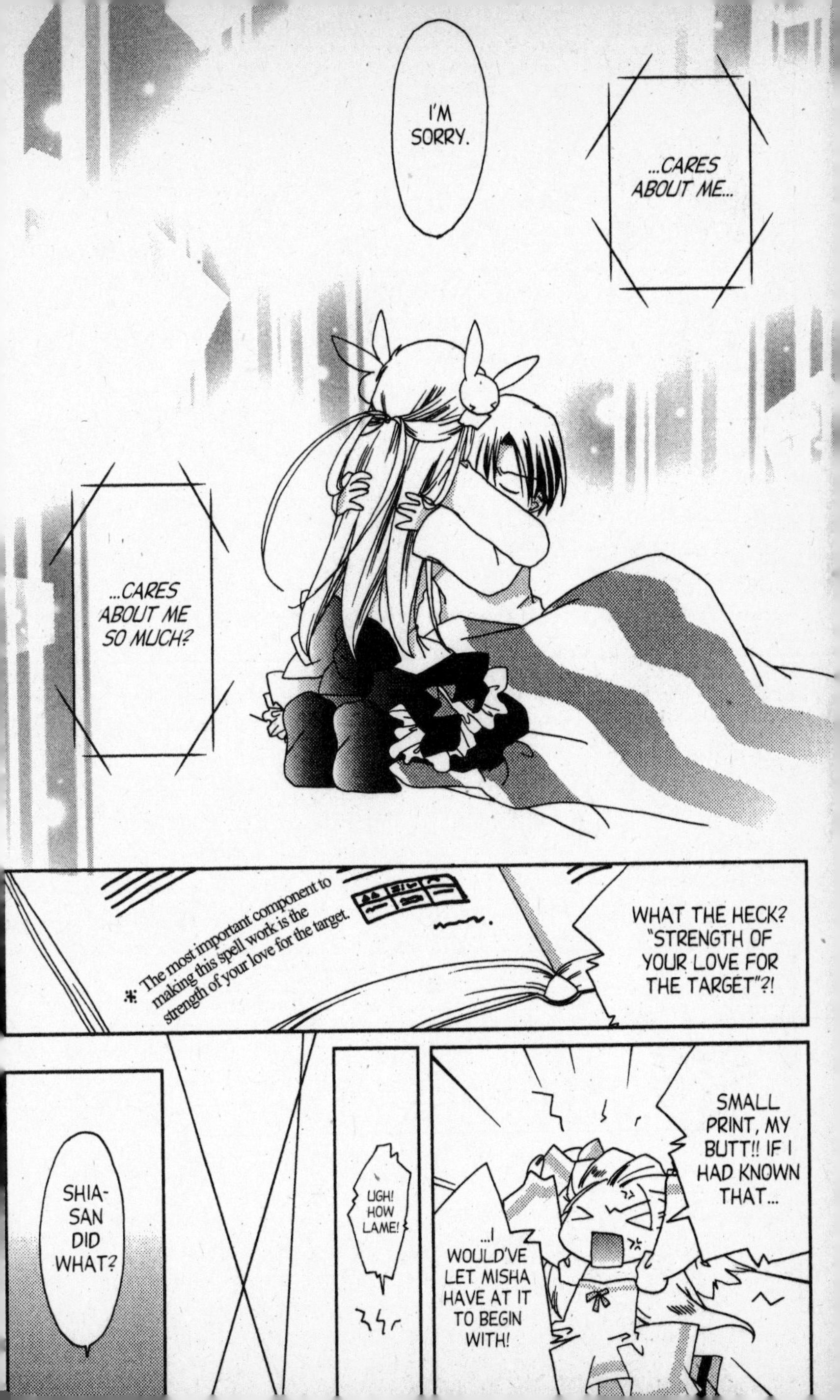
I'M SORRY.
...CARES ABOUT ME...
...CARES ABOUT ME SO MUCH?
WHAT THE HECK? "STRENGTH OF YOUR LOVE FOR THE TARGET"?!
※ The most important component to making this spell work is the strength of your love for the target.
SMALL PRINT, MY BUTT!! IF I HAD KNOWN THAT...
...I WOULD'VE LET MISHA HAVE AT IT TO BEGIN WITH!
UGH! HOW LAME!
SHIA-SAN DID WHAT?

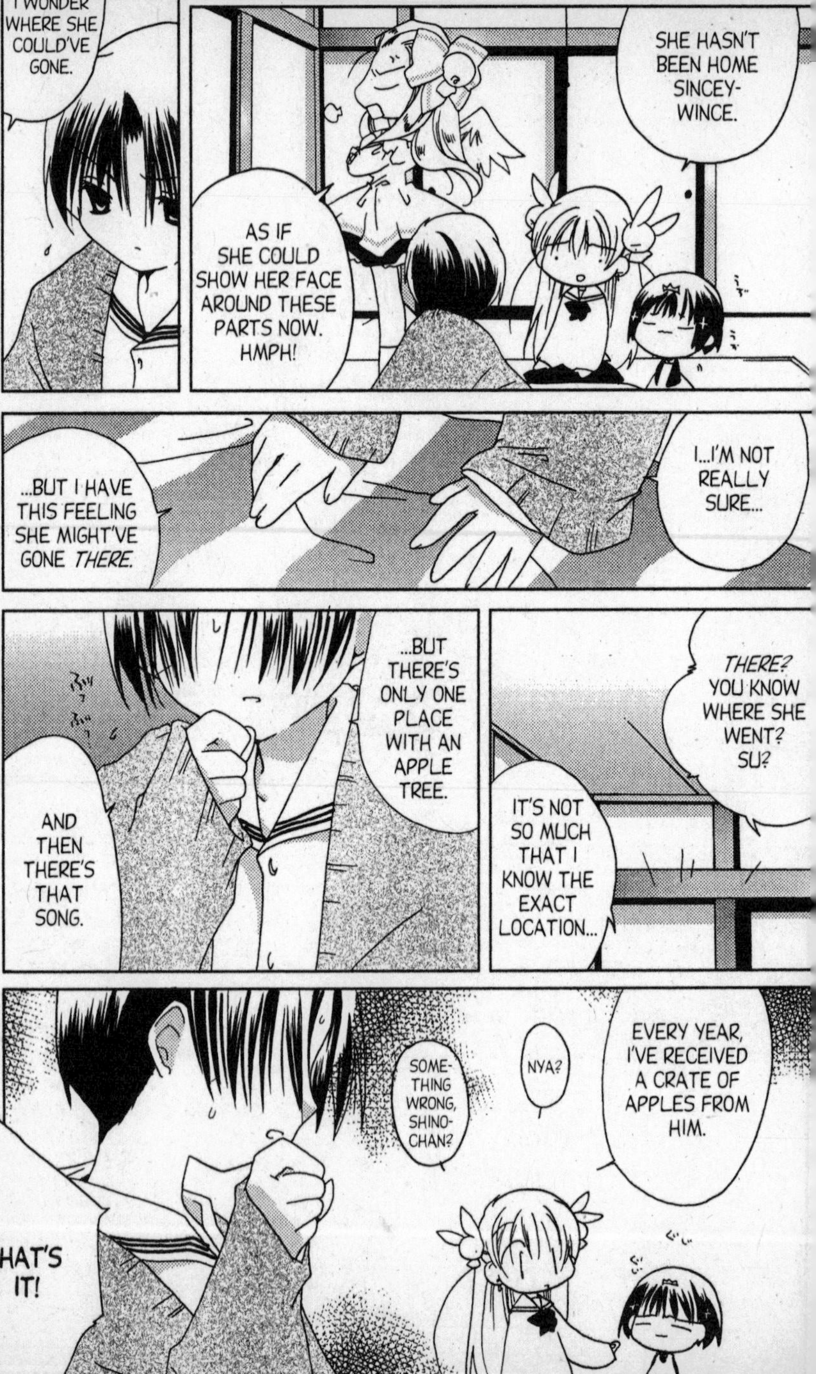
SHE HASN'T BEEN HOME SINCEY-WINCE.
AS IF SHE COULD SHOW HER FACE AROUND THESE PARTS NOW. HMPH!
I WONDER WHERE SHE COULD'VE GONE.
I...I'M NOT REALLY SURE...
...BUT I HAVE THIS FEELING SHE MIGHT'VE GONE *THERE.*
THERE? YOU KNOW WHERE SHE WENT? SU?
IT'S NOT SO MUCH THAT I KNOW THE EXACT LOCATION...
...BUT THERE'S ONLY ONE PLACE WITH AN APPLE TREE.
AND THEN THERE'S THAT SONG.
EVERY YEAR, I'VE RECEIVED A CRATE OF APPLES FROM HIM.
NYA?
SOME-THING WRONG, SHINO-CHAN?
THAT'S IT!

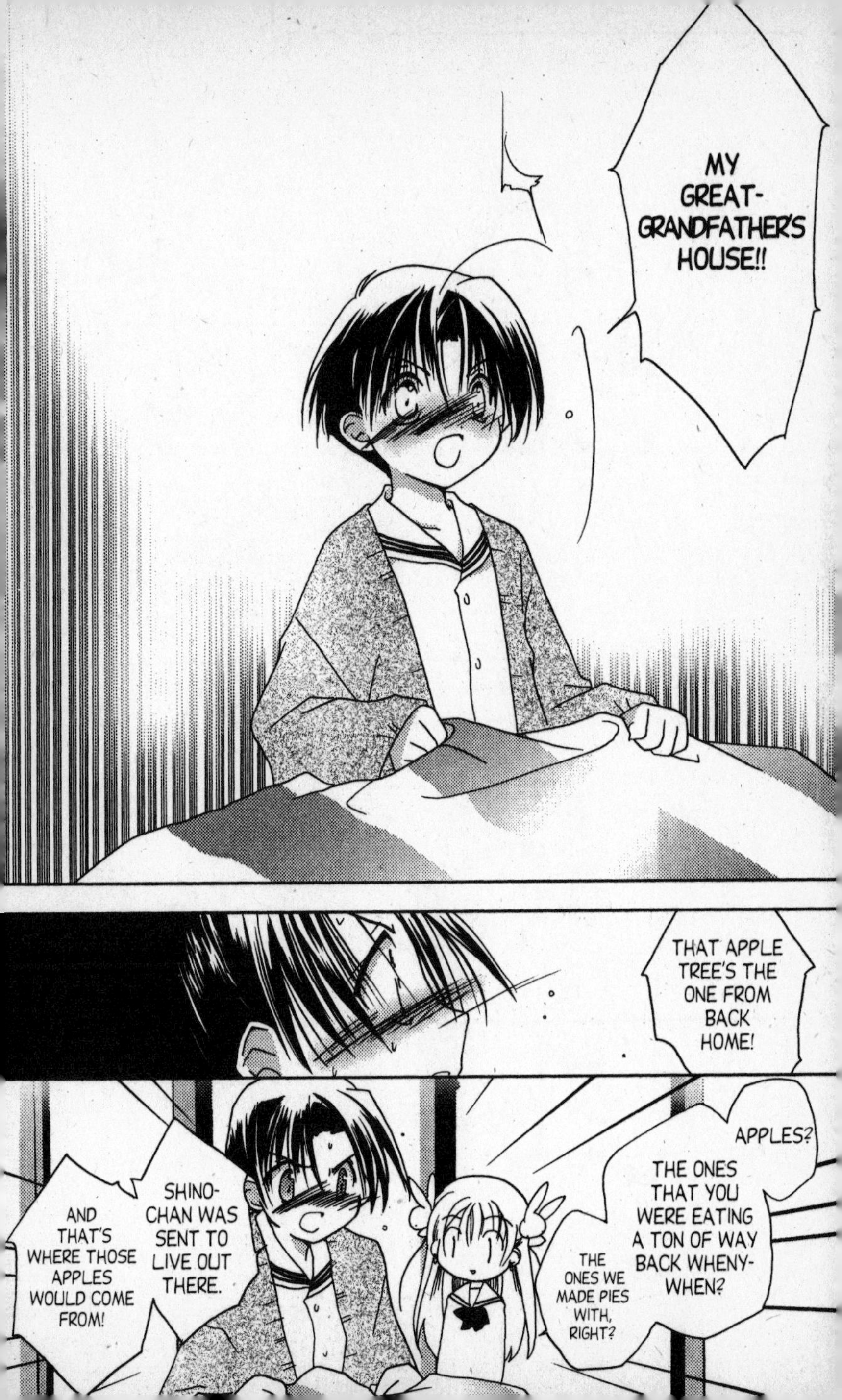
MY GREAT-GRANDFATHER'S HOUSE!!
THAT APPLE TREE'S THE ONE FROM BACK HOME!
APPLES?
THE ONES THAT YOU WERE EATING A TON OF WAY BACK WHENY-WHEN?
THE ONES WE MADE PIES WITH, RIGHT?
SHINO-CHAN WAS SENT TO LIVE OUT THERE.
AND THAT'S WHERE THOSE APPLES WOULD COME FROM!

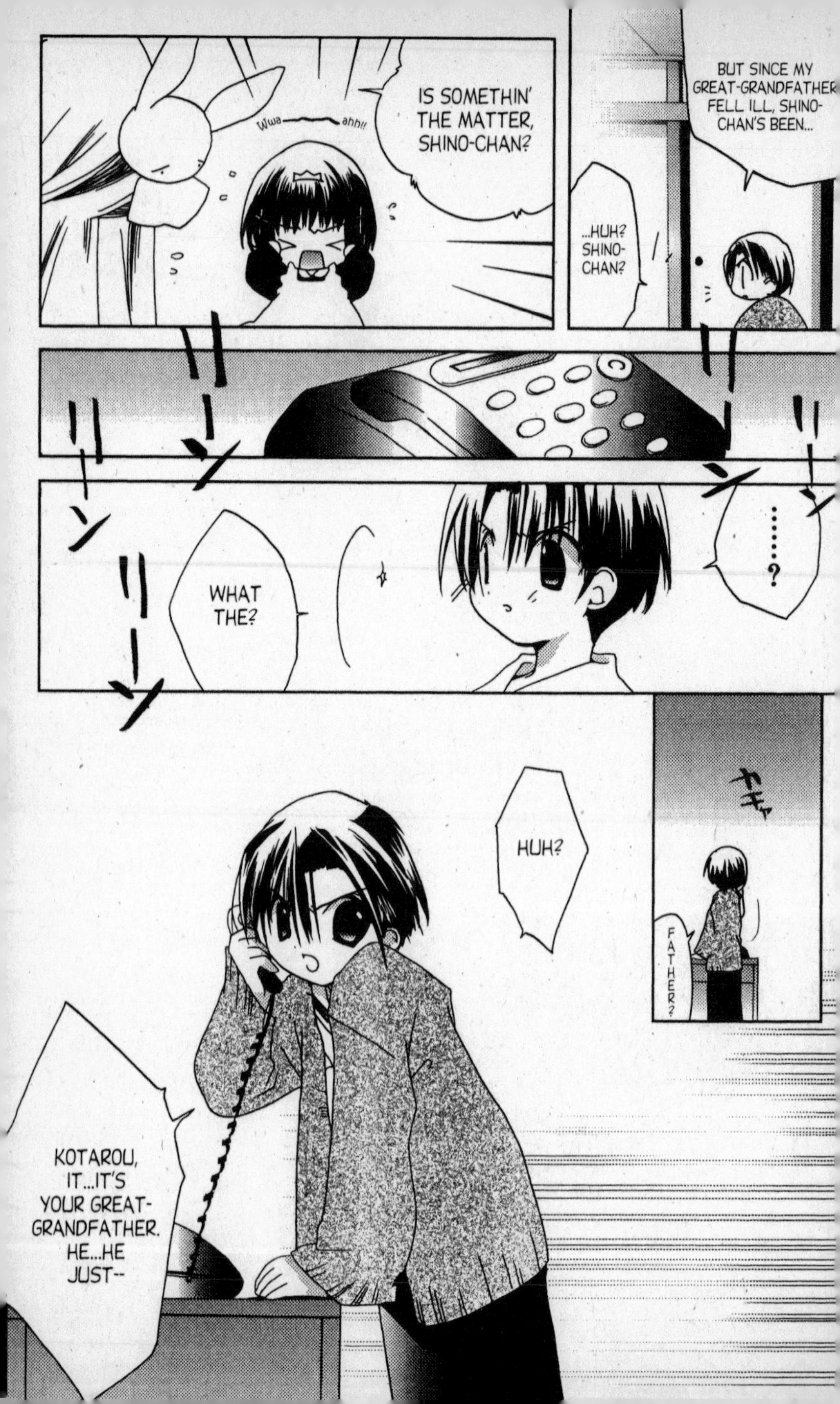
BUT SINCE MY GREAT-GRANDFATHER FELL ILL, SHINO-CHAN'S BEEN...
...HUH? SHINO-CHAN?
Wwa——ahh!!
IS SOMETHIN' THE MATTER, SHINO-CHAN?
......?
WHAT THE?
FATHER?
HUH?
KOTAROU, IT...IT'S YOUR GREAT-GRANDFATHER. HE...HE JUST--

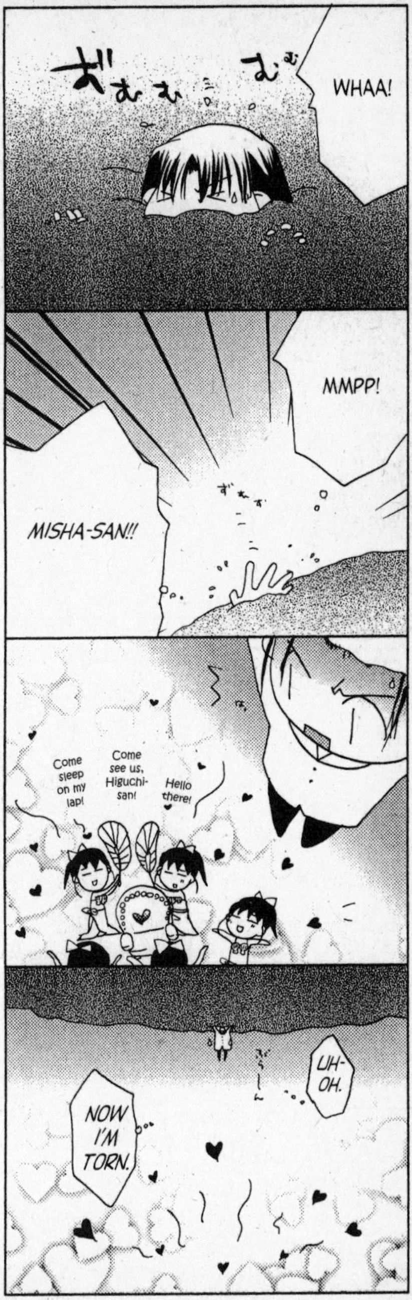
WHAA!
MMPP!
MISHA-SAN!!
Hello there!
Come see us, Higuchi-san!
Come sleep on my lap!
UH-OH.
NOW I'M TORN.

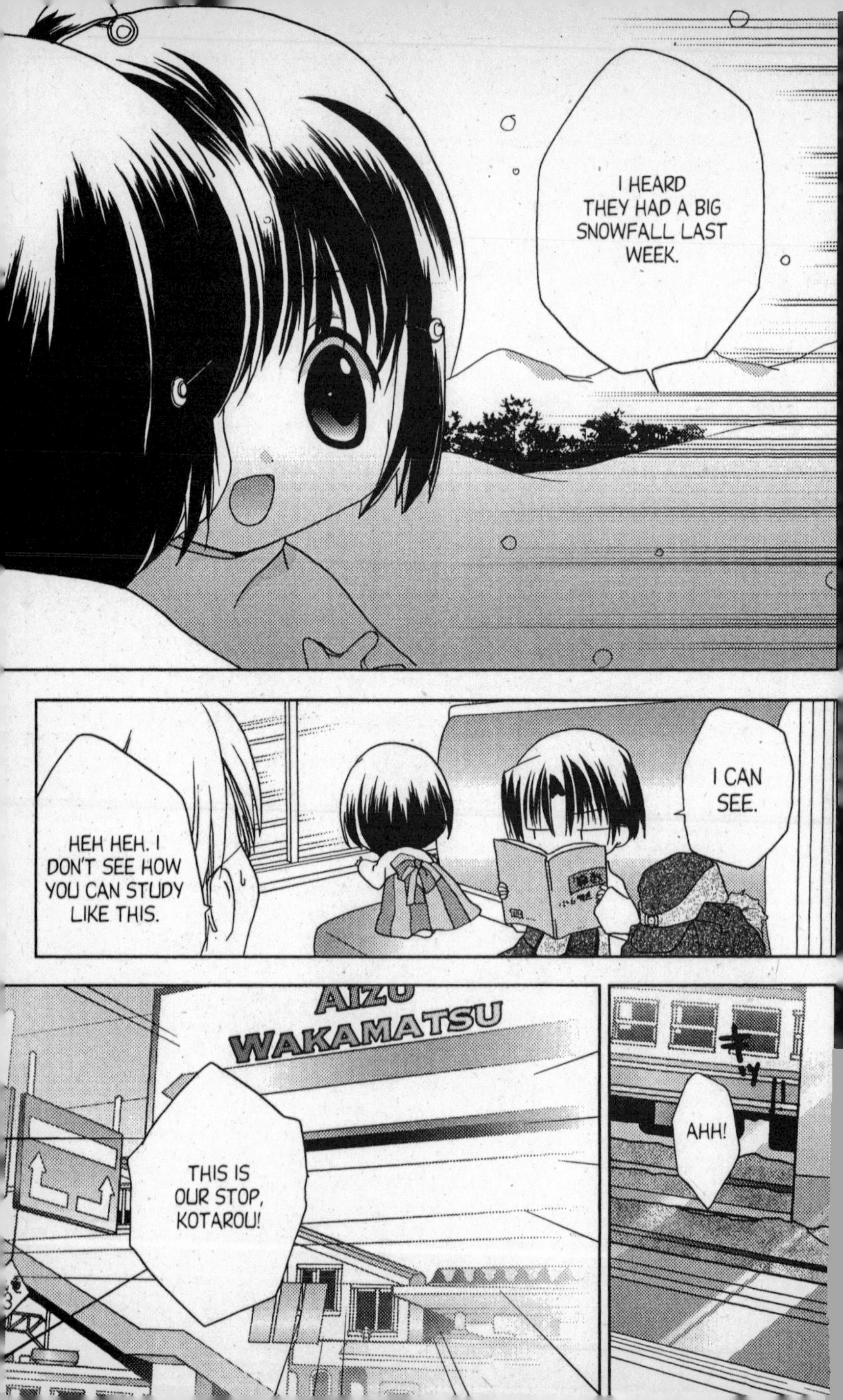
I HEARD THEY HAD A BIG SNOWFALL LAST WEEK.
I CAN SEE.
HEH HEH. I DON'T SEE HOW YOU CAN STUDY LIKE THIS.
AHH!
AIZU WAKAMATSU
THIS IS OUR STOP, KOTAROU!

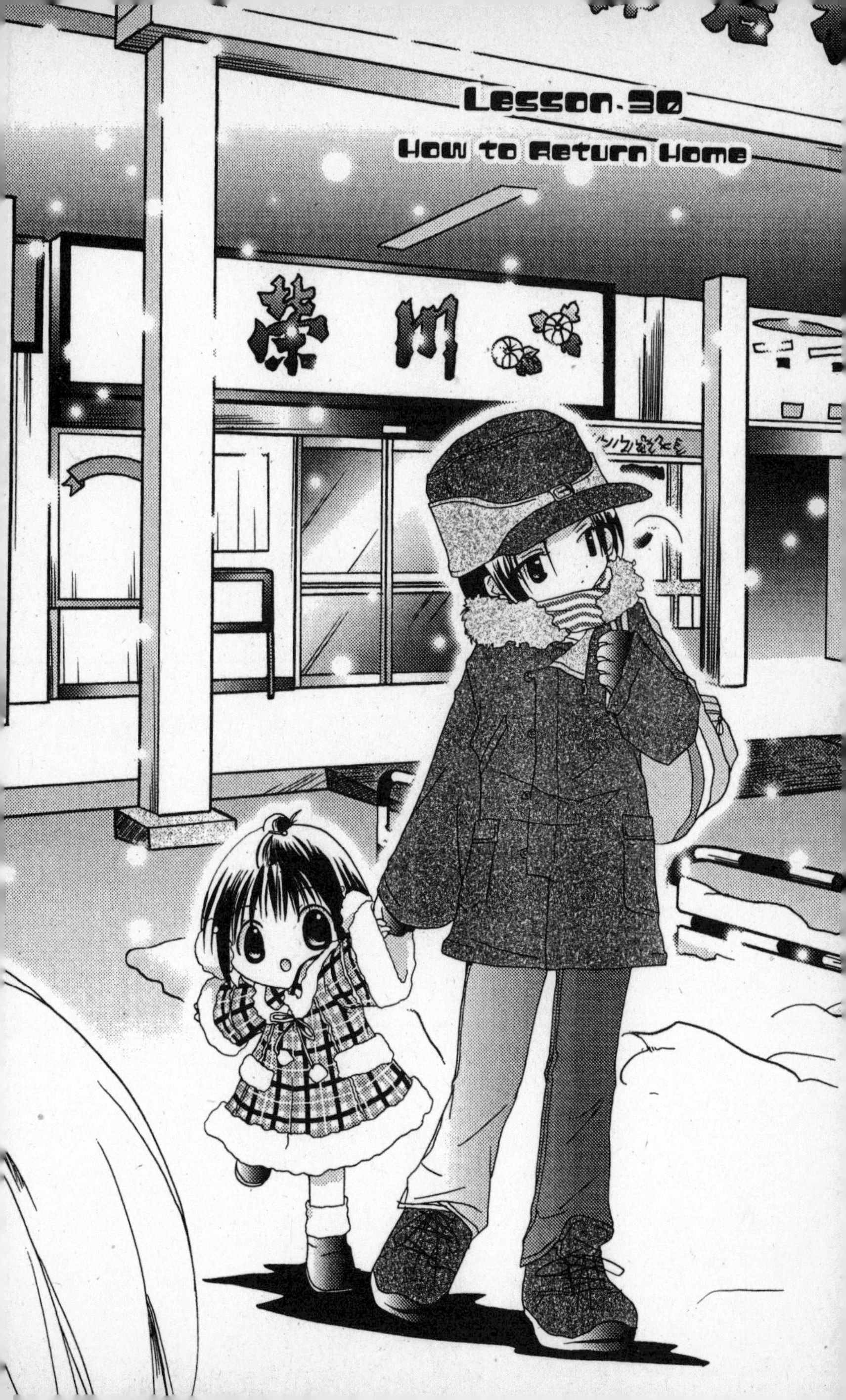
Lesson 30
How to Return Home

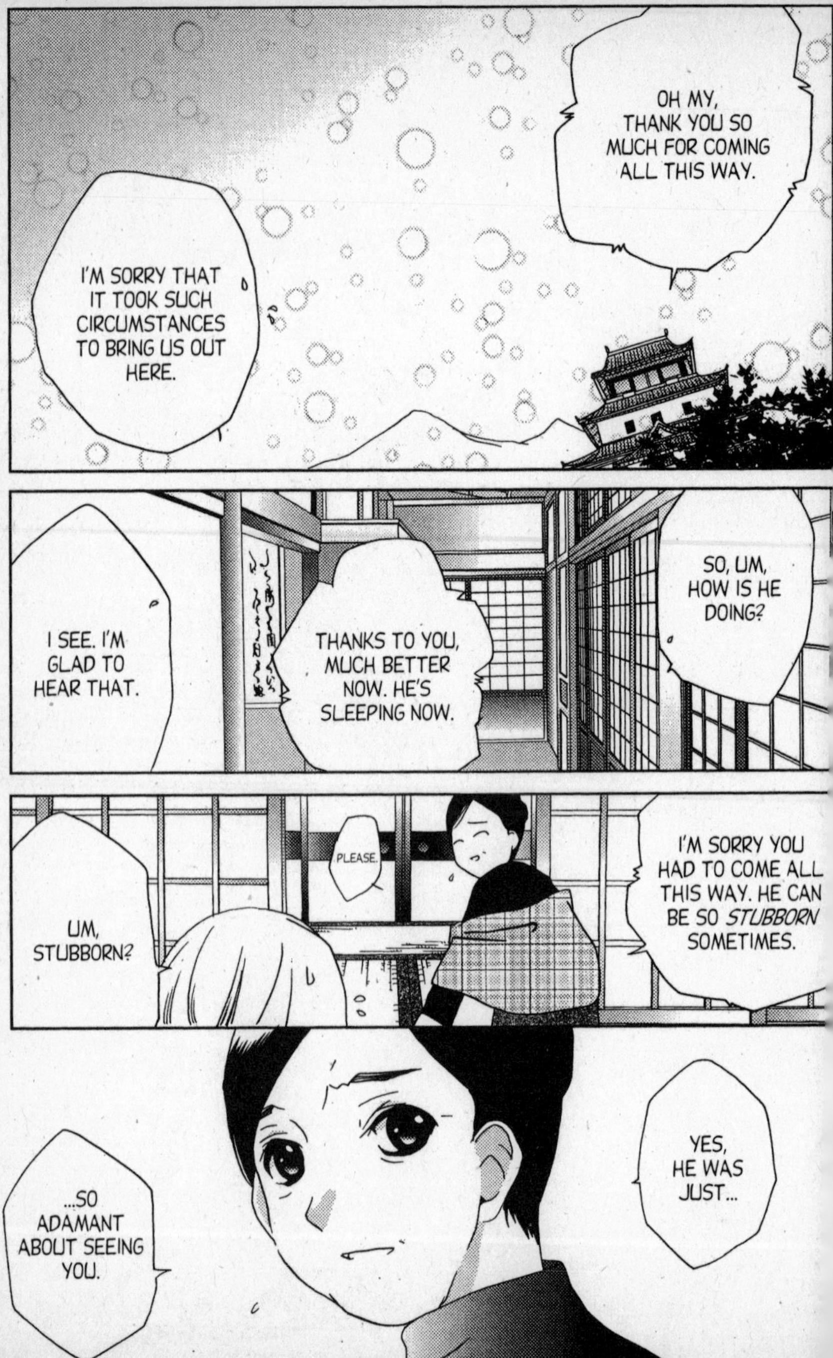
OH MY, THANK YOU SO MUCH FOR COMING ALL THIS WAY.
I'M SORRY THAT IT TOOK SUCH CIRCUMSTANCES TO BRING US OUT HERE.
SO, UM, HOW IS HE DOING?
THANKS TO YOU, MUCH BETTER NOW. HE'S SLEEPING NOW.
I SEE. I'M GLAD TO HEAR THAT.
I'M SORRY YOU HAD TO COME ALL THIS WAY. HE CAN BE SO *STUBBORN* SOMETIMES.
PLEASE.
UM, STUBBORN?
YES, HE WAS JUST...
...SO ADAMANT ABOUT SEEING YOU.

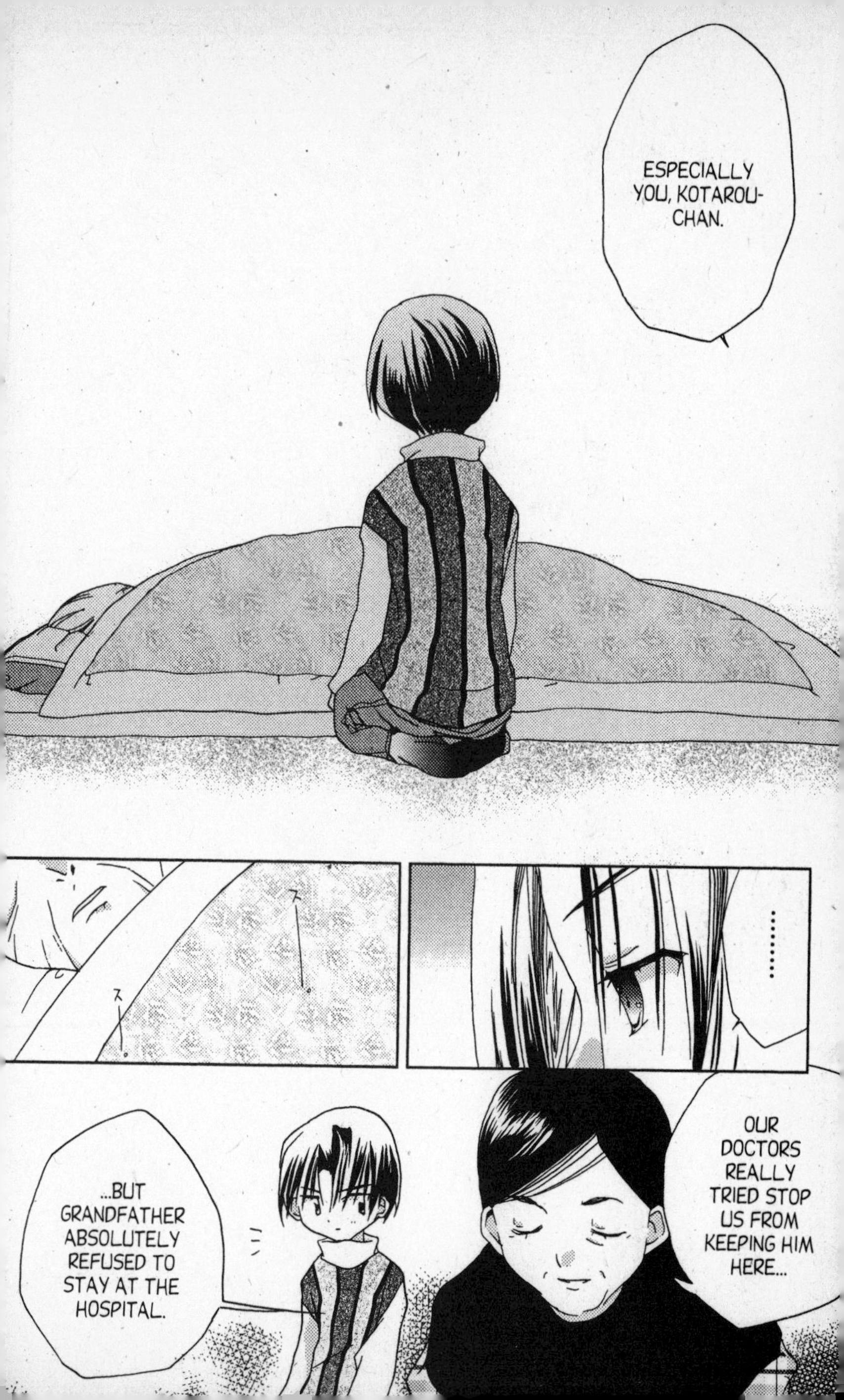
ESPECIALLY YOU, KOTAROU-CHAN.
......
ス
ス
OUR DOCTORS REALLY TRIED STOP US FROM KEEPING HIM HERE...
...BUT GRANDFATHER ABSOLUTELY REFUSED TO STAY AT THE HOSPITAL.

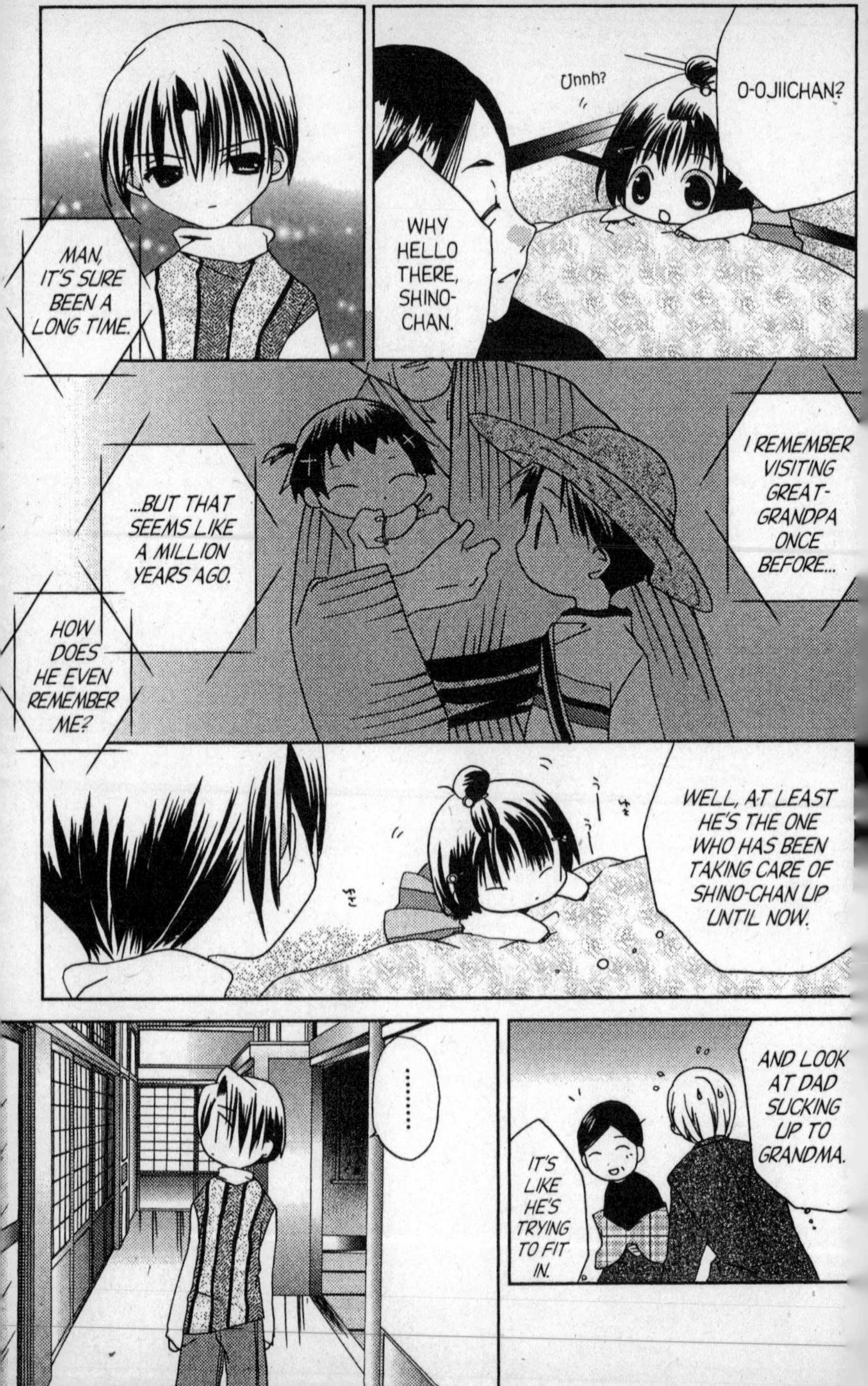
O-OJIICHAN?
Unnh?
WHY HELLO THERE, SHINO-CHAN.
MAN, IT'S SURE BEEN A LONG TIME.
I REMEMBER VISITING GREAT-GRANDPA ONCE BEFORE...
...BUT THAT SEEMS LIKE A MILLION YEARS AGO.
HOW DOES HE EVEN REMEMBER ME?
WELL, AT LEAST HE'S THE ONE WHO HAS BEEN TAKING CARE OF SHINO-CHAN UP UNTIL NOW.
AND LOOK AT DAD SUCKING UP TO GRANDMA.
IT'S LIKE HE'S TRYING TO FIT IN.
....

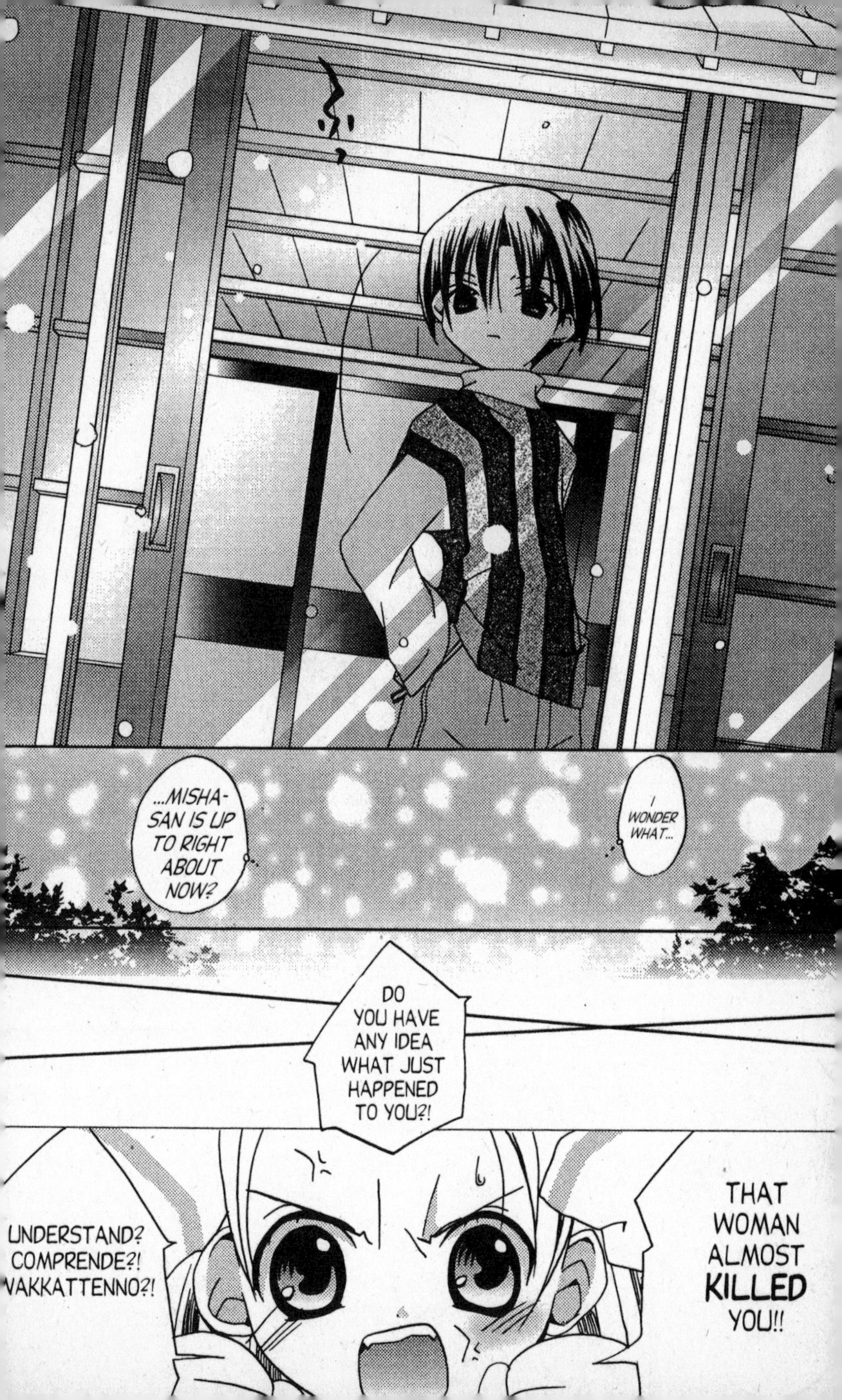
I WONDER WHAT...
...MISHA-SAN IS UP TO RIGHT ABOUT NOW?
DO YOU HAVE ANY IDEA WHAT JUST HAPPENED TO YOU?!
THAT WOMAN ALMOST KILLED YOU!!
UNDERSTAND? COMPRENDE?! VAKKATTENNO?!

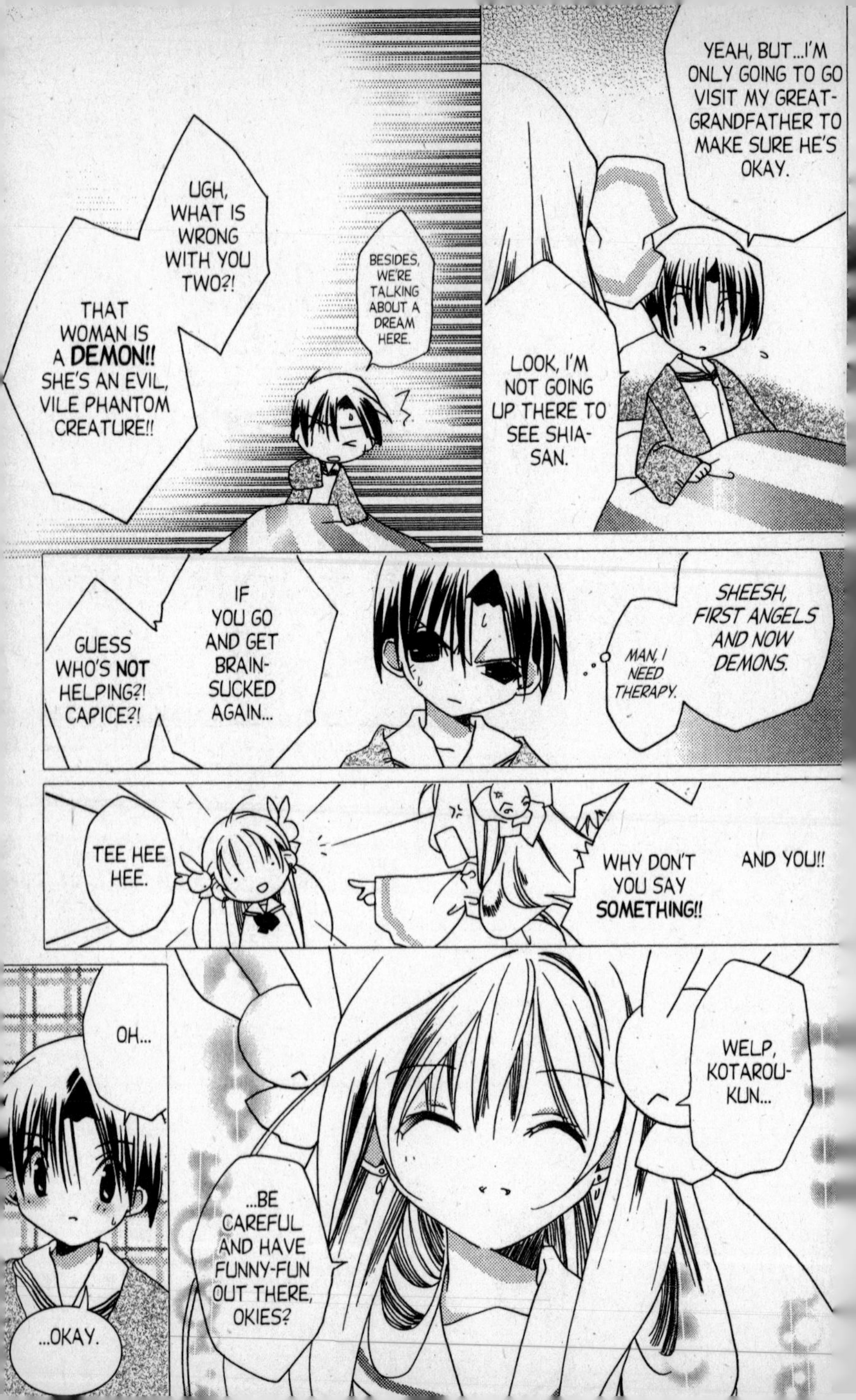
YEAH, BUT...I'M ONLY GOING TO GO VISIT MY GREAT-GRANDFATHER TO MAKE SURE HE'S OKAY.
LOOK, I'M NOT GOING UP THERE TO SEE SHIA-SAN.
BESIDES, WE'RE TALKING ABOUT A DREAM HERE.
UGH, WHAT IS WRONG WITH YOU TWO?!
THAT WOMAN IS A **DEMON!!** SHE'S AN EVIL, VILE PHANTOM CREATURE!!
SHEESH, FIRST ANGELS AND NOW DEMONS.
MAN, I NEED THERAPY.
IF YOU GO AND GET BRAIN-SUCKED AGAIN...
GUESS WHO'S **NOT** HELPING?! CAPICE?!
AND YOU!!
WHY DON'T YOU SAY **SOMETHING!!**
TEE HEE HEE.
WELP, KOTAROU-KUN...
...BE CAREFUL AND HAVE FUNNY-FUN OUT THERE, OKIES?
OH...
...OKAY.

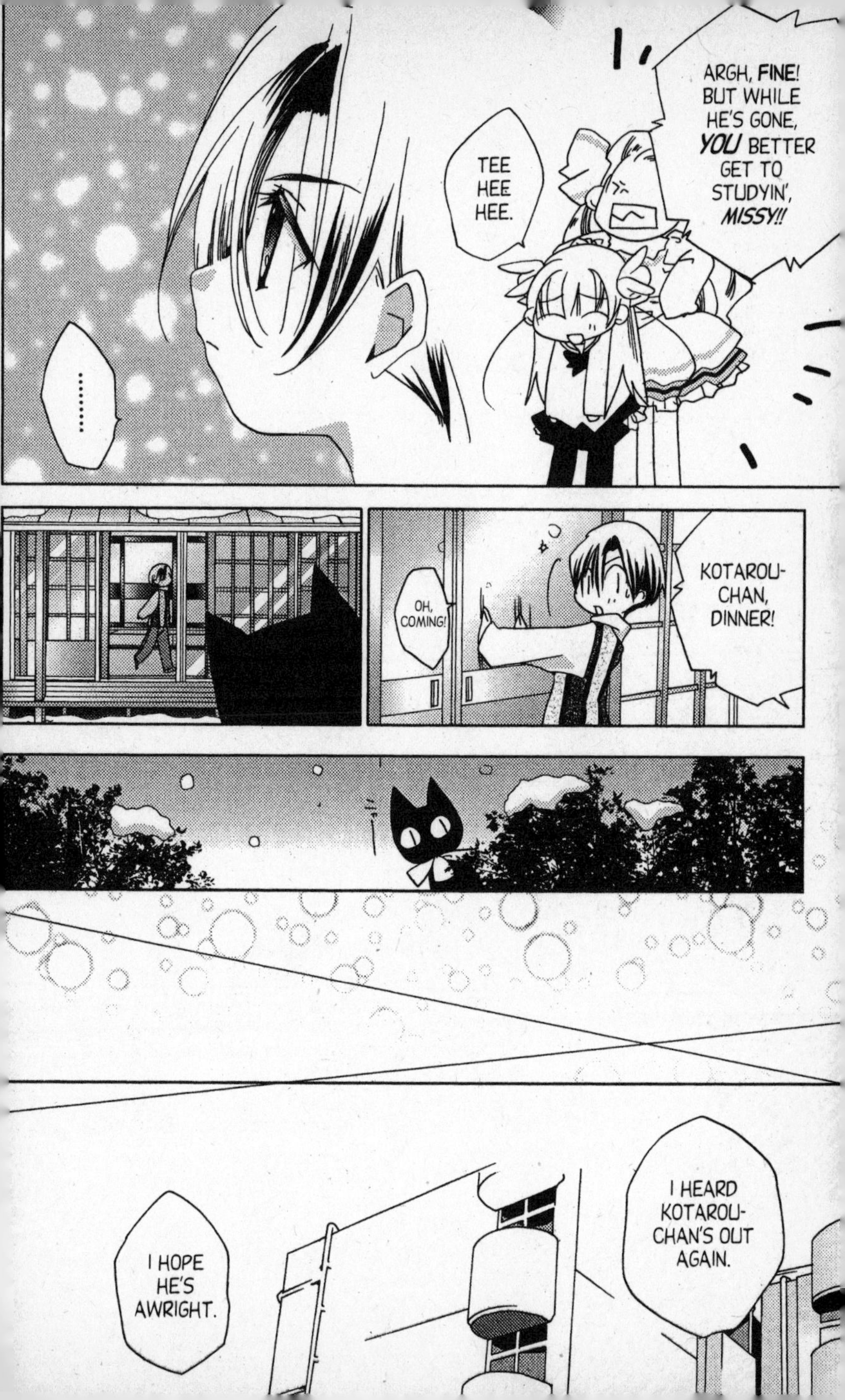
ARGH, FINE! BUT WHILE HE'S GONE, YOU BETTER GET TO STUDYIN', MISSY!!
TEE HEE HEE.
......
KOTAROU-CHAN, DINNER!
OH, COMING!
I HEARD KOTAROU-CHAN'S OUT AGAIN.
I HOPE HE'S AWRIGHT.

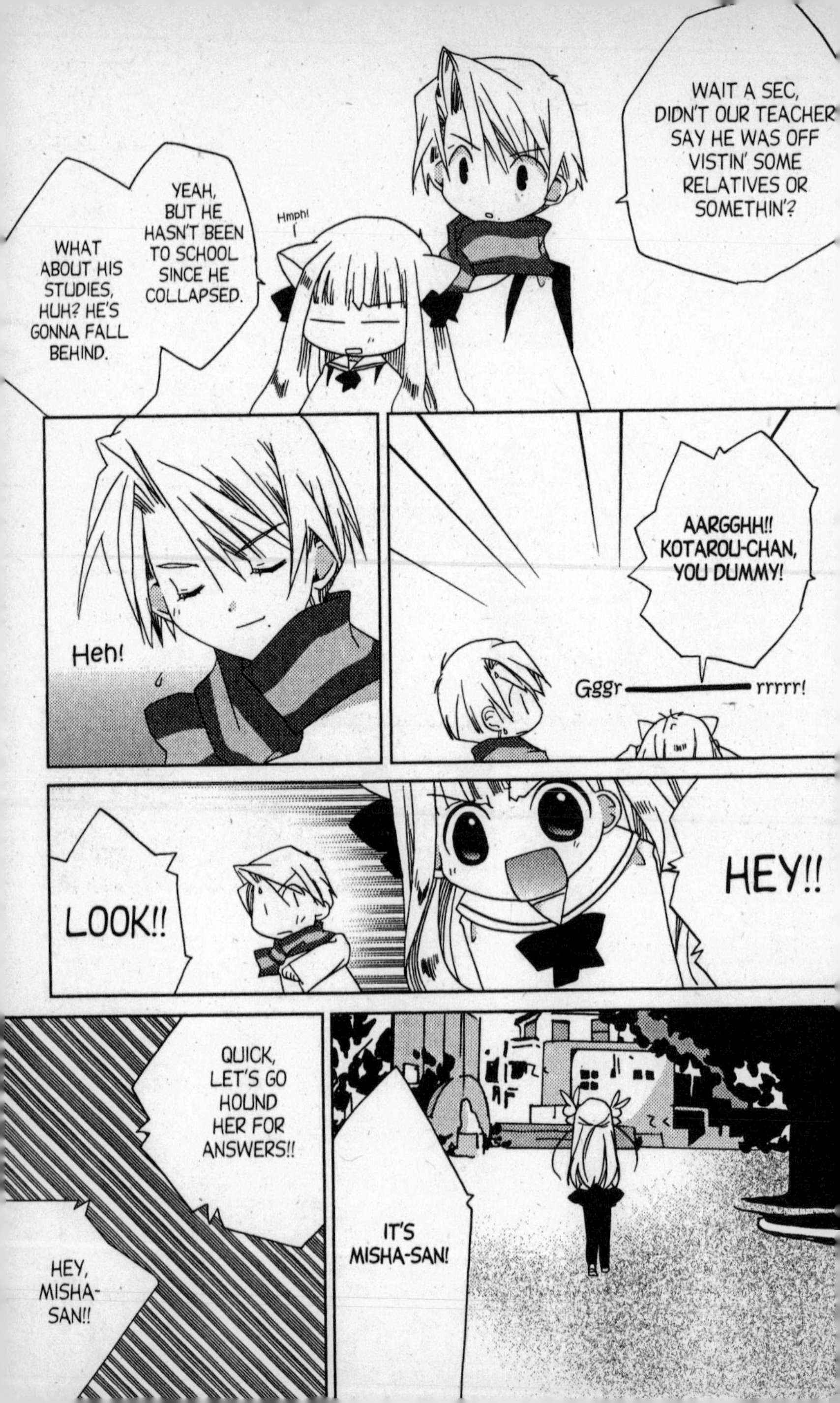
WAIT A SEC, DIDN'T OUR TEACHER SAY HE WAS OFF VISTIN' SOME RELATIVES OR SOMETHIN'?
Hmph!
YEAH, BUT HE HASN'T BEEN TO SCHOOL SINCE HE COLLAPSED.
WHAT ABOUT HIS STUDIES, HUH? HE'S GONNA FALL BEHIND.
AARGGHH!! KOTAROU-CHAN, YOU DUMMY!
Gggr——rrrr!
Heh!
HEY!!
LOOK!!
IT'S MISHA-SAN!
QUICK, LET'S GO HOUND HER FOR ANSWERS!!
HEY, MISHA-SAN!!

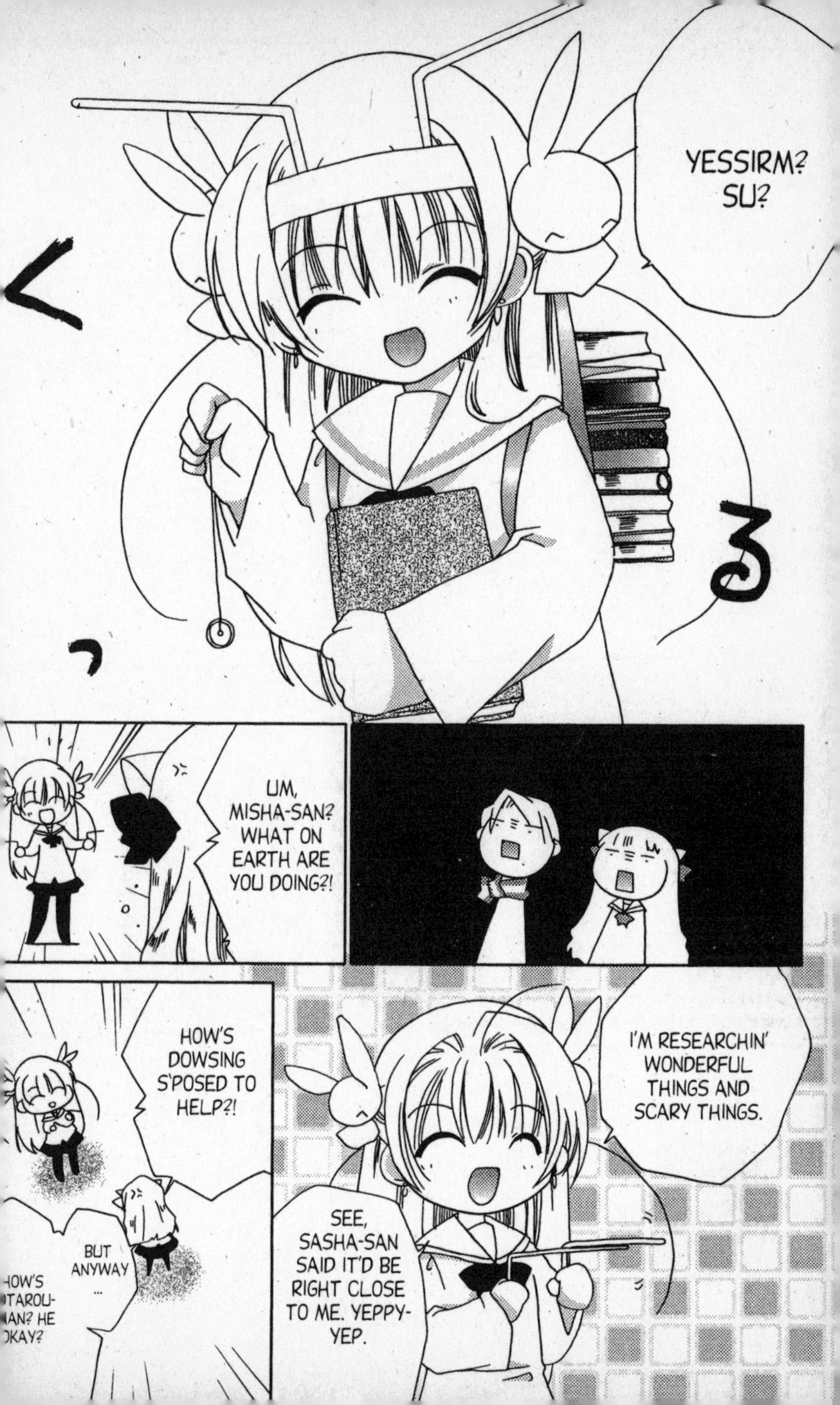
YESSIRM? SU?
UM, MISHA-SAN? WHAT ON EARTH ARE YOU DOING?!
I'M RESEARCHIN' WONDERFUL THINGS AND SCARY THINGS.
SEE, SASHA-SAN SAID IT'D BE RIGHT CLOSE TO ME. YEPPY-YEP.
HOW'S DOWSING S'POSED TO HELP?!
BUT ANYWAY ...
HOW'S TAROU- AN? HE KAY?

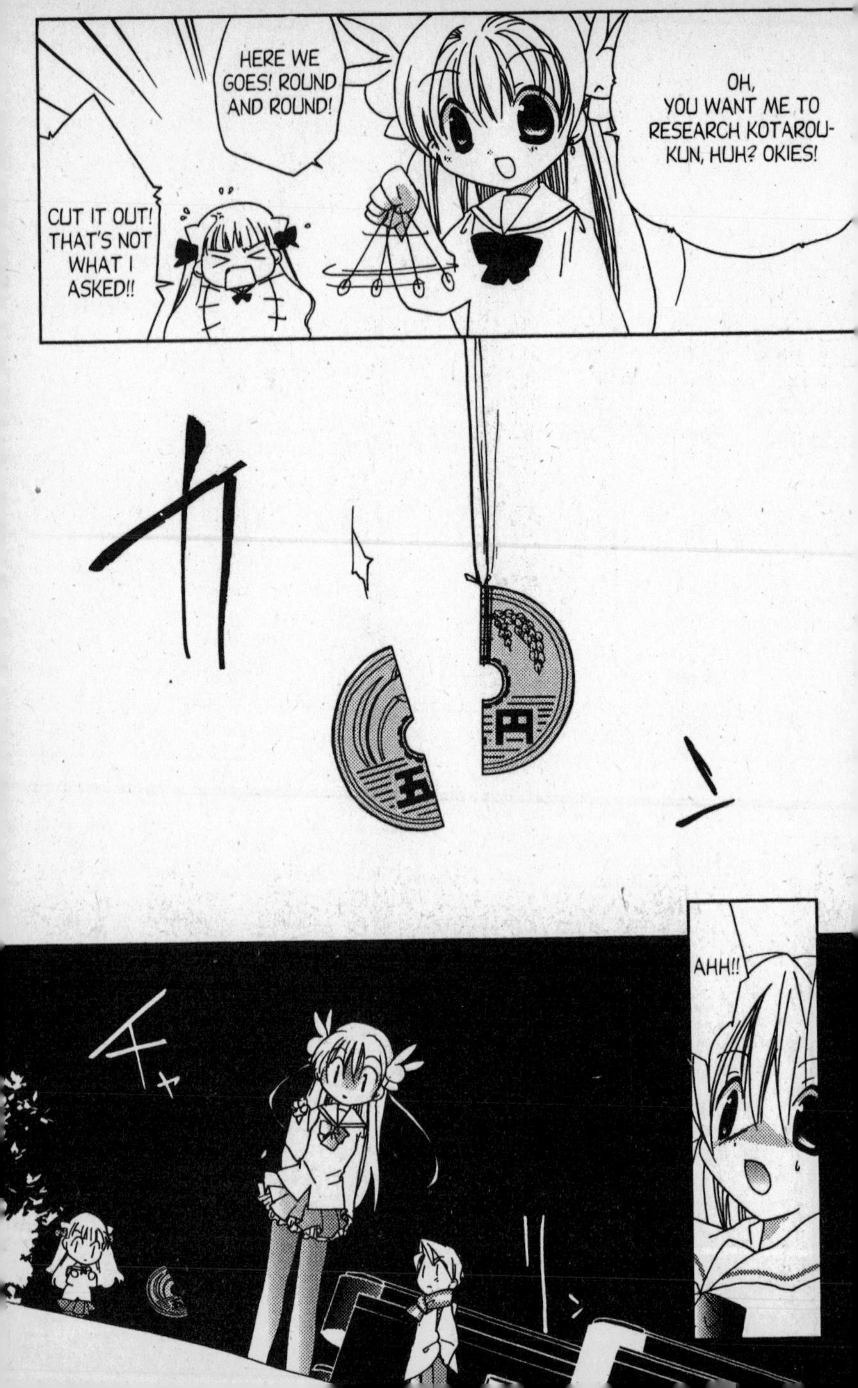
OH, YOU WANT ME TO RESEARCH KOTAROU-KUN, HUH? OKIES!
HERE WE GOES! ROUND AND ROUND!
CUT IT OUT! THAT'S NOT WHAT I ASKED!!
AHH!!

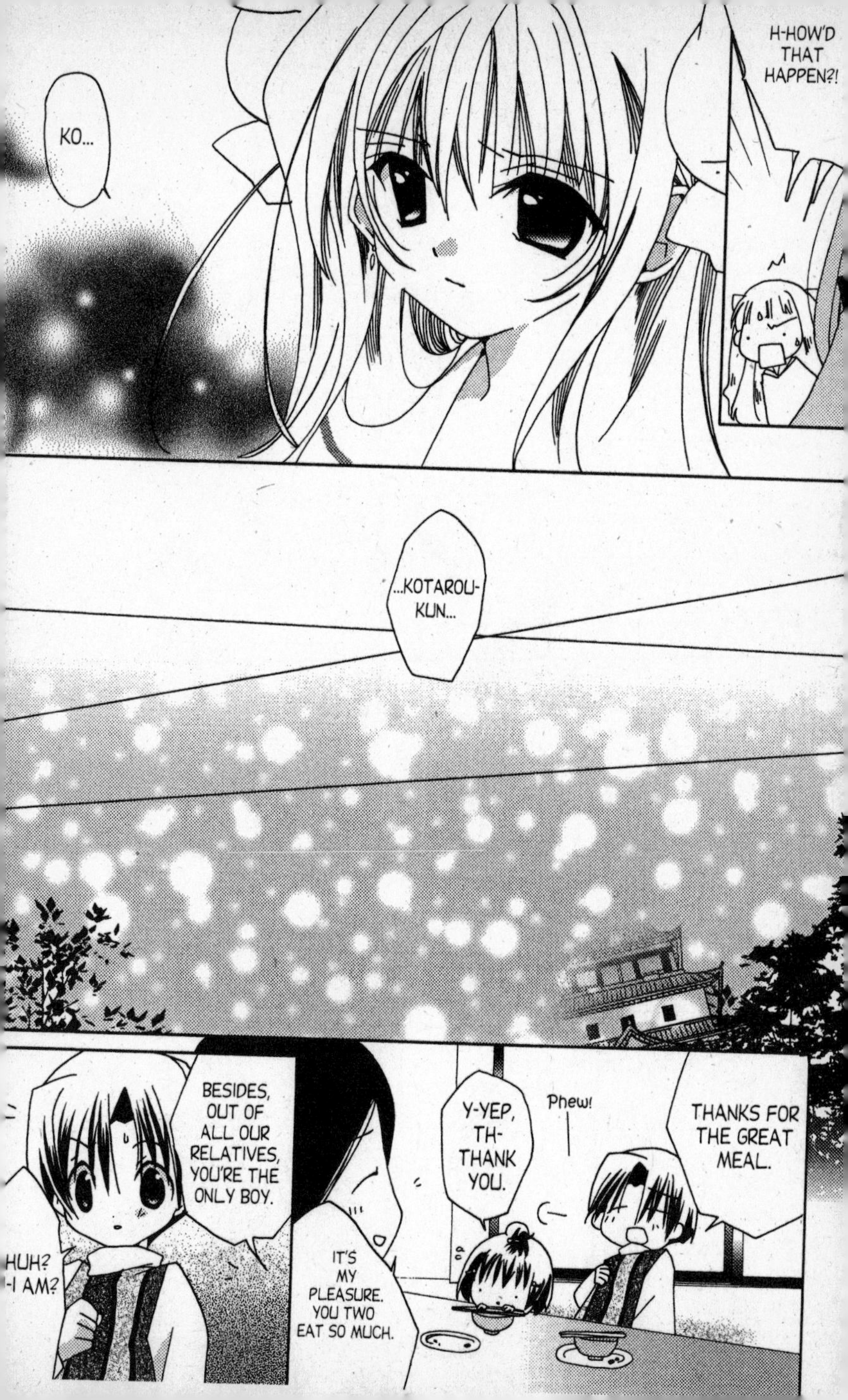
H-HOW'D THAT HAPPEN?!
KO...
...KOTAROU-KUN...
THANKS FOR THE GREAT MEAL.
Phew!
Y-YEP, TH-THANK YOU.
IT'S MY PLEASURE. YOU TWO EAT SO MUCH.
BESIDES, OUT OF ALL OUR RELATIVES, YOU'RE THE ONLY BOY.
HUH? -I AM?

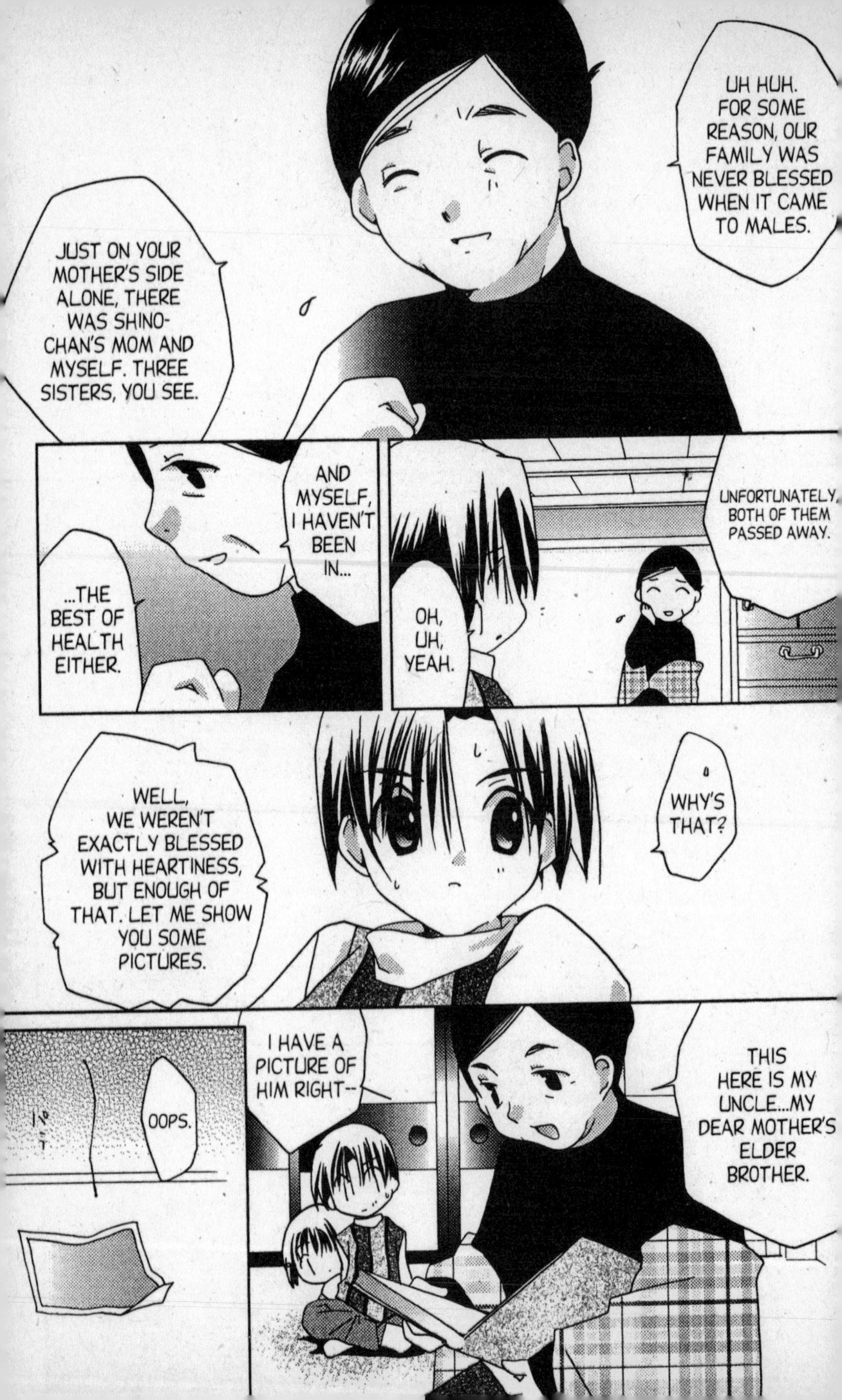
UH HUH. FOR SOME REASON, OUR FAMILY WAS NEVER BLESSED WHEN IT CAME TO MALES.
JUST ON YOUR MOTHER'S SIDE ALONE, THERE WAS SHINO-CHAN'S MOM AND MYSELF. THREE SISTERS, YOU SEE.
UNFORTUNATELY, BOTH OF THEM PASSED AWAY.
OH, UH, YEAH.
AND MYSELF, I HAVEN'T BEEN IN...
...THE BEST OF HEALTH EITHER.
WHY'S THAT?
WELL, WE WEREN'T EXACTLY BLESSED WITH HEARTINESS, BUT ENOUGH OF THAT. LET ME SHOW YOU SOME PICTURES.
THIS HERE IS MY UNCLE...MY DEAR MOTHER'S ELDER BROTHER.
I HAVE A PICTURE OF HIM RIGHT--
OOPS.

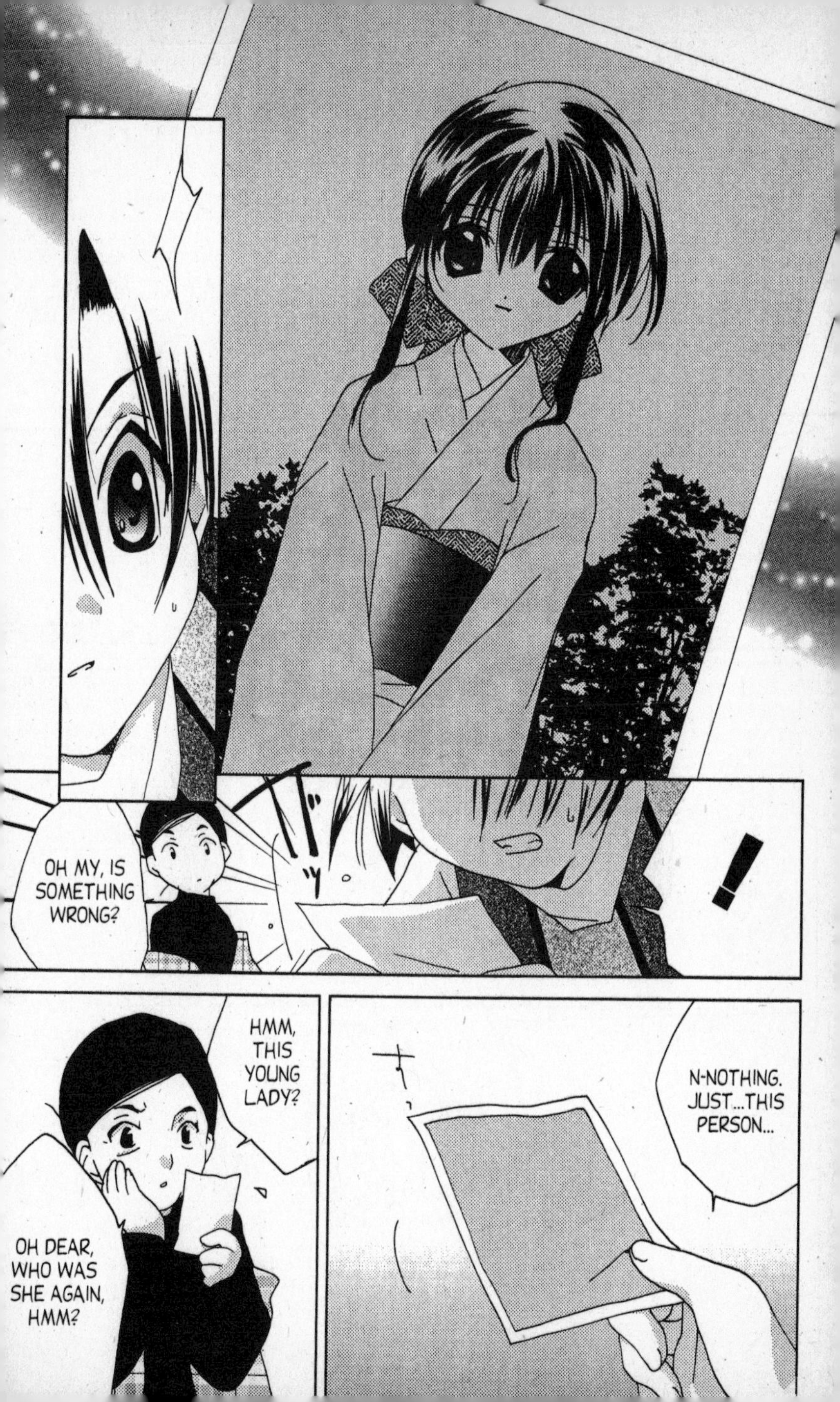
!
OH MY, IS SOMETHING WRONG?
N-NOTHING. JUST...THIS PERSON...
HMM, THIS YOUNG LADY?
OH DEAR, WHO WAS SHE AGAIN, HMM?

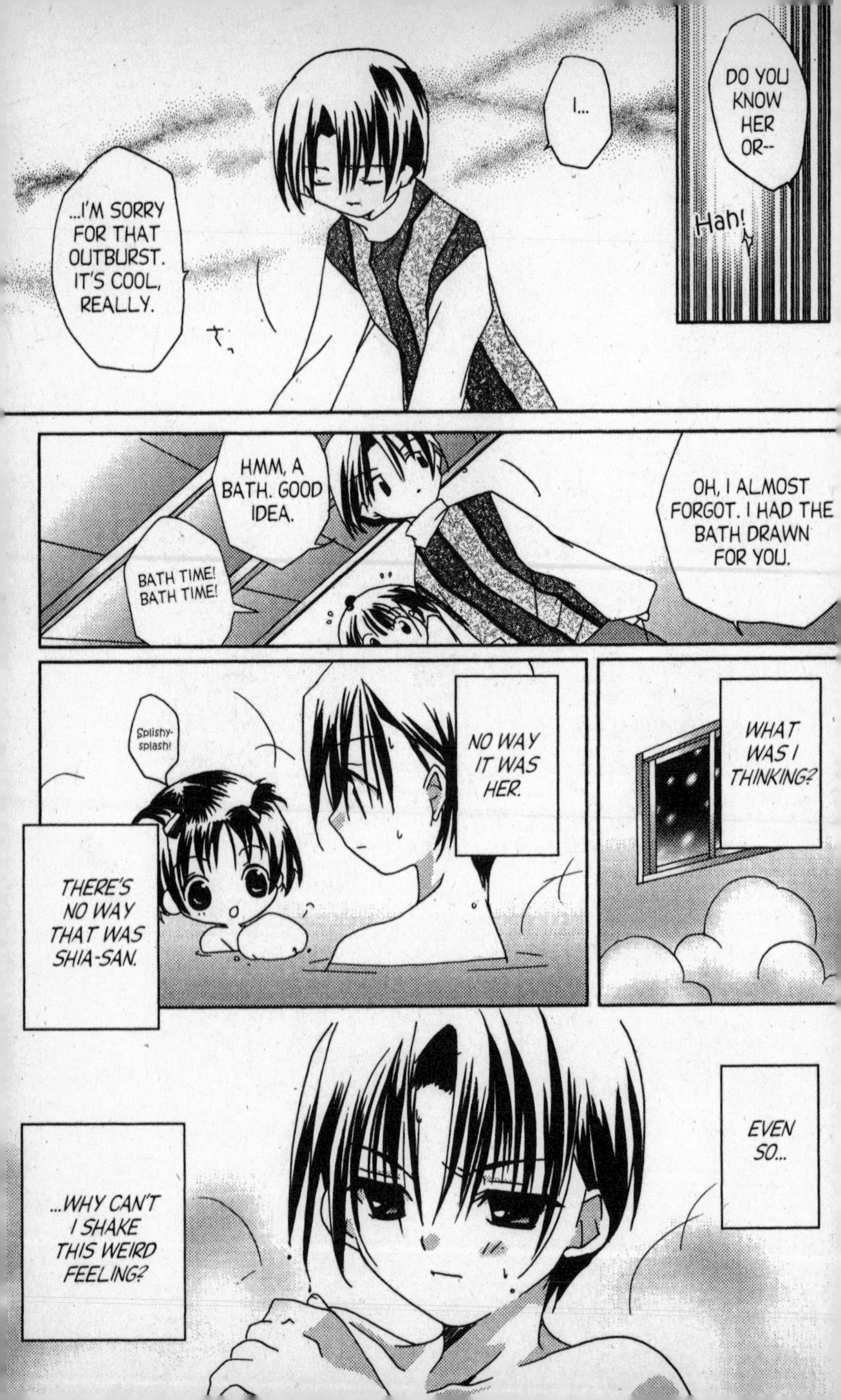
DO YOU KNOW HER OR--
Hah!
I...
...I'M SORRY FOR THAT OUTBURST. IT'S COOL, REALLY.
OH, I ALMOST FORGOT. I HAD THE BATH DRAWN FOR YOU.
HMM, A BATH. GOOD IDEA.
BATH TIME! BATH TIME!
WHAT WAS I THINKING?
NO WAY IT WAS HER.
Splishy-splash!
THERE'S NO WAY THAT WAS SHIA-SAN.
EVEN SO...
...WHY CAN'T I SHAKE THIS WEIRD FEELING?

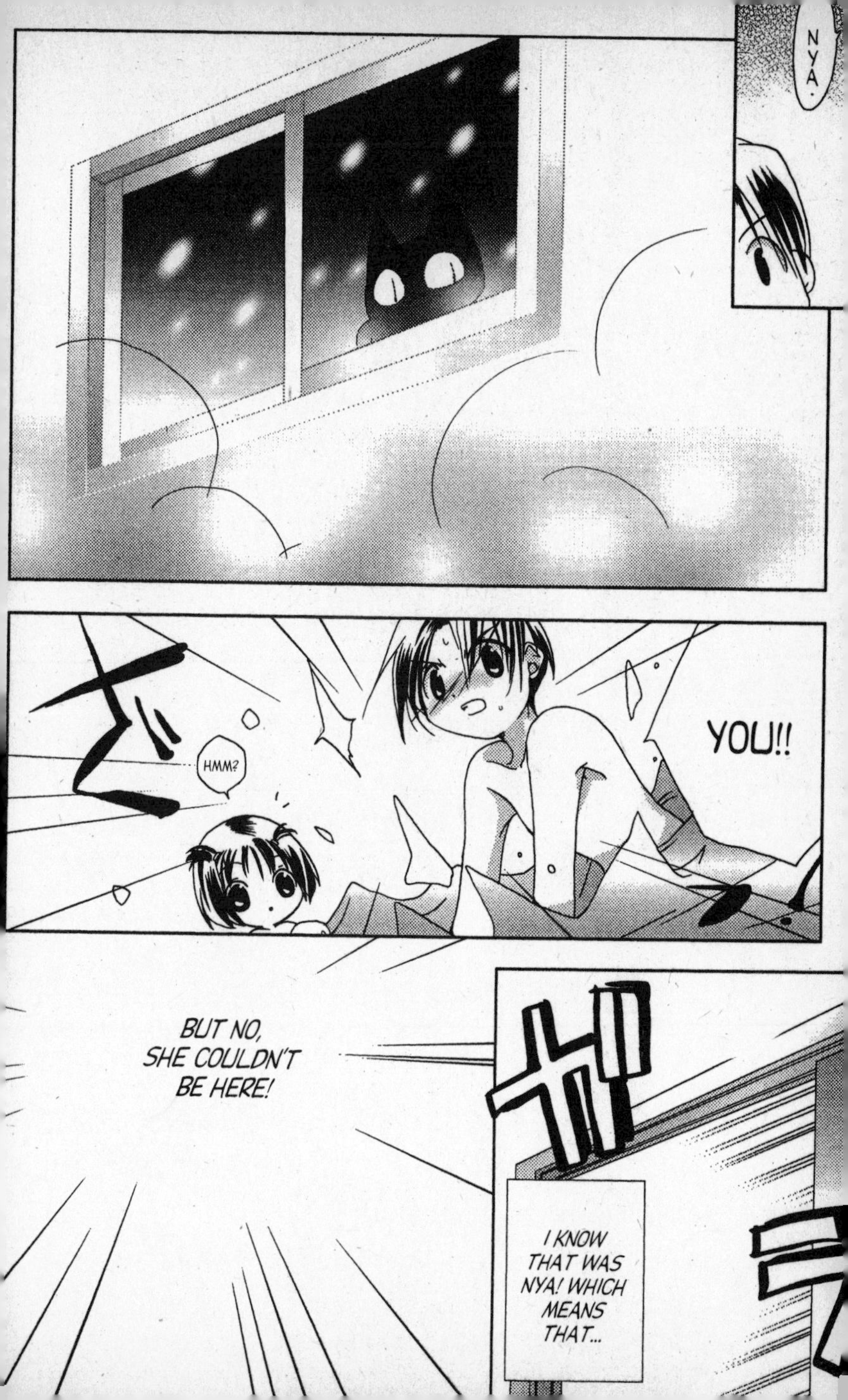
NYA.
YOU!!
HMM?
I KNOW THAT WAS NYA! WHICH MEANS THAT...
BUT NO, SHE COULDN'T BE HERE!

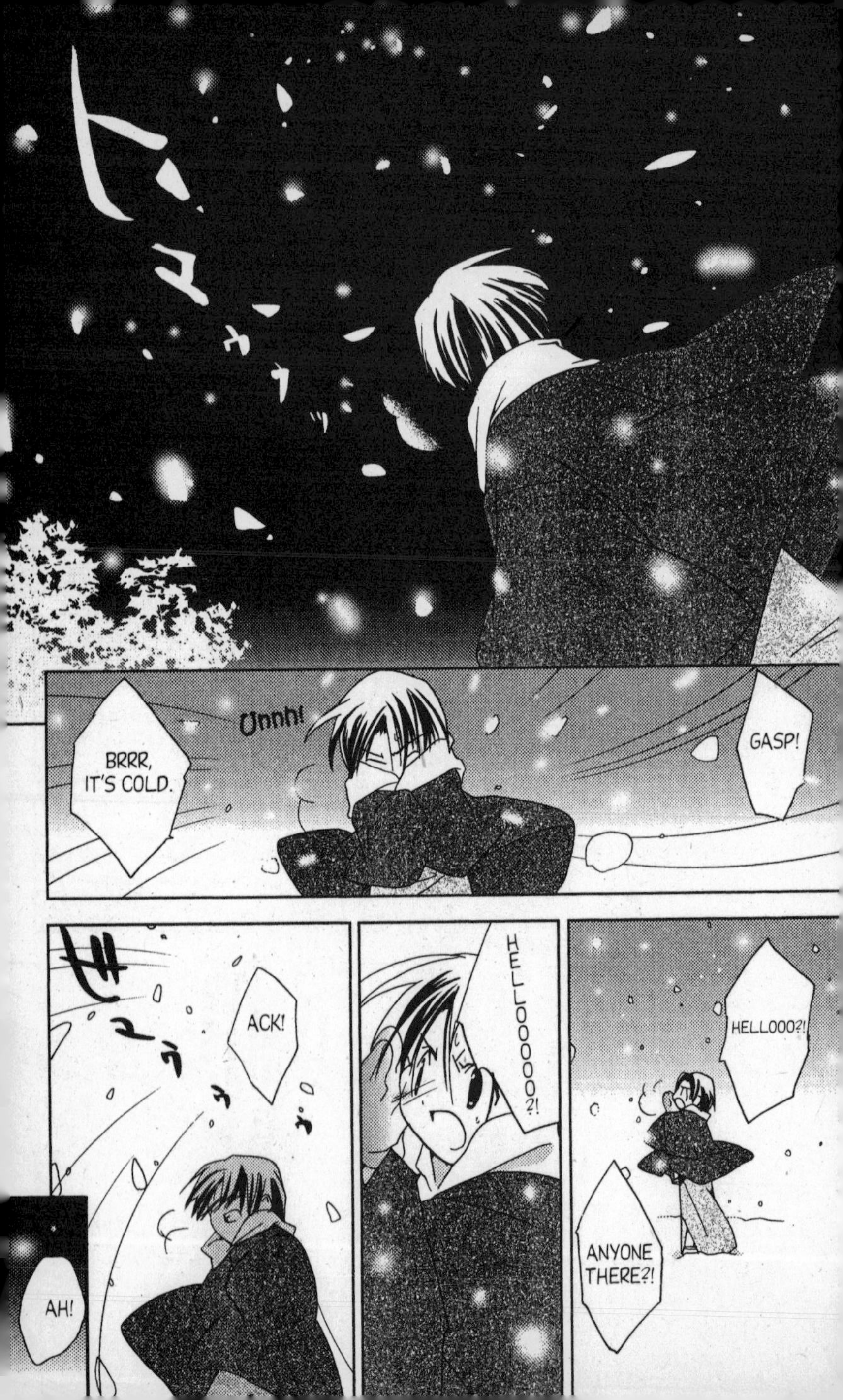
GASP!
Unnh!
BRRR, IT'S COLD.
HELLOOO?!
ANYONE THERE?!
HELLOOOOOO?!
ACK!
AH!

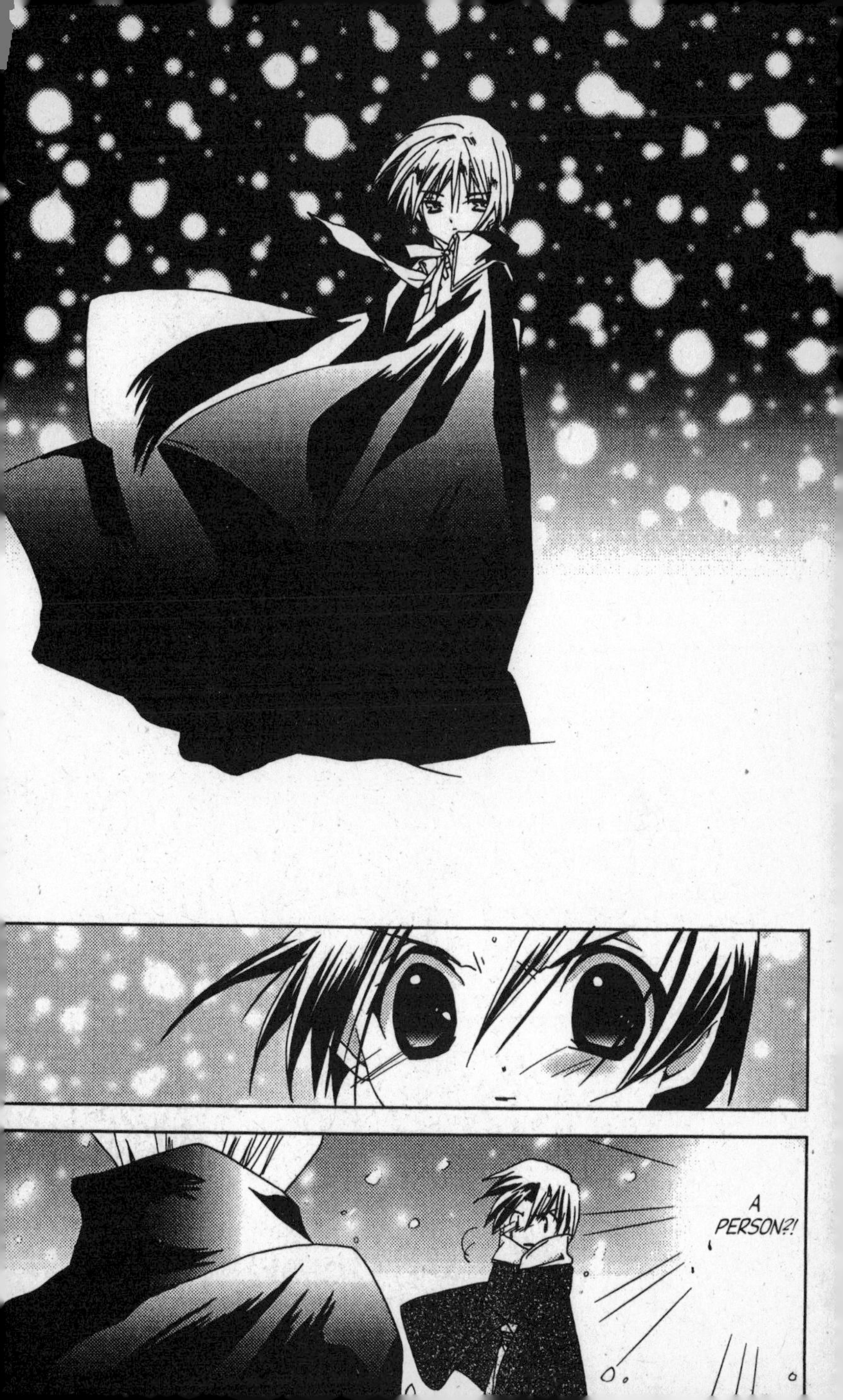
A PERSON?!

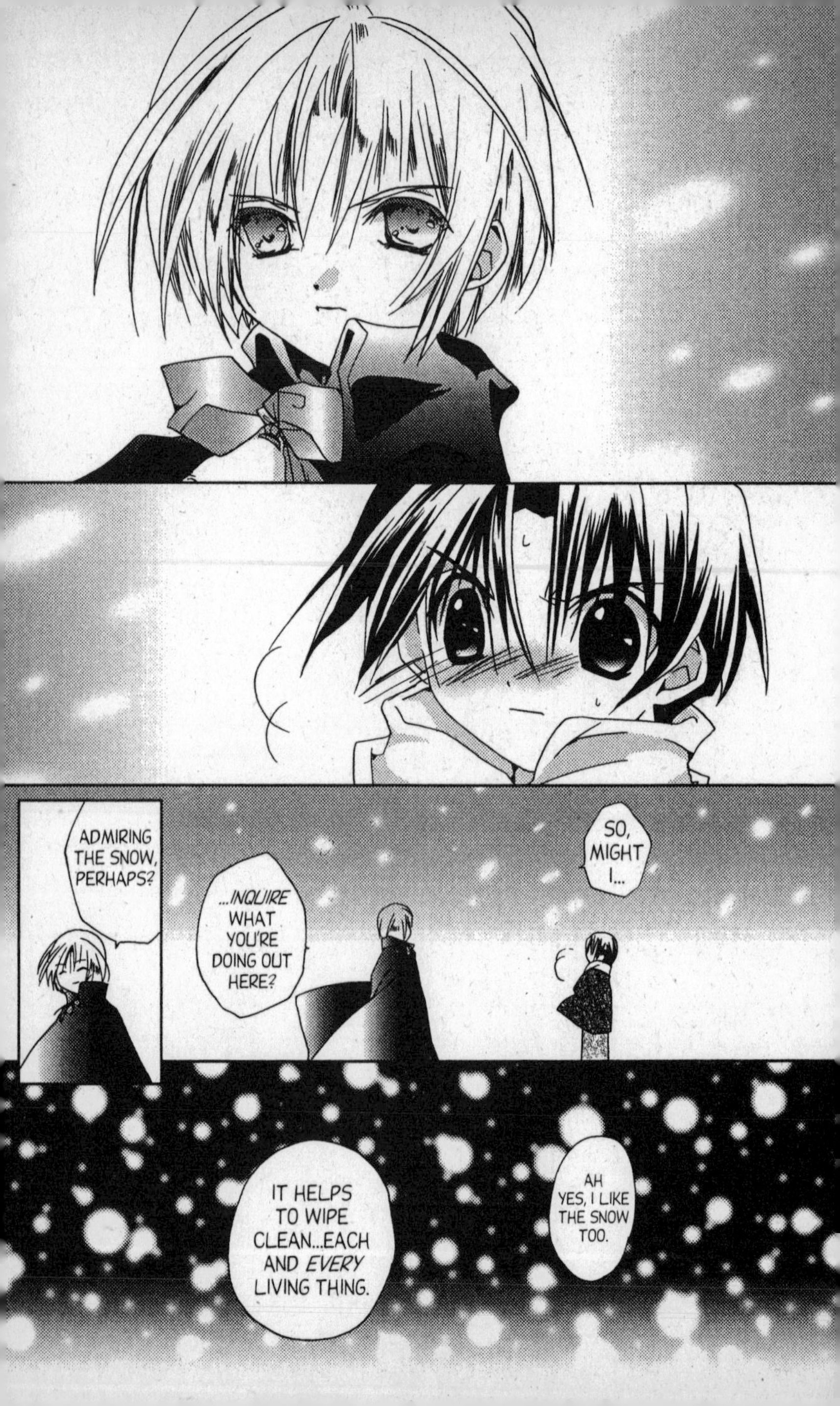
SO, MIGHT I...
...*INQUIRE* WHAT YOU'RE DOING OUT HERE?
ADMIRING THE SNOW, PERHAPS?
AH YES, I LIKE THE SNOW TOO.
IT HELPS TO WIPE CLEAN...EACH AND *EVERY* LIVING THING.

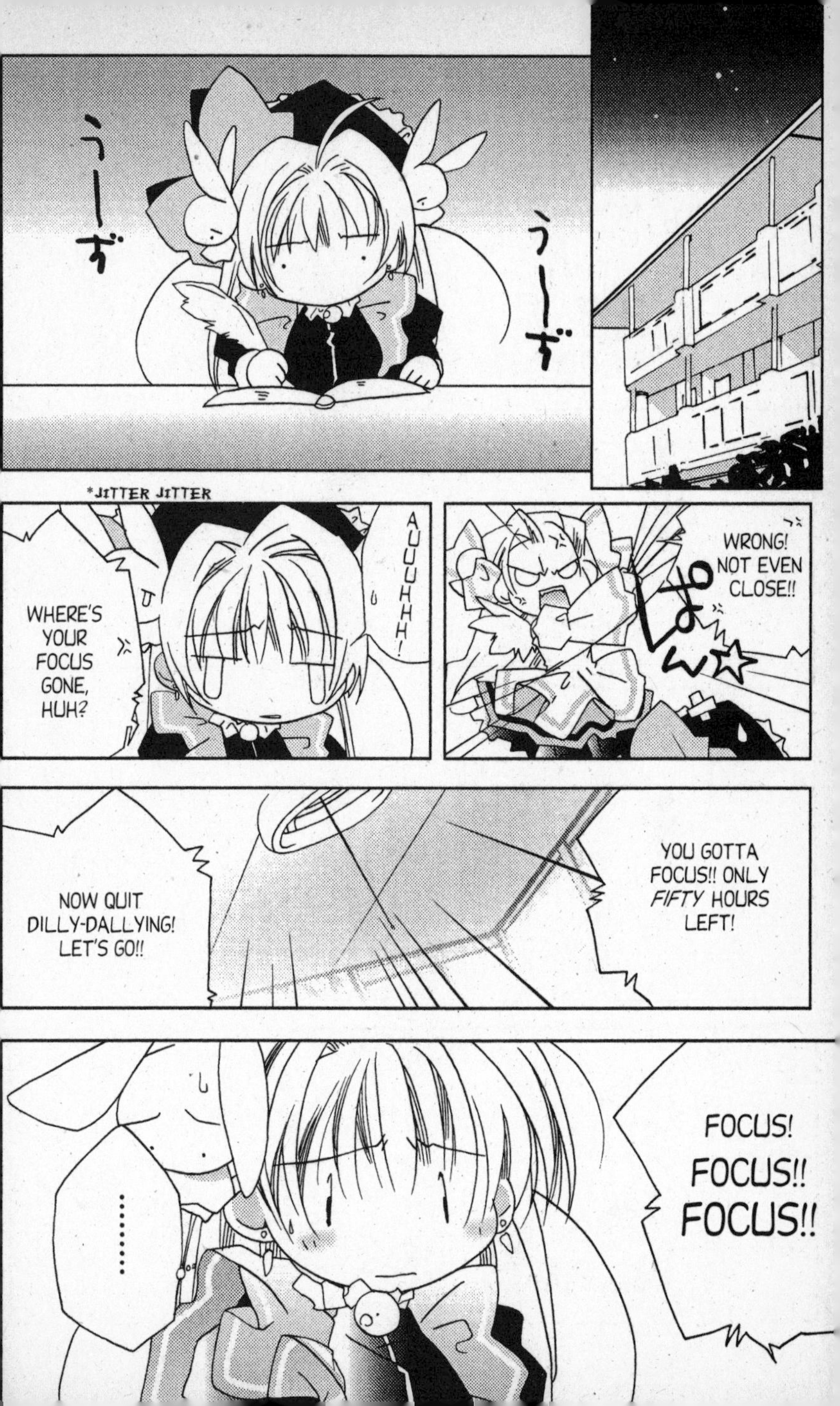

うーず
うーず
*JITTER JITTER
WRONG! NOT EVEN CLOSE!!
ぱしん☆
AUUUHHH!
WHERE'S YOUR FOCUS GONE, HUH?
YOU GOTTA FOCUS!! ONLY FIFTY HOURS LEFT!
NOW QUIT DILLY-DALLYING! LET'S GO!!
FOCUS! FOCUS!! FOCUS!!
......

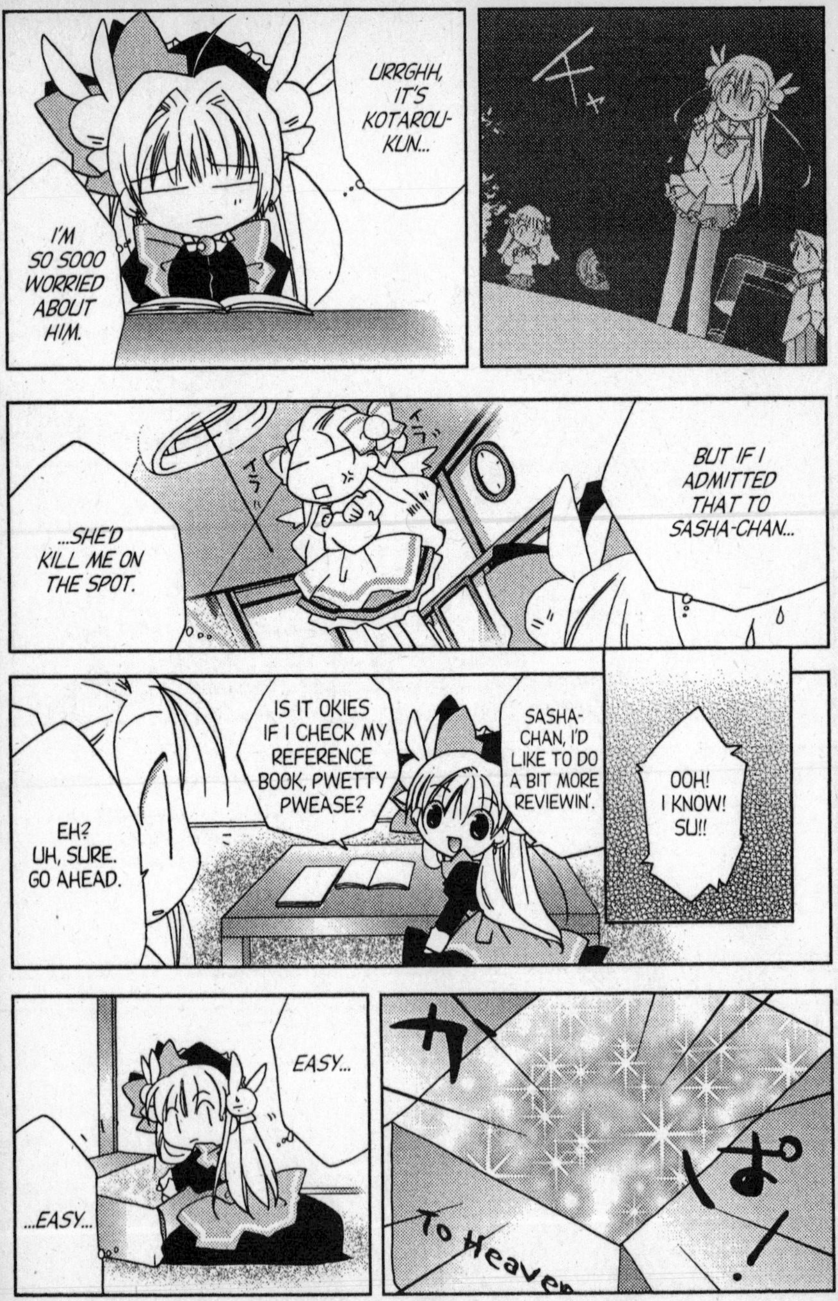
URRGHH, IT'S KOTAROU-KUN...
I'M SO SOOO WORRIED ABOUT HIM.
BUT IF I ADMITTED THAT TO SASHA-CHAN...
...SHE'D KILL ME ON THE SPOT.
OOH! I KNOW! SU!!
SASHA-CHAN, I'D LIKE TO DO A BIT MORE REVIEWIN'.
IS IT OKIES IF I CHECK MY REFERENCE BOOK, PWETTY PWEASE?
EH? UH, SURE. GO AHEAD.
カ
ぱっ!
To Heaven
EASY...
...EASY...

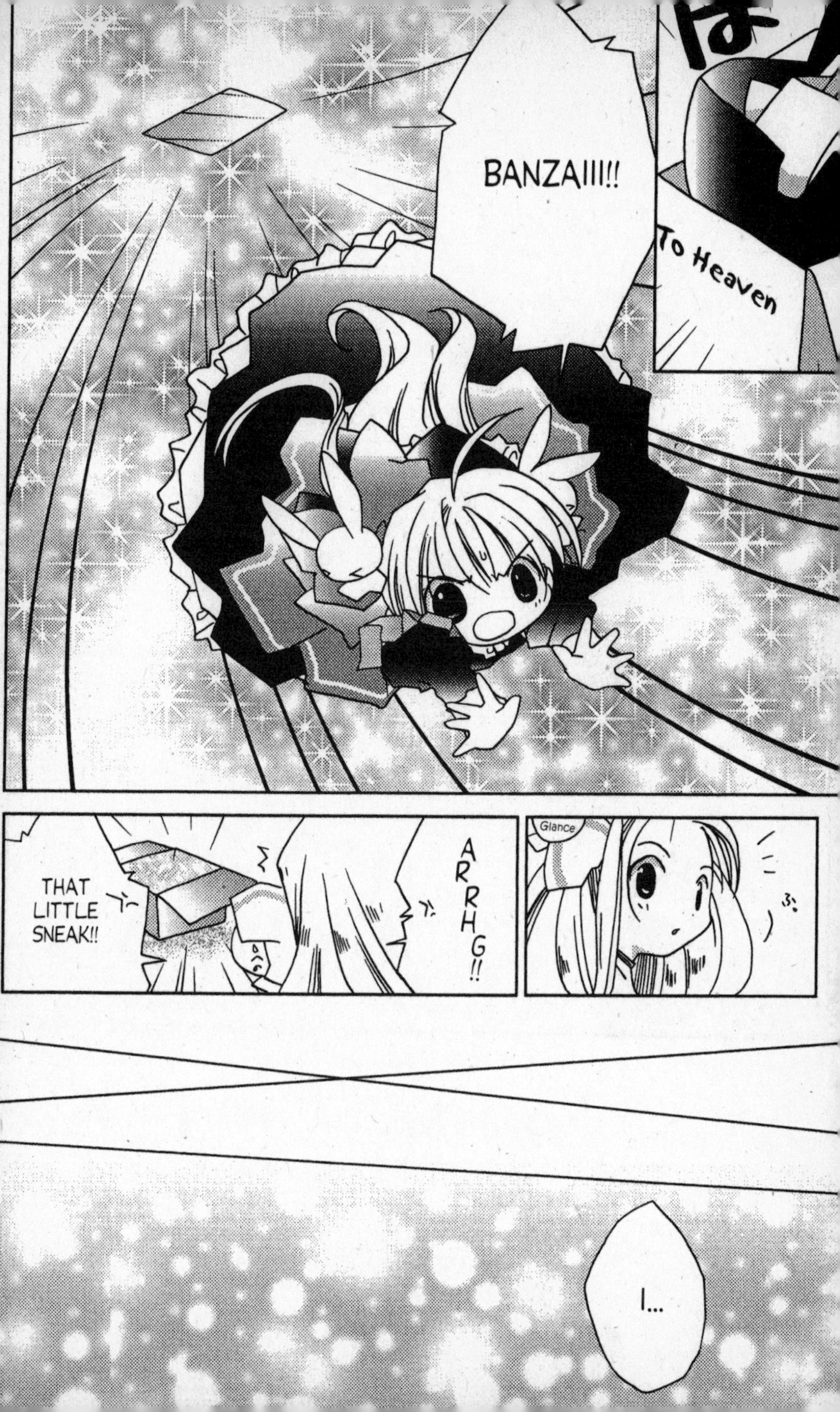
To Heaven
BANZAIIII!!
Glance
ARRHG!!
THAT LITTLE SNEAK!!
I...

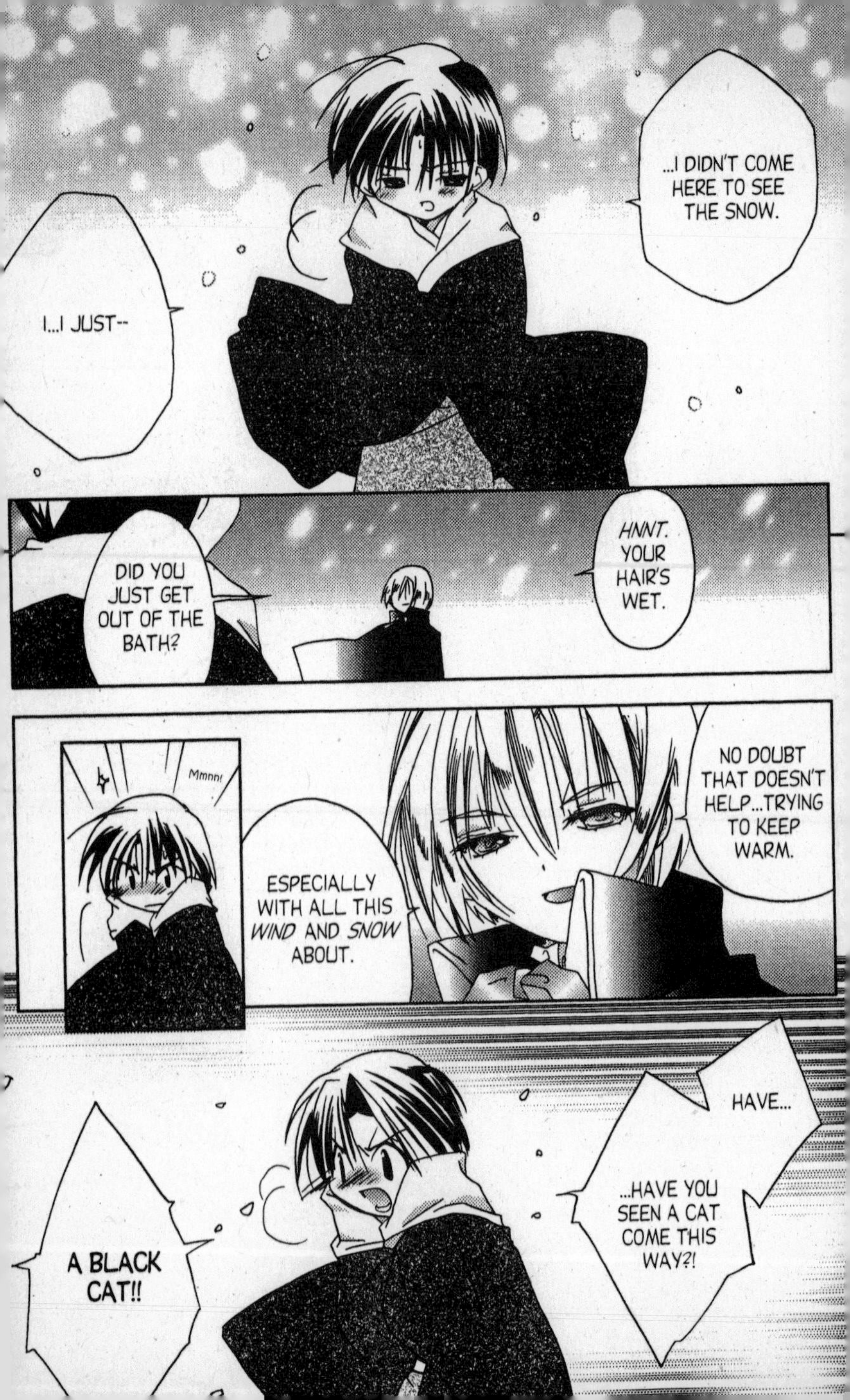
...I DIDN'T COME HERE TO SEE THE SNOW.
I...I JUST--
HNNT. YOUR HAIR'S WET.
DID YOU JUST GET OUT OF THE BATH?
NO DOUBT THAT DOESN'T HELP...TRYING TO KEEP WARM.
ESPECIALLY WITH ALL THIS WIND AND SNOW ABOUT.
Mmnn!
HAVE...
...HAVE YOU SEEN A CAT COME THIS WAY?!
A BLACK CAT!!

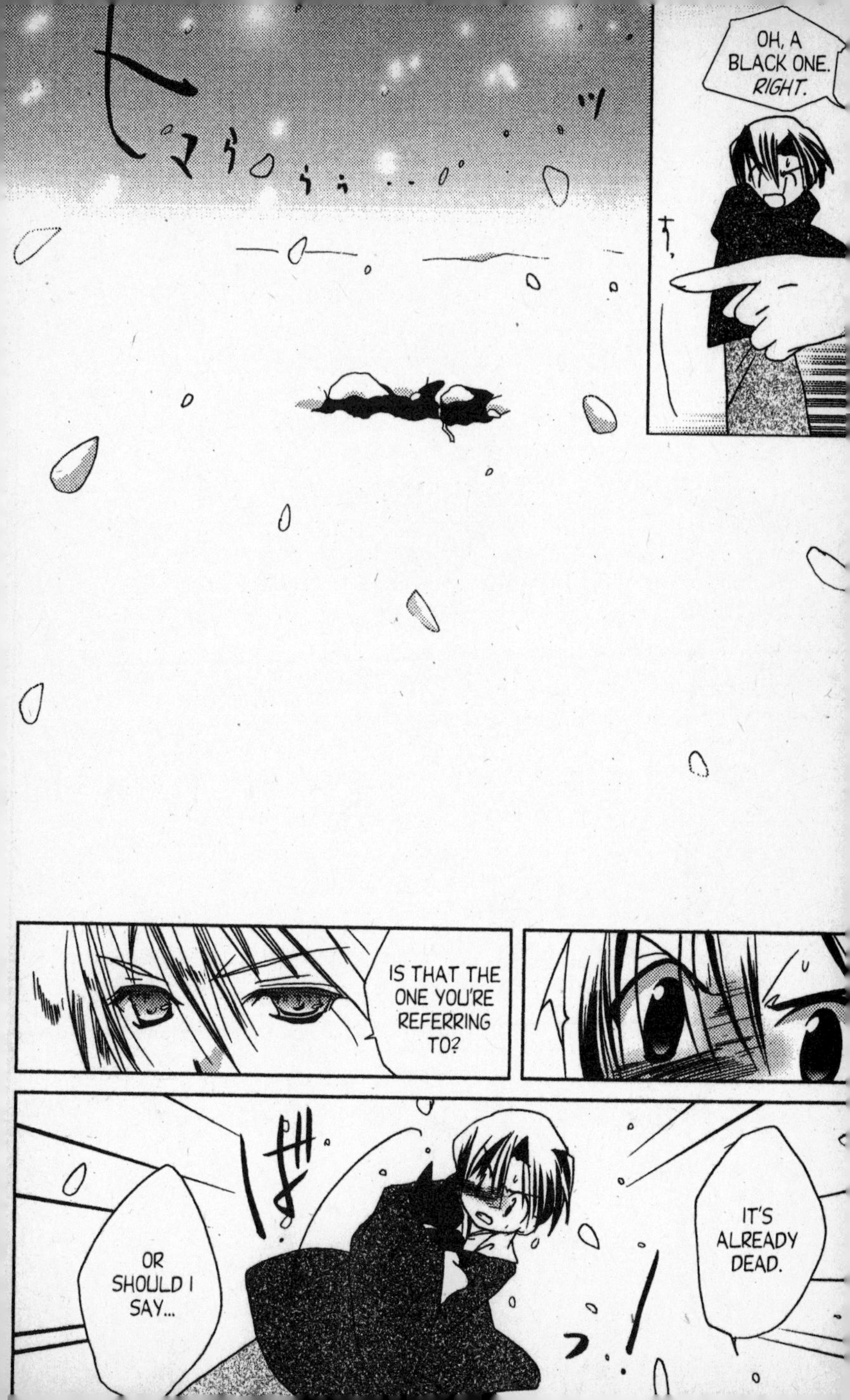
OH, A BLACK ONE. RIGHT.
IS THAT THE ONE YOU'RE REFERRING TO?
IT'S ALREADY DEAD.
OR SHOULD I SAY...

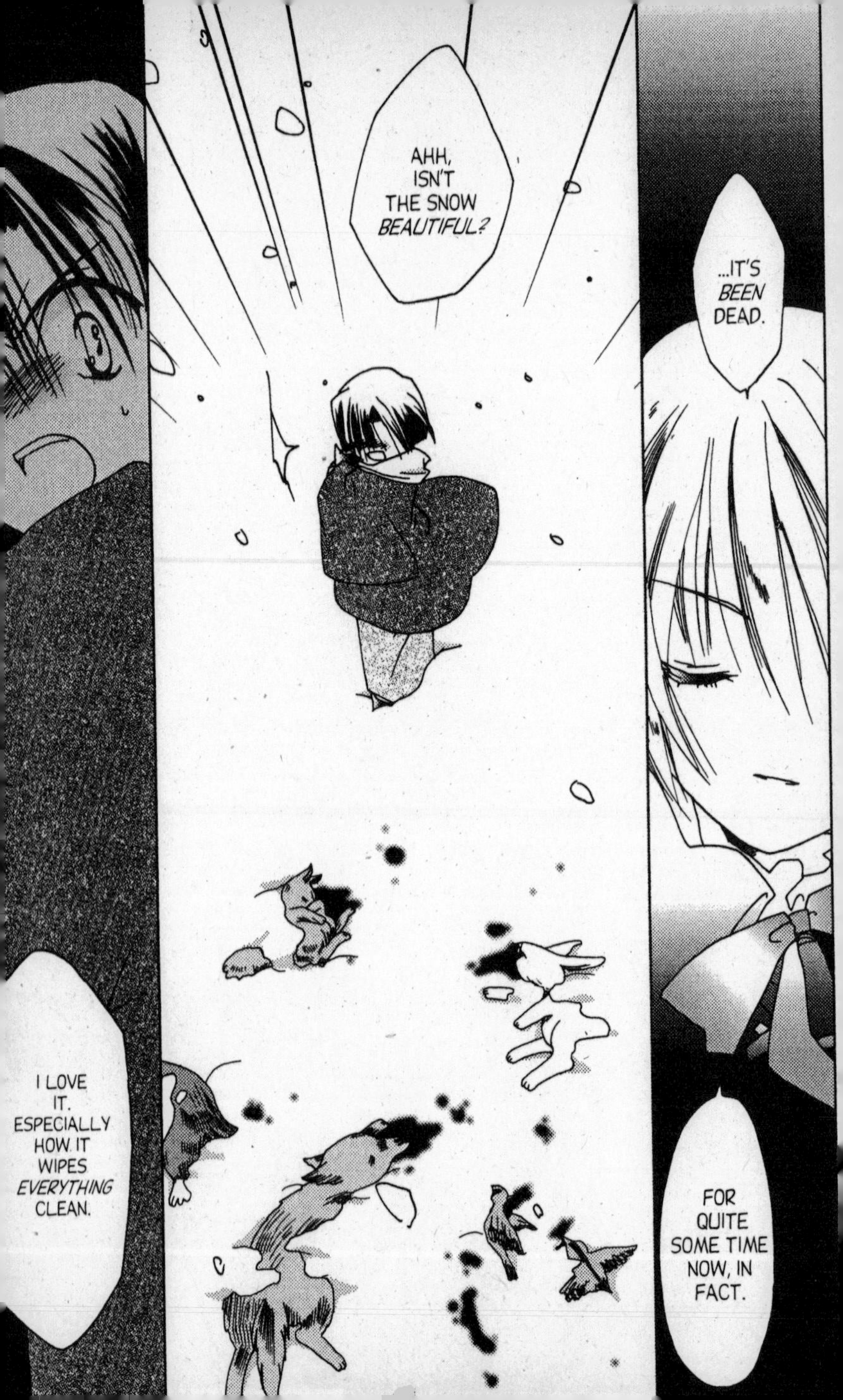
...IT'S *BEEN* DEAD.
FOR QUITE SOME TIME NOW, IN FACT.
AHH, ISN'T THE SNOW *BEAUTIFUL?*
I LOVE IT. ESPECIALLY HOW IT WIPES *EVERYTHING* CLEAN.

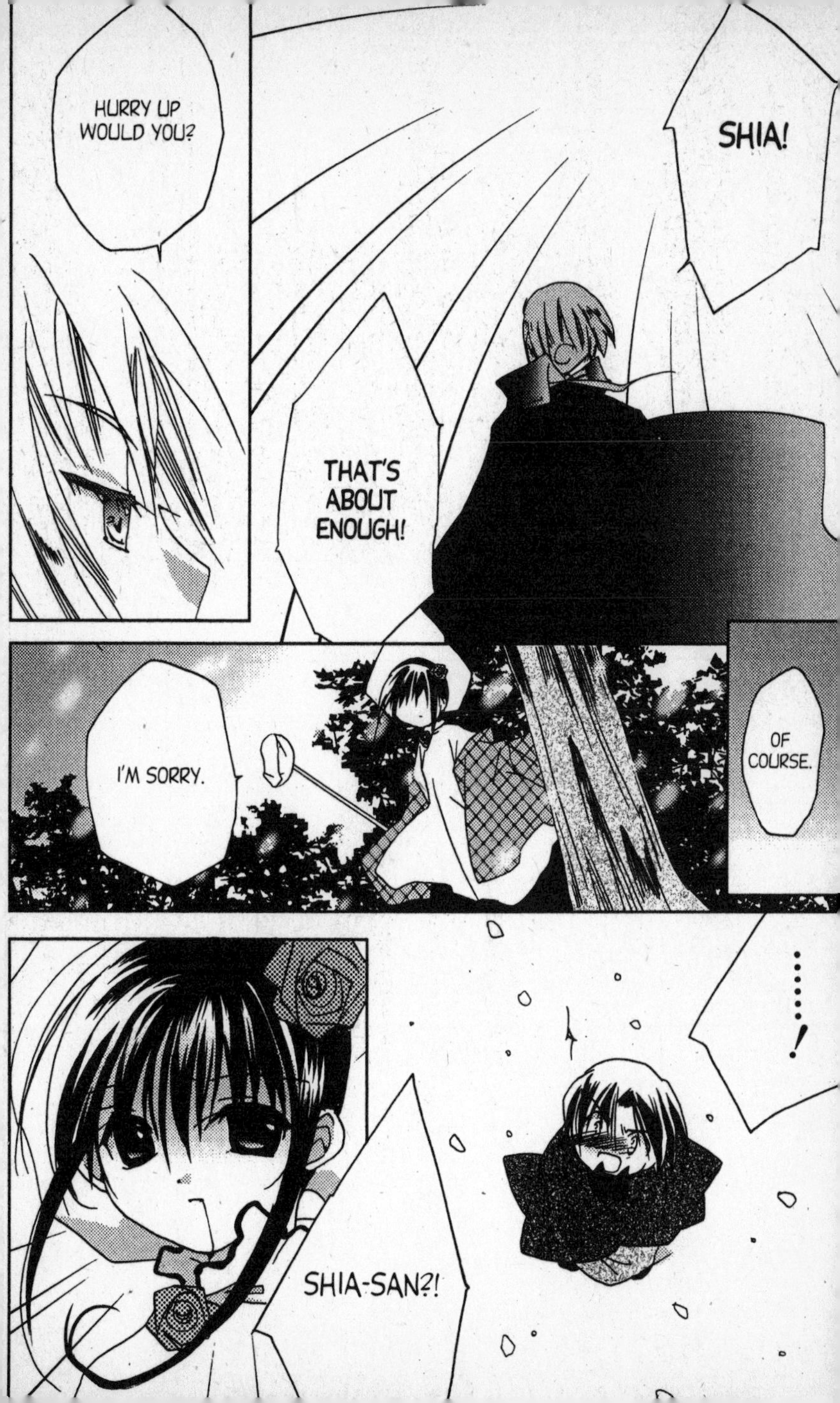
SHIA!
THAT'S ABOUT ENOUGH!
HURRY UP WOULD YOU?
OF COURSE.
I'M SORRY.
......!
SHIA-SAN?!

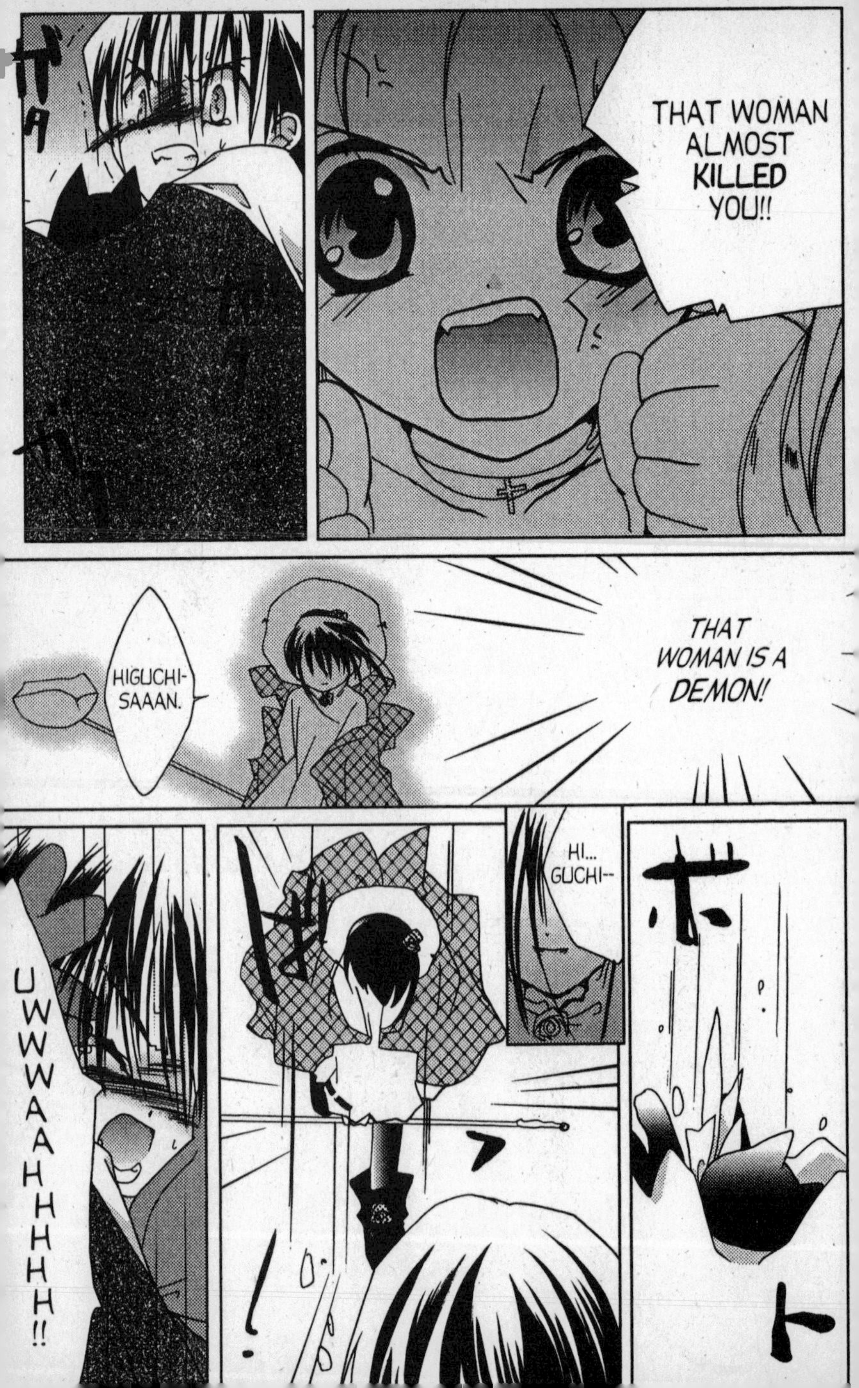
THAT WOMAN ALMOST KILLED YOU!!
THAT WOMAN IS A DEMON!
HIGUCHI-SAAAN.
HI... GUCHI--
UWWWAAHHHHHH!!

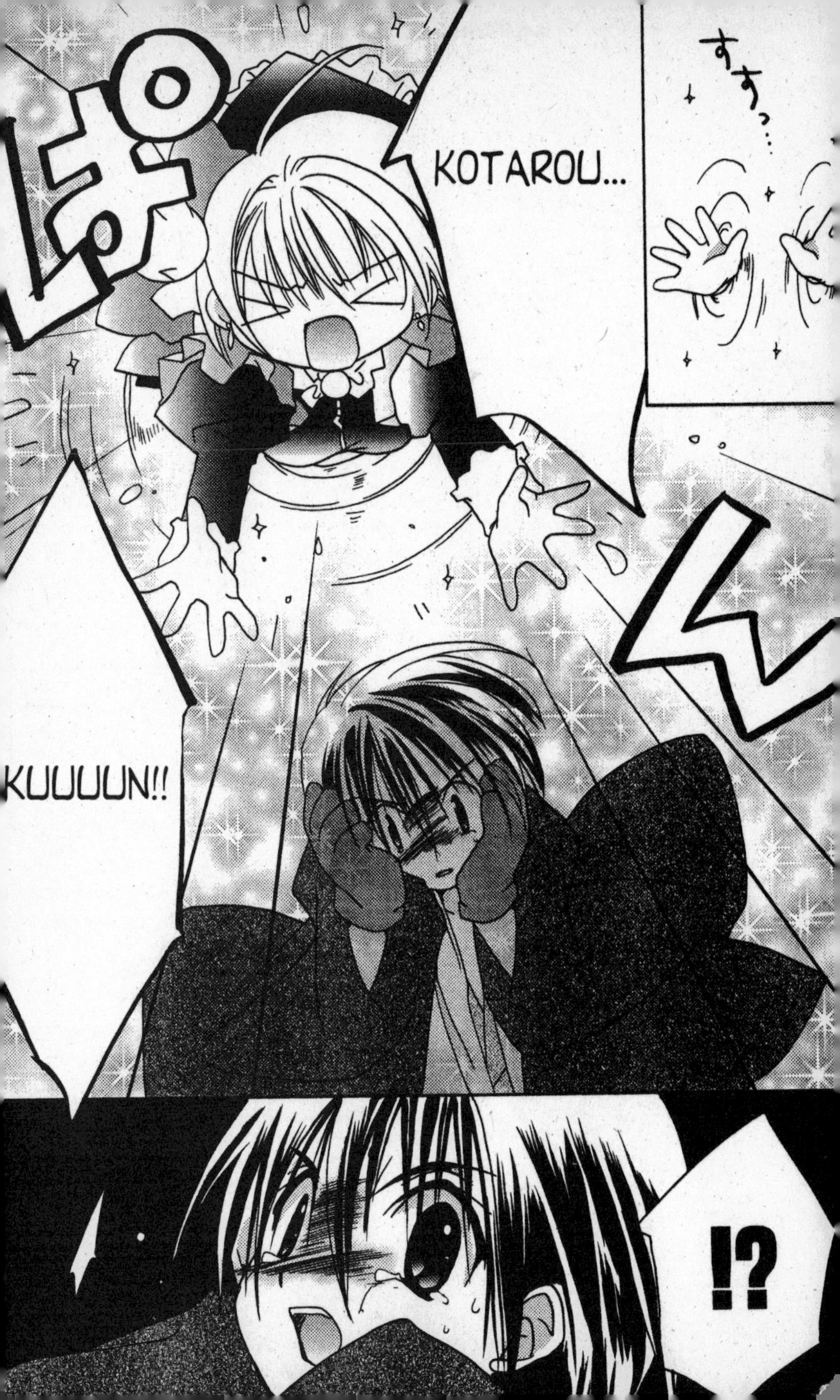

すすっ…
KOTAROU...
KUUUUN!!
!?

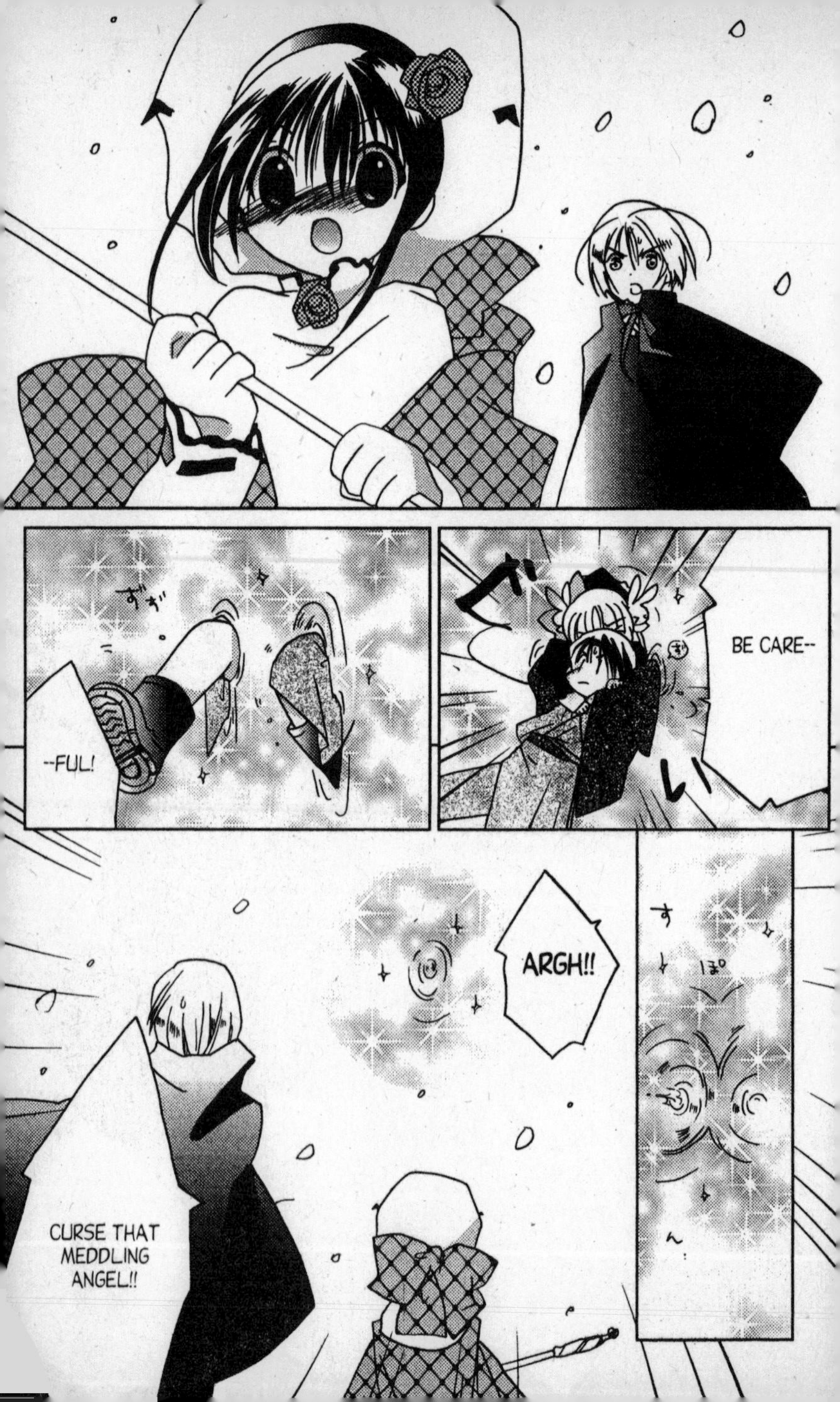
BE CARE--
--FUL!
ARGH!!
CURSE THAT MEDDLING ANGEL!!

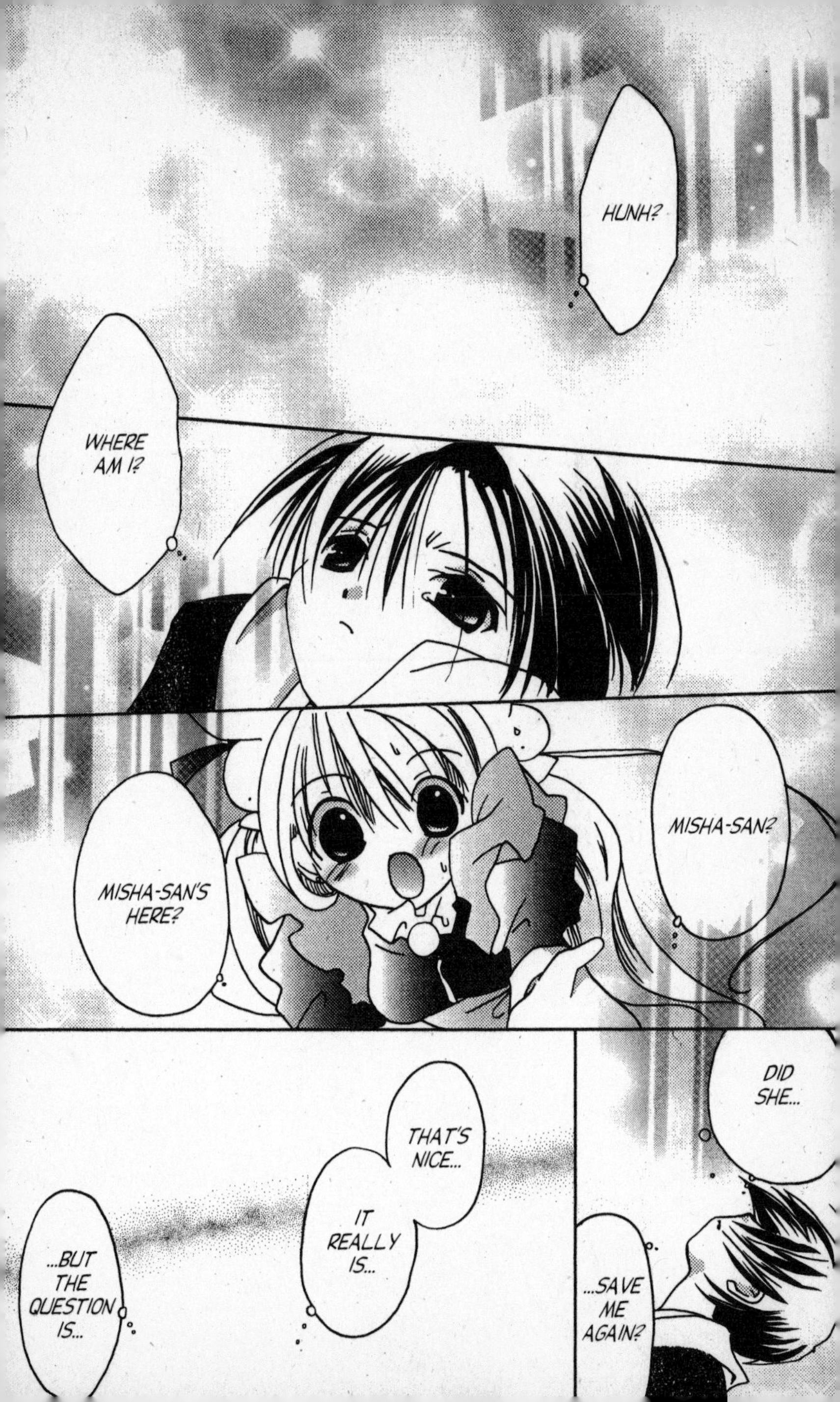
HUNH?
WHERE AM I?
MISHA-SAN?
MISHA-SAN'S HERE?
DID SHE...
...SAVE ME AGAIN?
THAT'S NICE...
IT REALLY IS...
...BUT THE QUESTION IS...

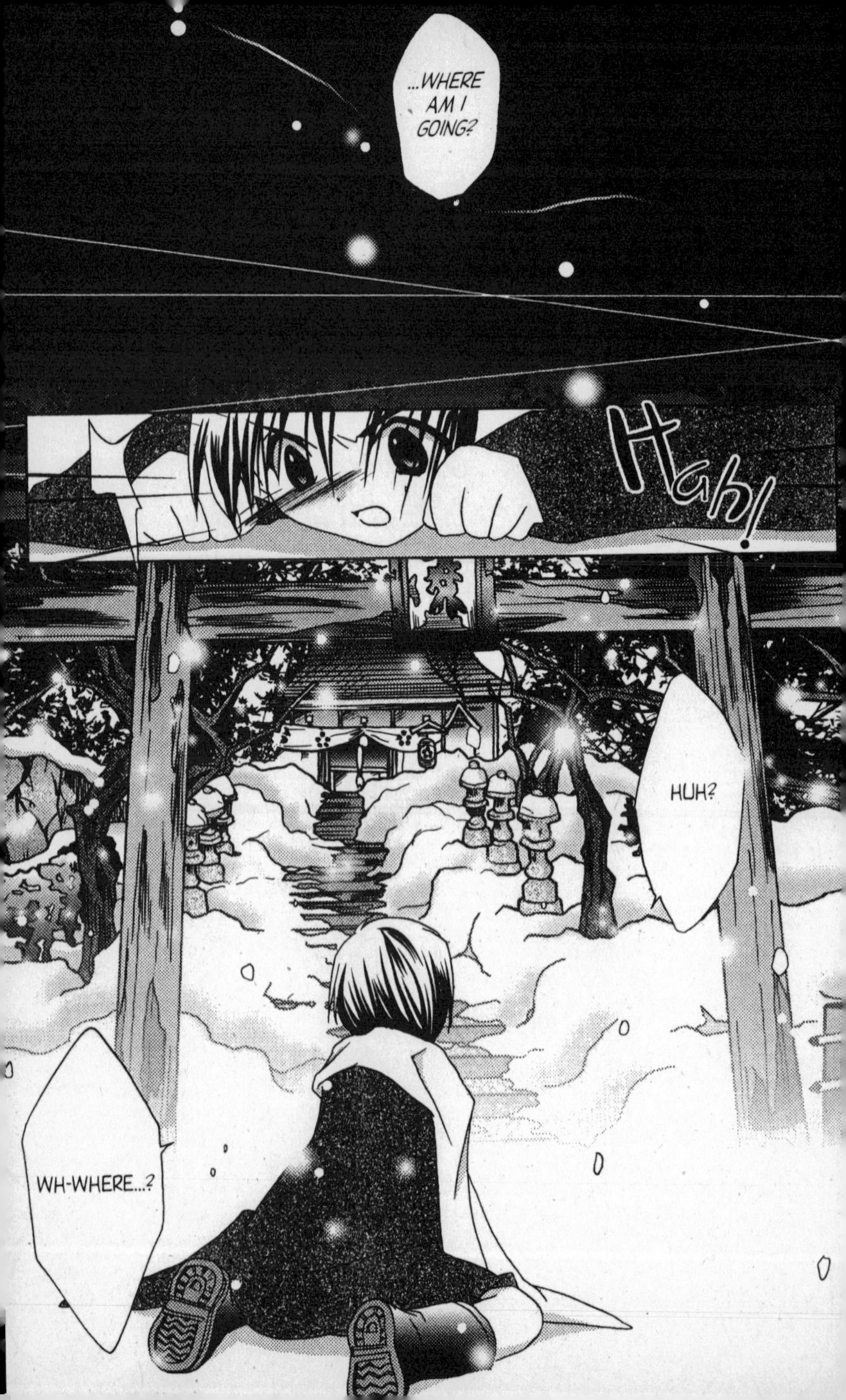
...WHERE AM I GOING?
Hah!
HUH?
WH-WHERE...?

◆Hello everyone!! Koge-Donbo here! *Pita-Ten's* finally in its fifth volume! I think I say this every single time, but the only reason I am blessed enough to continue releasing comics is because of you guys out there. So thank you so much!!

◆Every time I work on releasing a compilation like this one, I always find myself looking at the pages I drew half-a-year ago and thinking, "Oh my god! Look at those drawings!! *They suck!!*" (Every single time, I swear, I say this. It's almost annoying.) Recently I re-read Volume 1 and man was that a hard read, if I may say so myself. Absolutely no flow at all! Plus, it didn't help that the first chapter didn't have a lot of pages to begin with. The other thing I think is, it seems that this particular installment was run problem-free, but let me tell you, there were tons and tons of problems each and every time. The actual drawing part I'm pretty quick with, but it's the drafts that just take me *FOREVER* to do. Yup, I get stuck everywhere. It's like I'm trying to think of a story and weave it through, but...auhhhh...or, like, I'll have a good premise, but just no way of working it in or something. I think I'm an idiot half the time. Yeah... Thank you, Midorino-san, for all the help you provide me!

◆I'm very sorry that there's no real tying factor to the story...but I do have to admit that it was a lot of fun for me to draw all the traditional Japanese outfits that appear in the later episodes of this book!♥ I was actually quite pleasantly surprised with myself for drawing them with such detail.
Anyhow, I hope to see you again in Volume 6!! ♥♥ - 4.5.2002 - Koge-Donbo

Oh yeah, I forgot to mention that I was born and raised in Tokyo. So to be quite honest, I speak very normal Japanese. I had a lot of help from my assistant's friends, mothers, fathers and such with nailing the various dialects. So thank you, thank you again!

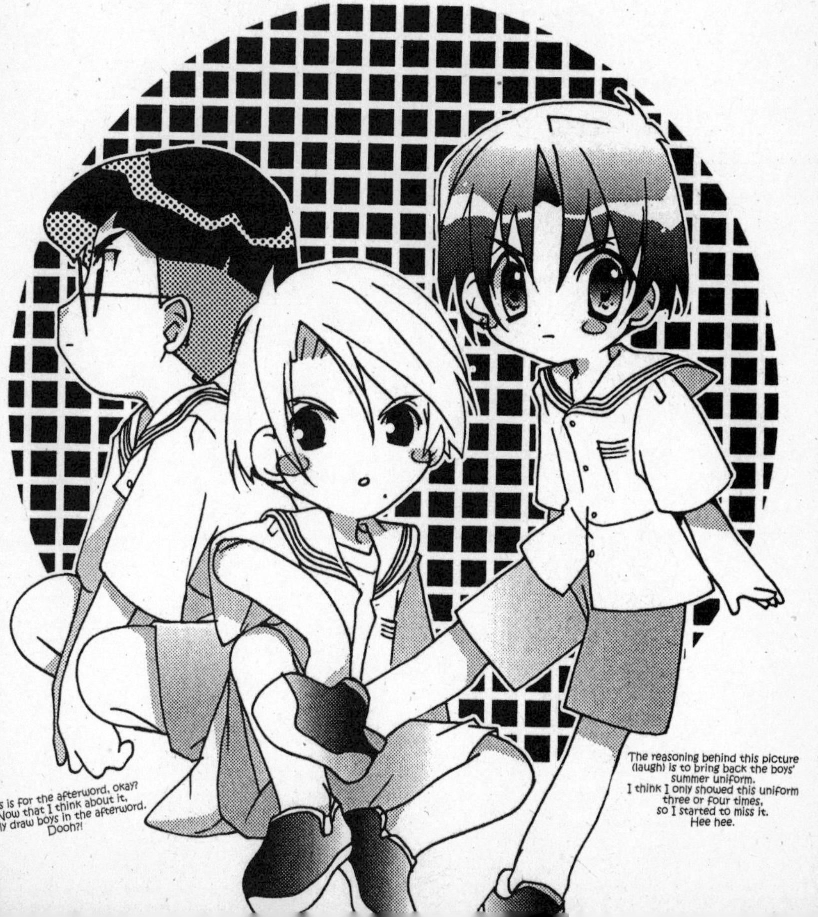
The reasoning behind this picture (laugh) is to bring back the boys' summer uniform.
I think I only showed this uniform three or four times, so I started to miss it.
Hee hee.
This is for the afterword, okay? Now that I think about it, only draw boys in the afterword. Dooh?!

Lesson 30

How to Peek Upon an Unknown Time
Part 1

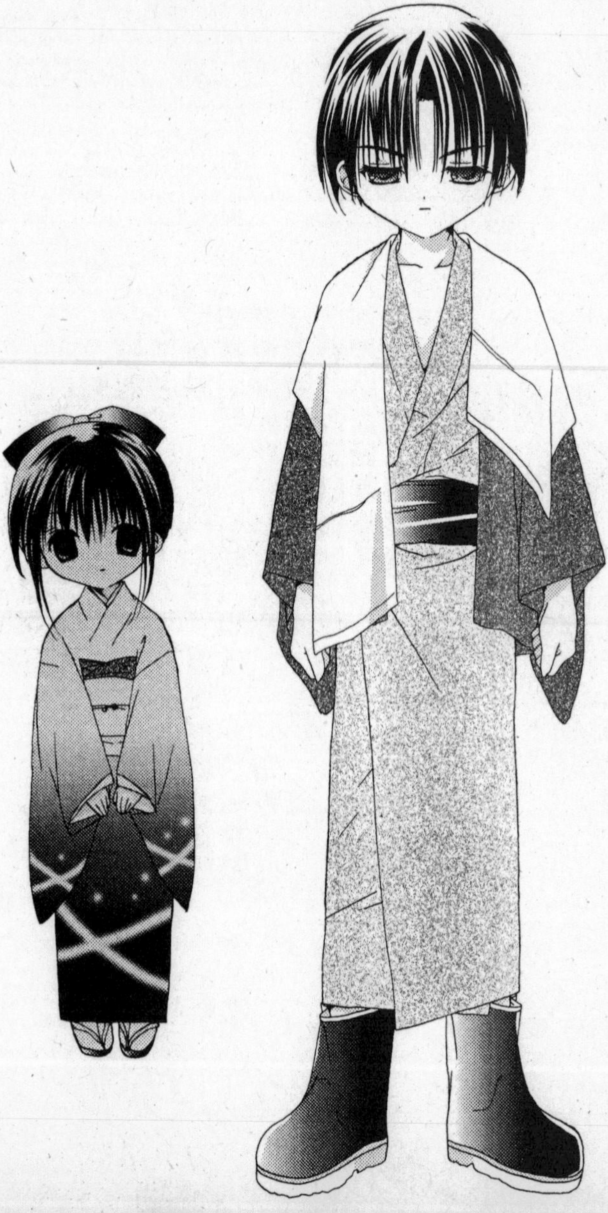

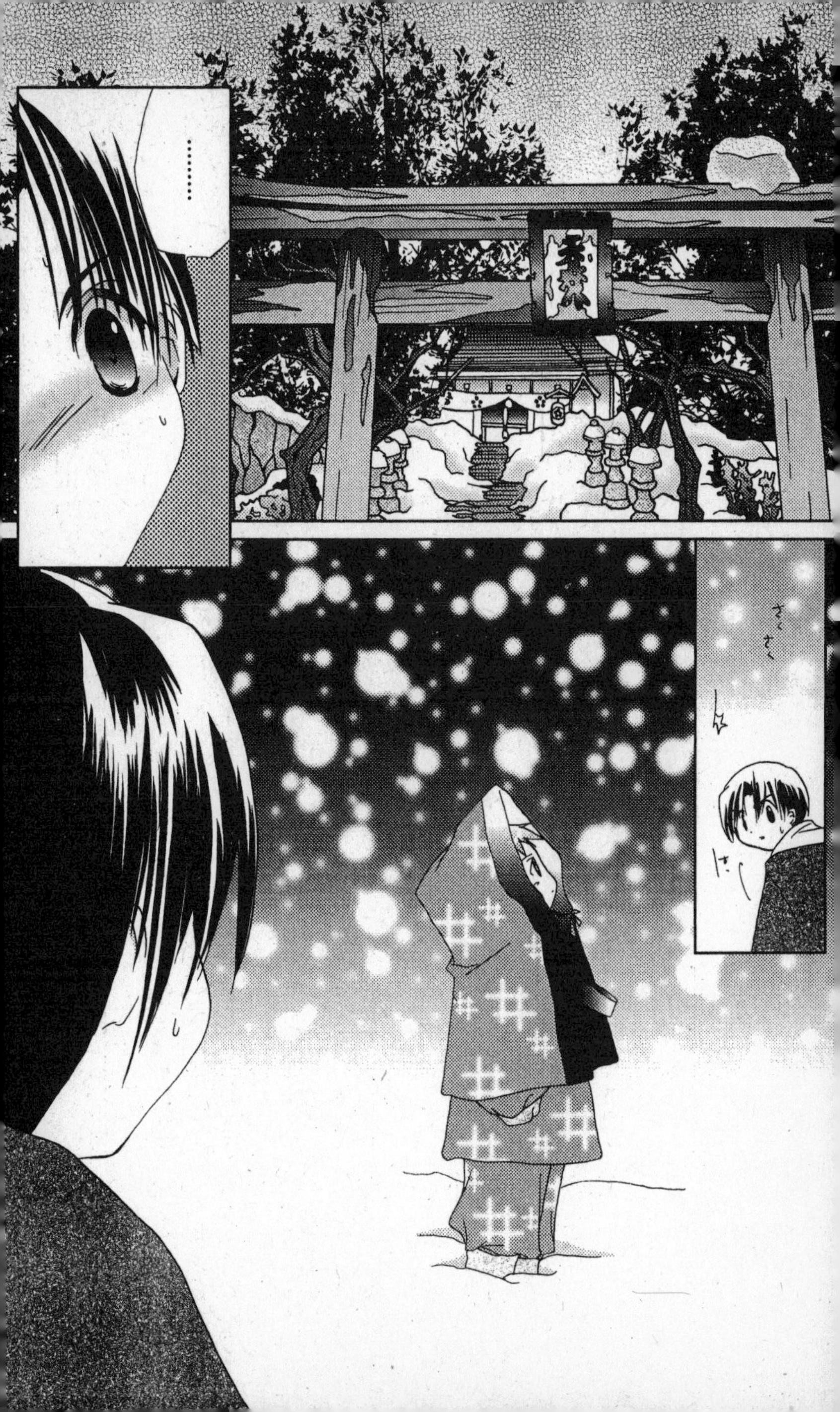
……
さく さく
はっ

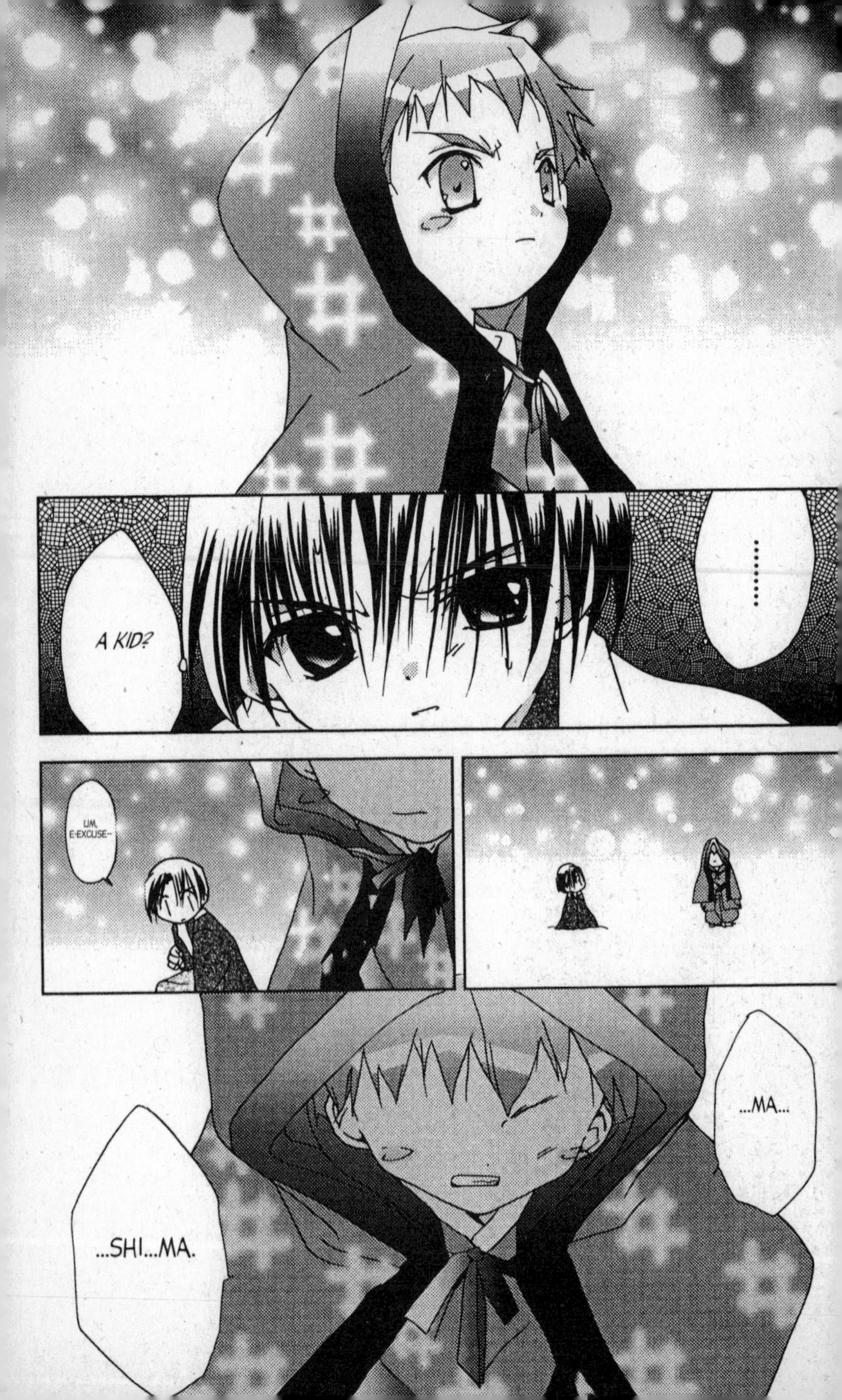
......
A KID?
UM, E-EXCUSE--
...MA...
...SHI...MA.

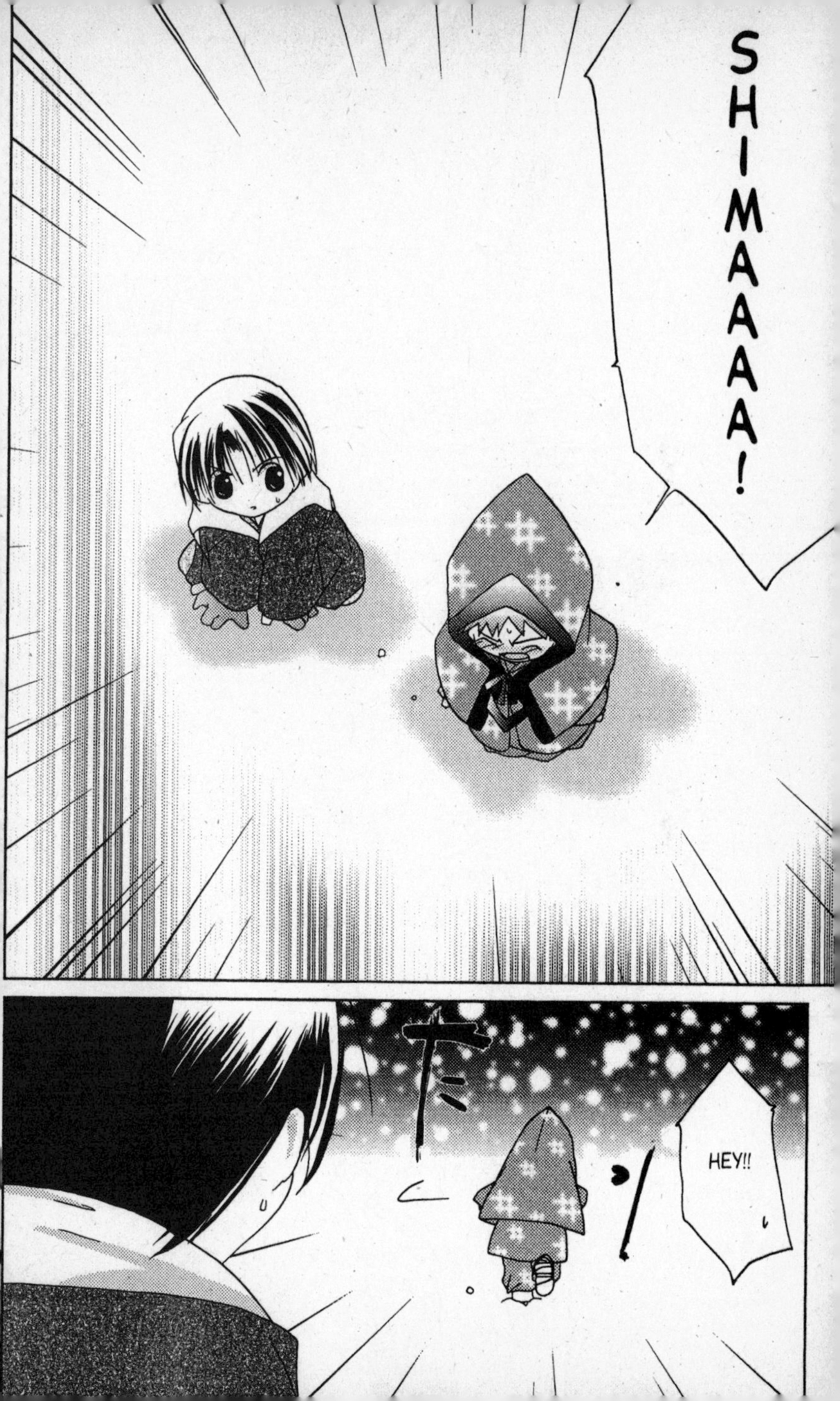
SHIMAAAAA!
HEY!!

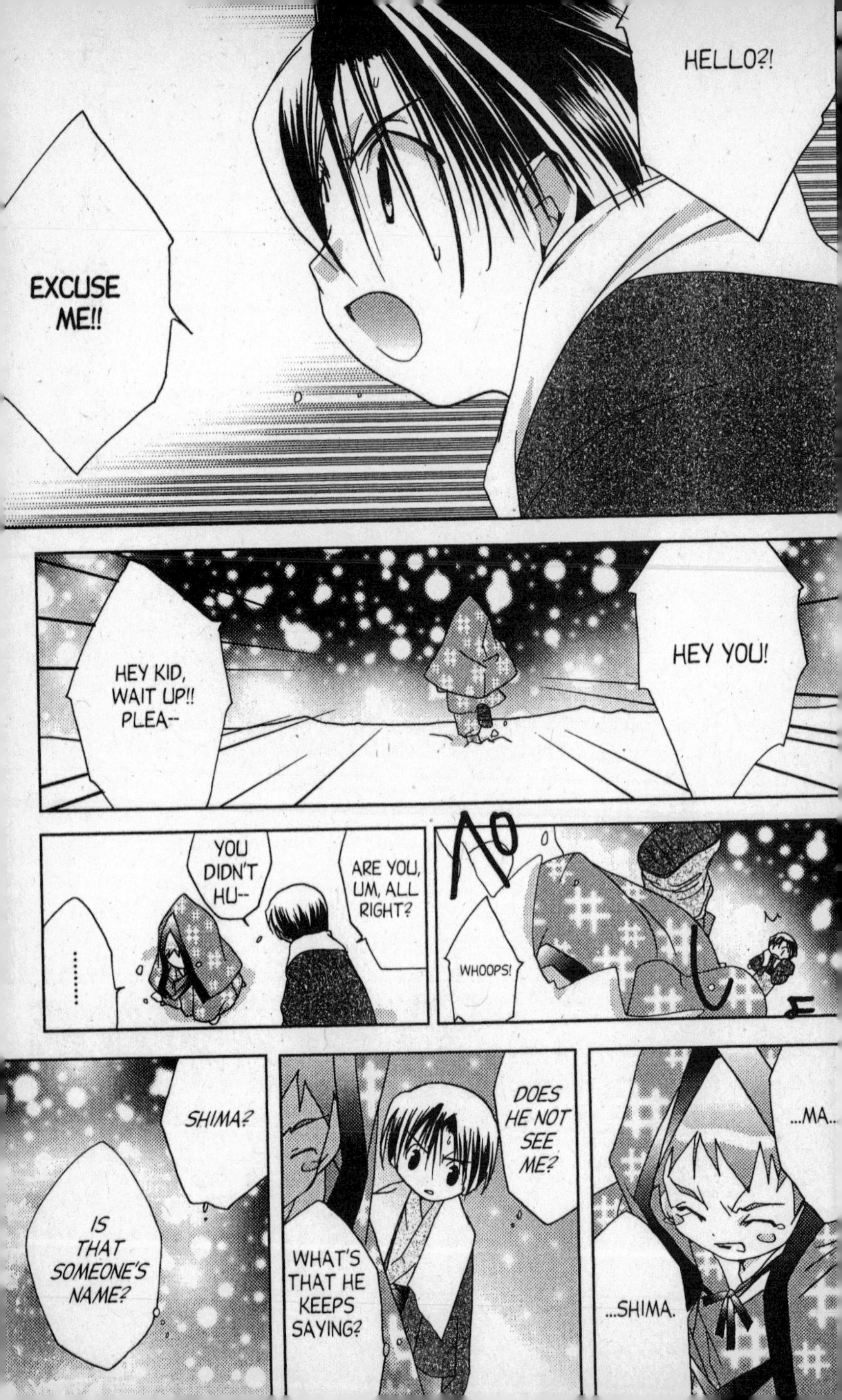
HELLO?!
EXCUSE ME!!
HEY YOU!
HEY KID, WAIT UP!! PLEA--
WHOOPS!
ARE YOU, UM, ALL RIGHT?
YOU DIDN'T HU--
......
...MA...
...SHIMA.
DOES HE NOT SEE ME?
WHAT'S THAT HE KEEPS SAYING?
SHIMA?
IS THAT SOMEONE'S NAME?

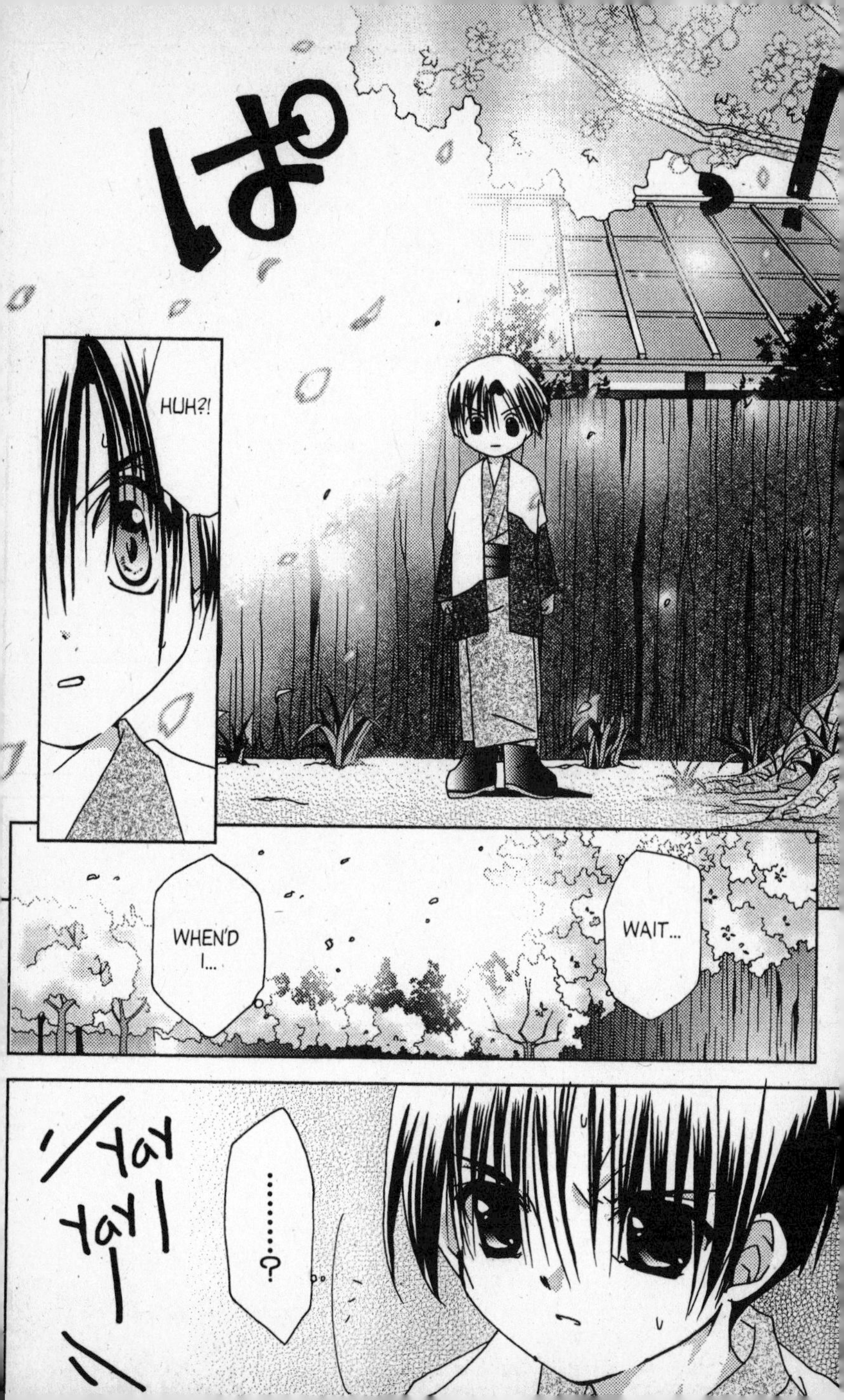
ぱっ!
HUH?!
WAIT...
WHEN'D I...
......?
YAY—YAY—

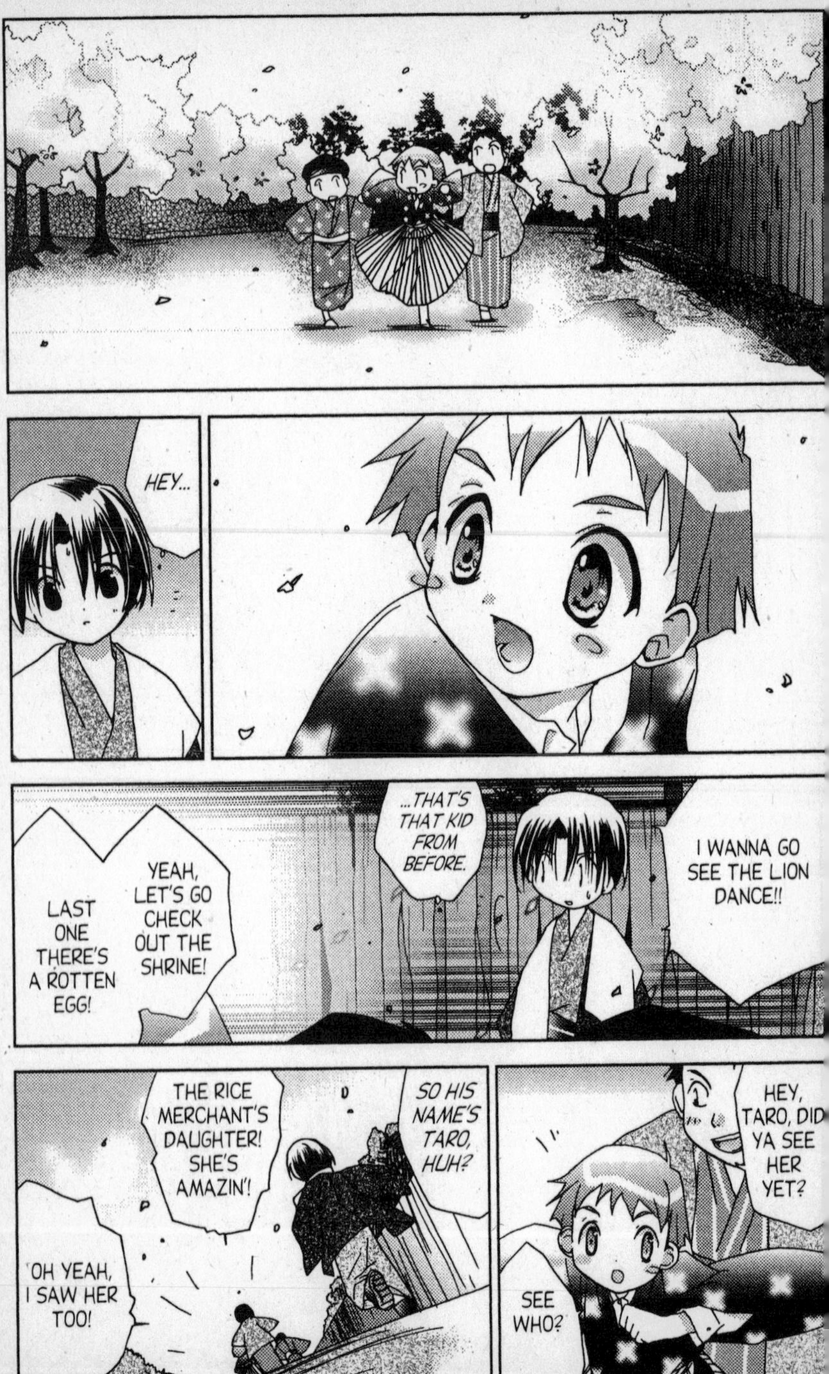
HEY...
I WANNA GO SEE THE LION DANCE!!
...THAT'S THAT KID FROM BEFORE.
YEAH, LET'S GO CHECK OUT THE SHRINE!
LAST ONE THERE'S A ROTTEN EGG!
HEY, TARO, DID YA SEE HER YET?
SEE WHO?
SO HIS NAME'S TARO, HUH?
THE RICE MERCHANT'S DAUGHTER! SHE'S AMAZIN'!
OH YEAH, I SAW HER TOO!

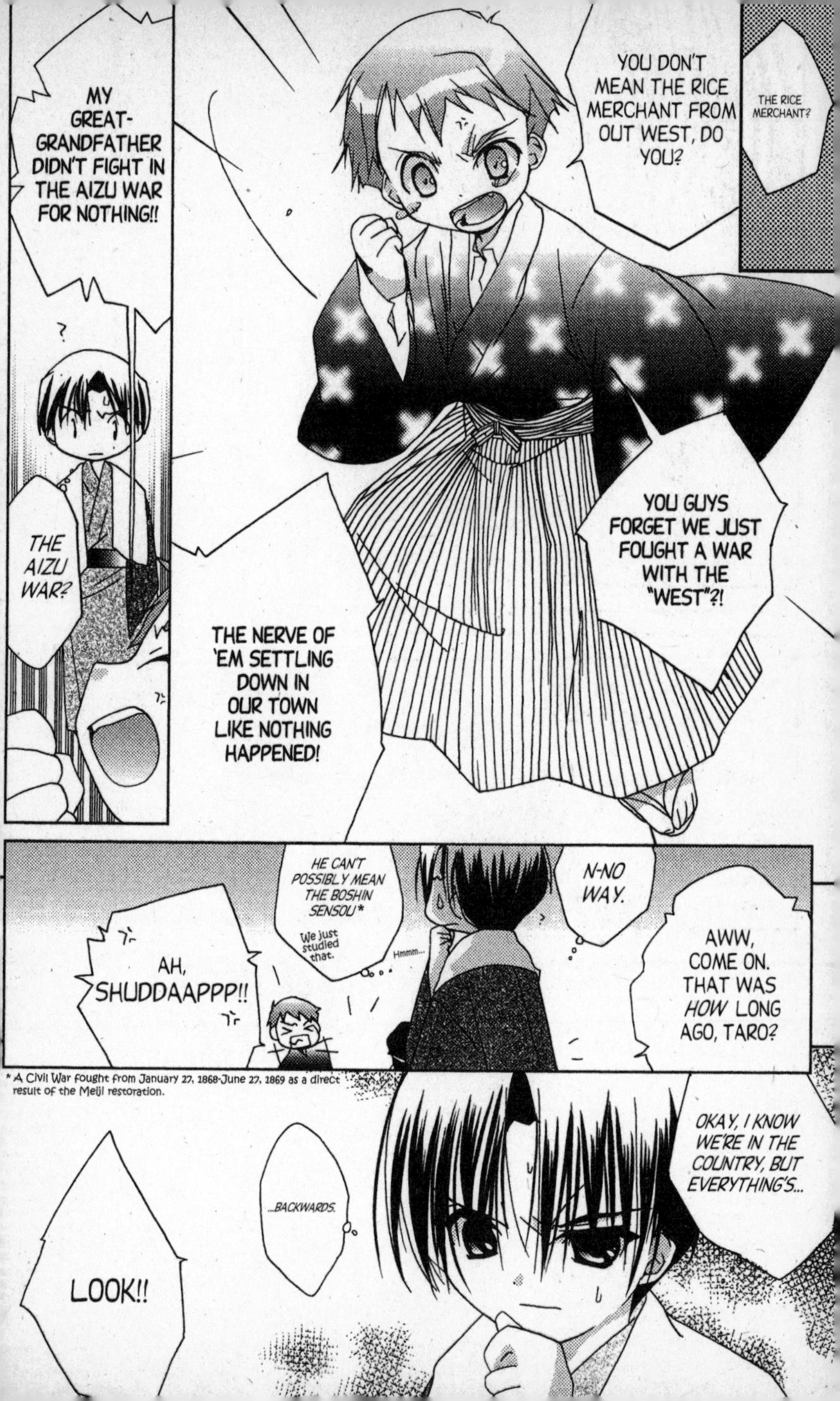
THE RICE MERCHANT?
YOU DON'T MEAN THE RICE MERCHANT FROM OUT WEST, DO YOU?
YOU GUYS FORGET WE JUST FOUGHT A WAR WITH THE "WEST"?!
THE NERVE OF 'EM SETTLING DOWN IN OUR TOWN LIKE NOTHING HAPPENED!
MY GREAT-GRANDFATHER DIDN'T FIGHT IN THE AIZU WAR FOR NOTHING!!
THE AIZU WAR?
AWW, COME ON. THAT WAS HOW LONG AGO, TARO?
N-NO WAY.
HE CAN'T POSSIBLY MEAN THE BOSHIN SENSOU*
We just studied that.
Hmmm...
AH, SHUDDAAPPP!!
OKAY, I KNOW WE'RE IN THE COUNTRY, BUT EVERYTHING'S...
...BACKWARDS.
LOOK!!

* A Civil War fought from January 27, 1868-June 27, 1869 as a direct result of the Meiji restoration.

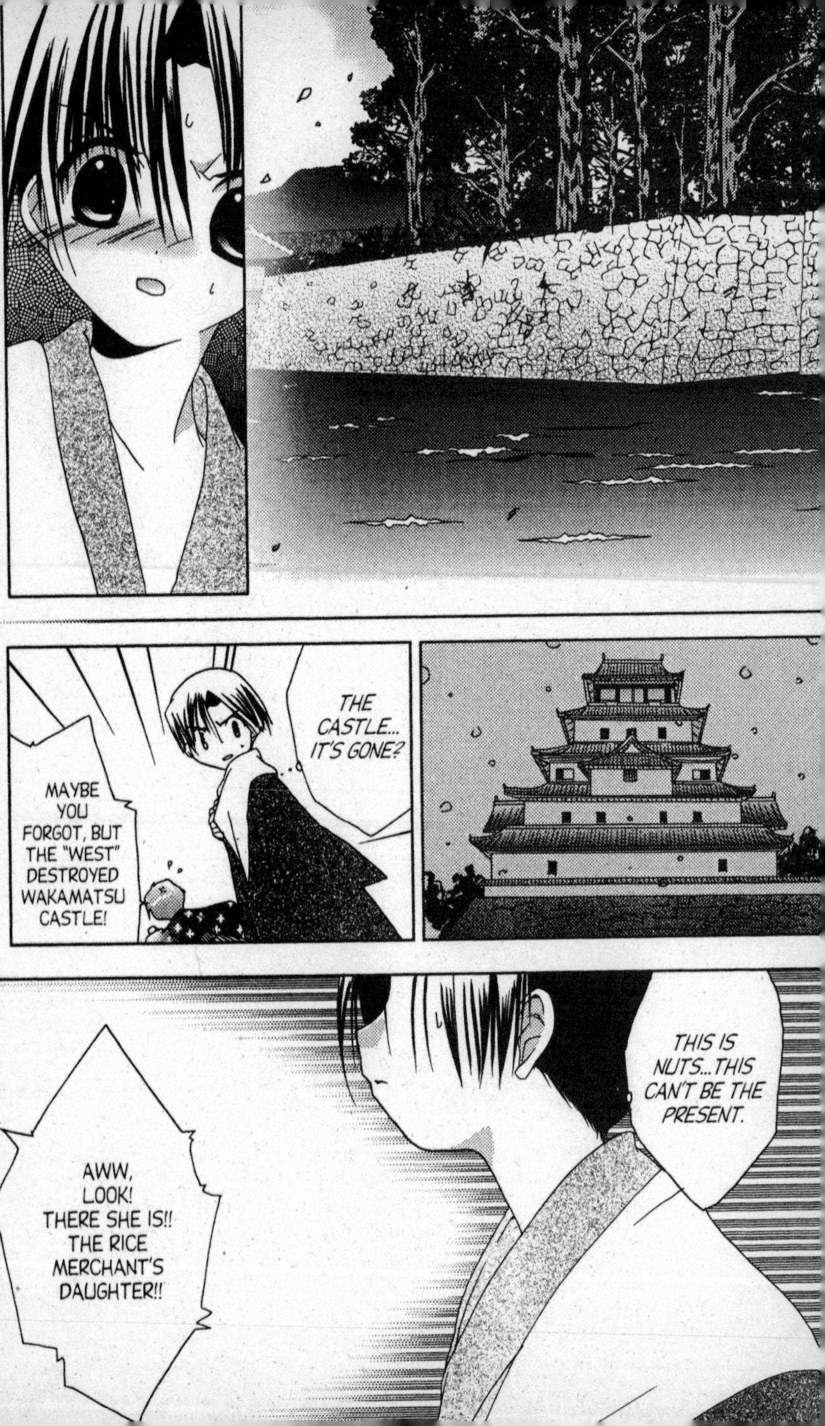
THE CASTLE... IT'S GONE?
MAYBE YOU FORGOT, BUT THE "WEST" DESTROYED WAKAMATSU CASTLE!
THIS IS NUTS...THIS CAN'T BE THE PRESENT.
AWW, LOOK! THERE SHE IS!! THE RICE MERCHANT'S DAUGHTER!!

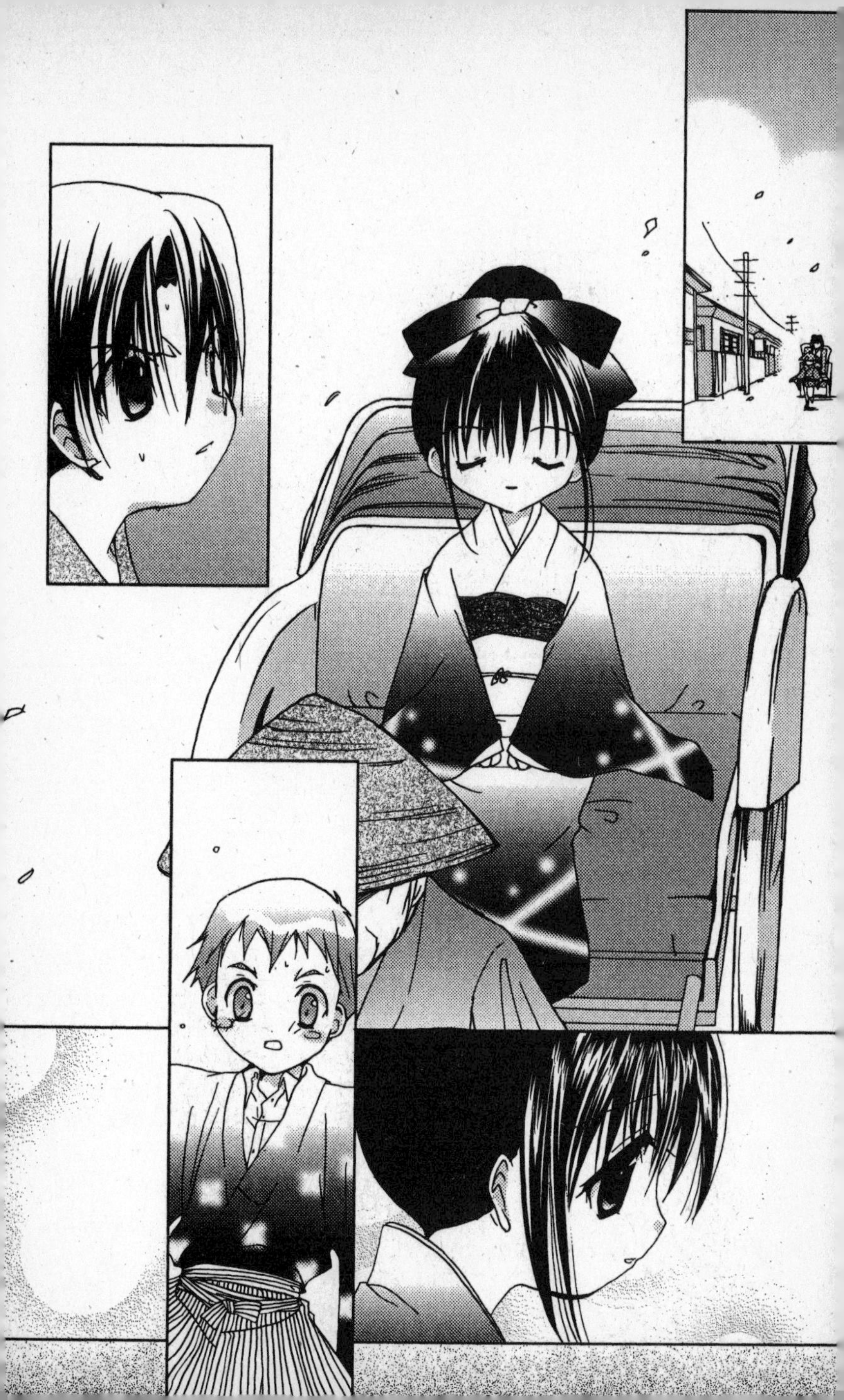

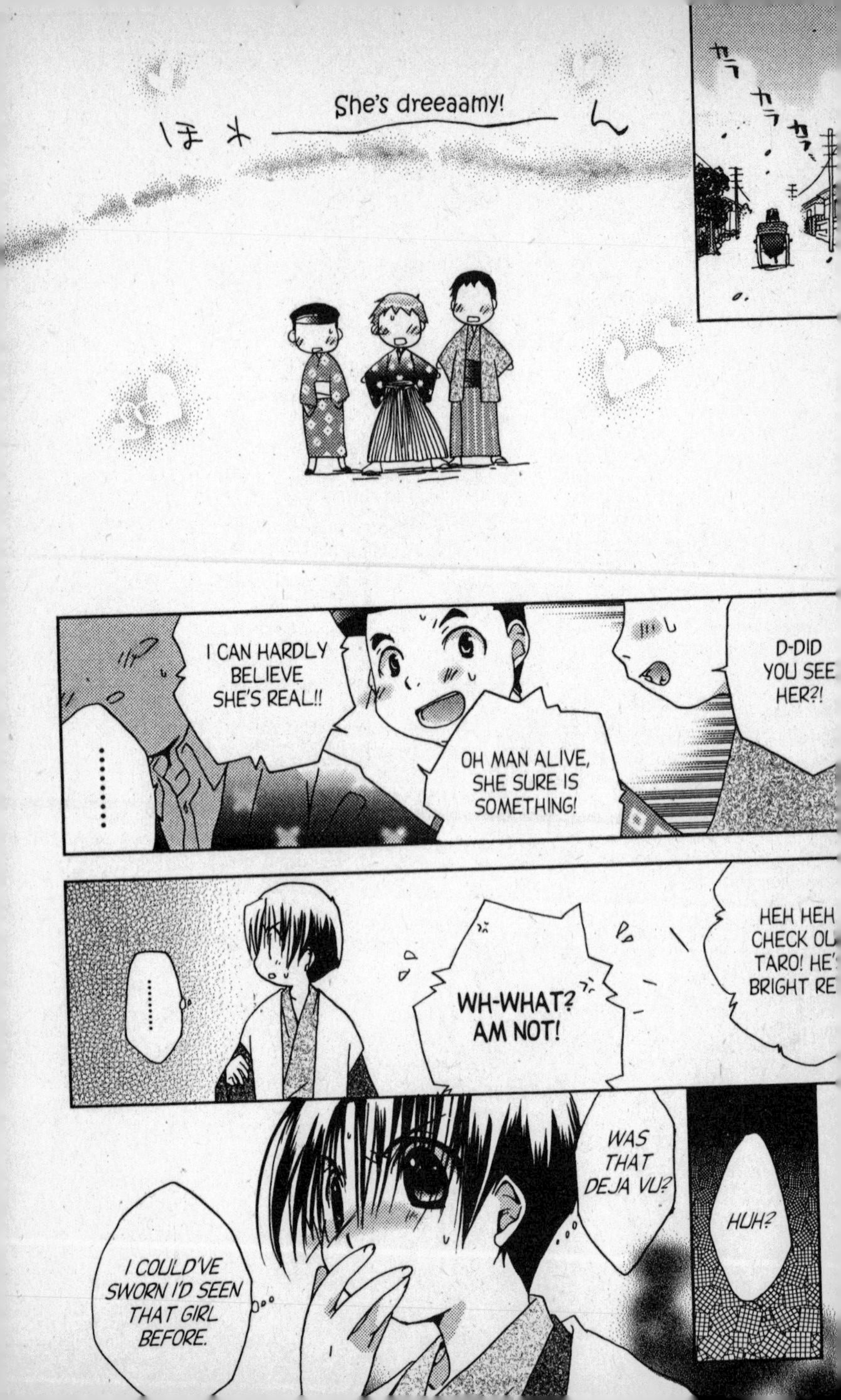

カラ カラ カラ
She's dreeaamy!
ほォ ん
D-DID YOU SEE HER?!
OH MAN ALIVE, SHE SURE IS SOMETHING!
I CAN HARDLY BELIEVE SHE'S REAL!!
....
HEH HEH CHECK OU TARO! HE' BRIGHT RE
WH-WHAT? AM NOT!
....
HUH?
WAS THAT DEJA VU?
I COULD'VE SWORN I'D SEEN THAT GIRL BEFORE.

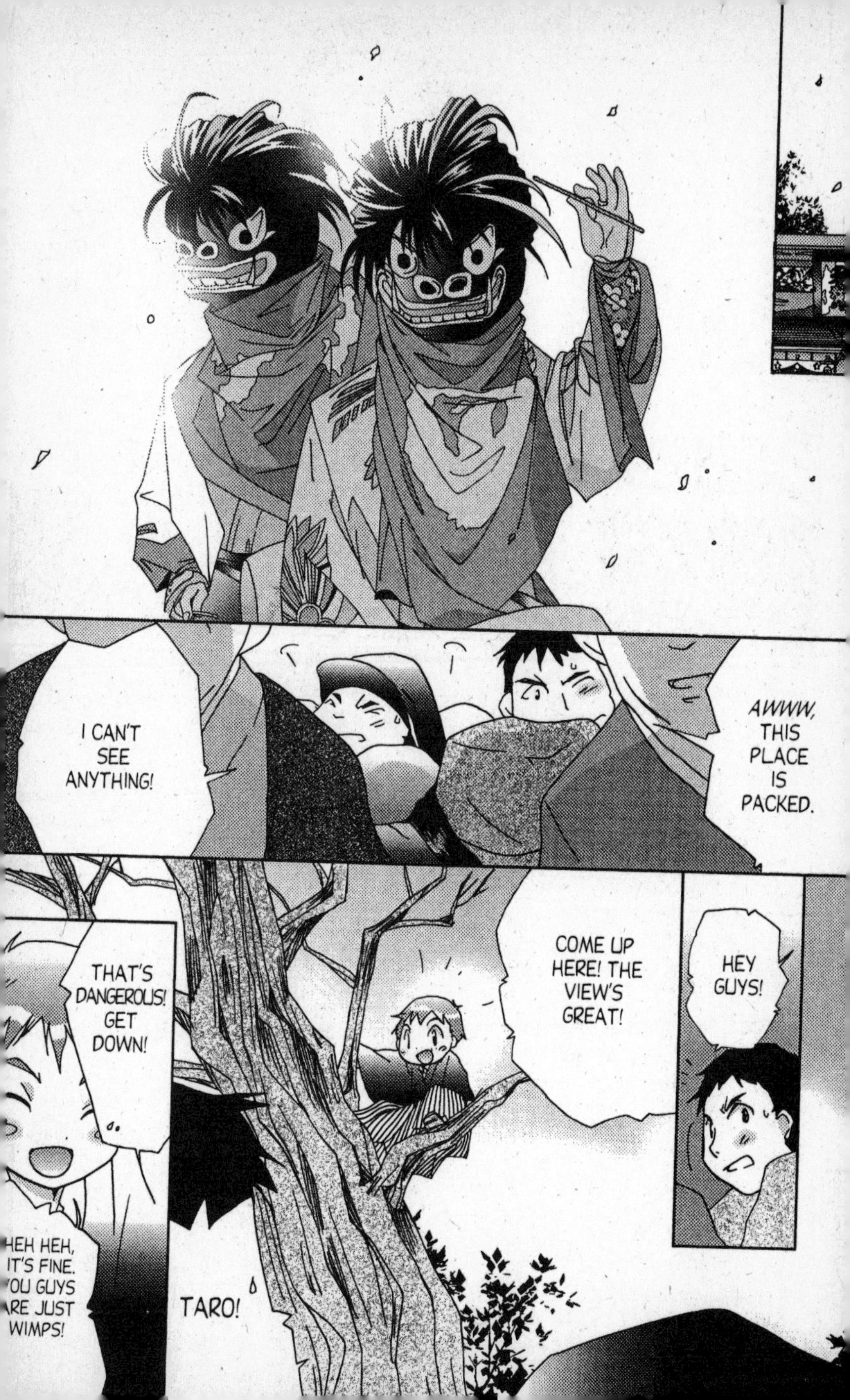
AWWW, THIS PLACE IS PACKED.
I CAN'T SEE ANYTHING!
HEY GUYS!
COME UP HERE! THE VIEW'S GREAT!
THAT'S DANGEROUS! GET DOWN!
TARO!
HEH HEH, IT'S FINE. YOU GUYS ARE JUST WIMPS!

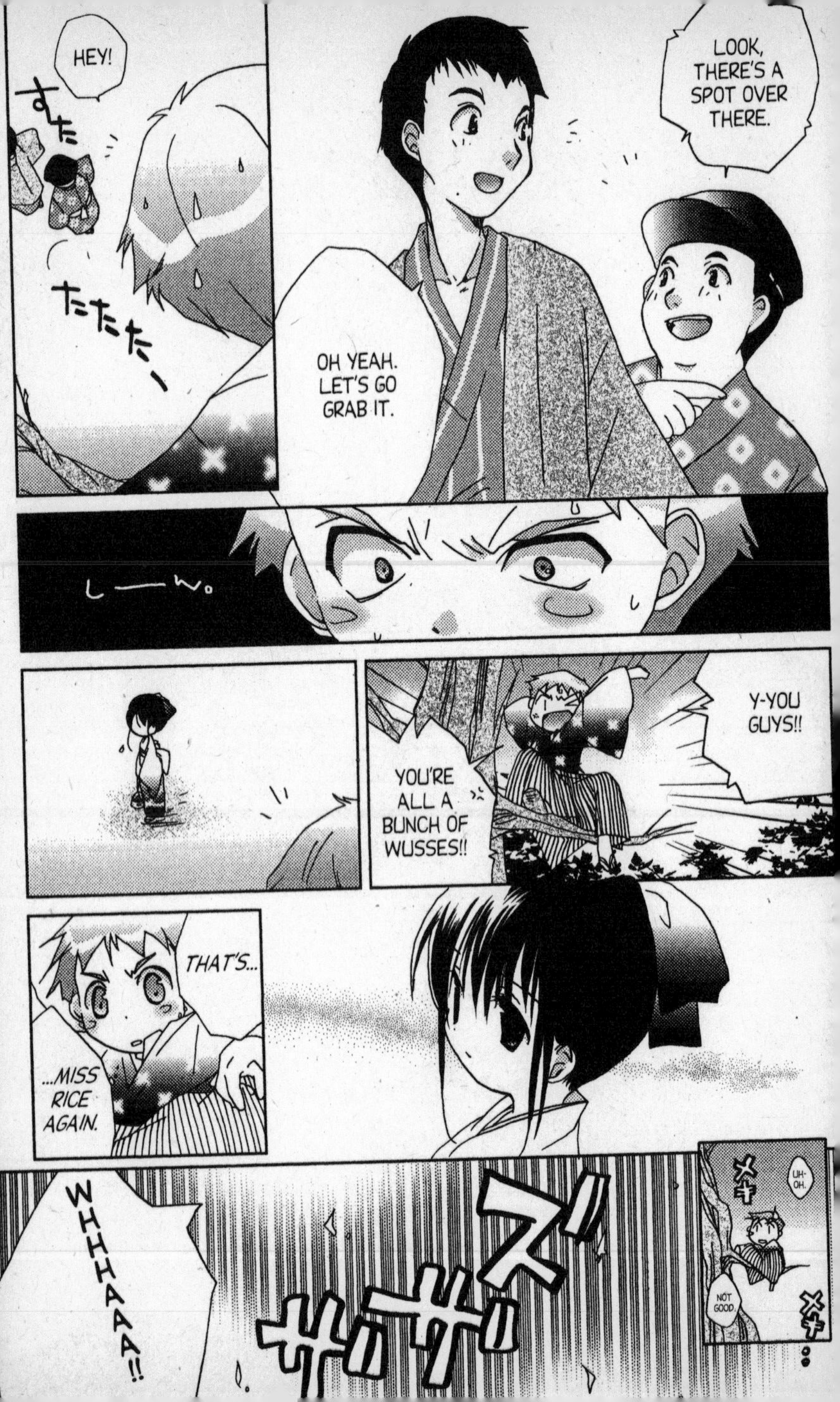
LOOK, THERE'S A SPOT OVER THERE.
OH YEAH. LET'S GO GRAB IT.
HEY!
すた
たたた、
しーん。
Y-YOU GUYS!!
YOU'RE ALL A BUNCH OF WUSSES!!
THAT'S...
...MISS RICE AGAIN.
メキ
UH-OH.
NOT GOOD.
メキ
ズザザ
WHHHAAAA!!

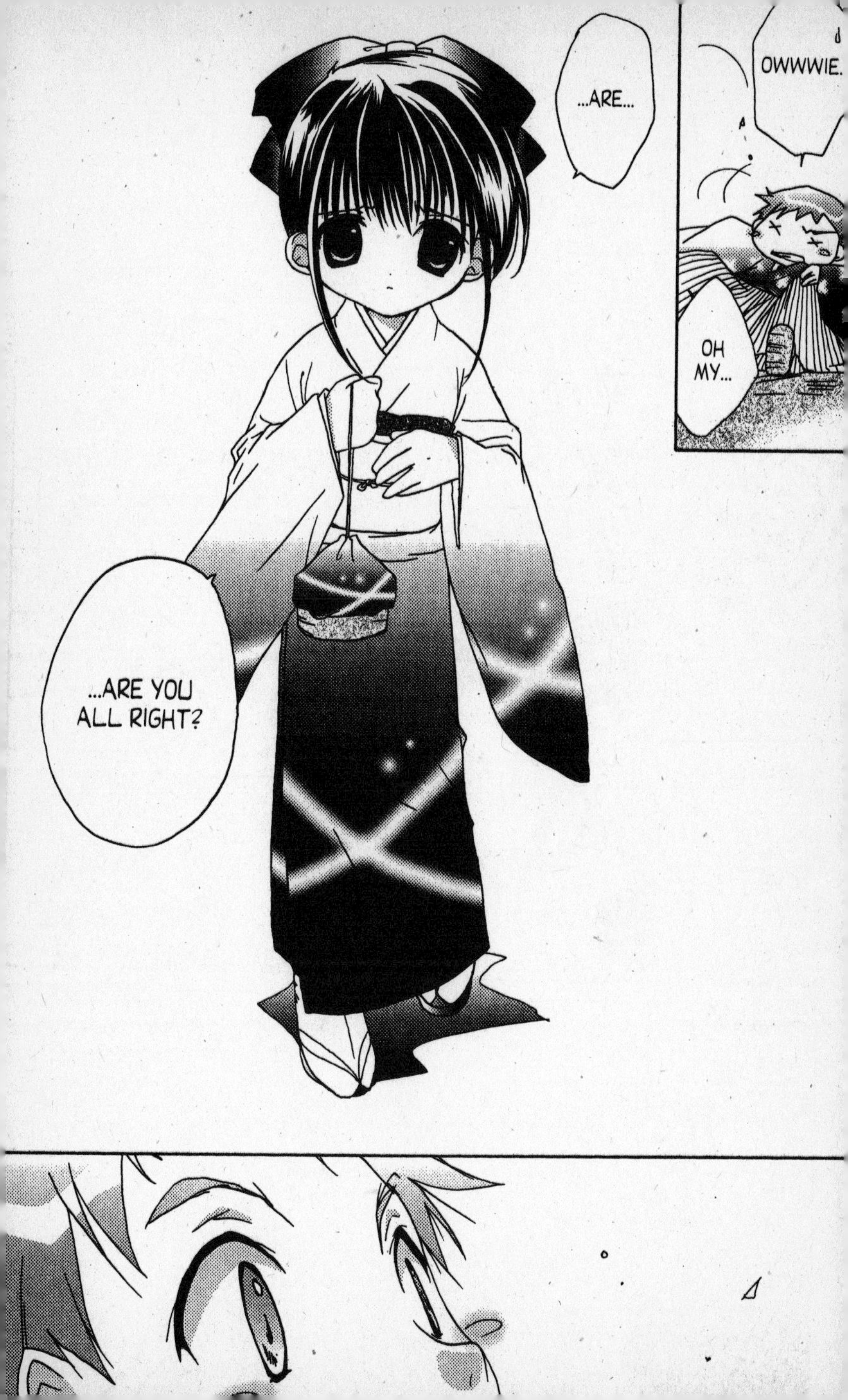
OWWWIE.
OH MY...
...ARE...
...ARE YOU ALL RIGHT?

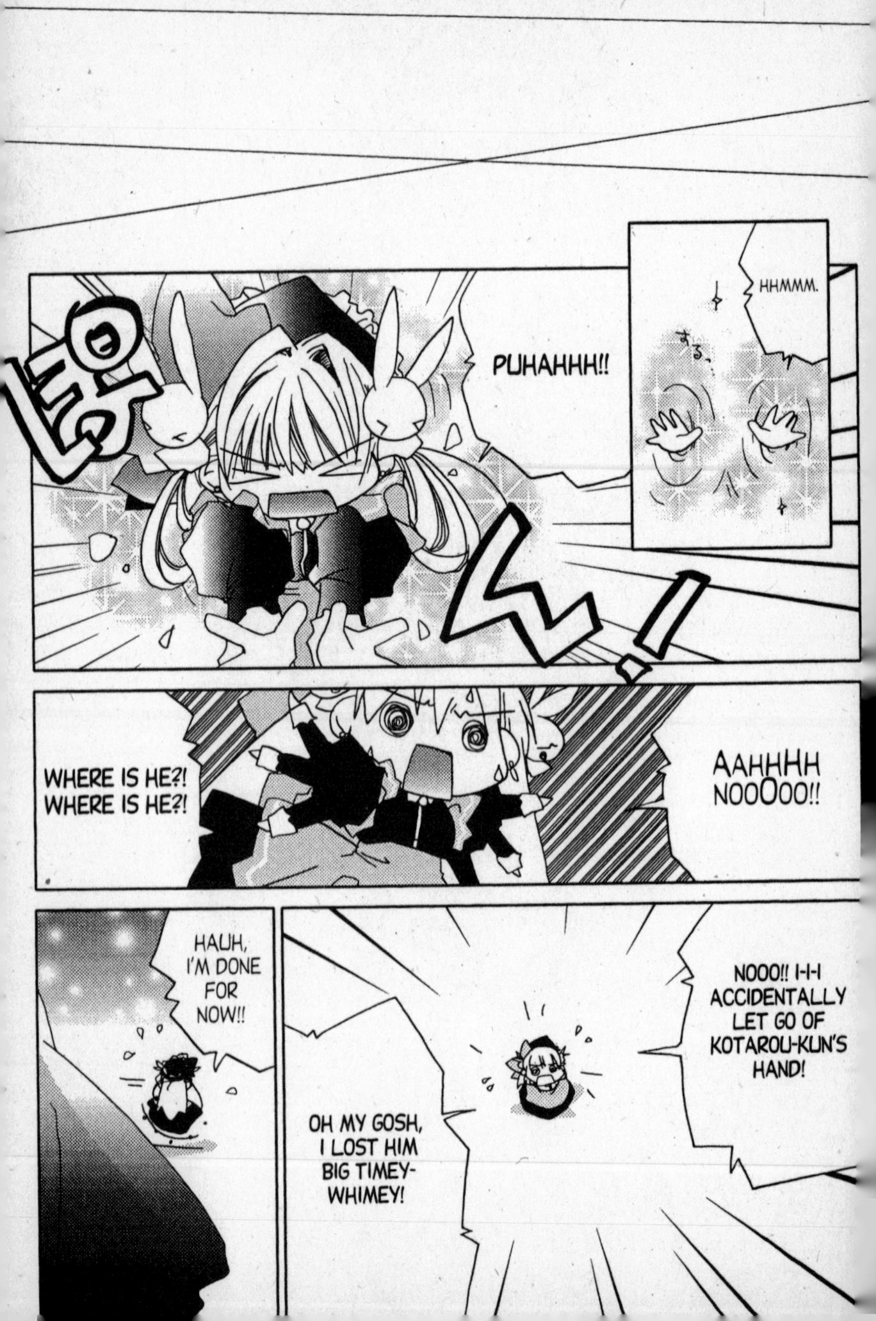

HHMMM.
する
PUHAHHH!!
AAHHHH NOOOOOO!!
WHERE IS HE?! WHERE IS HE?!
NOOO!! I-I-I ACCIDENTALLY LET GO OF KOTAROU-KUN'S HAND!
OH MY GOSH, I LOST HIM BIG TIMEY-WHIMEY!
HAUH, I'M DONE FOR NOW!!

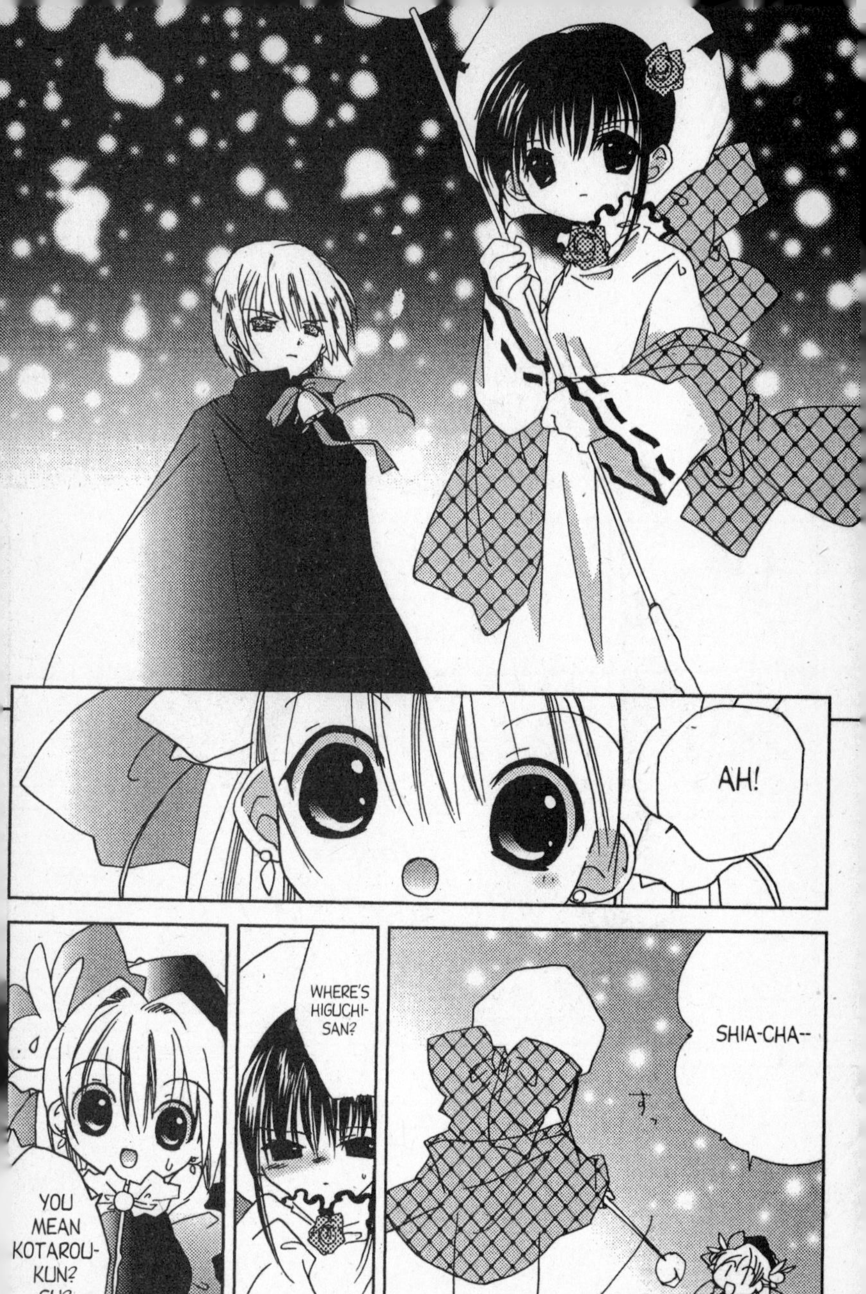
AH!
SHIA-CHA--
WHERE'S HIGUCHI-SAN?
YOU MEAN KOTAROU-KUN? SU?

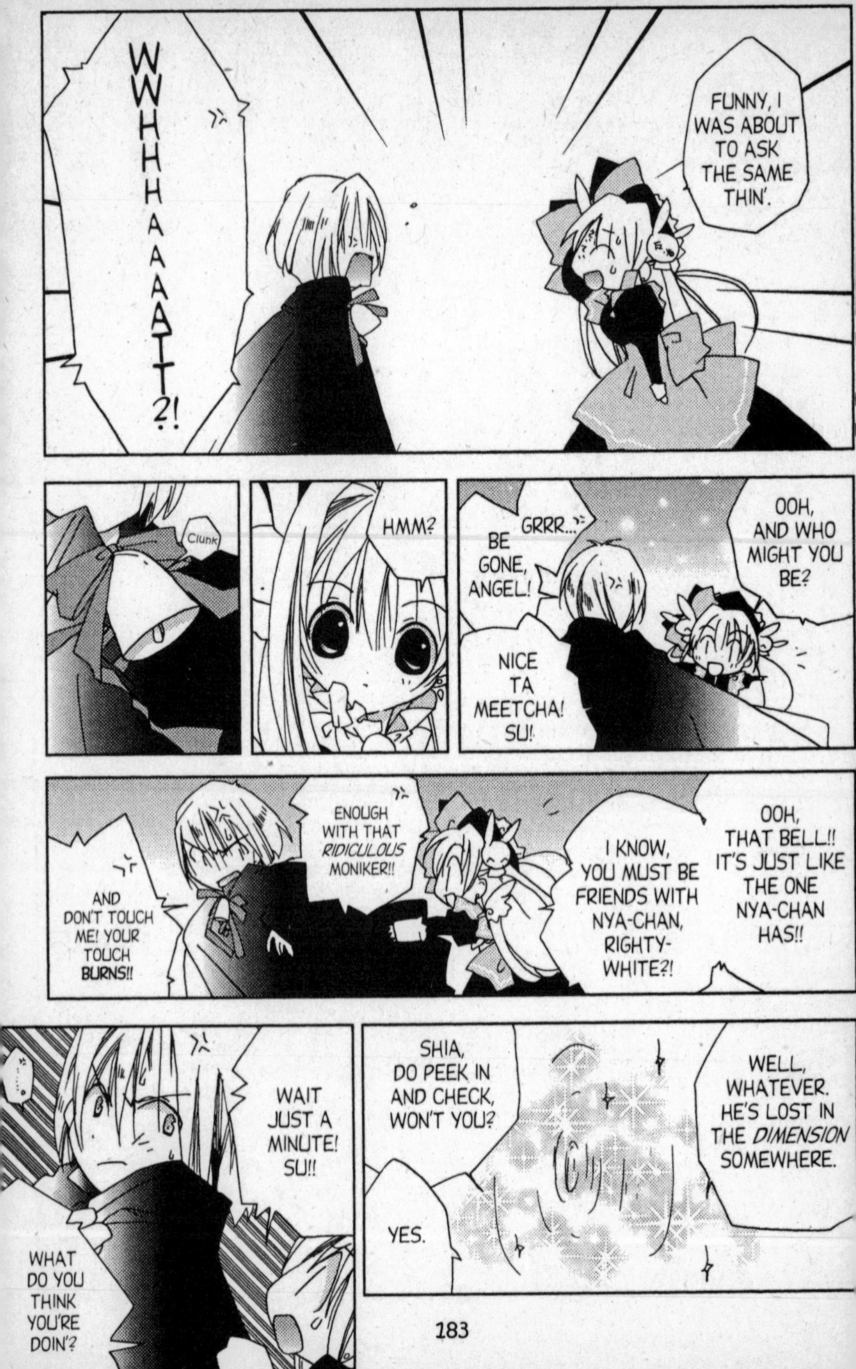
FUNNY, I WAS ABOUT TO ASK THE SAME THIN'.
WWHHHAAAATT?!
OOH, AND WHO MIGHT YOU BE?
NICE TA MEETCHA! SU!
GRRR...
BE GONE, ANGEL!
HMM?
Clunk
OOH, THAT BELL!! IT'S JUST LIKE THE ONE NYA-CHAN HAS!!
I KNOW, YOU MUST BE FRIENDS WITH NYA-CHAN, RIGHTY-WHITE?!
ENOUGH WITH THAT *RIDICULOUS* MONIKER!!
AND DON'T TOUCH ME! YOUR TOUCH **BURNS**!!
WELL, WHATEVER. HE'S LOST IN THE *DIMENSION* SOMEWHERE.
SHIA, DO PEEK IN AND CHECK, WON'T YOU?
YES.
WAIT JUST A MINUTE! SU!!
WHAT DO YOU THINK YOU'RE DOIN'?

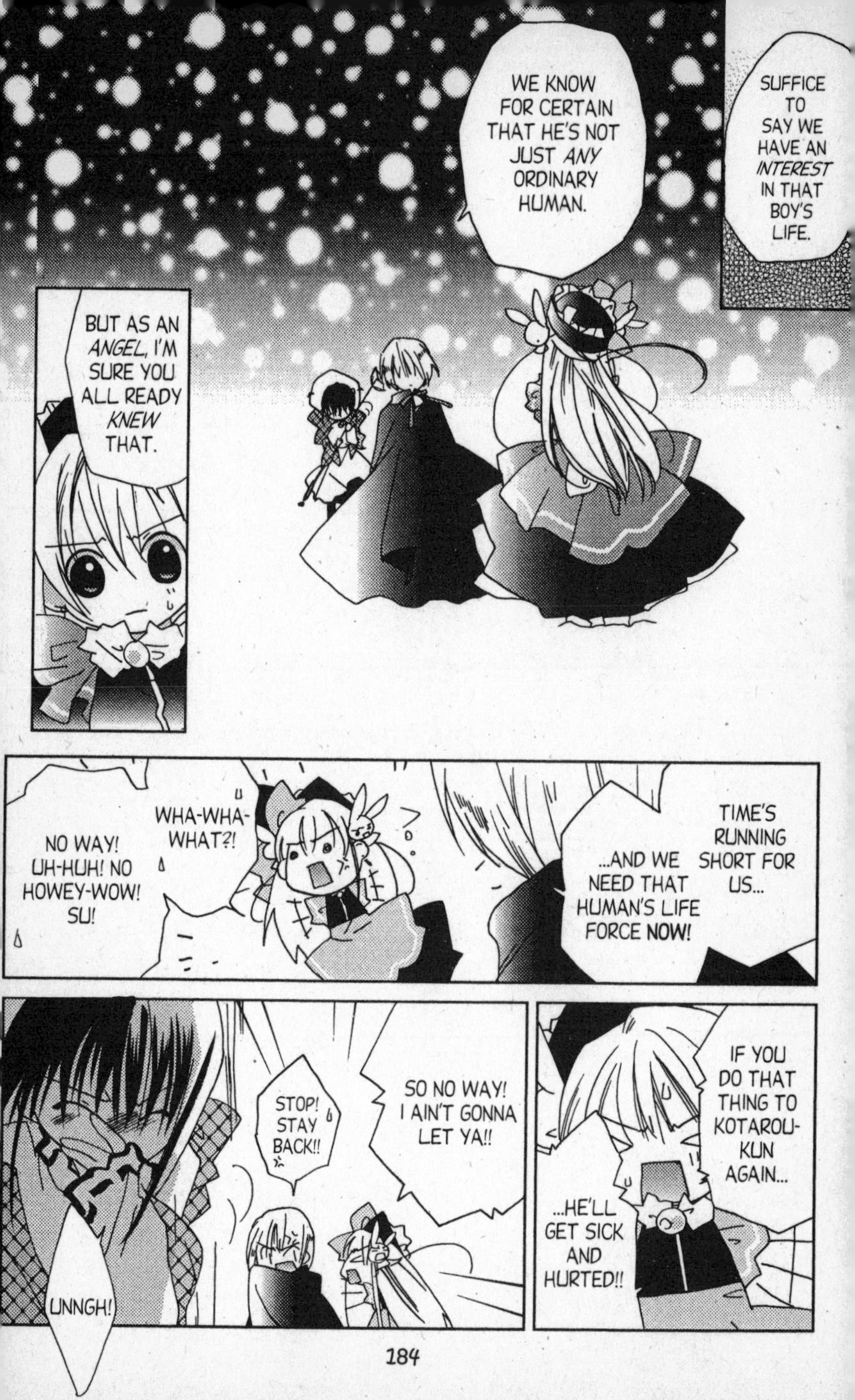
SUFFICE TO SAY WE HAVE AN *INTEREST* IN THAT BOY'S LIFE.
WE KNOW FOR CERTAIN THAT HE'S NOT JUST *ANY* ORDINARY HUMAN.
BUT AS AN *ANGEL*, I'M SURE YOU ALL READY *KNEW* THAT.
TIME'S RUNNING SHORT FOR US...
...AND WE NEED THAT HUMAN'S LIFE FORCE **NOW!**
WHA-WHA-WHAT?!
NO WAY! UH-HUH! NO HOWEY-WOW! SU!
IF YOU DO THAT THING TO KOTAROU-KUN AGAIN...
...HE'LL GET SICK AND HURTED!!
SO NO WAY! I AIN'T GONNA LET YA!!
STOP! STAY BACK!!
UNNGH!

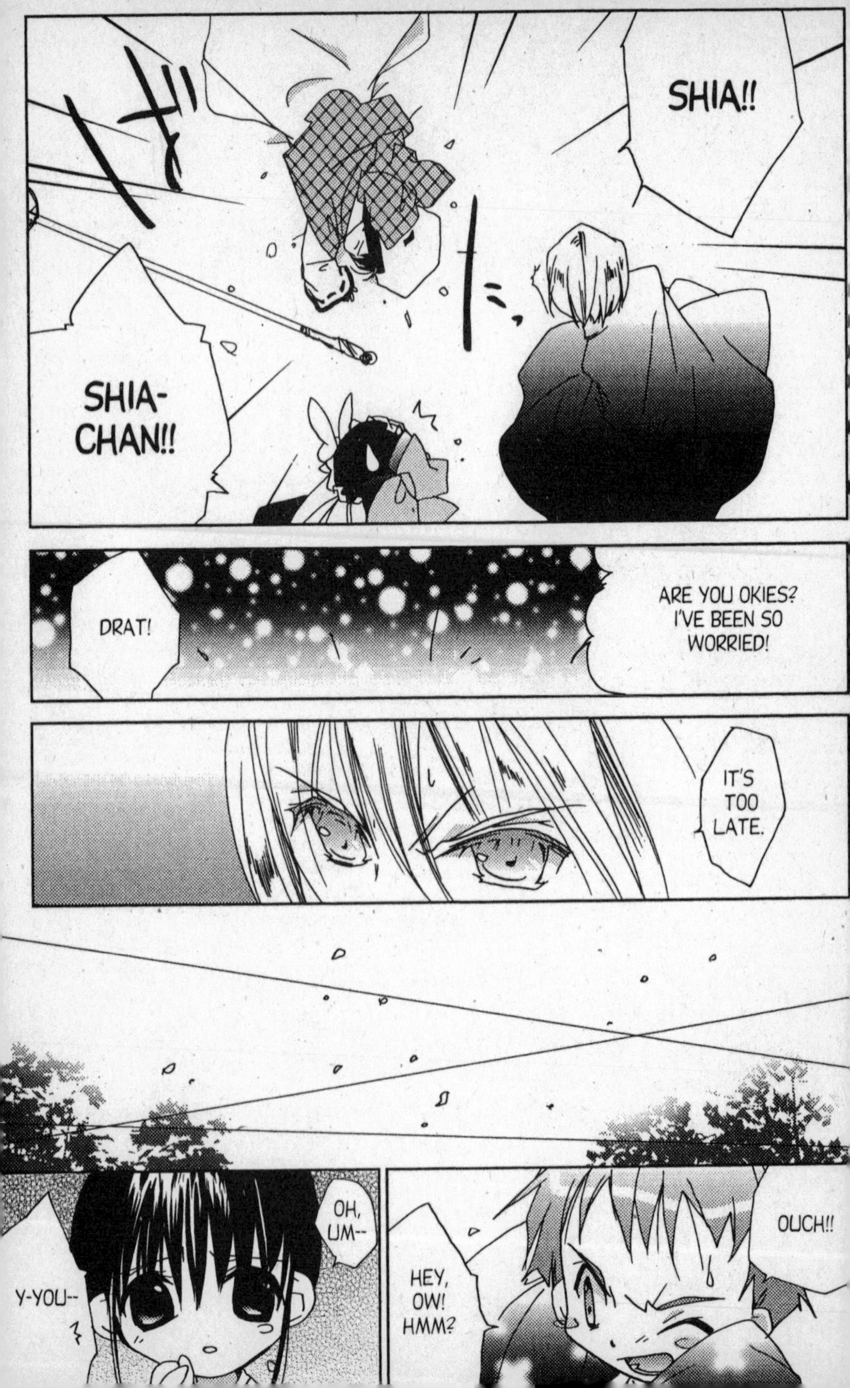
SHIA!!
SHIA-CHAN!!
ARE YOU OKIES? I'VE BEEN SO WORRIED!
DRAT!
IT'S TOO LATE.
OUCH!!
HEY, OW! HMM?
OH, UM--
Y-YOU--

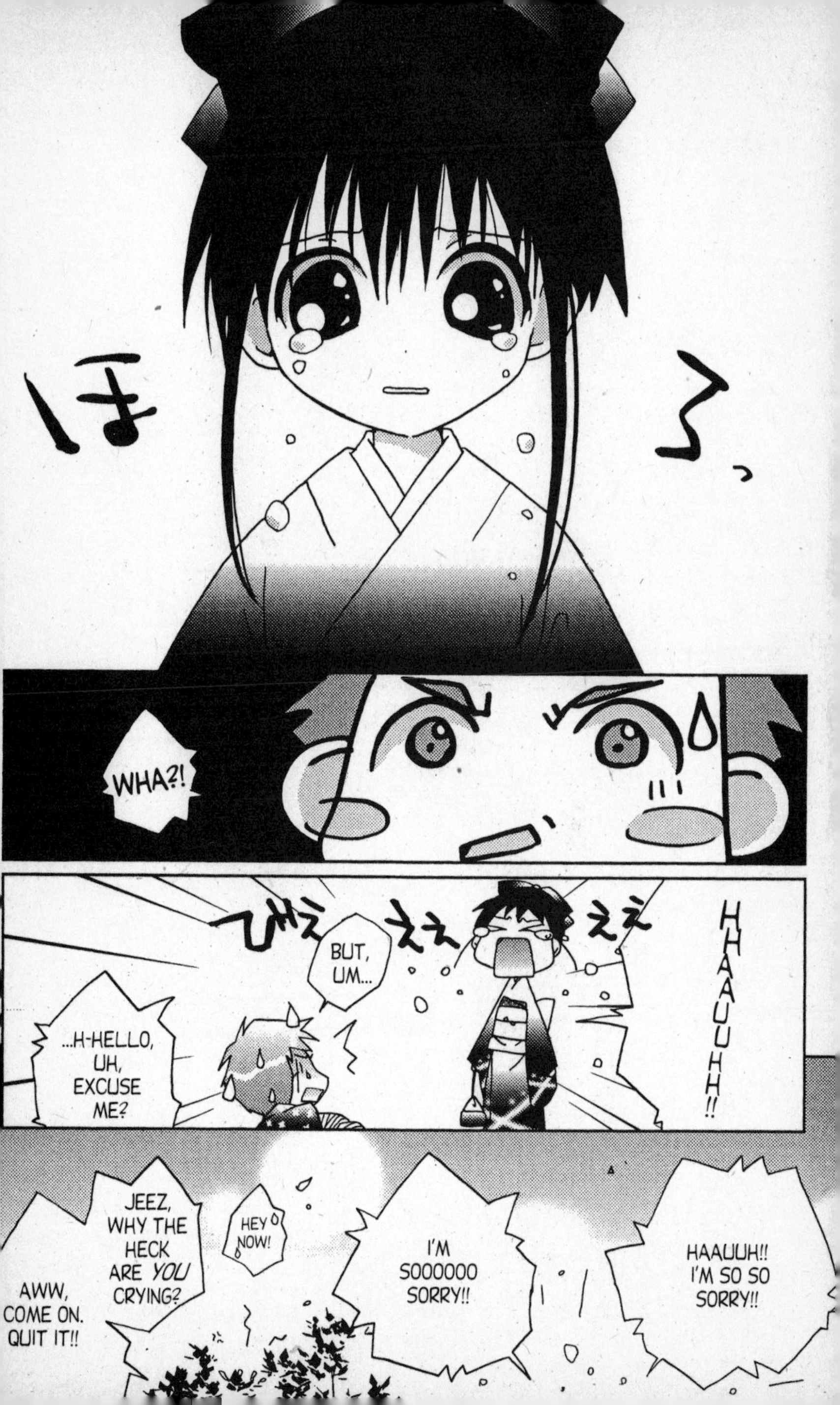

ほろっ
WHA?!
HHAAUUHH!!
ひええええええ
BUT, UM...
...H-HELLO, UH, EXCUSE ME?
HAAUUH!! I'M SO SO SORRY!!
I'M SOOOOOO SORRY!!
HEY NOW!
JEEZ, WHY THE HECK ARE *YOU* CRYING?
AWW, COME ON. QUIT IT!!

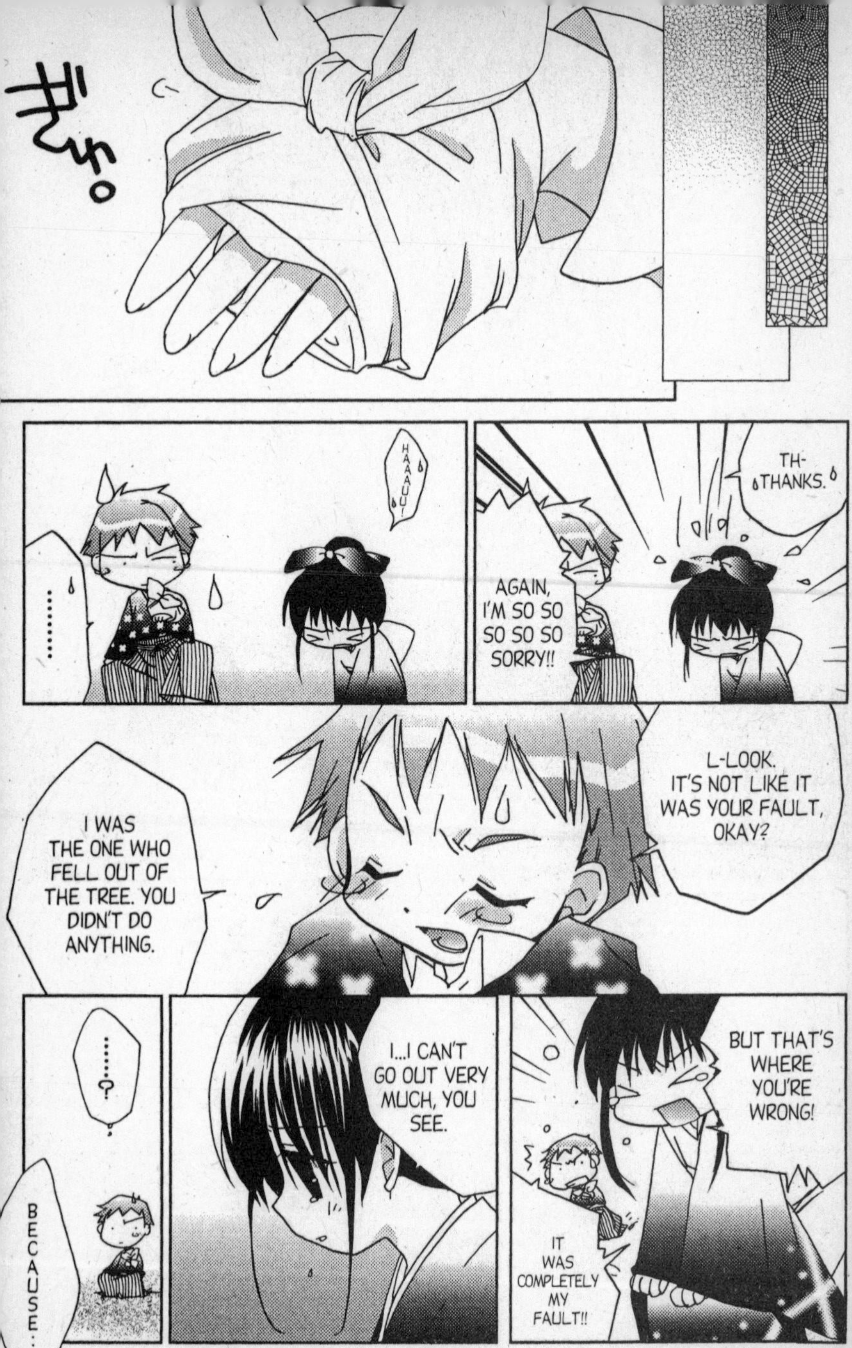
TH- THANKS.
AGAIN, I'M SO SO SO SO SO SORRY!!
HAAAUU!
....
L-LOOK. IT'S NOT LIKE IT WAS YOUR FAULT, OKAY?
I WAS THE ONE WHO FELL OUT OF THE TREE. YOU DIDN'T DO ANYTHING.
BUT THAT'S WHERE YOU'RE WRONG!
IT WAS COMPLETELY MY FAULT!!
I...I CAN'T GO OUT VERY MUCH, YOU SEE.
......?
BECAUSE...

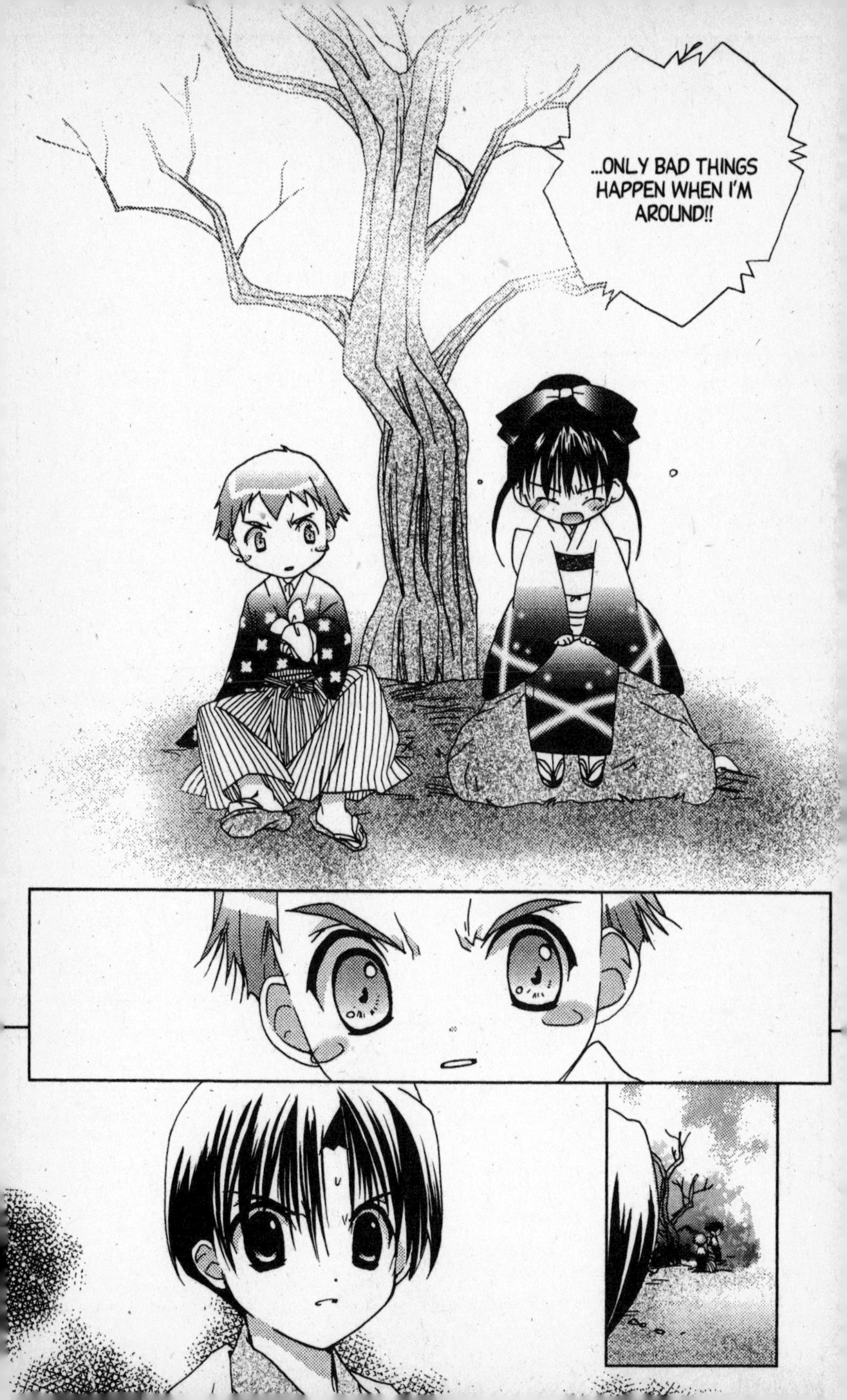
...ONLY BAD THINGS HAPPEN WHEN I'M AROUND!!

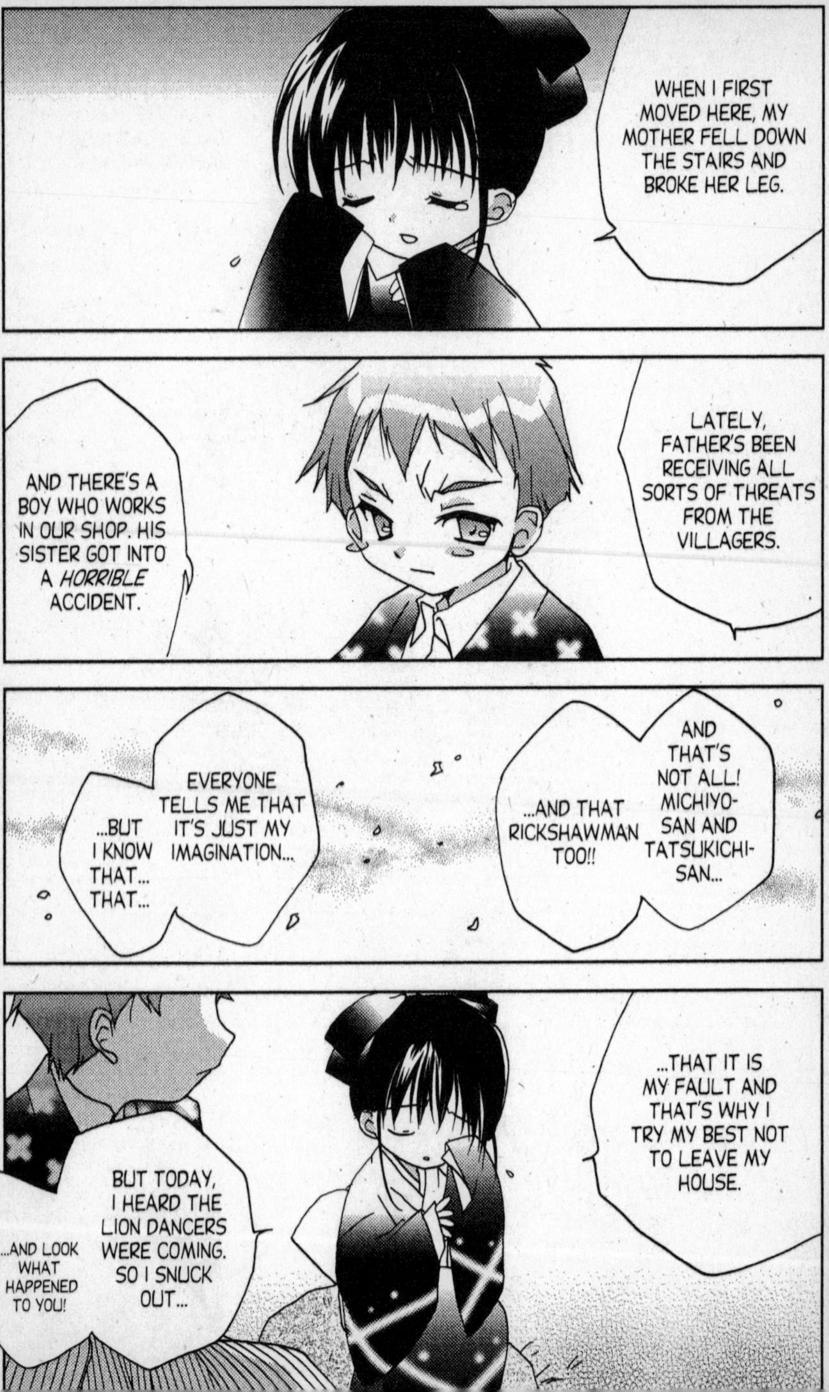
WHEN I FIRST MOVED HERE, MY MOTHER FELL DOWN THE STAIRS AND BROKE HER LEG.
LATELY, FATHER'S BEEN RECEIVING ALL SORTS OF THREATS FROM THE VILLAGERS.
AND THERE'S A BOY WHO WORKS IN OUR SHOP. HIS SISTER GOT INTO A *HORRIBLE* ACCIDENT.
AND THAT'S NOT ALL! MICHIYO-SAN AND TATSUKICHI-SAN...
...AND THAT RICKSHAWMAN TOO!!
EVERYONE TELLS ME THAT IT'S JUST MY IMAGINATION...
...BUT I KNOW THAT... THAT...
...THAT IT IS MY FAULT AND THAT'S WHY I TRY MY BEST NOT TO LEAVE MY HOUSE.
BUT TODAY, I HEARD THE LION DANCERS WERE COMING. SO I SNUCK OUT...
...AND LOOK WHAT HAPPENED TO YOU!

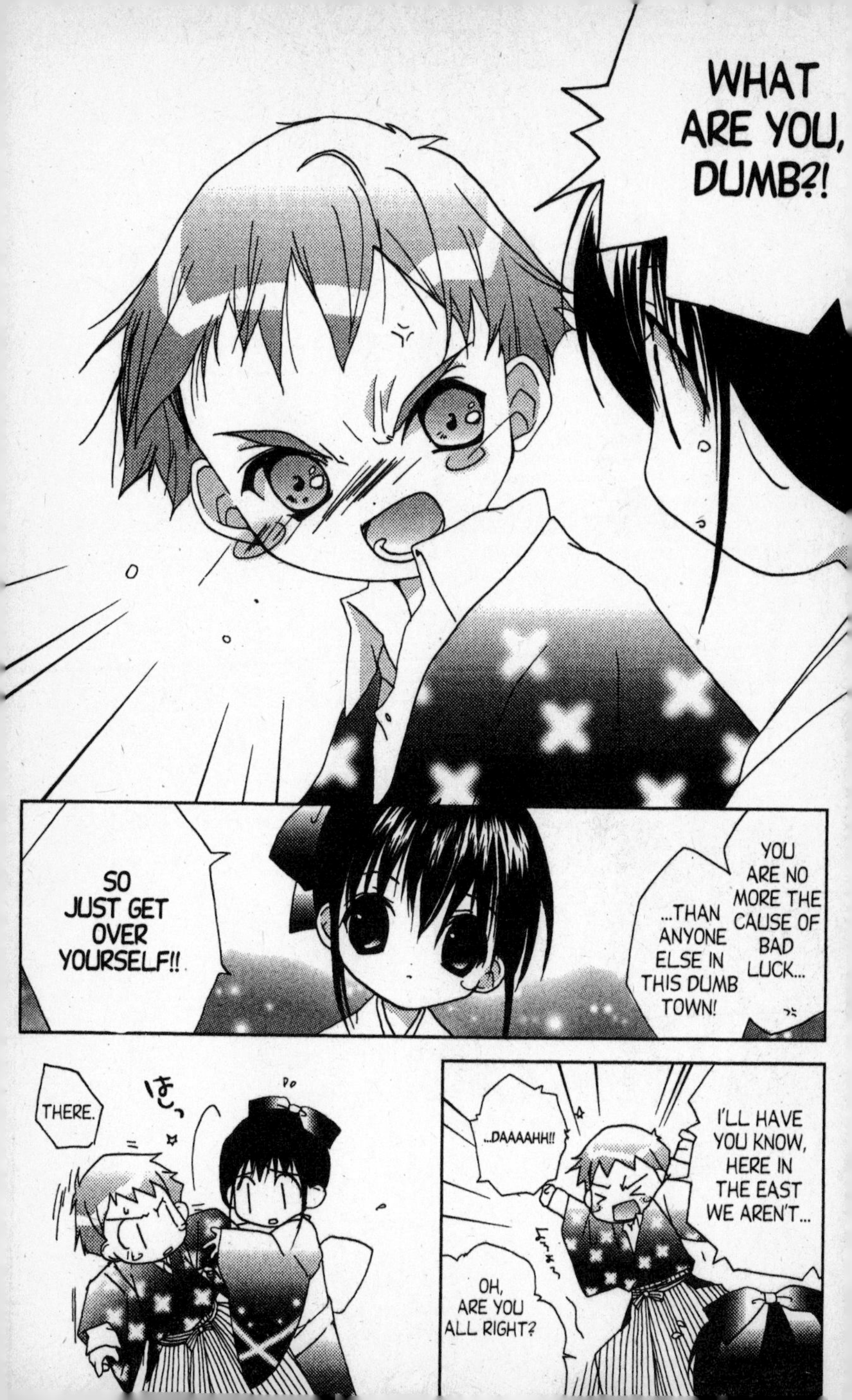
WHAT ARE YOU, DUMB?!
YOU ARE NO MORE THE CAUSE OF BAD LUCK...
...THAN ANYONE ELSE IN THIS DUMB TOWN!
SO JUST GET OVER YOURSELF!!
I'LL HAVE YOU KNOW, HERE IN THE EAST WE AREN'T...
...DAAAAHH!!
OH, ARE YOU ALL RIGHT?
THERE.

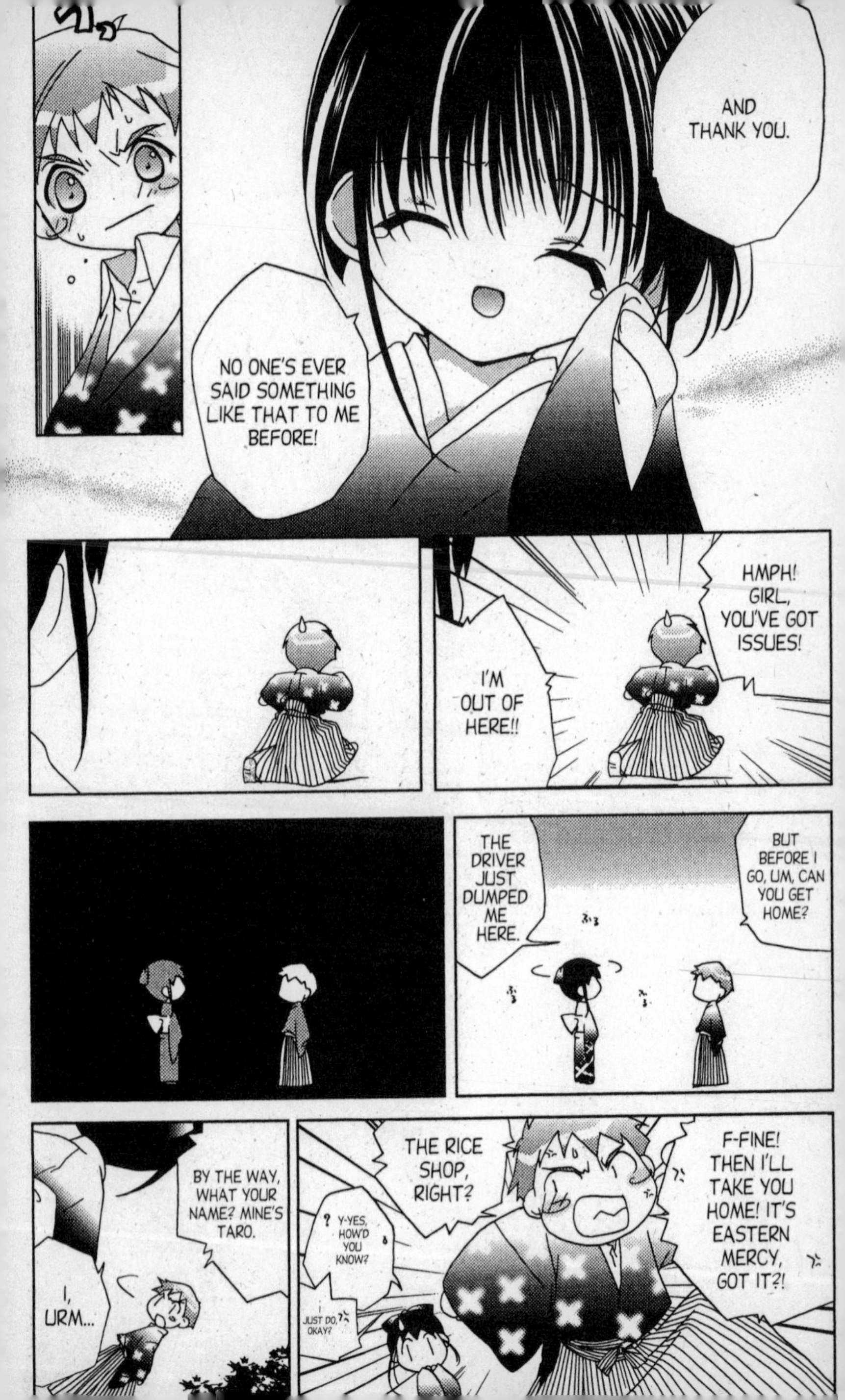
NO ONE'S EVER SAID SOMETHING LIKE THAT TO ME BEFORE!
AND THANK YOU.
HMPH! GIRL, YOU'VE GOT ISSUES!
I'M OUT OF HERE!!
BUT BEFORE I GO, UM, CAN YOU GET HOME?
THE DRIVER JUST DUMPED ME HERE.
F-FINE! THEN I'LL TAKE YOU HOME! IT'S EASTERN MERCY, GOT IT?!
THE RICE SHOP, RIGHT?
Y-YES, HOW'D YOU KNOW?
I JUST DO, OKAY?
BY THE WAY, WHAT YOUR NAME? MINE'S TARO.
I, URM...

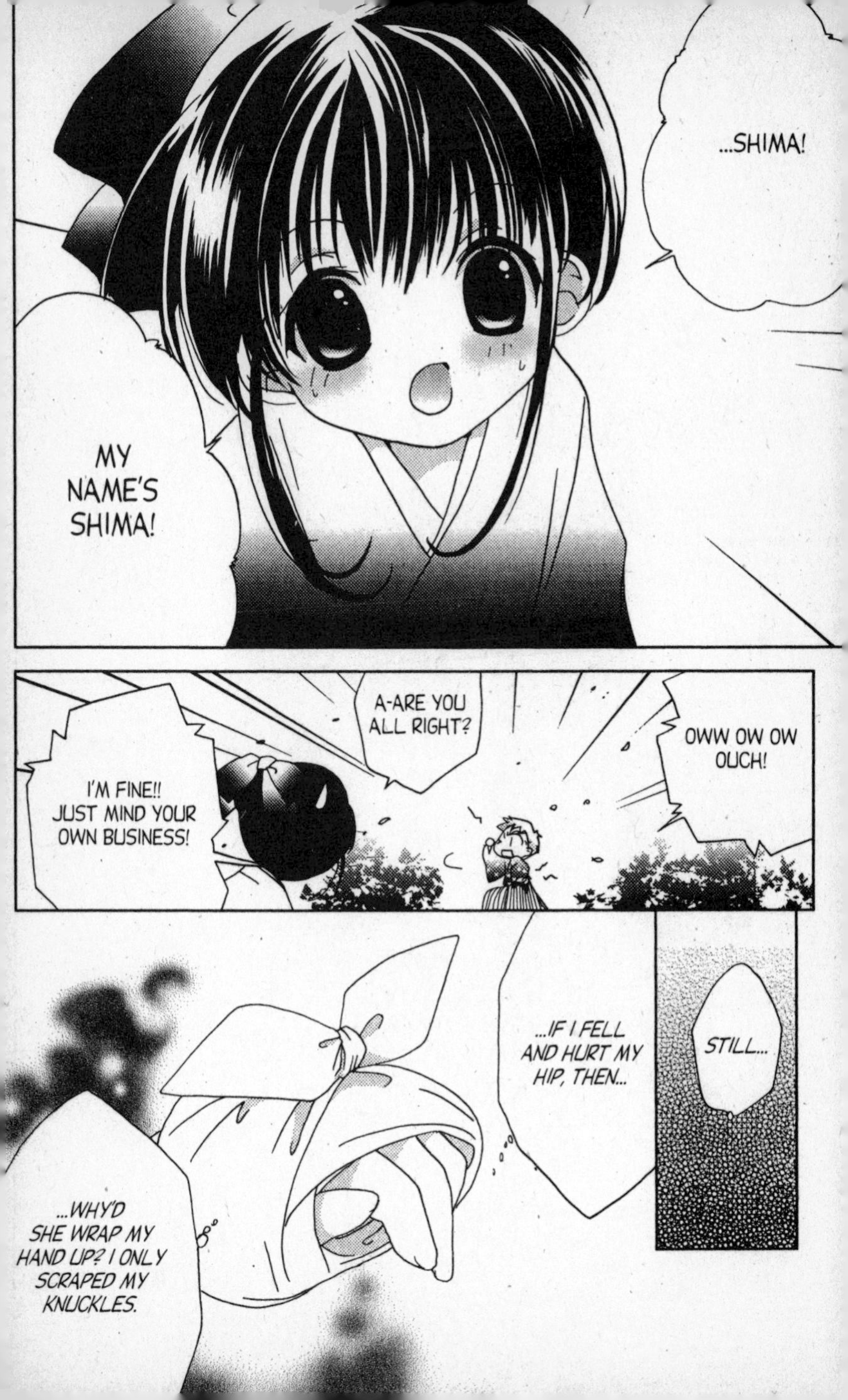
...SHIMA!
MY NAME'S SHIMA!
OWW OW OW OUCH!
A-ARE YOU ALL RIGHT?
I'M FINE!! JUST MIND YOUR OWN BUSINESS!
STILL...
...IF I FELL AND HURT MY HIP, THEN...
...WHY'D SHE WRAP MY HAND UP? I ONLY SCRAPED MY KNUCKLES.

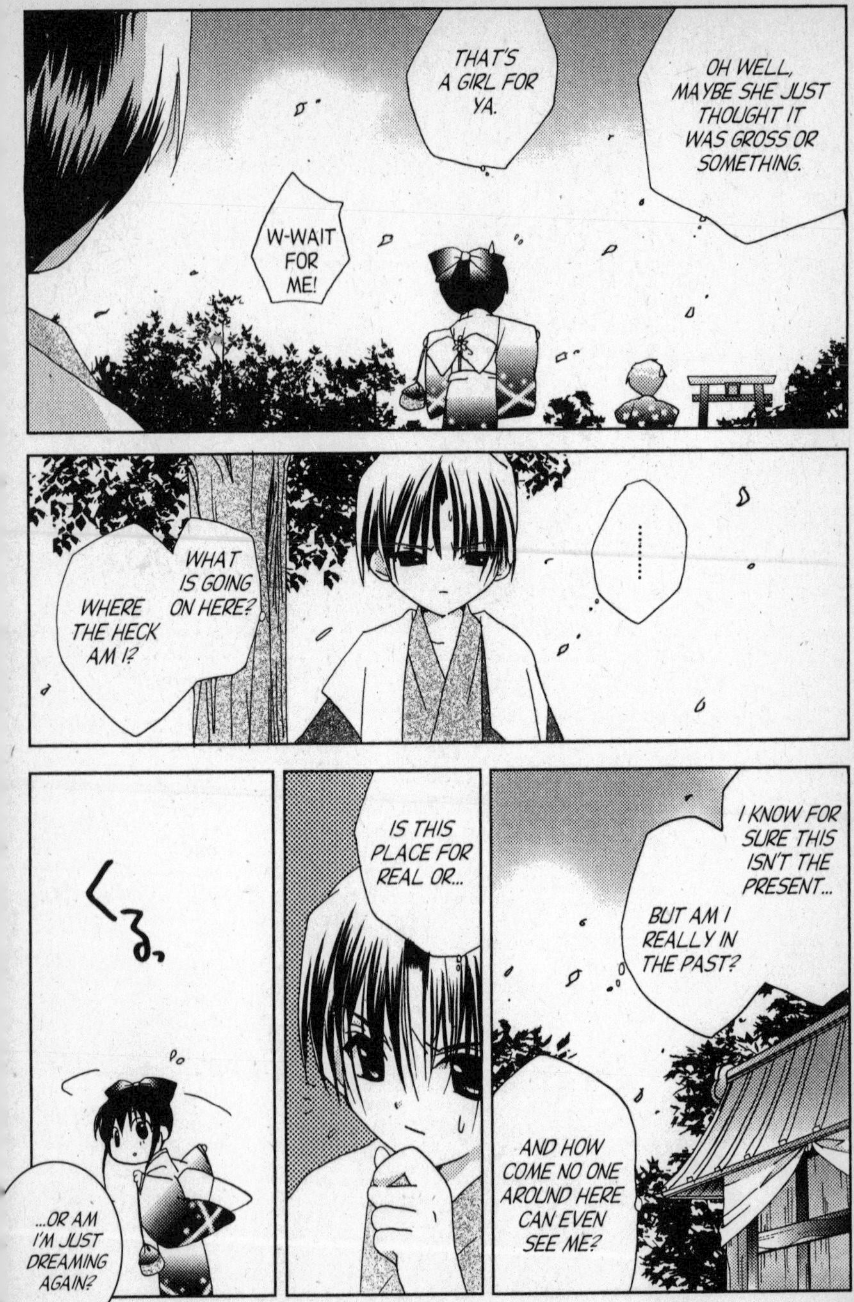
OH WELL, MAYBE SHE JUST THOUGHT IT WAS GROSS OR SOMETHING.
THAT'S A GIRL FOR YA.
W-WAIT FOR ME!
......
WHAT IS GOING ON HERE?
WHERE THE HECK AM I?
I KNOW FOR SURE THIS ISN'T THE PRESENT...
BUT AM I REALLY IN THE PAST?
AND HOW COME NO ONE AROUND HERE CAN EVEN SEE ME?
IS THIS PLACE FOR REAL OR...
くる
...OR AM I'M JUST DREAMING AGAIN?

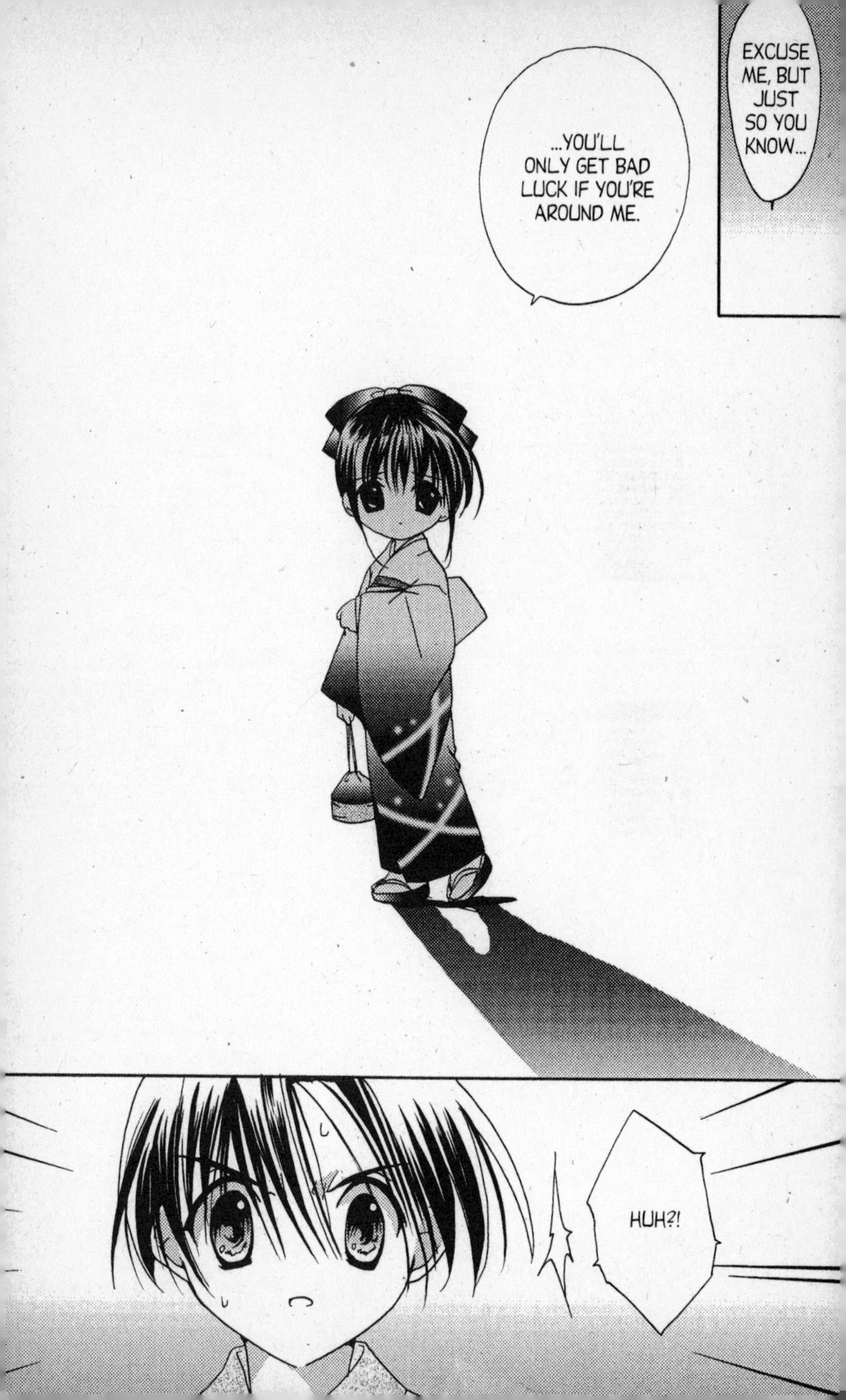
EXCUSE ME, BUT JUST SO YOU KNOW...
...YOU'LL ONLY GET BAD LUCK IF YOU'RE AROUND ME.
HUH?!

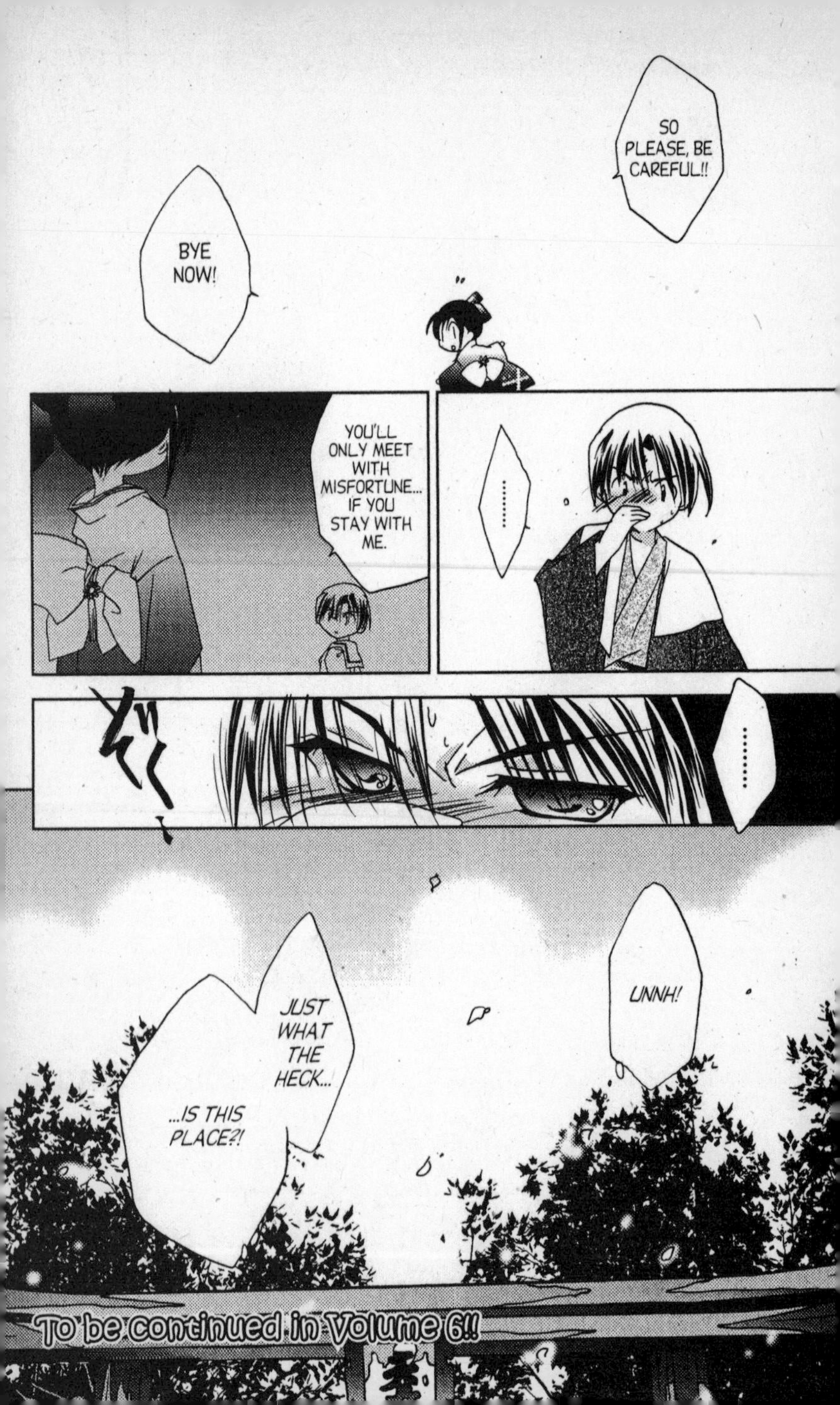
SO PLEASE, BE CAREFUL!!
BYE NOW!
......
YOU'LL ONLY MEET WITH MISFORTUNE... IF YOU STAY WITH ME.
......
UNNH!
JUST WHAT THE HECK...
...IS THIS PLACE?!
To be continued in Volume 6!!

In the Next Volume of...

PITA-TEN

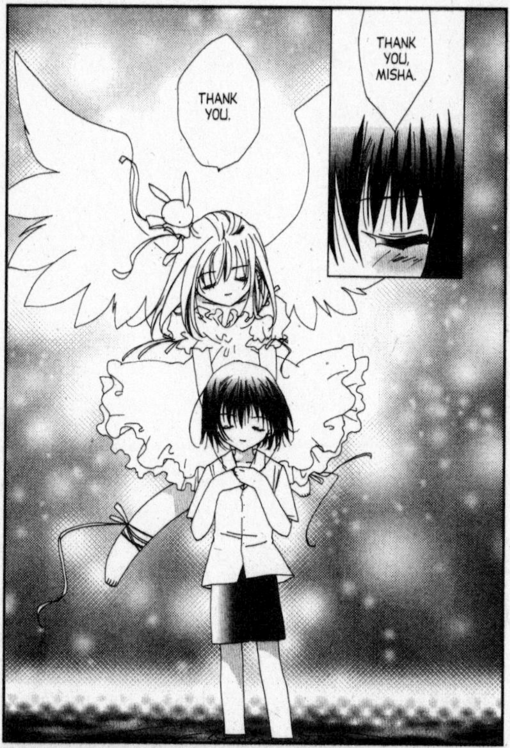
THANK YOU, MISHA.
THANK YOU.

In a revealing adventure of historic proportions, Kotarou tries to discover the truth behind his relation to Misha and Shia. The mystery, memories and mayhem of the past might just be the keys to unlocking the forgotten promises that will finally bring Kotarou, Misha and Shia together for a happy future...

ALSO AVAILABLE FROM TOKYOPOP®

MANGA

.HACK//LEGEND OF THE TWILIGHT
@LARGE
ABENOBASHI: MAGICAL SHOPPING ARCADE
A.I. LOVE YOU
AI YORI AOSHI
ANGELIC LAYER
ARM OF KANNON
BABY BIRTH
BATTLE ROYALE
BATTLE VIXENS
BRAIN POWERED
BRIGADOON
B'TX
CANDIDATE FOR GODDESS, THE
CARDCAPTOR SAKURA
CARDCAPTOR SAKURA - MASTER OF THE CLOW
CHOBITS
CHRONICLES OF THE CURSED SWORD
CLAMP SCHOOL DETECTIVES
CLOVER
COMIC PARTY
CONFIDENTIAL CONFESSIONS
CORRECTOR YUI
COWBOY BEBOP
COWBOY BEBOP: SHOOTING STAR
CRAZY LOVE STORY
CRESCENT MOON
CROSS
CULDCEPT
CYBORG 009
D•N•ANGEL
DEMON DIARY
DEMON ORORON, THE
DEUS VITAE
DIABOLO
DIGIMON
DIGIMON TAMERS
DIGIMON ZERO TWO
DOLL
DRAGON HUNTER
DRAGON KNIGHTS
DRAGON VOICE
DREAM SAGA
DUKLYON: CLAMP SCHOOL DEFENDERS
EERIE QUEERIE!
ERICA SAKURAZAWA: COLLECTED WORKS
ET CETERA
ETERNITY
EVIL'S RETURN
FAERIES' LANDING
FAKE
FLCL
FLOWER OF THE DEEP SLEEP
FORBIDDEN DANCE
FRUITS BASKET
G GUNDAM

GATEKEEPERS
GETBACKERS
GIRL GOT GAME
GIRLS EDUCATIONAL CHARTER
GRAVITATION
GTO
GUNDAM BLUE DESTINY
GUNDAM SEED ASTRAY
GUNDAM WING
GUNDAM WING: BATTLEFIELD OF PACIFISTS
GUNDAM WING: ENDLESS WALTZ
GUNDAM WING: THE LAST OUTPOST (G-UNIT)
GUYS' GUIDE TO GIRLS
HANDS OFF!
HAPPY MANIA
HARLEM BEAT
HYPER RUNE
I.N.V.U.
IMMORTAL RAIN
INITIAL D
INSTANT TEEN: JUST ADD NUTS
ISLAND
JING: KING OF BANDITS
JING: KING OF BANDITS - TWILIGHT TALES
JULINE
KARE KANO
KILL ME, KISS ME
KINDAICHI CASE FILES, THE
KING OF HELL
KODOCHA: SANA'S STAGE
LAMENT OF THE LAMB
LEGAL DRUG
LEGEND OF CHUN HYANG, THE
LES BIJOUX
LOVE HINA
LUPIN III
LUPIN III: WORLD'S MOST WANTED
MAGIC KNIGHT RAYEARTH I
MAGIC KNIGHT RAYEARTH II
MAHOROMATIC: AUTOMATIC MAIDEN
MAN OF MANY FACES
MARMALADE BOY
MARS
MARS: HORSE WITH NO NAME
MINK
MIRACLE GIRLS
MIYUKI-CHAN IN WONDERLAND
MODEL
MOURYOU KIDEN
MY LOVE
NECK AND NECK
ONE
ONE I LOVE, THE
PARADISE KISS
PARASYTE
PASSION FRUIT
PEACH GIRL
PEACH GIRL: CHANGE OF HEART

05.26.04T

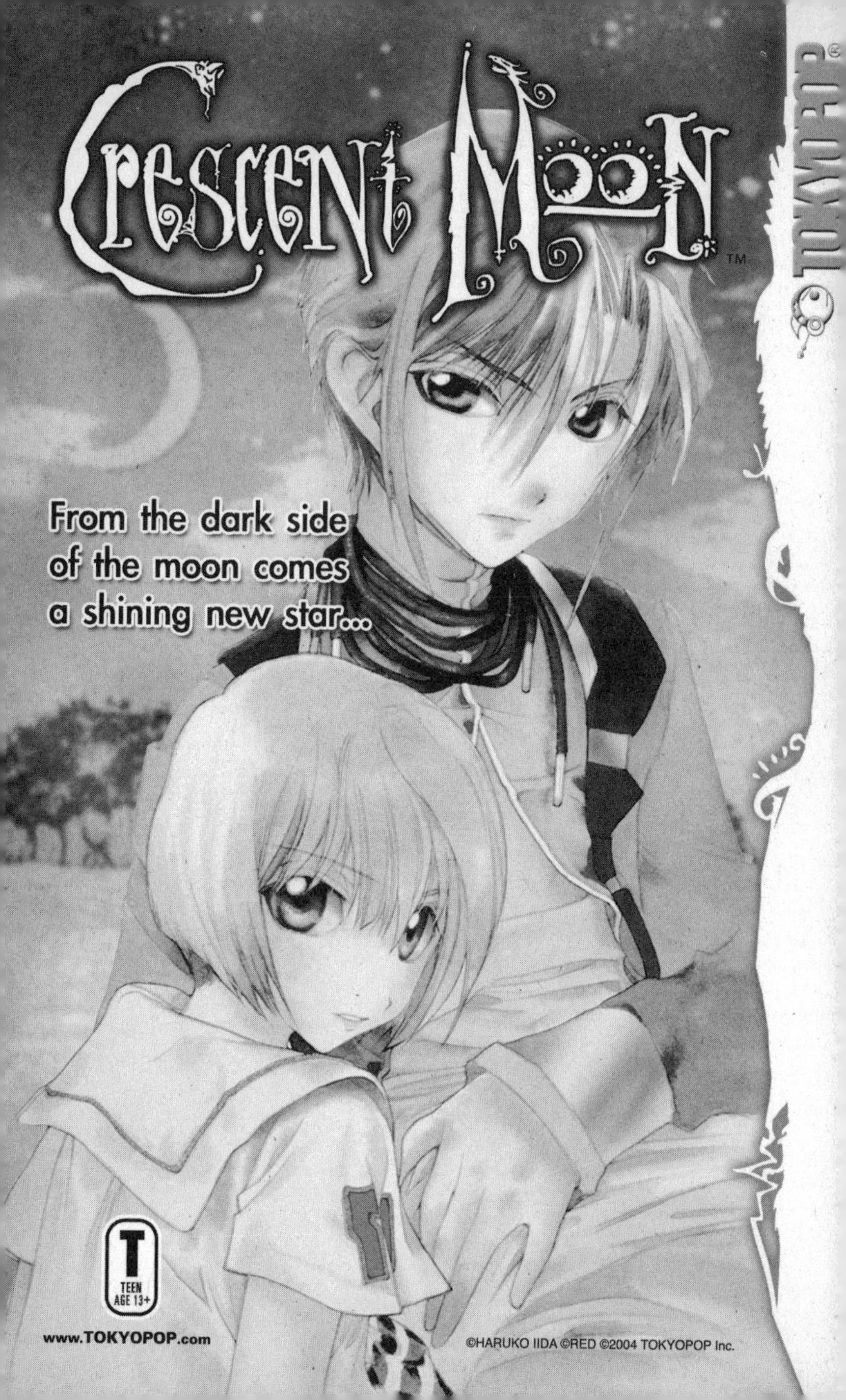
Crescent Moon™
TOKYOPOP®
From the dark side of the moon comes a shining new star...
T TEEN AGE 13+
www.TOKYOPOP.com
©HARUKO IIDA ©RED ©2004 TOKYOPOP Inc.

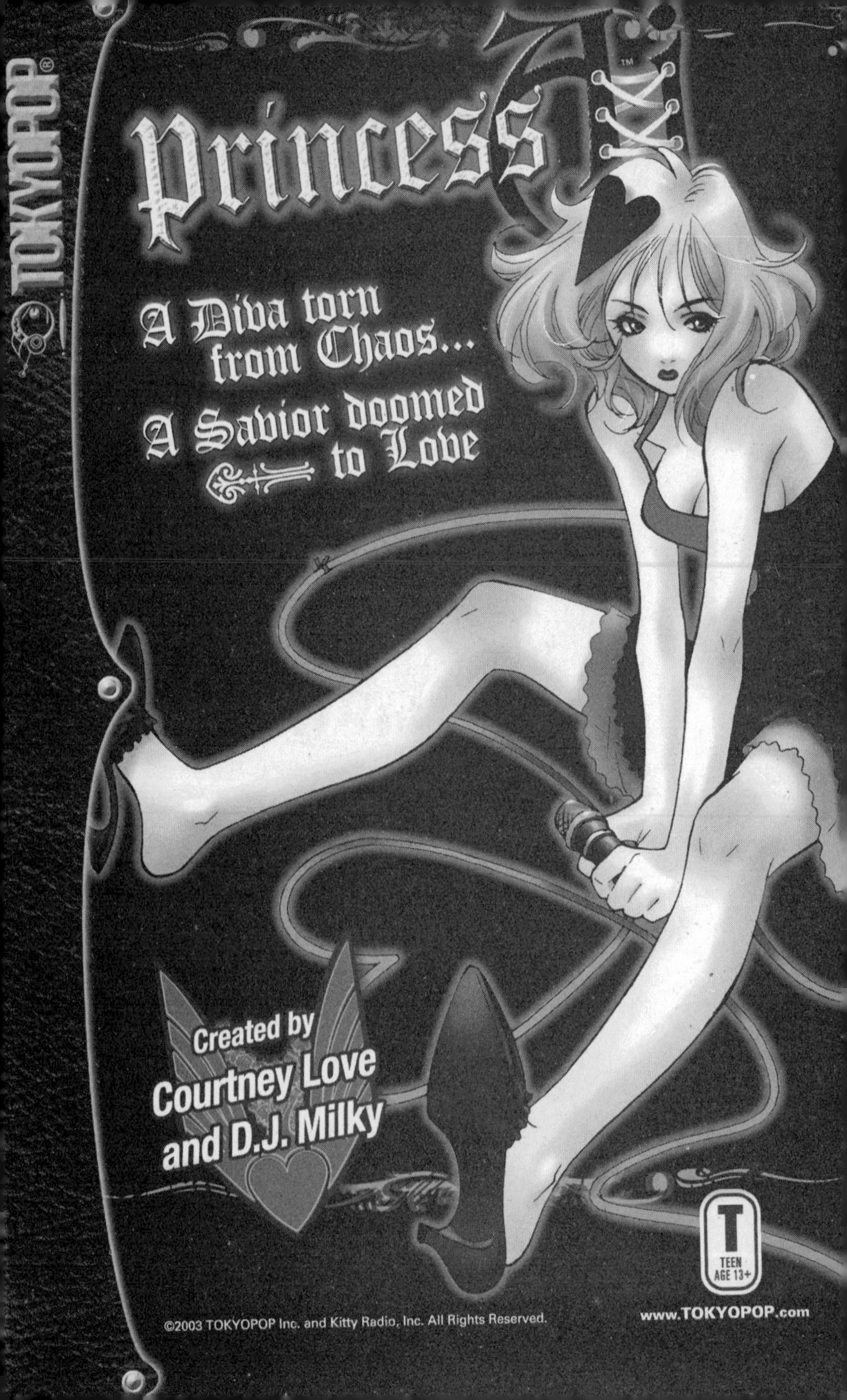
TOKYOPOP®
Princess Ai™
A Diva torn from Chaos...
A Savior doomed to Love
Created by
Courtney Love
and D.J. Milky
T
TEEN
AGE 13+
©2003 TOKYOPOP Inc. and Kitty Radio, Inc. All Rights Reserved.
www.TOKYOPOP.com

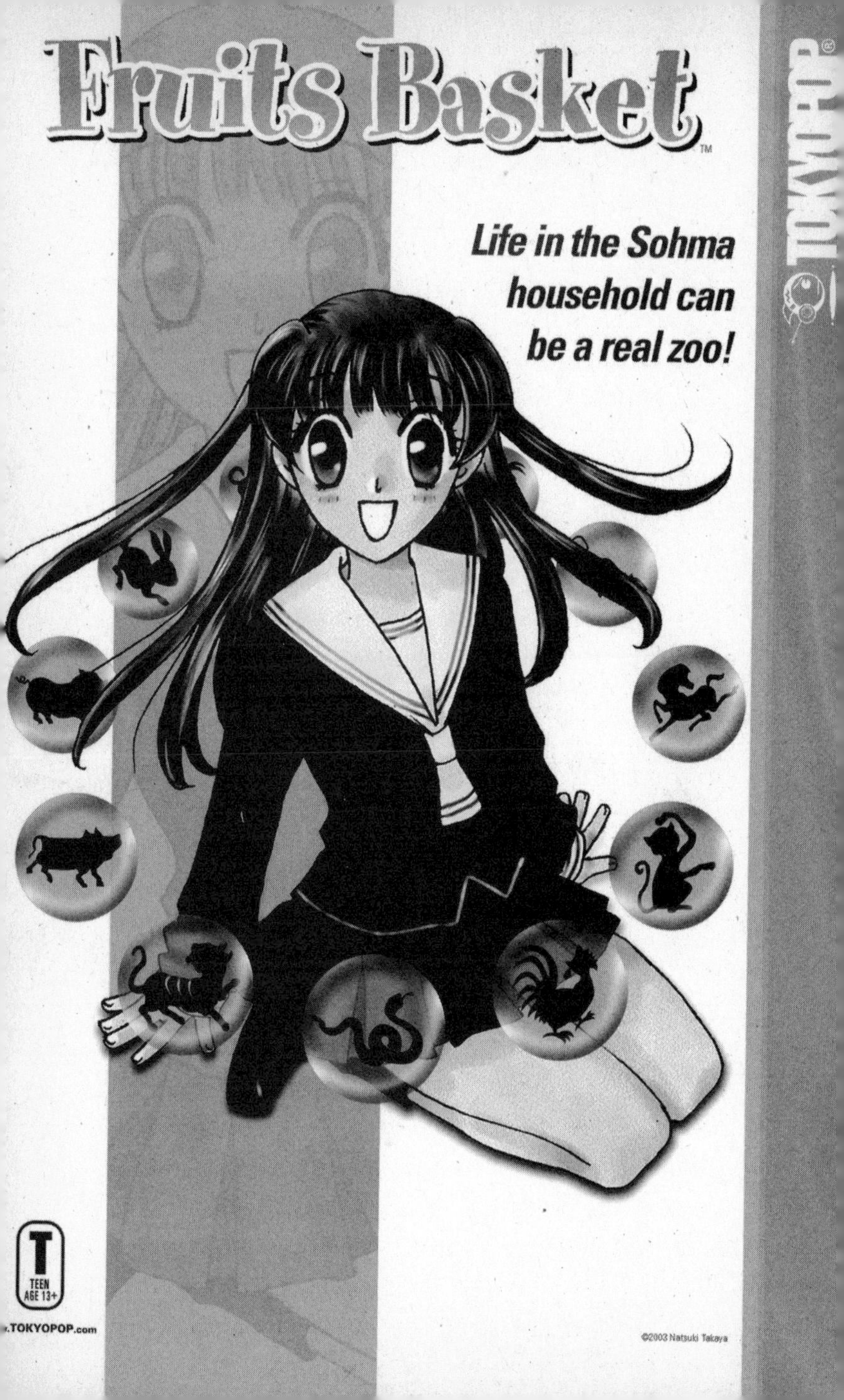
Fruits Basket™
TOKYOPOP
Life in the Sohma household can be a real zoo!
T TEEN AGE 13+
.TOKYOPOP.com
©2003 Natsuki Takaya

The One I Love

watashi no suki na hito

FROM THE CREATORS OF CLAMP ❄CHOBITS & TOKYO BABYLON

breathtaking stories of love and romance

T TEEN AGE 13+

www.TOKYOPOP.co

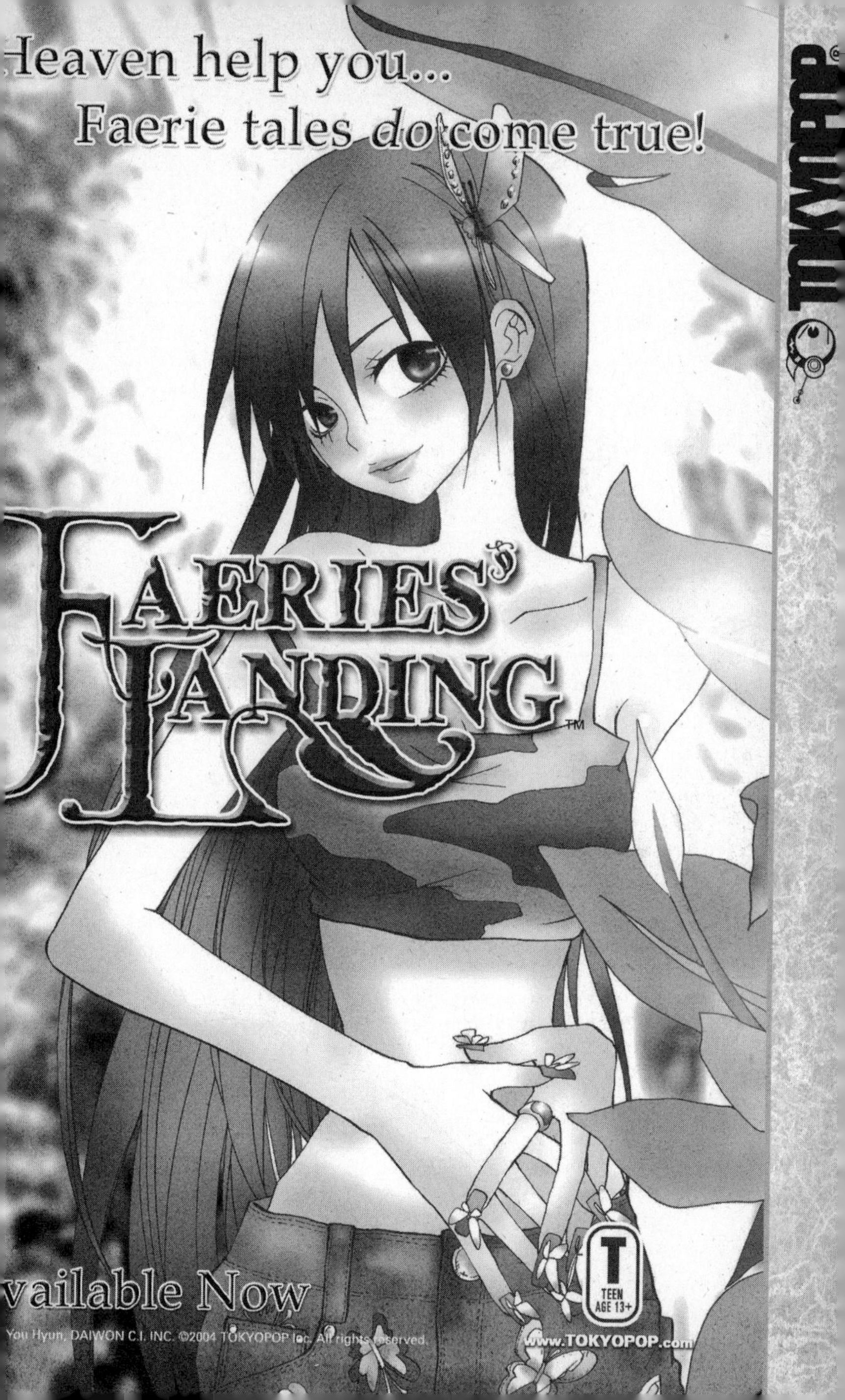
Heaven help you...
Faerie tales *do* come true!
TOKYOPOP
FAERIES' LANDING™
vailable Now
T TEEN AGE 13+
You Hyun, DAIWON C.I. INC. ©2004 TOKYOPOP Inc. All rights reserved.
www.TOKYOPOP.com

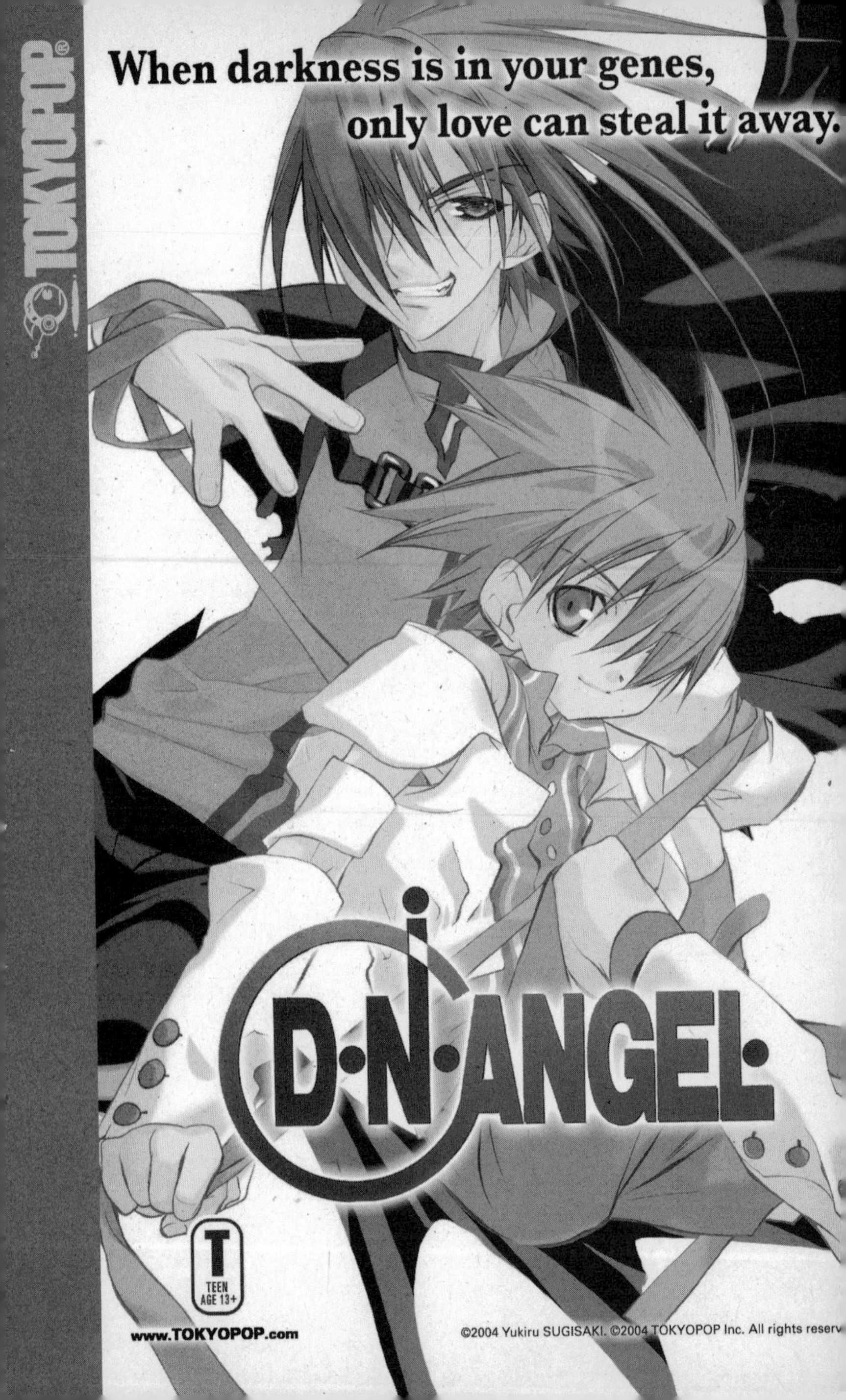
TOKYOPOP
When darkness is in your genes,
only love can steal it away.
D·N·ANGEL
T
TEEN
AGE 13+
www.TOKYOPOP.com
©2004 Yukiru SUGISAKI. ©2004 TOKYOPOP Inc. All rights reserv

STOP!

This is the back of the book. You wouldn't want to spoil a great ending!

This book is printed "manga-style," in the authentic Japanese right-to-left format. Since none of the artwork has been flipped or altered, readers get to experience the story just as the creator intended. You've been asking for it, so TOKYOPOP® delivered: authentic, hot-off-the-press, and far more fun!

DIRECTIONS

If this is your first time reading manga-style, here's a quick guide to help you understand how it works.

It's easy... just start in the top right panel and follow the numbers. Have fun, and look for more 100% authentic manga from TOKYOPOP®!

1
2
3
4
5
6
7
8
9
10

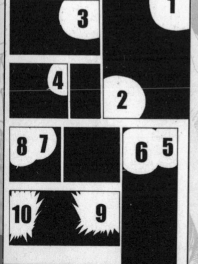

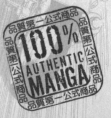